Lecture Notes in Computer Science   13383

More information about this series at https://link.springer.com/bookseries/558

Shamik Sural · Haibing Lu (Eds.)

Data and Applications Security and Privacy XXXVI

36th Annual IFIP WG 11.3 Conference, DBSec 2022
Newark, NJ, USA, July 18–20, 2022
Proceedings

 Springer

Editors
Shamik Sural
Department of Computer Science
and Engineering
Indian Institute of Technology Kharagpur
Kharagpur, West Bengal, India

Haibing Lu
Department of Information Systems
and Analytics
Santa Clara University
Santa Clara, CA, USA

ISSN 0302-9743   ISSN 1611-3349 (electronic)
Lecture Notes in Computer Science
ISBN 978-3-031-10683-5   ISBN 978-3-031-10684-2 (eBook)
https://doi.org/10.1007/978-3-031-10684-2

This Springer imprint is published by the registered company Springer Nature Switzerland AG
The registered company address is: Gewerbestrasse 11, 6330 Cham, Switzerland

Preface

This volume contains the papers selected for presentation at the 36th Annual IFIP WG11.3 Conference on Data and Applications Security and Privacy (DBSec 2022), held during July 18–20, 2022, in Newark, NJ, USA.

In response to the call for papers of this edition, 33 submissions were received, and all submissions were evaluated on the basis of their significance, novelty, and technical quality. The Program Committee, comprising 45 members, performed an excellent job, with the help of additional reviewers, of reviewing all submissions through a careful anonymous process (with three or more reviews per submission). The Program Committee's work was carried out electronically, yielding intensive discussions. Of the submitted papers, 12 full papers and six short papers were selected for presentation at the conference.

The success of DBSec 2022 depended on the volunteering effort of many individuals, and there is a long list of people who deserve special thanks. We would like to thank all the members of the Program Committee, and all the external reviewers, for all their hard work in evaluating the papers and for their active participation in the discussion and selection process. We are very grateful to all people who readily assisted and ensured a smooth organization process, in particular Jaideep Vaidya and Yuan Hong for their efforts as DBSec 2022 general co-chairs; Sara Foresti (IFIP WG11.3 chair) for her guidance and support; Hafiz Asif (publicity chair) for helping with publicity; and Lan Yao for helping with other arrangements for the conference. EasyChair made the conference review and proceedings process run very smoothly.

Last but certainly not least, thanks to all the authors who submitted papers and all the conference attendees. We hope you find the proceedings of DBSec 2022 interesting, stimulating, and inspiring for your future research.

June 2022

Shamik Sural
Haibing Lu

Organization

Program Committee

Vijay Atluri	Rutgers University, USA
Yang Cao	Kyoto University, Japan
Frédéric Cuppens	Polytechnique Montréal, Canada
Nora Cuppens-Boulahia	Polytechnique Montréal, Canada
Sabrina De Capitani di Vimercati	Università degli Studi di Milano, Italy
Giovanni Di Crescenzo	Peraton Labs, USA
Csilla Farkas	University of South Carolina, USA
Barbara Fila	INSA Rennes, IRISA, France
Sara Foresti	Università degli Studi di Milano, Italy
Steven Furnell	University of Nottingham, UK
Kambiz Ghazinour	Kent State University, USA
Ehud Gudes	Ben-Gurion University, Israel
Maanak Gupta	Tennessee Tech University, USA
Yuan Hong	University of Connecticut, USA
Sokratis Katsikas	Norwegian University of Science and Technology, Norway
Ram Krishnan	University of Texas at San Antonio, USA
Costas Lambrinoudakis	University of Piraeus, Greece
Adam J. Lee	University of Pittsburgh, USA
Xiang Li	Santa Clara University, USA
Yingjiu Li	University of Oregon, USA
Giovanni Livraga	University of Milan, Italy
Javier Lopez	Universidad de Málaga, Spain
Haibing Lu (Chair)	Santa Clara University, USA
Maryam Majedi	University of Toronto, Canada
Brad Malin	Vanderbilt University, USA
Sjouke Mauw	University of Luxembourg, Luxembourg
Meisam Mohammady	CSIRO, Australia
Samrat Mondal	Indian Institute of Technology Patna, India
Charles Morisset	Newcastle University, UK
Martin Olivier	University of Pretoria, South Africa
Stefano Paraboschi	Universita di Bergamo, Italy
Günther Pernul	Universität Regensburg, Germany
Silvio Ranise	University of Trento and Fondazione Bruno Kessler, Italy
Indrajit Ray	Colorado State University, USA

Contents

Privacy-Preserving Access and Computation

Quantum Security

Security Operations and Policies

Data Privacy

Assessing Differentially Private Variational Autoencoders Under Membership Inference

Daniel Bernau[1(✉)], Jonas Robl[1], and Florian Kerschbaum[2]

[1] SAP, Karlsruhe, Germany
{Daniel.Bernau,Jonas.Robl}@sap.com
[2] University of Waterloo, Waterloo, Canada
florian.kerschbaum@uwaterloo.ca

Abstract. We present an approach to quantify and compare the privacy-accuracy trade-off for differentially private Variational Autoencoders. Our work complements previous work in two aspects. First, we evaluate the strong reconstruction MI attack against Variational Autoencoders under differential privacy. Second, we address the data scientist's challenge of setting privacy parameter ϵ, which steers the differential privacy strength and thus also the privacy-accuracy trade-off. In our experimental study we consider image and time series data, and three local and central differential privacy mechanisms. We find that the privacy-accuracy trade-offs strongly depend on the dataset and model architecture. We do rarely observe favorable privacy-accuracy trade-offs for Variational Autoencoders, and identify a case where LDP outperforms CDP.

Keywords: Variational Autoencoders · Differential Privacy

1 Introduction

Generative machine learning models such as Variational Autoencoders (VAE) and Generative Adversarial Networks (GAN) infer rules about the distribution of training data to generate new images, tables or numeric datasets that follow the training data distribution. The decision whether to use GAN or VAE depends on the learning task and dataset. However, similar to machine learning models for classification [4,9,22,25,31] trained generative models leak information about individual training data records [5,11,12]. Anonymization of the training data or a training optimizer with differential privacy (DP) can reduce such leakage by limiting the privacy loss that an individual in the training would encounter when contributing their data [1,2,15]. Depending on the privacy parameter ϵ DP has a significant impact on the accuracy of the generative model since the perturbation affects how closely generated samples follow the training data distribution. Balancing privacy and accuracy for differentially private generative

---

D. Bernau and J. Robl—Authors contributed equally to this research.

© IFIP International Federation for Information Processing 2022
Published by Springer Nature Switzerland AG 2022
S. Sural and H. Lu (Eds.): DBSec 2022, LNCS 13383, pp. 3–14, 2022.
https://doi.org/10.1007/978-3-031-10684-2_1

models is a challenging task for data scientist since privacy parameter ϵ states an upper bound on the privacy loss. In contrast, quantifying the privacy loss under a concrete attack such as membership inference (MI) allows to quantify and compare the accuracy-privacy trade-off between differentially private generative models. This paper compares the privacy-accuracy trade-off for differentially private VAE. This is motivated by previous work that has identified VAE are more prone to MI attacks than GAN [12]. Hence, data scientists may want to particularly consider the use of DP when training VAE. We formulate an experimental study to validate whether our methodology allows to identify sweet spots w.r.t. the privacy-accuracy trade-off in VAE. We conduct experiments for two datasets covering image and activity data, and for three different local and central DP mechanisms. We quantify the privacy-accuracy trade-off under MI attacks for differentially private image and motion data VAE. The interested reader may find further information in an extended version of this paper [3].

2   Preliminaries

We use Variational Autoencoders (VAE) [18] to learn the joint probability distribution $p(X, Y)$ of features X and labels Y of a training dataset $\mathcal{D}^{train}$. VAE consist of two neural networks: encoder E and decoder D. During training a record x is given to the encoder which outputs the mean $E_\mu(x)$ and variance $E_\Sigma(x)$ of a Gaussian distribution. A latent variable z is then sampled from the Gaussian distribution $N(E_\mu(x), E_\Sigma(x))$ and fed into the decoder D. After successful training the reconstruction $D(z)$ should be close to x. During training two terms are minimized. First, the *reconstruction error* $\|D(z) - x\|$. Second, the *Kullback-Leibler divergence* between the distribution of latent variables z and the unit Gaussian. The KL divergence term prevents the VAE from memorizing certain latent variables since the distribution should be similar to the unit Gaussian. Kingma et al. [18] motivate the training objective as a lower bound on the log-likelihood and suggest training E and D for a training objective by using the *reparameterization trick*. Samples $D(z)$ are generated from the VAE by sampling a latent variable $z \sim N(0, 1)$ and passing z through D. Similar to GAN conditional VAE generate samples for a specific label by utilizing a condition c as input to E and D. MI attacks against machine learning models aim to identify the membership or non-membership of an individual record w.r.t. the training dataset $\mathcal{D}^{train}$ of a target model. To exploit differences in the generated samples of a trained target model the MI adversary $\mathcal{A}_{\text{MI}}$ uses a statistical attack model. Therefore, $\mathcal{A}_{\text{MI}}$ computes a similarity or error metric for individual records x. After having calculated such a metric for a set of records $\mathcal{A}_{\text{MI}}$ labels the records with the highest similarity, or lowest error, as members and all other records as non-members. For VAE the reconstruction loss quantifies how close a reconstructed training record is to the original training data record. Based on the reconstruction loss Hilprecht et al. formulate the reconstruction attack against VAE that outperforms prior work [12]. The reconstruction attack assumes that a reconstructed training record will have a smaller reconstruction loss than a reconstructed test record and repeatedly computes the reconstruction $\hat{x} = D(z)$

for a record x by drawing the latent variable z from the record-specific latent distribution $\mathcal{N}(\mathbb{E}_\mu(x), \mathbb{E}_\sigma(x))$. The mean reconstruction distance for N samples is then calculated by $f_{reconstruction} = -\frac{1}{N}\sum_i^N d(\hat{x} - x)$. Furthermore, the reconstruction attack depends on the availability of a distance measure d. In this work we use the generic Mean Squared Error (MSE) and the image domain specific Structural Similarity Index Measure (SSIM) as distance measures. A record x is likely a training record in case of small mean reconstruction distances for MSE or a similarity close to 1 for SSIM.

For a dataset $\mathcal{D}$ DP [6] can either be used centrally to perturb a function $f(\mathcal{D})$ or locally to perturb individual records $x \in \mathcal{D}$. In central DP (CDP) an aggregation function $f(\cdot)$ is first evaluated and then perturbed by a trusted server. Due to perturbation it is no longer possible for an adversary to confidently determine whether $f(\cdot)$ was evaluated on $\mathcal{D}$, or some neighboring dataset $\mathcal{D}'$ differing in one record. Privacy is provided to records in $\mathcal{D}$ as their impact on $f(\cdot)$ is limited. Mechanisms $\mathcal{M}$ that follow Definition 1 in the Appendix are used for perturbation of $f(\cdot)$. CDP holds for all possible differences $\|f(\mathcal{D}) - f(\mathcal{D}')\|_2$ by scaling noise to the global sensitivity [7]. To apply CDP in VAE we use a differentially private version of the Adam stochastic gradient optimizer[1] (DP-Adam). Per update step DP-Adam adds differentially private noise from the (ϵ, δ)-DP Gaussian mechanism to the gradients [1]. DP-Adam bounds the sensitivity of the computed gradients by specifying a clipping norm $\mathcal{C}$. We measure the privacy loss under composition by composing the Gaussian mechanism σ under Renyi DP [21]. Similar to related work we set $\delta = \frac{1}{|\mathcal{D}|}$ in our experiments [1,2]. We refer to the perturbation of records $x \in \mathcal{D}$ as local DP (LDP) [29] and use a local randomizer $\mathcal{LR}$ [17] as of Definition 2 in the Appendix to perturb each feature in a record $x \in \mathcal{D}$ independently. A series of $\mathcal{LR}$ executions per record composes to ϵ-LDP [17], where ϵ is a summation of all composed $\mathcal{LR}$ privacy losses. We use the $\mathcal{LR}$ by Fan [8] for LDP image pixelization. Their $\mathcal{LR}$ applies the ϵ-DP Laplace mechanism [7] to each pixel and small privacy parameters ϵ will result in random black and white images. We furthermore use a domain independent LDP mechanism specifically for VAE, to which we refer as VLDP. VLDP by Weggenmann et al. [30] allows a data scientist to use VAE as LDP mechanism to perturb data. This is achieved by limiting the encoders mean and adding noise to the encoders standard deviation before sampling the latent code z during training. After training, the resulting VAE is used to perturb records with $\epsilon = \frac{\Delta f \sqrt{2 \log(1.25/\delta)}}{\sigma}$. In this work we limit the resulting mean of the encoder to $[-3, 3]$ by using the tanh activation function.

3 Accuracy and Privacy for Variational Autoencoders

We compare the privacy-accuracy trade-off for differentially private VAE to support a data scientist $\mathcal{DS}$ in choosing privacy parameters ϵ. For this we formulate a framework to quantify privacy and accuracy as well as the privacy-accuracy trade-off for differentially private VAE with LDP and CDP. A visual representation of

---

[1] We use Tensorflow Privacy: https://github.com/tensorflow/privacy.

the framework can be found in the extended version of this paper [3]. The framework first splits a dataset $\mathcal{D}$ into three distinct subsets: training data $\mathcal{D}^{train}$, validation data $\mathcal{D}^{val}$ and test data $\mathcal{D}^{test}$. The *target model* VAE is trained on $\mathcal{D}^{train}$ and optimized on $\mathcal{D}^{val}$. After training, the target model is used to generate a new dataset $\mathcal{D}^{gen}$ with the same distribution as $\mathcal{D}^{train}$. We use $\mathcal{D}^{gen}$ as input for the *target classifier*, a feed-forward neural network for classification trained on $\mathcal{D}^{gen}$ and evaluated on $\mathcal{D}^{test}$. This is a common approach to evaluate the accuracy of generative models [10,16,28]. We quantify privacy under an MI adversary $\mathcal{A}_{\texttt{MI}}$ performing a MI attack. The MI attack dataset $\mathcal{D}^{atk}$ for training and evaluating the MI attack model is sampled equally from $\mathcal{D}^{train}$ and $\mathcal{D}^{test}$. We use the framework to calculate the baseline, as well as CDP and LDP trade-off. The baseline trade-off is calculated from the baseline target classifier test accuracy and the MI attack without any DP mechanism. For the CDP trade-off the target model is trained with DP-Adam. To evaluate the accuracy of the MI attack we use Average Precision of the Precision-Recall curve (MI AP) which considers membership as sensitive information. The MI AP quantifies the integral under the precision-recall curve as a weighted mean of the precision P per threshold t and the increase in recall R from the previous threshold. Independently of the target model accuracy, $\mathcal{DS}$ might be interested in lowering MI AP below a predefined threshold. We quantify the relative trade-off between accuracy and privacy by φ [2] which considers the relative difference between the change in test accuracy for $\mathcal{DS}$ and MI AP for $\mathcal{A}_{\texttt{MI}}$. The LDP trade-off can be computed in three settings which we refer to as LDP-Train, LDP-Full, and VLDP. In LDP-Train a LDP mechanism is applied solely to $\mathcal{D}^{train}$, but not $\mathcal{D}^{val}$ and $\mathcal{D}^{test}$. We evaluated the LDP-Train setting and observed it to be mostly impractical for VAE since it introduces a transfer learning task. In particular, working on two different data distributions for $\mathcal{D}^{train}$ and $\mathcal{D}^{test}$ leads to distant latent representations and contrasting reconstructions. This neither benefits the target classifier test accuracy nor reduces MI attack performance in comparison to perturbing both training and test data. In LDP-Full, $\mathcal{D}$ is perturbed and the training objective of the target model and the target classifier is changed implicitly. VLDP perturbs generated data $\mathcal{D}^{gen}$ by training a perturbation model that follows the target model architecture to enforce LDP. The use of LDP also leads to MI attack variations. In particular, the MI attack can either be evaluated against perturbed or unperturbed records in $\mathcal{D}^{atk}$. We argue that in the LDP-Full setting the MI attack performance against unperturbed records is particularly relevant from the viewpoint of $\mathcal{DS}$, since the unperturbed records represent the actual sensitive information and otherwise the attack model would solely learn the to differentiate two distributions by the perturbation skew. Hence, we exclusively consider the MI attack against unperturbed $\mathcal{D}^{train}$ for LDP.

4   Evaluation

Instead of comparing privacy parameter ϵ we designed and performed an experiment to compare the privacy-accuracy trade-off in different DP settings. We discuss the experiment for two reference datasets in four parts. First, we state the *baseline* test accuracy of the target classifier on non-generated data to provide information on the general drop in test accuracy between generated and non-generated data. Second and third, we discuss CDP and LDP results. Fourth, the results for VLDP are presented. For each mechanism we depict the results in two figures, stating target classifier accuracy and MI AP over ϵ. We also state the original target classifier test accuracy and MI AP for unperturbed data.

The target model is trained for 1000 epochs after which the target model test loss did not decrease significantly, and the target classifier accuracy did not increase anymore for the two reference datasets considered in this paper. The target classifier is trained on generated samples from the VAE until the target classifier test data loss is stagnating (i.e., early stopping). This experiment design avoids overfitting and increases real-world relevance of our results. For CDP we use DP-Adam which samples noise from a Gaussian distribution with scale $\sigma = $ noise multiplier $z \times$ clipping norm $\mathcal{C}$. $\mathcal{C}$ is set to the median of norms of the unclipped gradients over the course of 100 training epochs [1]. We evaluate increasing CDP noise regimes for the target model by evaluating noise multipliers $z \in \{0.001, 0.01, 0.1, 0.5, 1\}$. The noise levels cover a wide range from baseline accuracy to naive majority vote. The exact CDP (ϵ, δ) and summarized LDP ϵ are provided in an extended version of this paper [3]. VLDP perturbation models are trained with $\sigma \in \{0.1, 1, 10, 100, 1000\}$.

4.1   Datasets and Learning Tasks

Labeled Faces in the Wild (LFW) is a reference dataset for image classification [14]. We resize the 250×250 images to 64×64 by using a bilinear filter and normalize pixels to $[0, 1]$ for improved accuracy. Images are distributed unbalanced across the classes. We consider the most frequent 20 and 50 classes to which we refer as LFW20 and LFW50. In total, LFW20 consists of 1906 records and LFW50 consists of 2773 records. 50% of the data is allocated to $\mathcal{D}^{train}$, 20% to $\mathcal{D}^{val}$ and 30% to $\mathcal{D}^{test}$. Our VAE target model [3] is an extension of the architecture by Hou et al. [13]. E consists of four convolutional layers with 4×4 kernels, a stride of two and Leaky ReLU as activation function. D comprises a dense layer followed by four convolutional layers with 3×3 kernels, a stride of one and Leaky ReLU as activation function. Before each convolutional layer we perform upsampling by a scale of two with the nearest neighbor method. New data is generated by randomly drawing z from a multivariate Gaussian distribution which is passed through the decoder to create a new record. The target classifier is built upon a pre-trained VGG-Very-Deep-16 (VGG16) model [26]. Examples for reconstructed training and test records can be found in the extended version of this paper [3].

MotionSense (MS) is a reference dataset for human activity recognition with 70610 accelerometer and gyroscope sensor measurements [20]. Each measurement consists of twelve datapoints. Measurements are labeled with activities such as walking downstairs, jogging, and sitting. The associated learning task is to label a time series of measurements with the corresponding activity. The VAE target model shall reconstruct such a time series. We normalize the data to

$[-1, 1]$ and group the measurements to time series of 10 s. Similar to related work [5,11,12] we allocate 10% of the data to $\mathcal{D}^{train}$ and $\mathcal{D}^{val}$ each, and the remaining 80% is allocated to $\mathcal{D}^{test}$. For the target model we use a multitask approach in which E consists of a simple LSTM layer followed by two dense layers for μ and σ [3]. μ and σ are used to sample z through the reparameterization trick. D starts with a repeat vector unit for z. This allows us to create sequences and pass z to an LSTM layer. To support the reconstruction task, we input μ to a classifier. We sample z from the class-specific latent distribution since the latent space is clustered as a consequence of the multitask classifier. The overall loss is balanced with $\lambda_1 = 0.01$, $\lambda_2 = 50$, $\lambda_3 = 0.5$ for KL-loss, reconstruction loss and classifier loss respectively. The target classifier is based on the Human Activity Recognition Convolutional Neural Network architecture for time series data by Saeed [24]. Each convolutional layer is followed by a dropout layer which we set to 0.3 to learn a more general representation of the data. The final two fully-connected layers are used for classification.

4.2   Labeled Faces in the Wild

On non-generated baseline images, the target classifier achieves baseline test accuracies of 0.78 and 0.66 for LFW20 and LFW50. For generated images we provide two accuracy metrics: the SSIM of the images generated by the target model and the test accuracy of the target classifier. Figure 1a states the accuracy metrics for unperturbed and CDP perturbed VAE. The unperturbed VAE does not generate images with close proximity to the baseline images. However, the images still suffice to produce target classifier test accuracies well above majority voting. Shapes of the head, hair, and some facial expressions as well as the background are observable in reconstructed images [3]. Figure 1d illustrates that the reconstruction attack with SSIM as distance metric yields an MI AP of 1 for unperturbed VAE, due to the large gap between train and test SSIM.

Figure 1a states CDP test accuracy over ϵ. The steady accuracy decrease is due to the closing target model train-test gap. The resulting regularization also lowers the SSIM of the generated images. A particular sharp drop in SSIM is observable for $z = 0.5$ ($\epsilon \approx 350$). For this datapoint posterior collapse occurs when E produces noisy μ and σ leading to unstable latent codes z which in turn are ignored by D. In consequence, D produces reconstructions independently of z leading to a increased reconstruction loss, while μ and σ become constant and minimize the KL-loss [19]. As a consequence, the target classifier resorts to majority vote. The CDP MI AP over ϵ is stated in Fig. 1d. The increased regularization caused by CDP is at the same time lowering MI AP. In addition, due to the inherent label imbalance in LFW the VAE reconstruction of loosely populated classes is worse than the reconstruction for classes with more records. Still, the resulting privacy-accuracy trade-off leaves space for compromise. When $\mathcal{DS}$ would for example be willing to accept an MI AP of up to 0.6 this would require setting $z \leq 0.1$ ($\epsilon \approx 10^5$). $z = 0.1$ leads to target classifier test accuracy of 0.31. However, if $\mathcal{DS}$ raise their threshold to 0.75 this would allow for $z = 0.01$ ($\epsilon \approx 10^8$) and a target classifier test accuracy of 0.52.

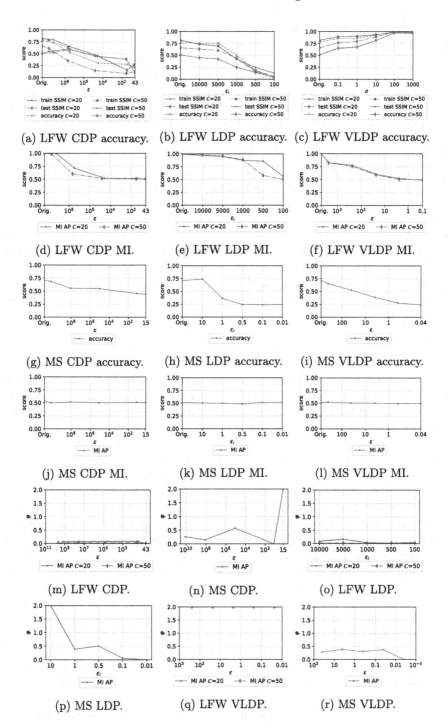

Fig. 1. LFW and MS accuracy, privacy and φ.

For LDP we use differentially private image pixelization to create LDP training and test datasets within neighborhood $m = \sqrt{64 \times 64}$. Figure 1b presents the LDP test accuracy and SSIM over ϵ_i. In contrast to the CDP experiments the target classifier test accuracy and target model SSIM metrics do not show a regularization effect caused by the introduced noise. The train-test gap narrows only slightly [3] and the noise introduced in the dataset makes the reconstruction task for the VAE more difficult. Thus, the MI AP in Fig. 1e remains nearly unchanged until $\epsilon_i \leq 500$ at which the target model SSIM and the target classifier test accuracy are at poor levels and little room for compromise exists.

VLDP accuracy over ϵ is presented in Fig. 1c. Counterintuitively, the test accuracy even rises over ϵ and the train-test gap and SSIM gap narrow. This is due to the VLDP perturbation model which reconstructs only essential facial features and leaves the background grey when faced with small ϵ. Hence the learning task for the target classifier and the reconstruction task for the VAE are simplified. The reconstruction attack against VLDP in Fig. 1f also decreases as the SSIM gap closes. All in all, the results point towards an advantage of the VLDP mechanism over the LDP image pixelization mechanism. The main disadvantage of the VLDP mechanism over image pixelization is the increased effort to optimize perturbation model hyperparameters.

4.3   MotionSense

Due to the absence of a domain specific accuracy metric we solely consider test accuracy for this dataset. The target classifier for MS achieves a baseline test-accuracy of 0.99 for non-generated data. Figure 1g states the test accuracy for original and CDP perturbed data over ϵ. The test accuracy is dropping to 0.71 for generated data, which is due to the target model being unable to reconstruct time series for all activities equally well. The reconstruction attack has not been used for a time series data in previous work and we suggest using MSE as reconstruction attack distance metric. The original MI attack performance is depicted in Fig. 1j and achieves an MI AP 0.52. We see three main reasons for the low MI AP in comparison to LFW. First, MS is more balanced in comparison to LFW. Second, there are significantly more records in MS than in LFW and thus more records per class allow to learn a more general representation. Third, sensor measurements exhibit ambiguities and thus the target model tends to learn more general trends instead of absolute values.

The CDP target classifier test accuracy slightly worsens with increasing noise as illustrated in Fig. 1g. This is due to the target classifier resorting to majority vote for particular activities with increasing noise. It resorts to majority vote for classes 0 to 3 which represent different types of movements but is still able to distinguish classes 4 and 5 which represent standing and sitting. The latter two activities are of different nature than the movements and remain distinguishable under noise. The majority vote analysis is more elaborate in the extended version of this paper [3]. The MI AP illustrated in Fig. 1j underlines the ineffectiveness of the reconstruction attack against the MS time series data.

For LDP we use the Laplace mechanism to perturb each measurement and specify the sensitivity per sensor as the maximum of all corresponding observed values to create differentially private time series. Figure 1h shows the target classifier accuracy over ϵ_i. Notably, the target classifier test accuracy increases slightly before dropping sharply over ϵ_i. Here, small noise levels are actually positively influencing the target model training and hence also allow the target classifier to better distinguish between different classes. In general, the simple LDP mechanism used within this experiment seems to prevent the target model from inferring structural information and thus limits reconstruction and meaningful generation of records. Figure 1k presents the MI attack performance. The MI AP decreases to 0.5 already at the largest ϵ_i and remains close to the baseline.

VLDP test accuracy over ϵ is depicted in Fig. 1i. In comparison to LFW the MS perturbation models do not focus on the essential features of the data and in turn the target classifier cannot benefit from increased perturbation. Due to this the predictions also shift to a majority vote for class 5 and lower the test accuracy significantly. The VLDP MI AP over ϵ is illustrated in Fig. 1l. Note that at $\sigma = 0.1$ ($\epsilon \approx 40$) an outlier is present where the target model did not learn a continuous latent space and thus the reconstruction of records from $\mathcal{D}^{test}$ suffered. However, the VLDP results show trends similar to LDP results.

5   Related Work

Torkzadehmahani et al. [28] propose the DP-cGAN framework to generate differentially private data and labels. Similar to our work they train target classifiers on the generated data to evaluate model accuracy. We consider VAE with LDP and CDP. Jordon et al. [16] extend the differentially private federated learning architecture PATE [23] to GAN. Similar to us, they analyze the accuracy of a target classifier for various privacy parameters, yet Jordon et al. do not discuss privacy aside from privacy parameter ϵ. Frigerio et al. [10] evaluate a CDP GAN for time series data also w.r.t. MI attacks. We also consider LDP and quantify the trade-off between privacy and accuracy. Takahashi [27] propose an enhanced version of the DP-SGD for VAE by adjusting the noise that is injected to the loss terms. We use DP-Adam where their improvement is not applicable.

Hayes et al. [11] propose LOGAN for MI attacks against GANs. For their black-box attacks they train a separate discriminator model to distinguish between members and non-members. In contrast, we consider statistical MI attack models, allowing for MI attacks against generative models without the need to train a separate attack model. Hilprecht et al. [12] propose the reconstruction attack and are the first to consider this attack under DP. Chen et al. [5] extend the reconstruction attack to a partial black-box setting where $\mathcal{A}_{\mathrm{MI}}$ solely has access to the latent space z, but not the internal parameters of the generative model. Their attack composes different losses targeting various aspects of a model. We ran all experiments within this paper also for their attack and the consideration of latent representation did lead to strictly weaker MI AP.

6   Discussion

The reconstruction attack has been shown effective for image data in prior work [5,12], despite being fairly simple and only taking one metric for disparate behaviour of the target model into consideration. This is in line with the identified gap in image reconstruction for LFW which was exploited by using SSIM as a distance measure. For MS we were not able to identify a measure that provides equal success. Since activity measurements exhibit many ambiguities the target model learns to reconstruct relative trends instead of concrete measurements that represent a specific movement. Therefore, the target model generalizes more and is less prone to MI attacks. Additionally, previous work has shown that large datasets with few classes are generally less vulnerable to MI attacks [22,25].

For CDP and image data we observe small noise to yield favorable trade-offs. The relative accuracy drop for $\mathcal{DS}$ largely exceeds the MI AP loss for $\mathcal{A}_{MI}$ throughout the LFW CDP experiments. This trend is illustrated in Fig. 1m which highlights that the drop in target classifier test accuracy is always larger than the privacy gain by reduced MI AP. For MS the reconstruction attack against original data solely achieves a performance close to random guessing. Hence, small noise is already sufficient to push the MI AP to random guessing. This is reflected in Fig. 1n, where we see an optimal φ already for $z = 0.001$. Similarly for LDP Figs. 1o and 1p for LFW and MS show only few favorable φ. These few favorable trade-offs again indicate that DP image pixelization and the Laplace mechanism disproportionately harm model accuracy over protecting privacy. LDP shows better trade-offs for small privacy parameters whereas $\mathcal{DS}$ gives up more accuracy compared to the gain in privacy.

The VLDP yielded the best trade-off between target classifier test accuracy and MI AP. This finding is supported by φ depicted in Figs. 1q and 1r. We identified the interaction between the perturbation models, that retain essential image features, and the targeted classification task as primary reason for the superior trade-off. φ for the VLDP experiments highlight that small noise bounds are protecting from the reconstruction attack. For larger noise bounds φ only offers limited informative value since the MI AP reaches random guessing while the target classifier test accuracy is bound by the classification baseline.

Our results indicate that CDP leads to a regularization effect and directly addresses a driver for MI AP. However, CDP also requires additional hyper-parameter optimization and increases computational costs. LDP mechanisms consume information within the data to foster protection and hence the test accuracy decrease heavily depends on how the LDP mechanism alters the training data. This effect is clearly visible for the MS dataset, where the decrease in target classifier accuracy is similar to the overall classification baseline. When this characteristic is present MI is affected mostly as a consequence of diminishing model performance. This is facilitated by the lack of regularization effect which keeps a present relative gap for the MI attacks to exploit. The VLDP mechanism preserves essential features of the LFW dataset during perturbation. The preservation of essential features is beneficial for the classification task as the test accuracy remains high while the MI AP decreases.

Appendix

Definition 1 ((ϵ, δ)-Central DP). *A mechanism $\mathcal{M}$ gives (ϵ, δ)-central DP if $\mathcal{D}, \mathcal{D}' \subseteq \mathcal{DOM}$ differing in at most one element, and all outputs $\mathcal{S} \subseteq \mathcal{R}$*

$$\Pr[\mathcal{M}(\mathcal{D}) \in \mathcal{S}] \leq e^{\epsilon} \cdot \Pr[\mathcal{M}(\mathcal{D}') \in \mathcal{S}] + \delta$$

Definition 2 (Local Differential Privacy). *A local randomizer (mechanism) $\mathcal{LR} : \mathcal{DOM} \rightarrow \mathcal{S}$ is ϵ-local differentially private, if $\epsilon \geq 0$ and for all possible inputs $v, v' \in \mathcal{DOM}$ and all possible outcomes $s \in \mathcal{S}$ of $\mathcal{LR}$*

$$\Pr[\mathcal{LR}(v) = s] \leq e^{\epsilon} \cdot \Pr[\mathcal{LR}(v') = s]$$

References

1. Abadi, M., et al.: Deep learning with differential privacy. In: Proceedings of the Conference on Computer and Communications Security CCS (2016)
2. Bernau, D., Robl, J., Grassal, P.W., Schneider, S., Kerschbaum, F.: Comparing local and central differential privacy using membership inference attacks. In: Proceedings of Conference on Data and Applications Security and Privacy. DBSEC (2021)
3. Bernau, D., Robl, J., Kerschbaum, F.: Assessing differentially private variational autoencoders under membership inference (2022)
4. Carlini, N., Liu, C., Erlingsson, U., Kos, J., Song, D.: The secret sharer. In: Proceedings of USENIX Security Symposium (2019)
5. Chen, D., Yu, N., Zhang, Y., Fritz, M.: GAN-leaks. In: Proceedings of Conference on Computer and Communications Security. CCS (2020)
6. Dwork, C.: Differential privacy. In: Proceedings of Colloquium on Automata, Languages and Programming. ICALP (2006)
7. Dwork, C., Roth, A.: The algorithmic foundations of differential privacy. Found. Trends Theor. Comput. Sci. 9(3–4), 211–407 (2014)
8. Fan, L.: Image pixelization with differential privacy. In: Proceedings of Conference on Data and Applications Security and Privacy. DBSec (2018)
9. Fredrikson, M., Jha, S., Ristenpart, T.: Model inversion attacks that exploit confidence information and basic countermeasures. In: Proceedings of Conference on Computer and Communications Security. CCS (2015)
10. Frigerio, L., de Oliveira, A.S., Gomez, L., Duverger, P.: Differentially private generative adversarial networks for time series, continuous, and discrete open data. In: Proceedings of Conference on ICT Systems Security and Privacy Protection (2019)
11. Hayes, J., Melis, L., Danezis, G., De Cristofaro, E.: LOGAN. In: Proceedings on Privacy Enhancing Technologies. PETS (2019)
12. Hilprecht, B., Härterich, M., Bernau, D.: Monte Carlo and reconstruction membership inference attacks against generative models. In: Proceedings on Privacy Enhancing Technologies. PETS (2019)
13. Hou, X., Shen, L., Sun, K., Qiu, G.: Deep feature consistent variational autoencoder. In: Proceedings of Conference on Applications of Computer Vision. WACV (2017)

14. Huang, G.B., Mattar, M., Lee, H., Learned-Miller, E.: Learning to align from scratch. In: Proceedings of Conference on Neural Information Processing Systems. NIPS (2012)
15. Jayaraman, B., Evans, D.: Evaluating differentially private machine learning in practice. In: Proceedings of USENIX Security Symposium (2019)
16. Jordon, J., Yoon, J., Schaar, M.V.D.: PATE-GAN. In: Proceedings of Conference on Learning Representations. ICLR (2019)
17. Kasiviswanathan, S.P., Lee, H.K., Nissim, K., Raskhodnikova, S., Smith, A.: What can we learn privately? SIAM J. Comput. **40**(3), 793–826 (2008)
18. Kingma, D.P., Welling, M.: Auto-encoding variational bayes. In: Proceedings of Conference on Learning Representations. ICLR (2014)
19. Lucas, J., Tucker, G., Grosse, R.B., Norouzi, M.: Dont blame the ELBO! A linear VAE perspective on posterior collapse. In: Proceedings of Conference on Neural Information Processing Systems. NIPS (2019)
20. Malekzadeh, M., Clegg, R.G., Cavallaro, A., Haddadi, H.: Protecting sensory data against sensitive inferences. In: Proceedings of Workshop on Privacy by Design in Distributed Systems. W-P2ds (2018)
21. Mironov, I.: Rényi differential privacy. In: Proceedings of Computer Security Foundations Symposium (CSF) (2017)
22. Nasr, M., Shokri, R., Houmansadr, A.: Comprehensive privacy analysis of deep learning. In: Proceedings of Symposium on Security and Privacy. S&P (2019)
23. Papernot, N., Song, S., Mironov, I., Raghunathan, A., Talwar, K., Erlingsson, Ú.: Scalable private learning with PATE. In: Proceedings of Conference on Learning Representations. ICLR (2018)
24. Saeed, A.: Implementing a CNN for Human Activity Recognition in Tensorflow. http://aqibsaeed.github.io/2016-11-04-human-activity-recognition-cnn/
25. Shokri, R., Stronati, M., Song, C., Shmatikov, V.: Membership inference attacks against machine learning models. In: Proceedings of Symposium on Security and Privacy. S&P (2017)
26. Simonyan, K., Zisserman, A.: Very deep convolutional networks for large-scale image recognition. In: Proceedings of Conference on Learning Representations. ICLR (2015)
27. Takahashi, T., Takagi, S., Ono, H., Komatsu, T.: Differentially Private Variational Autoencoders with Term-wise Gradient Aggregation (2020)
28. Torkzadehmahani, R., Kairouz, P., Paten, B.: DP-CGAN. In: Proceedings of Conference on Computer Vision and Pattern Recognition Workshops. CVPRW (2019)
29. Wang, T., Blocki, J., Li, N., Jha, S.: Locally differentially private protocols for frequency estimation. In: Proceedings of USENIX Security Symposium (2017)
30. Weggenmann, B., Rublack, V., Andrejczuk, M., Mattern, J., Kerschbaum, F.: DP-VAE. In: Proceedings of Web Conference. WWW (2022)
31. Zhu, L., Liu, Z., Han, S.: Deep leakage from gradients. In: Proceedings of Conference on Neural Information Processing Systems. NeurIPS (2019)

Utility and Privacy Assessment of Synthetic Microbiome Data

Markus Hittmeir[1]([⊠])(iD), Rudolf Mayer[1,2](iD), and Andreas Ekelhart[1](iD)

[1] SBA Research gGmbH, Floragasse 7, Vienna, Austria
{mhittmeir,rmayer,aekelhart}@sba-research.org
[2] Vienna University of Technology, Favoritenstraße 9-11, Vienna, Austria

Abstract. The microbial communities of the human body are subject to extensive research efforts. The individual variations in the human microbiome reveal information about our diet, exercise habits and general well-being, and are useful for investigations on the prediction and therapy of diseases. On the other hand, these variations allow for microbiome-based identification of individuals, thus posing privacy risks in microbiome studies. Synthetic microbiome datasets hold the promise of reducing said risks while simultaneously keeping the utility of the data for research as high as possible. In this paper, we conduct an empirical evaluation of two open-source data synthetization tools on several publicly available microbiome datasets. In particular, we generate synthetic training data and investigate its performance for a variety of machine learning tasks on microbiome samples. Our findings indicate the suitability of synthetic microbiome data for analysis and for privacy protection.

1 Introduction

The composition of bacteria, viruses, fungi and protists on different sites of the human body appear to have a great influence on our health. Research on the human microbiome and its potential for prediction, diagnosis and therapy of diseases has been flourishing for several years. In this context, a particularly well-studied body site is the gastrointestinal tract. Distinct changes in the gut microbiome are related to gastrointestinal diseases [2], obesity [8], diabetes [12], and depression [17]. A most recent study appears to have found a link to the risk for developing post-acute COVID-19 syndrome [10]. While there is a huge potential for analysis in clinical settings, previous research studies have demonstrated that it is important to regard the human microbiome as personal and sensitive medical data. The genetic sequence data obtained from the samples allows for microbiome-based forensic identification of individuals [3,23]. However, even the processed, tabular microbiome profiles obtained via the extraction of metagenomic features such as operational taxonomic units (OTUs) show a high individual and temporal stability. In 2015, Franzosa et al. [4] revealed that individual variations in such metagenomic features extracted from microbiome readings allow for the re-identification of individuals among populations of hundreds. Comparing initial microbiome samples with follow-up samples collected

© IFIP International Federation for Information Processing 2022
Published by Springer Nature Switzerland AG 2022
S. Sural and H. Lu (Eds.): DBSec 2022, LNCS 13383, pp. 15–27, 2022.
https://doi.org/10.1007/978-3-031-10684-2_2

30–300 days later, up to 80% of individuals could still be matched correctly. The authors concluded that the demonstrated possibility of Personal Microbiome Identification (PMI) poses privacy threats to individuals participating in microbiome studies. The findings of Franzosa et al.'s original study have been further aggravated in a recent analysis [7], which uses a distance-based approach for the comparison of microbiome samples. Reaching a true-positive identification rate of up to 94%, this technique underlines the need for solutions to protect the privacy of individuals in microbiome databases.

Methods for enhancing the privacy in genomic datasets [1] and specific approaches related to human DNA sequence data [9,11] have been studied and improved in the last years. In 2016, Wagner et al. used secure two-party computation, which protects the inputs to the computation, for the analysis of microbiome data [22]. Besides that, research on privacy-preserving techniques for microbiome data is less advanced. In this paper, we discuss the generation of synthetic data as a solution for privacy-preserving data publishing and for preventing PMI on microbiome reports. The idea of data synthetization is to learn the global properties of an original dataset (that cannot easily be shared), and generate a synthetic dataset, with the aim of preserving these properties and relations between the attributes and without actually revealing the individuals described by the data. The synthetic data can then be shared much more easily and holds the promise to allow data analysis with similar results. For example, we hope to train machine learning models on the synthetic data that ultimately achieve effectiveness comparable to models trained on the real data. Previous publications have shown that the approach of generating synthetic data reduces privacy risks on microdata by simultaneously preserving the utility for performing machine learning tasks (e.g., [5]). We will demonstrate that the same conclusion can be drawn for tasks on metagenomic microbiome profiles.

The remainder of the paper is structured as follows: In Sect. 2, we will discuss microbiome data, the mentioned techniques for PMI and the data synthetization tools in greater detail. In Sect. 3, we consider the privacy threats due to PMI and how synthetization can help with reducing these threats. In Sect. 4, the reader can find the results of our experiments. Section 5 contains concluding remarks, and the appendix provides some additional analysis results.

2   Preliminaries and Related Work

We start by discussing the contents of metagenomic microbiome profiles. The datasets in our experiments are tables containing individuals (i.e., sample vectors) described by hundreds to thousands of columns (attributes) that contain the National Center for Biotechnology Information (NCBI) genome identifiers of RefSeq-based OTUs [14], which classify groups of closely related organisms found in the microbiome., After preprocessing, the values in the tables are the relative abundances of the respective OTU in the sample vector, i.e. they are normalized row-wise to a unit-vector length. Hence, the attributes contain decimal numbers between 0 and 1 that represent the relative proportion of the OTU in the complete sample of the individual. As a result, the values in each sample vector sum up to 1.

Next, let us briefly discuss the two methods for PMI on metagenomic profiles mentioned in the introduction. In Franzosa et al.'s approach [4], a feature is understood as either present or absent, depending on feature detection limits for the relative abundance count (e.g., one limit used is 0.001). Their PMI method then aims to find so-called metagenomic codes that are unique for each individual. These codes are a small subset of features that are present in the individual sample but, in this combination, are not present in any other sample of the dataset. It is then demonstrated in experiments that these codes are stable enough over time such that their comparison may be used to find pairs of samples that belong to the same individual. The second PMI approach [7], a distance-based extension of Franzosa et al.'s technique, consists of three phases. In the first phase, the abundance values in the sample vectors are transformed to integral values by using feature abundance limits. The second phase concerns the determination of possible matches. In order to check a specific sample s against a dataset D, one computes the most similar (the "nearest-neighbor") sample $\bar{s}$ of s in D. By doing so, one obtains $(s, \bar{s})$ as candidate for a pair of samples belonging to the same individual. In the third phase, a threshold criteria is introduced to decrease the false positive count. The candidate pair is accepted only if $\bar{s}$ is a "reverse nearest-neighbor" of s, i.e., if there is no sample in D that is closer to $\bar{s}$ than s. The method in [7] shows an increased identification rate over the method in [4] on most considered body sites. In particular, one observes an increase of the percentage of true positive identifications of 30% on the gut microbiome, averaged over four different metagenomic feature types.

The present paper is concerned with the mitigation of privacy risks resulting from the PMI techniques, based on the generation of synthetic data. The workflow of synthetic data generation tools may be summarized as follows:

1. Learn the properties of the original dataset, i.e. the distribution of its features and the correlations between them, and store them in some kind of model.
2. Use the model to generate synthetic data samples, e.g. by drawing random data entries from the learned distributions.

By generating enough synthetic samples, we can obtain a synthetic dataset of length equal to the original dataset (or any other arbitrary size). While there is no 1-to-1 correspondence between synthetic samples and real individuals, the hope is that we can use synthetic data for analysis without a significant loss of performance. One of the earliest usages of synthetic data was in the partial synthetic data approach by Rubin [18], where certain columns are generated synthetically. An overview on more than 20 approaches is given in [19], categorizing the approaches into fully or partially synthetic.

For selecting the synthetic data generation tools included in our analysis, we focused on recent methods that are open-source implementations and utilize generative models to ensure robust and high-quality data. In addition, the techniques need to be able to deal with the relatively large (hundreds to thousands) number of attributes in metagenomic microbiome profiles. We identified the following two tools.

The **Synthetic Data Vault** (SDV) has been developed by Patki et al. in 2016 [15][1]. The SDV allows to synthesize both single table datasets and relational databases. The user can choose between different models for learning the patterns on the original data, such as fitting Gaussian Copulas or using GANs.

The **synthpop** (SP) package for the statistical analysis language R [13][2] uses as the default synthesis method the CART (Classification and Regression Trees) algorithm. However, the user is able to specify a different method.

Another tool, the Data Synthesizer [16], is not included in our analysis due to efficiency issues during the construction of its Bayesian network. Possible speed-ups for this tool are a prospect for future work (see Sect. 5).

3　Threat Model and Goal of Synthetization

We now discuss the notions related to a privacy violation of microbiome data. In addition, we will consider our goal to mitigate these threats by publishing synthetic instead of original microbiome datasets.

Victim. An individual who provided their microbiome samples in the course of medical studies, diagnosis and therapy of diseases, personal health and fitness advise, or similar. Their microbiome data, and possible analysis results or metadata, are publicly available, e.g. in the form of (possibly deidentified) samples.

Adversary. A party in possession of microbiome samples with the intention to link them to other microbiome samples. The purpose is to reveal the identity of the underlying individuals and/or to obtain more information about them. The adversary's options to obtain microbiome samples include public microbiome databases, cyberattacks against healthcare and research facilities, data exfiltration via insiders, and potentially, directly from the victim (e.g., saliva).

Threats. Assume that an adversary possesses a sample of a certain individual. We discuss four reasons for the adversary to match the sample against another database.

 (i) To find out if an individual participated in a certain study, i.e. a form of membership disclosure. This might allow them to obtain sensitive information, e.g. in the case where the study has been conducted in the context of specific diseases.
 (ii) The attacker may be able to obtain previously unknown metadata linked to the identified sample from the new database (e.g., medical and personal data provided in the course of a study or treatment, or questionnaires).
(iii) Even in the absence of metadata, the attacker may be able to get hold of new microbiome samples from the same individual and could thereby learn about changes over time in the individual's human microbiome. Such changes could, e.g., point to physical diseases, depression, and changes in diet.

---

[1] https://github.com/HDI-Project/SDV.
[2] https://www.synthpop.org.uk/ resp. https://github.com/bnowok/synthpop.

(iv) Ongoing research efforts increasingly associate microbiome samples with several other individual traits, such as the age or geographical background [24]. Therefore, collecting and linking multiple samples from the same individual could also aid an attacker in identifying the person behind a sample.

We will use synthetization to reduce the risks of the threats (i)–(iv). As we have already discussed in Sect. 2, there is no 1-to-1 correspondence between synthetic and real samples. An adversary may still try to apply PMI techniques to match a sample in their possession against a synthetic dataset. However, any match that is potentially found must be considered incidental, as no synthetic sample is related to a particular individual. In addition, no metadata is linked to the samples in a synthetic dataset, which eliminates threat (ii). Since identity disclosure in the form discussed above does not appear to be possible, previous publications about privacy risks on synthetic data [6, 20] have focused on the notion of *attribute disclosure*. It refers to the risk that, on structured tabular datasets, an adversary might learn the victim's value of a sensible attribute. It has been concluded that attribute disclosure can happen without identity disclosure, and that there remains a risk for attribute disclosure on synthetic data. However, it appears that this conclusion does not translate to microbiome datasets. The attributes in these tables are particularly numerous. While the complete composition of the microbiome is rich with information, it is much less obvious that knowledge about a single, specific feature in a sample could be particularly sensitive. While we do not completely disregard the possibility of attribute disclosure, we will not investigate it further in the present paper.

The promise of synthetic data is a close similarity of its global properties to the original data. From a privacy-preserving point of view, this would ideally come with a substantial dissimilarity of its local properties. Synthetic samples that are very similar to real ones might still allow to deduce local information about the original dataset, even without the immediate threat of identity disclosure. In previous publications (e.g., [5]), this question has been investigated by considering the distance between synthetic samples and their nearest-neighbor in the original dataset. We will conduct a similar analysis in Sect. 4.2.

4   Evaluation

Our experiments are based on the publicly available datasets from "Knights-lab"'s microbiome machine learning repository[3] [21]. In total, the repository contains data for 33 curated machine learning tasks, mainly for binary classification. We utilized six medium-sized datasets: two for distinguishing healthy microbiome samples from those where the hosts suffer from Morbus Crohn (the "Gevers" datasets in the repository), two further datasets with tasks on Irritable Bowel Disease (the "Morgan" datasets), one for distinguishing lean from obese individuals (the "Turnbaugh" dataset), and one for detecting tumors (the

---

[3] https://knights-lab.github.io/MLRepo/.

"dataset"). In each case, we will use data containing RefSeq-based OTU abundance counts to compare our results directly to the baselines shown in [21, p. 5]. Table 1 provides an overview of the original dataset properties.

Table 1. Dataset characteristics prior to any preprocessing

Dataset	Task	# Samples	# Features
Gevers Ileum	control vs crohn's disease	140	943
Gevers Rectum	control vs crohn's disease	160	943
Morgan CD	healthy vs crohn's disease	128	829
Morgan UC	healthy vs ulcerative colitis	128	829
Turnbaugh	lean vs obese	142	557
Kostic	healthy vs tumor biopsy	172	908

For their case study benchmarking, the authors of [21] used an experimental setup including feature preprocessing steps and a repeated 5-fold cross-validation. We will use a similar setup and briefly summarize it here:

1. The OTU counts in the original tables are converted to relative abundance, such that the sum of all values in each sample vector equals 1. In addition, the counts were filtered at a minimum of 10% prevalence across samples and collapsed at a complete-linkage correlation of 95%.
2. The relative abundances in the tables are transformed by using the same feature abundance limits as in [7], namely $t_i = 0.00005 \cdot 10^i$ for $i = 0, 1, 2, 3, 4$. For each cell value x, we then set $x \leftarrow 0$ if $x < t_0$, $x \leftarrow i$ if $t_{i-1} \leq x < t_i$ for some $1 \leq i \leq 4$, and $x \leftarrow 5$ if $x \geq t_4$.
3. Like the authors of the original publication [21], we apply a 5-fold cross validation to split up our datasets into training and test data. Note that the samples are assigned to the folds such that the target class is equally balanced within each fold, i.e. the folds are stratified.
4. For each fold, we applied the tools discussed in Sect. 2 to the training dataset to generate synthetic training data of equal length. For synthpop, we used the CART ("Classification and Regression Trees") model and set the "minbucket" parameter[4] to 1. For the Synthetic Data Vault, we used the GaussianCopula model, and passed an argument to the model that a categorical transformer should be used for the target column.[5]

---

[4] This parameter refers to the minimum number of observations in any terminal note. A higher value leads to synthetic data with larger differences to original samples.
[5] The default transformation for the GaussianCopula model is One Hot Encoding. We noticed that, with this default setting, it often occurred that only one of the two possible values of the target column is generated, leading to a constant column in the synthetic training data. Using the categorical transformation solves this problem.

5. Finally, we train our machine learning models on both the original and the synthetic training datasets, and compare their performances on the test dataset of the respective fold. We applied Random Forest and Support Vector Machines (SVM) with radial and linear kernel and default parameters.
6. This entire process is repeated ten times, and the mean class probabilities are used to calculate the ROC-AUC score (see Sect. 4.1).

To summarize, we use the very same experimental setup as the authors of [21][6], with one notable difference: we apply the feature abundance limits in Step 2 to transform the floating point numbers in the sample vectors to integer values that represent the abundance. The main idea behind this is to split up the complete range of values in an (geometrically) even way, emphasizing the corresponding levels of abundance. Comparing the performance baselines established in [21, p. 5] to our results on the original data in the subsequent subsection, we observe increased AUC-scores for Support Vector Machines. This indicates a slight benefit from this data preprocessing step.

4.1 Task Utility

We now consider the results of the experiment described above. For comparing the performance of the machine learning algorithms, we used a Receiver Operating Characteristic (ROC) curve just like in the original publication [21]. The following plots compare sensitivity (or "true-positive rate") on the y-axis to specificity (or "true-negative rate") on the x-axis for various probability thresholds. The Area Under the Curve (AUC) scores are listed within the plots and colored according to the ML model they refer to.

Let us start by summarizing the results of the two "Gevers" datasets (Fig. 1). Comparing the scores of ML models trained on SDV data instead of the original data, we can see that there are only minor differences in the effectiveness. Data generated via synthpop also shows scores that are very close to the original data. It is notable that we even have a slightly better score of SVM Linear on both datasets.

Let us proceed with the two "Morgan" datasets (Fig. 1). On SDV data, we again have very close scores on the first dataset, with a slightly larger drop for the Random Forest model. On the second dataset, Random Forest performed even better than on the original data, but SVM Linear performed substantially worse and shows a drop of the AUC score of 8%. Similar conclusions can be drawn for synthpop, which performed slightly better on the first dataset and slightly worse on the second. On the "Turnbaugh" dataset (Fig. 2), we again obtain good scores for both the SDV and synthpop. However, synthpop shows better results than the SDV, and the difference is particularly pronounced for

---

[6] An implementation of their experiments in the programming language R can be found on Github (https://github.com/knights-lab/MLRepo). We have modified their code and called Python scripts (e.g. for the SDV) with the package 'reticulate' (https://rstudio.github.io/reticulate/index.html).

SVM Linear. These roles are reversed on the "Kostic" dataset (Fig. 2), where SDV shows a particular high score on the Random Forest model.

On average, we observe a satisfying performance on synthetic data that is on par with previous experimental results for the evaluation of synthetic microdata for machine learning tasks (e.g., see [5]). SDV and synthpop are on a similar performance level. However, both methods appear to work better or worse in certain scenarios. For example, SVM with a linear kernel appears to perform exceptionally well on some of the synthpop datasets, while Random Forest performs well on some of the SDV datasets.

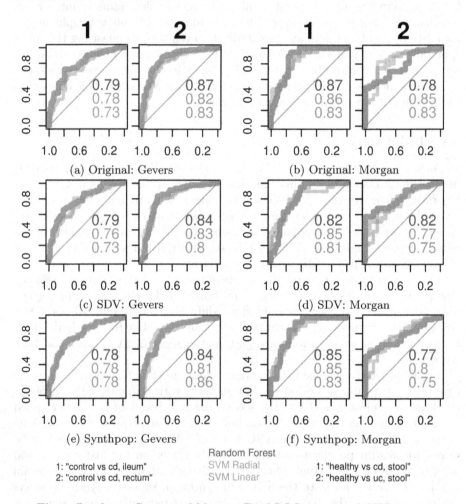

Fig. 1. Results on Gevers and Morgan: Final ROC curves and AUC scores

4.2 Sample Similarity and Privacy Risks

The goal of the synthetization is to keep the *global* dataset properties as close to the original data as possible. On the other hand, we do not want to preserve the

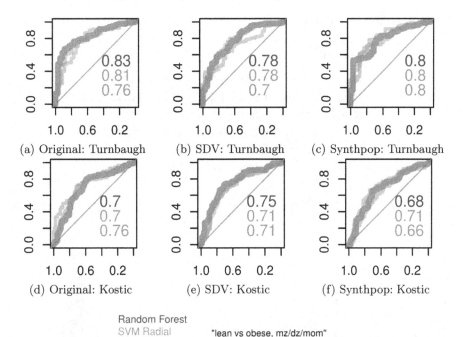

(a) Original: Turnbaugh   (b) SDV: Turnbaugh   (c) Synthpop: Turnbaugh

(d) Original: Kostic   (e) SDV: Kostic   (f) Synthpop: Kostic

Random Forest
SVM Radial   "lean vs obese, mz/dz/mom"
SVM Linear   "healthy vs tumor biopsy, paired"

Fig. 2. Results on Turnbaugh and Kostic

local properties of the original data, as these may allow to deduce information about real individual samples (see Sect. 3). While there is no 1-to-1 relation between synthetic and original samples, there may be privacy risks related to close local similarities between original and synthetic data samples, leading to near-matches. We measure this similarity as follows:

1. For each synthetic sample s, we computed the nearest neighboring original sample, i.e., the sample with minimal euclidean distance d_s to s.
2. We compute the mean and the variance of these minimal distances, i.e., the mean and the variance over d_s for all samples s in the synthetic dataset.

The results of a randomly chosen synthetic dataset for each of the processed original datasets are reported in Table 2. We can see that the distances d_s are on average reasonably large on both the SDV and on synthpop. In a direct comparison, however, synthpop's samples are considerably closer to the original ones than those obtained from SDV. In addition, synthpop shows a large variance in these local similarities of the datasets, and some samples are close or even equal to original data samples. Hence, datasets produced by synthpop seem to contain local information that is very similar to original data, thus leading to increased privacy risks for those vulnerable samples. SDV does not show the same behavior and may hence provide an increased reduction of privacy vulnerabilities.

Table 2. Mean minimal distance between original and synthetic nearest neighbors

Dataset	SDV	SPO
Gevers Ileum	11.322 ± 1.386	8.688 ± 24.527
Gevers Rectum	10.925 ± 1.240	7.510 ± 21.120
Morgan CD	14.301 ± 0.565	10.744 ± 20.577
Morgan UC	14.048 ± 0.735	9.772 ± 22.701
Turnbaugh	12.824 ± 0.588	9.141 ± 24.413
Kostic	14.970 ± 0.627	11.299 ± 30.380

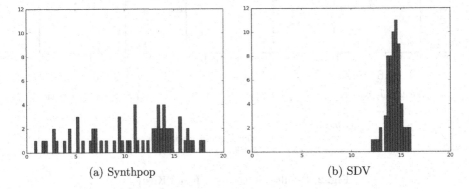

(a) Synthpop   (b) SDV

Fig. 3. Distance plots for the Morgan CD dataset

In Fig. 3, we provide a histogram showing the minimal distances for the "Morgan" CD dataset. The plot visualizes the tendencies observed in Table 2 and looks similar for the other considered datasets.

5   Conclusions and Future Work

In this paper, we evaluated two data synthetization methods, the *Synthetic Data Vault* and *synthpop*, for machine learning tasks on microbiome data. Both the SDV and synthpop performed well on the considered tasks, with AUC scores mostly deviating about $\pm 3\%$ from those on the original data. In our assessment of the privacy risks, we observed that synthpop generates a number of synthetic microbiome samples very close to original ones, indicating that there may remain higher privacy risks on synthpop than on SDV. However, we point out that synthpop comes with parameters (e.g., the already discussed 'minbucket' parameter) allowing to generate datasets with smaller or larger deviations from the original data. Since there is a trade-off between the utility and the privacy risk reduction on synthetic data, the option to customize the synthetic datasets may be useful in specific scenarios.

Our future work will concern the development of speed-ups for the Data Synthesizer and similar tools based on Bayesian networks. While models based on these networks usually generate data of high quality, the large number of features in microbiome tables leads to problems related to the efficient construction of these networks. Moreover, a comparison with other privacy-preserving data publishing methods, such as k-anonymity or micro-aggregation, would help to put the achieved performance of synthetic data into perspective.

Acknowledgements. This work was partially funded by the Austrian Research Promotion Agency FFG under grant 877173 (GASTRIC). SBA Research (SBA-K1) is a COMET Centre within the framework of COMET - Competence Centers for Excellent Technologies Programme and funded by BMK, BMDW, and the federal state of Vienna. The COMET Programme is managed by FFG.

Appendix: Heatmap Comparison

Figure 4 shows heatmaps for the "Kostic" dataset to demonstrate the ability of the synthesizers to preserve correlations between attributes. Red color in the feature matrix indicates a positive (Pearson) correlation coefficient between the respective features, while blue color indicates a negative coefficient. Synthpop's heatmap shows great similarities to the original. The heatmap on the SDV dataset is also similar, but to a lesser extent. In addition, there are features on the SDV dataset that are constant, and for which the correlation coefficient is not defined. Similar patterns can also be observed on the other datasets.

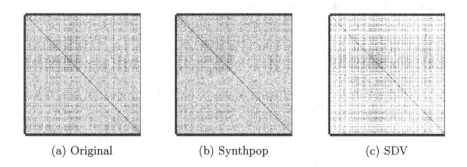

(a) Original   (b) Synthpop   (c) SDV

Fig. 4. Heatmaps on the Kostic dataset

References

1. Berger, B., Cho, H.: Emerging technologies towards enhancing privacy in genomic data sharing. Genome Biol. **20**(128) (2019). https://doi.org/10.1186/s13059-019-1741-0
2. Distrutti, E., Monaldi, L., Ricci, P., Fiorucci, S.: Gut microbiota role in irritable bowel syndrome: new therapeutic strategies. World J. Gastroenterol. **22**(7), 2219 (2016)

3. Fierer, N., Lauber, C.L., Zhou, N., McDonald, D., Costello, E.K., Knight, R.: Forensic identification using skin bacterial communities. PNAS **107**(14), 6477–6481 (2010)
4. Franzosa, E., Huang, K., Meadow, J., Gevers, D., Lemon, K., Bohannan, B.: Identifying personal microbiomes using metagenomic codes. PNAS **112**(22), E2930–E2938 (2015)
5. Hittmeir, M., Ekelhart, A., Mayer, R.: On the utility of synthetic data: an empirical evaluation on machine learning tasks. In: International Conference on Availability, Reliability and Security. ARES. ACM Press, Canterbury (2019). https://doi.org/10.1145/3339252.3339281
6. Hittmeir, M., Mayer, R., Ekelhart, A.: A baseline for attribute disclosure risk in synthetic data. In: ACM Conference on Data and Application Security and Privacy. CODASPY. ACM, New Orleans, March 2020. https://doi.org/10.1145/3374664.3375722
7. Hittmeir, M., Mayer, R., Ekelhart, A.: Distance-based techniques for personal microbiome identification. In: International Conference on Availability, Reliability and Security, ARES. ACM, Vienna, August 2022. https://doi.org/10.1145/3538969.3538985
8. Ley, R., Turnbaugh, P., Klein, S., Gordon, J.: Microbial ecology: human gut microbes associated with obesity. Nature **444**(7122), 1022–1023 (2006)
9. Li, G., Wang, Y., Su, X.: Improvements on a privacy-protection algorithm for DNA sequences with generalization lattices. Comput. Methods Programs Biomed. **108**(1), 1–9 (2012)
10. Liu, Q., et al.: Gut microbiota dynamics in a prospective cohort of patients with post-acute COVID-19 syndrome. Gut **71**(3) (2022). https://doi.org/10.1136/gutjnl-2021-325989
11. Malin, B.A.: Protecting genomic sequence anonymity with generalization lattices. Methods Inf. Med. **44**(5), 687–692 (2005)
12. Musso, G., Gambino, R., Cassader, M.: Obesity, diabetes, and gut microbiota: the hygiene hypothesis expanded? Diabetes Care **33**(10), 2277–2284 (2010)
13. Nowok, B., Raab, G., Dibben, C.: synthpop: Bespoke creation of synthetic data in R. J. Stat. Softw. Art. **74**(11) (2016). https://doi.org/10.18637/jss.v074.i11
14. O'Leary, N., Wright, M., Brister, J., et al.: Reference sequence (RefSeq) database at NCBI: current status, taxonomic expansion, and functional annotation. Nucleic Acids Res **44**, D733–D745 (2016)
15. Patki, N., Wedge, R., Veeramachaneni, K.: The synthetic data vault. In: IEEE International Conference on Data Science and Advanced Analytics (DSAA). Montreal, QC, Canada, 17–19 October 2016
16. Ping, H., Stoyanovich, J., Howe, B.: Datasynthesizer: privacy-preserving synthetic datasets. In: International Conference on Scientific and Statistical Database Management. Chicago, IL, USA, 27–29 June 2017
17. Rogers, G., Keating, D., Young, R., Wong, M., Licinio, J., Wesselingh, S.: From gut dysbiosis to altered brain function and mental illness: mechanisms and pathways. Mol. Psychiatry **21**(6), 738–748 (2016)
18. Rubin, D.B. (ed.): Multiple Imputation for Nonresponse in Surveys. Wiley Series in Probability and Statistics, Wiley, Hoboken (1987). https://doi.org/10.1002/9780470316696
19. Surendra, H., Mohan, H.S.: A review of synthetic data generation methods for privacy preserving data publishing. Int. J. Sci. Technol. Res. **6**(3), 95–101 (2017)

20. Taub, J., Elliot, M., Pampaka, M., Smith, D.: Differential correct attribution probability for synthetic data: an exploration. In: Domingo-Ferrer, J., Montes, F. (eds.) PSD 2018. LNCS, vol. 11126, pp. 122–137. Springer, Cham (2018). https://doi.org/10.1007/978-3-319-99771-1_9

21. Vangay, P., Hillmann, B.M., Knights, D.: Microbiome Learning Repo (ML Repo): a public repository of microbiome regression and classification tasks. GigaScience 8(5) (2019). https://doi.org/10.1093/gigascience/giz042

22. Wagner, J., Paulson, J.N., Wang, X., Bhattacharjee, B., Corrada Bravo, H.: Privacy-preserving microbiome analysis using secure computation. Bioinformatics 32(12) (2016). https://doi.org/10.1093/bioinformatics/btw073

23. Woerner, A.E., et al.: Forensic human identification with targeted microbiome markers using nearest neighbor classification. Forensic Sci. Int. Genet. 38, 130–139 (2019)

24. Yatsunenko, T.: Human gut microbiome viewed across age and geography. Nature 486(7402), 222–227 (2012)

Combining Defences Against Data-Poisoning Based Backdoor Attacks on Neural Networks

Andrea Milakovic[1] and Rudolf Mayer[1,2]([⊠]) [iD]

[1] Vienna University of Technology, Favoritenstraße 9-11, Vienna, Austria
[2] SBA Research gGmbH, Floragasse 7, Vienna, Austria
rmayer@sba-research.org

Abstract. Machine learning-based systems are increasingly used in critical applications such as medical diagnosis, automotive vehicles, or biometric authentication. Because of their importance, they can become the target of various attacks. In a data poisoning attack, the attacker carefully manipulates some input data, e.g. by superimposing a pattern, e.g. to insert a backdoor (a wrong association of the specific pattern to a desired target) into the model during the training phase. This can later be exploited to control the model behaviour during prediction, and attack its integrity, e.g. by identifying someone as the wrong user or not correctly identifying a traffic sign, thus causing road incidents.

Poisoning of the training data is difficult to detect, as often, only small amounts of the data need to be manipulated to achieve a successful attack. The backdoors inserted into the model are hard to detect as well, as its unexpected behaviour manifests only when the specific backdoor trigger, which is only known to the attacker, is presented. Nonetheless, several defence mechanisms were proposed, and in the right setting, they can yield usable results; however, they still show shortcomings and insufficient effectiveness in several cases. In this work, we thus try to answer the extent to which combinations of these defences can improve their individual effectiveness. To this end, we first build successful attacks for two datasets and investigate factors influencing the attack success. Our evaluation shows a substantial impact of the type of neural network models and datasets on the effectiveness of the defence. We also show that the choice of the backdoor trigger has a big impact on the attack and its success. Finally, our evaluation shows that a combination of defences can improve existing defences in several cases.

Keywords: Machine Learning · Poisoning Attacks · Defences

1 Introduction

With the emergence of Deep Learning (DL), Machine Learning (ML) systems have delivered even more impressive performance in a variety of application domains, from pattern recognition tasks like speech and object recognition,

© IFIP International Federation for Information Processing 2022
Published by Springer Nature Switzerland AG 2022
S. Sural and H. Lu (Eds.): DBSec 2022, LNCS 13383, pp. 28–47, 2022.
https://doi.org/10.1007/978-3-031-10684-2_3

employed in self-driving cars and robots, to cybersecurity tasks like spam and malware detection [8]. With an increased dependency of daily life on machine-learning-based systems, they also increasingly become the target of attacks.

Commonly discussed attacks include evasion and poisoning [2], which attack the availability or integrity of a machine learning model – and consequently the system employing it. Evasion attacks happen during prediction time, while poisoning attacks manipulate the training data and thus the model itself. In a poisoning integrity attack, the attacker's objective is to create a backdoor that allows inputs manipulated by the attacker, using the backdoor key, to be predicted as a target label of the attacker's choice. For example, against a face recognition system, this enables the attacker to impersonate another person and subsequently mislead the authentication system into identifying the attacker as a person that has access to a resource. A backdoored model should perform well on most benign inputs (including inputs that the end-user may hold out as a validation set), but cause targeted misclassifications of the model for inputs that satisfy the secret, attacker-chosen property – the backdoor key or trigger.

Research mostly focuses on current state-of-the-art methods such as Convolutional Neural Networks (CNNs), which are often employed in image analysis and computer vision. Many DL approaches are black-box models that are difficult to interpret – thus also malicious behaviour is challenging to detect.

Nonetheless, a few defence mechanisms against backdoor attacks are proposed. For CNNs, it has been shown that different parts of the network are specialised for learning the normal classification behaviour versus the backdoor, i.e. the association of the specific trigger pattern and the desired target. This is what several defences try to exploit. Activation clustering, e.g. tries to separate the inputs into groups of "normal" and "poisoned" inputs to discard the latter. On the other hand, fine-pruning tries to remove the parts of the network that are triggered by the backdoor pattern. Depending on several aspects, these defences can achieve good results against poisoning attacks; however, they still show shortcomings and insufficient effectiveness in many cases. In this work, we thus aim to answer the question of to what extent combinations of these defences can improve their effectiveness. Our main contributions are:

- We generate three poisoned versions of datasets for common tasks such as traffic sign and face recognition and publish them online (see footnote 5).
- We build successful backdoor attacks against three different neural networks (CNNs) to investigate the impact of several aspects, such as the backdoor trigger shape and size or the attacked model.
- We show that there is a substantial impact of the match-up of the neural network models and datasets on the effectiveness of current defences
- We show that a combination of defences can improve the stand-alone defences in several cases and can thus lead to a more robust and trustworthy machine learning system in adversarial environments.

1.1   Threat Model

We consider a user that wants to train a model, using a training dataset D_{train}. The attacker's goal is to return a model that will classify correctly all the inputs

Table 1. Categorisation of attacks against machine learning (based on [2])

	Integrity	Availability	Confidentiality
Test data	Evasion (e.g. adversarial examples)	–	Model stealing, model inversion,
Training data	Poisoning (to allow subsequent intrusions) - e.g. backdoors	Poisoning (to maximise classification error)	–

that do not contain the backdoor trigger and uniquely misclassify only the inputs that contain the trigger. To achieve this, we assume an attacker that has the capability to alter the training data and insert different patterns that can be used as a backdoor trigger and can add an arbitrary number of poisoned training inputs and modify any clean training inputs.

The remainder of this paper is organised as follows. Section 2 discusses related work, before Sect. 3 describes our evaluation setup. We then discuss results in Sect. 4, and provide conclusions and future work in Sect. 5.

2 Related Work

Adversarial Machine Learning comprises several attacks on a machine learning pipeline. They can be grouped, e.g., using the categorisation proposed in [2], which is based on the attacker's goals and capabilities to manipulate training and test data. An attacker can have one of the following goals along the axes of the well-known CIA (Confidentiality, Integrity, and Availability) triad, which is used analogously for other assets in cybersecurity:

- Availability: misclassifications that compromise normal system operation
- Integrity: misclassifications that do not compromise normal system operation
- Confidentiality/privacy: reveal confidential information on the learning model or its users

Table 1 shows attacks against ML systems, categorised along these axes.

It is important to note the difference between a backdoor and an adversarial example [23]. The latter, a form of an evasion attack, aims to discover or manipulate inputs at prediction time, so that they lead to a wrong inference. Contrarily, poisoning attacks interfere during the training phase.

2.1 Backdoor Attacks

A backdoor in cybersecurity, in general, is often a piece of malicious code (or similar), embedded by an attacker into a software (e.g. an operating system or application). The code enables the attacker e.g. to obtain higher privileges e.g. by authenticating through a particular password of the attacker's choice.

In Machine Learning, a backdoor embedded into a model allows the attacker to steer the prediction of that model. The model ideally behaves normally on regular (clean) inputs and only behaves wrongly on inputs that trigger the backdoor.

A backdoor trigger is normally superimposed on the original input; for example, for images, it can be a specific pixel pattern (e.g. yellow square) or a part of another image (e.g. sunglasses), or it can even be invisible [12]. The trigger is only known to the attacker and is needed to leverage the backdoor.

Gu et al. [9] proposed a backdoor attack by poisoning the training data. The attacker chooses a target label and a trigger pattern to be superimposed. Then, a subset of training images is overlayed with the trigger pattern, and their labels are modified to the target label. By training a model on the original and poisoned data, the backdoor is embedded. The authors show that in many settings, 99%+ of the poisoned inputs were misclassified as intended. In this attack scenario, the adversary needs the capability to manipulate the training data.

A slightly different approach, called Trojan Attack, was proposed by Liu et al. [14]. Here, the assumption is that the attacker has access to the final trained model but can not interfere with the initial training process. The attacker generates a trigger pattern that optimises large activation values of selected neurons. The attacker then generates inputs that specifically lead to high confidence values of a selected output node; this process is to some extent comparable to a model inversion attack [6], which tries to re-generate training data from a model. With the trigger and the generated training data, the model is fine-tuned to obtain a backdoored model, which can then be re-distributed to victims.

Backdoor attacks have been demonstrated to text data in e-mail SPAM classification [16], Natural Language Processing [5], and speech recognition [14], but the most prominent setting is image recognition tasks on datasets such as natural image recognition (CIFAR, ImageNet, ..), traffic sign recognition, or face recognition. While some works also address feature-extraction and shallow learning methods [15], the majority of works focuses on CNNs.

2.2 Backdoor Defences

As a backdoored model is trained to perform well on benign test data, and it can only be activated with the correct trigger, it is difficult to detect whether a backdoor is present in a model. This is aggravated by the fact that many deep learning approaches are black-box models and difficult to interpret – thus, also malicious behaviour is difficult to spot. Nonetheless, several defences against poisoning attacks have been proposed. Most methods are untargeted, i.e. they do not try to identify the specific vulnerability (e.g. the used pattern), but rather try to identify a super-set of causes and treat them in the hope that this deactivates the backdoor. Methods can be categorised depending on the step in the ML process they operate on. Some methods operate **during** training and, e.g., try to detect poisoned images and remove them from the training data to obtain a non-backdoored model. Other methods **post-process** a trained model, trying to disinfect it; this is especially useful when the model was obtained from an untrusted source without knowledge of how the training was performed.

One of the earliest methods was proposed by Nelson et al. [16] and is a rather general, model-agnostic mechanism called *Reject On Negative Impact* (RONI). It measures the effect of each additional training instance. The defender first trains a classifier with a base training set, then adds a new instance, and trains another classifier. If this new instance causes a drop in accuracy, it is removed. RONI is infeasible for complex models such as CNNs, as it requires re-training for each instance to be analysed. CNNs require tens of thousands or more samples easily – and one single training run can take hours, days or even more.

The Data Provenance defence by Baracaldo et al. [1] is very similar to RONI – but instead of assessing individual samples, it does so with groups of samples, thus reducing the number of models that need to be trained Each group is evaluated by comparing the performance of the classifier trained with and without it. The groups are identified based on using the information of the origin and creation (i.e. the provenance) of the training data. This defence is thus primarily useful when the training data is created as a union of datasets from different sources, e.g. multiple sensors operated by different organisations.

Activation clustering (AC) by Chen et al. [3] is based on the assumption that the activations of poisoned data differ from those of clean data, and thus can be separated by clustering. The defence first trains a model with untrusted (possibly poisoned) data and then records the activations for the inputs. Independent component analysis (ICA) is performed to reduce these to 10–15 features. Subsequently, they are clustered via k-Means into two clusters. Then, a new model is trained while omitting the data that belongs to one of the clusters and is subsequently used to classify the removed clusters. If the removed cluster contained activations of clean data, it is expected that the data belonging to it will largely be classified correctly. If it contained activations of poisoned data instead, the model will now not have learned the pattern and will thus primarily classify the data as the source class. Once the poisoned cluster is identified, its data can be removed, and a new model is trained with (assumed) clean data.

A similar defence, proposed by Tran et al. [24] and called *Spectral Signatures* (SS)), is based on identifying poisoned samples as outliers. The defence first selects a specific layer that is believed to represent high-level features. During a forward pass, the representation vectors for each output class label are recorded, and a covariance matrix thereof is the basis for a singular value decomposition (SVD). This is used to compute an outlier score for each input. The inputs with the highest scores are flagged and removed from the training set. Finally, the model is re-trained without the removed inputs. AC and SS have a few key differences. First, AC uses activations of (one of) the last hidden layer, while SS uses layers representing features, thus, earlier layers. Further, AC splits the data into two sub-groups and tests which one to remove, while SS computes an outlier score for each input and identifies those with the highest scores as poisoned.

Gu et al. [9] demonstrate that backdoored inputs trigger larger activation values in neurons that are otherwise dormant in the presence of clean inputs, which motivates the approach to remove (prune) these neurons. Using validation data that is known to be clean, the defender records the average activation of each neuron on a backdoored model. The neurons with the least activation are then pruned. The authors recommend pruning one of the last convolutional layers, as these sparsely encode the features learned in earlier layers – pruning in these layers should have a larger impact on the behaviour of the network.

Liu et al. [13] show that pruning is not effective against an adaptive attacker that anticipates that defence and tries to force the clean and backdoor learning onto the same neurons, by an anticipatory removal of dormant neurons before learning from the poisoned samples. Thus, (some) neurons represent both clean and poisoned patterns. Later, the removed neurons are added back and serve as a decoy for the defender – who will likely first remove those, before active neurons are considered. To defend against the adaptive attack, [13] proposes "fine pruning" (FP), adding a second step of fine-tuning the model with clean data. This will also update the weights of neurons involved in backdoor behaviour.

Combining several defences has shown to gain improvements over individual methods for evasion attacks and adversarial examples, specifically [11,27].

3   Evaluation Setup

In general, our evaluation workflow is as follows: (i) we train a model with only clean images, to obtain a baseline for the effectiveness (e.g. accuracy) on the test data, (ii) we poison a certain percentage of the train data and train a model thereupon. For this model, we measure the (change in) effectiveness and also the rate of test images that are poisoned and classified as intended by the attacker, (iii) we apply the defence method, which might modify the current model, or optionally we need to re-train a model if, e.g. images that are identified as poisoned are removed, (iv) we compare the accuracy and attack defence rate on this defended model, to the baseline and the backdoored model.

3.1   Datasets and Models

We use three publicly available benchmark datasets, detailed in Table 2. For the fine-pruning defence, we use a part of the train set as the clean dataset required for this defence. We keep the *absolute* number of clean samples comparable, motivated by a similar effort spent for labelling on each dataset, thus the percentage varies for each dataset. We picked the model architectures shown in Table 3, which have shown to be working well with these datasets

The **German Traffic Sign Recognition Benchmark** (GTSRB) [21][1] contains 43 classes of traffic signs, and is split into 39,209 training and 12,630 test images. We use 10% of the train data as clean set for fine-pruning. We use the CNN proposed by Wang et al. [25], used, e.g. also in [7]. It consists of two convolutional layers, followed by a max-pooling layer, again two convolutional layers followed by a max-pooling layer, and finally, two fully connected layers.

YouTube Aligned Faces Dataset (YTAF) [26][2] is derived from the YouTube faces datasets, which contains 3,425 YouTube videos of 1,595 different people. It is used for face recognition and face verification tasks [18,20,22]. Similar to the literature, we filter out people that have less than 100 images, resulting

---

[1] https://benchmark.ini.rub.de/gtsrb_dataset.html.
[2] https://www.cs.tau.ac.il/~wolf/ytfaces/.

in a dataset with 599,967 images for 1,283 individuals. We split the data into train, test and clean set in the ratio of 75:20:5, to obtain similar sizes of train and test set as used in the literature. In line with the literature, we use DeepID [22], a CNN with four convolutional layers. The first three layers are followed by max-pooling, and both convolutions 3 and 4 output to a fully connected layer.

Labeled Faces in the Wild (LFW) [10][3] contains 5,749 people with 13,000 images, whereas 1,680 of the people pictured have two or more distinct photos. We filtered out people with less than 20 images, arriving at 57 classes and 2,923 images. We split these into a train, test, and clean set with a ratio of 70:20:10. We use a pre-trained VGG16-Face model [18][4], which was trained on 2.6 million images. We fine-tune the last layer of the model on our dataset, as it was done in [4]. Thus, also only the last layer is trained with poisoned samples.

Table 2. Datasets used

Domain	Dataset Details			
	Name	# Classes	Train Size	Test Size
Traffic Signs	GTSRB	43	35,288	12,630
Face	YTAF	1,283	529,172	59,996
Recognition	LFW	57	2,500	292

We then train the models on clean data with the hyperparameters specified in Table 3; for GTSRB and YTAF, these are based on [25], and achieve almost identical accuracy as the benchmarks reported in literature. For LFW with the VGG-Faces model, without a comparable setup from literature, we used a grid search to determine optimal parameters. We tested different values for following parameters: epochs (10, 20, 30, 50, 70, 100), batches (32, 64), optimiser (Adam, Adadelta) and learning rate (0.001, 0.01, 0.1). We do not have a comparison to literature in terms of accuracy for LFW with VGG16 model.

Our poisoned datasets as well as the trained models are available at Zenodo[5].

3.2   Backdoor Triggers

For GTSRB, we use five different patterns as triggers. A square pattern is used frequently in literature (e.g. [9,17,19], either yellow or white, and we use these in two sizes (2×2, 4×4 pixels); we complement these with an additional pattern of four pixels, following similar patterns used in e.g. [3,25]. We use the pattern in both yellow and white to see if the colour has an impact.

---

[3] http://vis-www.cs.umass.edu/lfw/.
[4] https://www.robots.ox.ac.uk/~vgg/software/vgg_face/.
[5] Datasets: DOI 10.5281/zenodo.6588632; models: DOI 10.5281/zenodo.6588730.

Table 3. Models used and clean dataset results

	Model			Accuracy	
Dataset	Name	Layers	Hyper-parameters	Ours	Literature
GTSRB	Custom al. [25]	6 Conv + 2 Dense	epochs=10, batch=32, optimizer=Adam, lr=0.001	97.21%	96.83% ([25])
YTAF	DeepID [22]	4 Conv + 1 Dense	epochs=10, batch=32, optimizer=Adadelta, lr=0.1	99.33%	98.14% ([25])
LFW	VGG-Faces [18]	13 Conv + 3 Dense	epochs= 50, batch=32, optimizer=Adadelta, lr=0.1 Only last layer re-trained	84.98%	N/A

In literature, a common approach is to put the trigger **outside** of the actual traffic sign – but this does not transfer to real-world settings or physical attacks. Since all traffic sign images are centred, we thus placed the trigger around the middle of the image. For the attack, we need to select which (source) class should be misclassified into which (target) class. Randomly selecting several combinations showed that there is little difference between the specific selection. We discuss in the following the results for one pair ("120 km/h" → "stop").

For face recognition, in literature, funky and attention-drawing sunglasses in bright colours are the most frequently used for face recognition datasets [4,13] However, their appearance is rather unusual, and it is rare that people wear such sunglasses – especially not politicians or businessmen. Thus, to provide a more realistic and less suspicious attack scenario, we include as well black sunglasses (of the same shape). We use the same triggers for YTAF and LFW, namely green and black sun-glasses, as depicted in Figs. 5 and 6. The trigger image was added manually using a web application[6]. Due to practical limitations of generating poisoned images, we thus focused on a randomly selected source class.

3.3   Evaluation and Metrics

To evaluate backdoor attacks and defences we considered the accuracy of the model and its change, as well as the backdoor success, similar to [13]. To be not noticeable, a backdoor attack should not decrease this accuracy a lot (e.g. less than 5%). The desired backdoor success depends on the use case, but in general, the attacker wants it as high as possible. However, we also performed attacks that have lower success to see the effectiveness of the defences against those. Backdoor defences should substantially decrease backdoor success; ideally, they would not affect (lower) the accuracy on the clean data at all – which is, however, in general, the case. Thus, the defender wants to minimise the loss in accuracy on clean data, while being effective enough against the attack.

---

[6] https://insertface.com/.

3.4 Evaluated Defences and Implementation

We apply the following defences: Spectral Signature (SS) [24], Data Provenance (DP) [1], Activation Clustering (AC) [3] and Fine Pruning (FP) [13]. SS is reported successful by the authors with 5% and 10% of poisoned images; DP with 10% to 70% poisoned data; AC with 10%, 15% and 33%; and FP is tested differently for each domain, with 10% for the face recognition task, approx. 15% for speech recognition, and 50% for traffic sign recognition.

We primarily use the implementations in the IBM Adversarial Robustness Toolbox (ART)[7]. Fine-Pruning is not provided by ART, and we thus adapt the code provided by the authors of the defence [13][8] to a similar stack as ART.

4   Results

Regarding the baseline attack success, Figs. 1a to 1e show that for different trigger patterns on GTSRB, a varying number of poisoned images is needed to achieve a high backdoor success rate. For e.g. 95% success, the lowest ratio of poisoned images is needed for the big yellow square pattern with 4%, while the white square and the white pattern require 27%. This confirms that both the size and the colour of the pattern have an impact on the backdoor's success.

For face recognition, a high backdoor success is important when e.g. in an authentication system, the attacker has only limited attempts to authenticate before being blocked. On YTAF, to achieve a 100% attack success rate when using the green glasses, we need to poison 10% of the the images in the source class (cf. Fig. 1f). For the black glasses, we achieved only 90% backdoor success. For LFW, with green glasses and 10% poisoning, the attack success was only 20%. While success steadily increases when poisoning up to 30%, it then plateaus at 70% success (cf. Fig. 1g). For black glasses, a similar glass ceiling is reached, but only when least poisoning 40%. Both face recognition datasets thereby confirm the importance of colour respectively contrast for the attack.

From our tested defences, Spectral Signature (SS) and Data Provenance (DP) did not produce useful results with any of our models and datasets. SS needs two hyper-parameters to be set: (i) the expected percentage of poisoned images (which is normally not known), and (ii) an internal multiplication factor that would increase recall at the cost of false positives. We performed an extensive grid search, including the true poison percentages, but no setting prevailed. To the best of our knowledge, this defence was only used by the original authors, on the CIFAR-10 dataset, and with a very special one-pixel backdoor pattern. We suspect that our choice of datasets or trigger is the reason for the low performance. Data Provenance requires provenance information, which is not available for any of our benchmark datasets. We tried various runs with randomly assigning samples into different sources, but the defence was never successful. Both defences might only work in the specific settings evaluated by their authors. We thus focus on the other, successful defences.

---

[7] https://github.com/Trusted-AI/adversarial-robustness-toolbox.
[8] https://github.com/kangliucn/Fine-pruning-defence/tree/master/face.

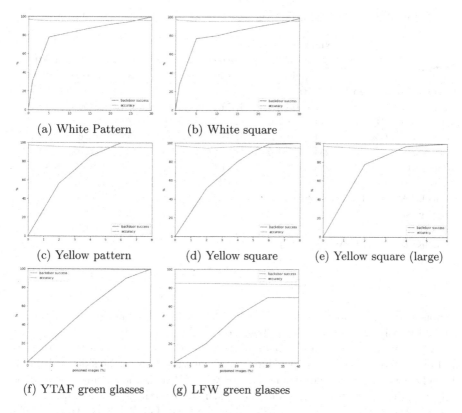

(a) White Pattern   (b) White square

(c) Yellow pattern   (d) Yellow square   (e) Yellow square (large)

(f) YTAF green glasses   (g) LFW green glasses

Fig. 1. Change in accuracy and backdoor success when increasing percentage of poisoned images: GTSRB (a–e), YTAF (f), LFW (g)

4.1 Activation Clustering Defence

We present and discuss the success of the defences against an attack with a percentage of poisoned data as above identified as a successful attack. The first backdoor defence applied is activation clustering. One important parameter is the metric used for cluster similarity computation. For all our cases, the distance-based metric would lead to all data being recognised as poisoned, which made this metric ineffective.

The results for AC with the size-based metric can be seen in the left half of Table 4 (absolute values are shown in Table 7). Even though the defence detects a relatively large portion of poisoned images in several settings, it also produces many false positives, i.e. clean data labelled as poisoned. For GTSRB models, the defence removed 31–33% of clean data, while for some settings (yellow square with lower percentage and the big yellow square), it did not remove any poisoned images. For YTAF, we can note a large difference depending on the pattern: for the green glasses, 21.11% of clean and 75% of poisoned images were removed, while for the black glasses, a lot more clean images (33.94%), but only 6.25%

Table 4. Accuarcy and attack success after applying Activation Clustering

Trigger	poisoned	Number of images removed poisoned	removed clean	Accuracy clean data	Δ Acc.	Attack success	Δ Attack success
German Traffic Sign (GTSRB)							
Yellow square (7%)	52	67.31%	31.79%	99.63%	+4.04%	100.00%	+0.74%
Yellow square (2%)	14	0.00%	32.82%	96.36%	+0.63%	60.00%	+16.55%
Yellow pattern (6%)	44	88.64%	31.98%	95.46%	+0.12%	99.26%	−0.74%
White square	258	75.19%	31.31%	95.19%	−0.40%	93.70%	−1.57%
White pattern	258	76.36%	31.24%	94.47%	−2.07%	100.00%	+1.12%
Big yellow square	29	0.00%	29.75%	96.52%	+3.80%	100.00%	+2.67%
Youtube Aligned Faces (YTAF)							
Green glasses	16	75.00%	21.11%	97.49%	−1.99%	30.00%	−70.00%
Black glasses	16	6.25%	33.94%	98.80%	−0.72%	90.00%	0%
Labelled Faces in the Wild (LFW)							
Green glasses	30	66.67%	28.82%	84.04%	−0.43%	50.00%	−28.57%
Black glasses	40	62.50%	33.55%	81.91%	−1.29%	50.00%	−28.57%

of poisoned images were removed. For LFW, green glasses perform better than black, but still worse than green glasses on YTAF.

After removing the data recognised as poisoned, the models were re-trained and evaluated on clean and poisoned data, shown on the right side of Table 4. The effectiveness varies substantially. For GTSRB, it is mostly ineffective, and only marginally reduced backdoor success in two settings: the yellow pattern (−0.74%) and white square (−1.57%). For the other GTSRB models, the backdoor success increased; this can be explained with the now more favourable proportion against clean images, as relatively fewer poisoned than clean images were removed.

For face recognition, we can observe a substantial reduction of attack success with the green glasses trigger on YTAF, from 100% to only 30%. For LFW, backdoor success decreased by 20% to 50%, for both colours. For both datasets, as expected, accuracy on the clean dataset drops as well, between 0.43% to 1.99%. On LFW, both green and black glasses lead to the same backdoor success (albeit with different percentage of poisoned images), and also the defence has the same effect. But different trigger colour makes a huge impact on YTAF; there, for black glasses, this defence did not decrease the backdoor success at all.

From the results for GTSRB, it seems that the percentage of poisoned data also has an impact on this defence. For models that have a small number of poisoned images (one of the yellow square settings, and the big yellow square), none of these are removed, and the backdoor success increased more than for the other GTSRB models – which is expected, since the ratio of poisoned to clean is even worse. To understand that impact, we studied this in detail for the yellow square pattern, increasing the percentage from 2% in a 1% step size, shown in Fig. 2. We can see that the defence always removes a lot and almost constant amount of clean images, namely 31–33%. In models with up to 4%

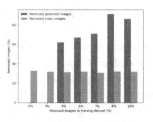 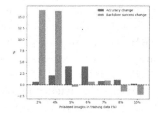

(a) Removed images   (b) Change in accuracy and attack success

Fig. 2. GTSRB: Activation clustering against yellow square pattern, different poisoning percentages

Table 5. Accuarcy and attack success after applying Fine Pruning

Model	2nd-to-last conv layer				Last conv layer			
	Removed neurons	Δ accuracy (clean data)	Attack success	Δ Attack Success	Removed neurons	Δ accuracy (clean data)	Attack success	Δ Attack Success
German Traffic Sign (GTSRB)								
Yellow square (7%)	76/128	+0.63%	92.96%	−6.35%	105/128	+0.02%	86.67%	−12.68%
Yellow square (2%)	101/128	+0.40%	45.13%	−13.30%	91/128	+2.29%	35.19%	−29.70%
Yellow pattern (6%)	98/128	+0.35%	95.92%	−4.08%	98/128	+0.21%	92.96%	−7.04%
White square	101/128	−1.39%	91.19%	−4.20%	99/128	+0.45%	90.74%	−4.67%
White pattern	96/128	−0.58%	85.83%	−13.31%	105/128	−0.98%	74.44%	−23.23%
Big yellow square	79/128	+2.44%	72.96%	−25.10%	99/128	+2.77%	68.15%	−30.02%
Youtube Aligned Faces (YTAF)								
Green glasses	10/60	−0.58%	70.00%	−30.00%	18/80	−0.40%	80.00%	−20.00%
Black glasses	16/60	−0.53%	60.00%	−33.33%	25/80	−0.47%	90.00%	0%
Labelled Faces in the Wild (LFW)								
Green glasses	127/512	−8.26%	30.00%	−42.86%	75/512	−7.98%	40.00%	−42.86%
Black glasses	127/512	−9.40%	60.00%	−14.29%	75/512	−11.11%	70.00%	0%

poisoned training data, no true positives were identified; beyond this percentage, the number increases sharply, and can reach up to 90%. A similar trend was observed for the big yellow square (not depicted). We might speculate that this stems from the utilised clustering algorithm, that is potentially not able to group the poisoned images together if they are too infrequent. Figure 2b shows that removing more true positives results in a drop of backdoor success, rather than an increase. However, the defence is still relatively ineffective. This is likely due to the fact that the backdoor pattern is still very prominent, and can be learned from fewer examples as well, as indicated in Fig. 1, where we observe that even with small percentage of poisoned data, the attack is already successful.

4.2 Fine Pruning Defence

For this defence, we prune neurons until the accuracy starts to drop more than 4% on the tuning set, as recommended in [13]. The authors of [13] do not specify which layer to prune, but just mention "later convolutional layers". Thus, we compare pruning on the last and second to last convolutional layer. After that, we fine-tune the model and evaluate it against clean and poisoned data separately, as shown in Table 5.

For GTSRB, we obtain a larger attack success reduction when we select the last convolutional layer, and they are substantially different for many trigger types, e.g. 29.7% instead of 13.3% reduction for the yellow square with less poisoned images. While the defence in general is maybe not as effective as it would be required, we can observe that in several cases, fine pruning did not reduce, but increase the accuracy for some of GTSRB models, i.e. pruning redundant neurons also improved generalisation in some cases.

On the other hand, on the face recognition models, we achieve better results when selecting the second to last convolutional layer. For example, for the black glasses pattern, pruning the last convolutional layer does not reduce the attack success at all, it just affects the clean data accuracy. But pruning the second to last layer, we reduce the attack success by 33.33% for YTAF and 14.28% for LFW. The biggest side effect of fine pruning is visible for LFW, where the accuracy was significantly decreased for both glasses colours.

When analysing the difference in the activations on clean and poisoned inputs, it can be observed that for GTSRB, there are several "dormant" neurons, not activated with clean inputs, on the last layer, as shown in Figs. 7 and 8. For the face recognition models, these are rather found on the second-to-last layer. This implies that a defender with a good understanding of the model and the ability to investigate neuron activations for clean samples may be able to chose the best layer.

We further varied the threshold for pruning – in addition to the suggested 4%, we also prune until a 2% and 6% accuracy drop, as shown in Fig. 3. We applied fine pruning with these new thresholds against selected GTSRB (yellow square) and YTAF and LFW (green glasses) attacks. We pruned as above: for GTSRB the last, and for YTAF and LFW, the second to last convolutional layer. For all cases, increasing the pruning threshold causes the accuracy on clean images to drop, as expected – but very marginally, except for LFW.

Figures 3a and 3b also show that for the GTSRB models, the backdoor success decreases when the threshold increases. The decrease is much bigger between 2% and 4% thresholds, than between 4% and 6%. For YTAF shown in Fig. 3c, at the 2% threshold, the backdoor success is not reduced, and for 4% and 6% the reduction is the same. For LFW shown in Fig. 3d, the defence effectiveness is the same for all thresholds, but accuracy decreases drastically with a higher threshold – already using just the 2% threshold, the accuracy reduction is around 7%, which might be unacceptable in many settings.

It is difficult to recommend one threshold valid for each setting – and the choice also depends on how much accuracy the defender is willing to give up. For the GTSRB models, it would be recommend to use the 6% threshold, since the accuracy does not drop much. For YTAF, the 4% threshold is the best choice, since it has the same backdoor success drop as the 6% threshold, but higher accuracy. In a real-world setting and no knowledge on the attack, this decision becomes more difficult, as it can be based only on the accuracy change.

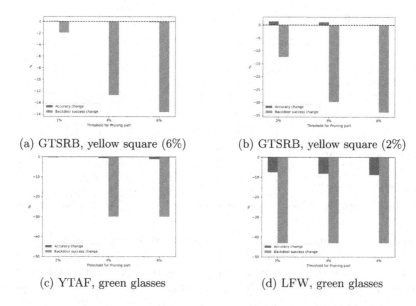

(a) GTSRB, yellow square (6%)   (b) GTSRB, yellow square (2%)

(c) YTAF, green glasses   (d) LFW, green glasses

Fig. 3. Change in accuracy and backdoor success caused by fine pruning

4.3 Combined Defence

We combined the defences in a different order, to analyse if this impacts the effectiveness. Table 6 recaps the effect of the individual defences in the 2nd and 3rd column, and then the impact of the combinations. Regarding accuracy on clean data, there is no big difference between the combination of defences and single defences, thus there is no penalty for combining.

First, we apply fine pruning (FP) after activation clustering (AC). The combination is an improvement over AC on GTSRB – but we need to keep in mind that defence did not actually decrease the attack on that dataset. There are some cases where the combination outperforms both individual defences, e.g. on the yellow square with a larger percentage of poisoned images, with a reduction of more than 25%, or the yellow pattern and white square, with around 12% higher reduction. For the big yellow square, there is no improvement over AC alone. For the remaining patterns, there is an improvement over AC, but the combination is worse than FP alone. When it comes to face recognition, the combination improved the results for all cases except the green glasses on YTAF, where the defence removed only 8 of 60 neurons, much below the other cases.

Comparing fine pruning and this combination, the latter returned better results in the case of LFW models, but equal or worse in the case of YTAF models. For GTSRB, the combination improved on three attacked models. Overall, this method obtained better or equal results than fine pruning for 6 out of 10 cases, and better or equal results than activation clustering for 9 out of 10 cases.

Results from applying activation clustering after fine pruning are depicted in the right half of Table 6. This combination reduced the attack success more

Table 6. Accuracy and attack success when combining Defences.

Model	Single Defence		Activation Clustering → FinePruning				FinePruning → Activation Clustering # images				
	AC	FP	Conv Layer	Removed Neurons	Accuracy clean data	Attack success	Poisoned	Removed Poisoned	Removed Overall	Accuracy clean data	Attack success
German Traffic Sign (GTSRB)											
Yellow square (7%)	100.00%	86.67%	Last	98/128	95.96%	62.96% (++)	44	0	10,873 (31%)	96.53%	97.78% (-)
Yellow square (2%)	60.00%	35.19%	Last	106/128	96.34%	48.15% (-)	14	0	11,578 (33%)	95.57%	52.29% (--)
Yellow pattern (6%)	99.26%	92.96%	Last	96/128	94.06%	89.26% (++)	44	38 (86%)	11,267 (32%)	95.76%	99.26% (-)
White square	93.70%	90.74%	Last	99/128	96.17%	78.89% (++)	258	0	11,110 (31%)	95.71%	94.07% (-)
White pattern	100.00%	74.44%	Last	100/128	96.00%	97.04% (-)	258	163 (63%)	11,488 (33%)	97.11%	98.52% (--)
Big yellow square	100.00%	68.15%	Last	101/128	95.82%	100.00% (--)	29	0	10,933 (31%)	96.30%	100.00% (-)
YouTube Aligned Faces (YTAF)											
Green glasses	30.00%	70.00%	2ndLast	8/60	98.97%	80.00% (-)	16	11 (69%)	151.531 (25%)	97.46%	20.00% (++)
Black glasses	90.00%	60.00%	2ndLast	15/60	98.54%	60.00% (--)	16	1 (6%)	153,707 (26%)	97.32%	90.00% (--)
Labelled Faces in the Wild (LFW)											
Green glasses	50.00%	30.00%	2ndLast	160/512	74.82%	20.00% (++)	30	22 (73%)	814 (33%)	79.08%	20.00% (++)
Black glasses	50.00%	60.00%	2ndLast	119/512	78.01%	30.00% (++)	40	8 (20%)	701 (28%)	79.43%	60.00% (-)

or equal than activation clustering for eight of 10 settings models – it is less effective only for GTSRB with the white square (very marginally), and LFW with the black glasses. Compared to fine pruning, this combination achieved less reduction in all GTSRB settings. In four out of six cases, activation clustering on a pruned model did not manage to to remove any poisoned image; when applying the defence alone, it failed to remove poisoned images only in two cases. On YTAF, the combination reduced substantially more of the attack success than only fine pruning for the green glasses pattern: down to 20.00%, compared to 70.00% after fine pruning only. With the black glasses on LFW, the combination achieved the same score as with fine pruning. The combination performed better on LFW with green glasses, where the attack success was reduced by 10%, down to 20.00%; for the black glasses, the reduction stayed the same, at 60.00%.

It is interesting to note that order of the defences did make an impact on the effectiveness. In general, the combination of activation clustering followed by fine pruning gave better results than the other way around. As a comparison, the first combination outperformed AC in 9, while the second combination outperformed only in 5 cases. Similarly, the first combination outperformed FP for 5 out of 10 models, but the second combination for only 2.

A likely explanation for this is as follows. When applying fine pruning, dormant neurons that are potentially used by poisoned images, as they represent the trigger pattern, are removed. Consequently, the activations of the poisoned images will produce less distinct patterns than clean data, and subsequently, the clustering algorithm is not able to separate these into poisoned or clean, but rather along other criteria, which are irrelevant for the poisoning detection.

4.4 Discussion

In our experiments, we observed that more contrast (by larger colour difference, e.g. green instead of the black glasses), as well as a larger size of the pattern, lead to an effective backdoor, already at a lower percentage of poisoned images.

Fine pruning (FP) was effective for every combination of the model and dataset. Activation clustering (AC) was much more effective on the YTAF and

LFW, independent of the used backdoor trigger; on GTSRB, it sometimes even had a negative effect, i.e. it increased the backdoor success in several cases. AC heavily depends on a good hyper-parameter for the metric used for clustering: the distance-based metric (falsely) recognises too many samples as poisoned, rendering the method useless; the size-based metric is thus preferable. FP depends primarily on two hyper-parameters: the layer to be pruned, and the pruning threshold. The choice of the layer can drastically increase the effectiveness, and is model dependent – and thus requires some domain knowledge to be correctly set, but with an inspection of the activations, it is likely feasible for many settings. The threshold parameter depends on the risk mitigation strategy of the model owner. Larger values incur a higher penalty on clean data accuracy, but provide a better defence. Which value is fitting is thus case and strategy dependent. However, we note that the recommendation from the authors of the method of 4% is not optimal in all settings.

Combining defences has only a marginal further impact on clean data accuracy – but generally reduces the attack success. In our evaluation, this positive effect was more substantial for the face classification datasets. Also, the order of the application of the combined defence matters, and applying AC first is recommended.

5 Conclusions and Future Work

In this paper, we investigated backdoor attacks and defence mechanisms. We utilised three different CNN models on three different image datasets – German Traffic Sign Recognition Benchmark (GTSRB), YouTube Aligned Faces (YTAF) and Labeled Faces in the Wild (LFW). We embedded backdoors by poisoning the dataset with different backdoor triggers, to show the impact of the trigger on the backdoor success. We observed that more contrast and a larger size of the pattern lead to an effective backdoor, already at low percentage of poisoned images.

We tested the effect of different defences, as well as combining the successful ones to become more effective. While fine pruning (FP) was effective for every combination of the model and dataset, activation clustering (AC) was much more effective on the YTAF and LFW, independent of the used backdoor trigger; on GTSRB, in contrast, it sometimes even had a negative effect. For both methods, setting the hyper parameters correctly is critical. Combining defences lead to only marginally further impact on clean data accuracy, but generally reduced the attack success. Thus, it is a valid and effective strategy to employ against suspected poisoning attacks, and should be considered by defenders.

Future work will focus on evaluating our results on an even larger range of datasets and models trained thereupon. Further, we will include other, novel defences not yet considered in this work.

Acknowledgements. SBA Research (SBA-K1) is a COMET Centre within the framework of COMET - Competence Centers for Excellent Technologies Programme and funded by BMK, BMDW, and the federal state of Vienna. The COMET Programme is managed by FFG.

Appendix

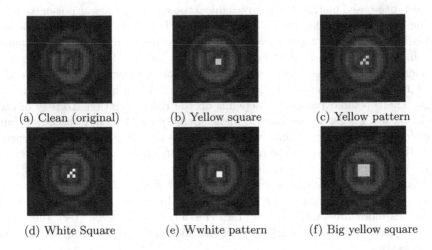

(a) Clean (original)   (b) Yellow square   (c) Yellow pattern

(d) White Square   (e) Wwhite pattern   (f) Big yellow square

Fig. 4. GTSRB: clean (a) and poisoned images with different patterns (b–f)

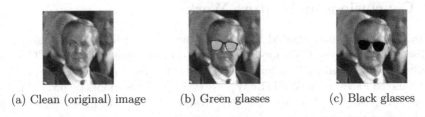

(a) Clean (original) image   (b) Green glasses   (c) Black glasses

Fig. 5. LFW (Donald Rumsfeld): clean and poisoned images with two colours

(a) Clean (original) image   (b) Green glasses   (c) Black glasses

Fig. 6. YTAF (Sarah Jessica Parker): clean and poisoned images with two colours

Table 7. Accuarcy and attack success after applying Activation Clustering (absolute image values)

Trigger	Number of images			Accuracy clean data	Δ Acc.	Attack success	Δ Attack success
	poisoned	removed poisoned	removed clean				
German Traffic Sign (GTSRB)							
Yellow square (7%)	52	35	11,203	99.63%	+4.04%	100.00%	+0.74%
Yellow square (2%)	14	0	11,578	96.36%	+0.63%	60.00%	+16.55%
Yellow pattern (6%)	44	39	11,271	95.46%	+0.12%	99.26%	−0.74%
White square	258	194	10,969	95.19%	−0.40%	93.70%	−1.57%
White pattern	258	197	10,943	94.47%	−2.07%	100.00%	+1.12%
Big yellow square	29	0	10,489	96.52%	+3.80%	100.00%	+2.67%
Youtube Aligned Faces (YTAF)							
Green glasses	16	12	94,968	97.49%	−1.99%	30.00%	−70.00%
Black glasses	16	1	152,736	98.80%	−0.72%	90.00%	0%
Labelled Faces in the Wild (LFW)							
Green glasses	30	20	581	84.04%	−0.43%	50.00%	−28.57%
Black glasses	40	25	673	81.91%	−1.29%	50.00%	−28.57%

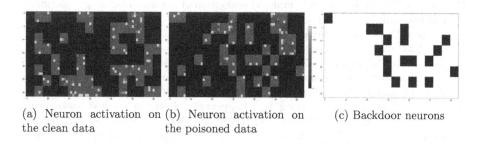

(a) Clean data   (b) Poisoned data   (c) Backdoor neurons

Fig. 7. GTSRB: neuron activations in second-to-last convolutional layer

(a) Neuron activation on the clean data   (b) Neuron activation on the poisoned data   (c) Backdoor neurons

Fig. 8. GTSRB: neuron activations in last convolutional layer

References

1. Baracaldo, N., Chen, B., Ludwig, H., Safavi, A., Zhang, R.: Detecting poisoning attacks on machine learning in IoT environments. In: IEEE International Congress on Internet of Things. ICIOT, IEEE, San Francisco, CA, July 2018. https://doi.org/10.1109/ICIOT.2018.00015

2. Biggio, B., Roli, F.: Wild patterns: ten years after the rise of adversarial machine learning. Pattern Recognit. **84**, 317–331 (2018). https://doi.org/10.1016/j.patcog.2018.07.023

3. Chen, B., et al.: Detecting backdoor attacks on deep neural networks by activation clustering. In: AAAI Workshop on Artificial Intelligence Safety. SafeAI, CEUR Workshop Proceedings, Honolulu, Hawaii, January 2019

4. Chen, X., Liu, C., Li, B., Lu, K., Song, D.: Targeted Backdoor Attacks on Deep Learning Systems Using Data Poisoning, December 2017

5. Dai, J., Chen, C., Li, Y.: A backdoor attack against LSTM-based text classification systems. IEEE Access **7** (2019). https://doi.org/10.1109/ACCESS.2019.2941376

6. Fredrikson, M., Jha, S., Ristenpart, T.: Model inversion attacks that exploit confidence information and basic countermeasures. In: ACM SIGSAC Conference on Computer and Communications Security. CCS. ACM, New York (2015). https://doi.org/10.1145/2810103.2813677

7. Fu, H., Veldanda, A.K., Krishnamurthy, P., Garg, S., Khorrami, F.: A feature-based on-line detector to remove adversarial-backdoors by iterative demarcation. IEEE Access **10** (2022). https://doi.org/10.1109/ACCESS.2022.3141077

8. Gu, J., et al.: Recent advances in convolutional neural networks. Pattern Recognit. **77** (2018). https://doi.org/10.1016/j.patcog.2017.10.013

9. Gu, T., Liu, K., Dolan-Gavitt, B., Garg, S.: BadNets: evaluating backdooring attacks on deep neural networks. IEEE Access **7** (2019). https://doi.org/10.1109/ACCESS.2019.2909068

10. Huang, G.B., Ramesh, M., Berg, T., Learned-Miller, E.: Labeled faces in the wild: a database for studying face recognition in unconstrained environments. Technical report 07–49, University of Massachusetts, Amherst, October 2007

11. Jankovic, A., Mayer, R.: An empirical evaluation of adversarial examples defences, combinations and robustness scores. In: Proceedings of the 2022 ACM on International Workshop on Security and Privacy Analytics. IWSPA, ACM, Baltimore, April 2022. https://doi.org/10.1145/3510548.3519370

12. Li, S., Xue, M., Zhao, B., Zhu, H., Zhang, X.: Invisible backdoor attacks on deep neural networks via steganography and regularization. IEEE Trans. Dependable Secure Comput. (2020). https://doi.org/10.1109/TDSC.2020.3021407

13. Liu, K., Dolan-Gavitt, B., Garg, S.: Fine-pruning: defending against backdooring attacks on deep neural networks. In: Bailey, M., Holz, T., Stamatogiannakis, M., Ioannidis, S. (eds.) RAID 2018. LNCS, vol. 11050, pp. 273–294. Springer, Cham (2018). https://doi.org/10.1007/978-3-030-00470-5_13

14. Liu, Y., et al.: Trojaning attack on neural networks. In: Network and Distributed System Security Symposium. NDSS, Internet Society, San Diego (2018). DOIurl-https://doi.org/10.14722/ndss.2018.23291

15. Mayerhofer, R., Mayer, R.: Poisoning attacks against feature-based image classification. In: ACM Conference on Data and Application Security and Privacy. CODASPY. ACM, Baltimore, April 2022. https://doi.org/10.1145/3508398.3519363

16. Nelson, B., et al.: Misleading learners: co-opting your spam filter. In: Machine Learning in Cyber Trust. Springer, Boston (2009).. https://doi.org/10.1007/978-0-387-88735-7_2

17. Nuding, F., Mayer, R.: Data poisoning in sequential and parallel federated learning. In: ACM on International Workshop on Security and Privacy Analytics. IWSPA. ACM, Baltimore, April 2022. https://doi.org/10.1145/3510548.3519372

18. Parkhi, O.M., Vedaldi, A., Zisserman, A.: Deep face recognition. In: British Machine Vision Conference. British Machine Vision Association, Swansea (2015). https://doi.org/10.5244/C.29.41

19. Rehman, H., Ekelhart, A., Mayer, R.: Backdoor attacks in neural networks – a systematic evaluation on multiple traffic sign datasets. In: Holzinger, A., Kieseberg, P., Tjoa, A.M., Weippl, E. (eds.) CD-MAKE 2019. LNCS, vol. 11713, pp. 285–300. Springer, Cham (2019). https://doi.org/10.1007/978-3-030-29726-8_18

20. Schroff, F., Kalenichenko, D., Philbin, J.: FaceNet: a unified embedding for face recognition and clustering. In: IEEE Conference on Computer Vision and Pattern Recognition, CVPR, IEEE Boston, June 2015. https://doi.org/10.1109/CVPR.2015.7298682

21. Stallkamp, J., Schlipsing, M., Salmen, J., Igel, C.: The German traffic sign recognition benchmark: a multi-class classification competition. In: International Joint Conference on Neural Networks, IJCNN, IEEE, San Jose, July 2011. https://doi.org/10.1109/IJCNN.2011.6033395

22. Sun, Y., Wang, X., Tang, X.: Deep learning face representation from predicting 10,000 classes. In: IEEE Conference on Computer Vision and Pattern Recognition. CVPR, IEEE, Columbus, June 2014. https://doi.org/10.1109/CVPR.2014.244

23. Szegedy, C., et al.: Intriguing properties of neural networks. In: International Conference on Learning Representations, ICLR, Banff, AB, Canada, April 2014

24. Tran, B., Li, J., Madry, A.: Spectral signatures in backdoor attacks. In: International Conference on Neural Information Processing Systems, NeurIPS. Curran Associates Inc., Montréal, December 2018

25. Wang, B., et al.: Neural Cleanse: identifying and mitigating backdoor attacks in neural networks. In: IEEE Symposium on Security and Privacy (SP). IEEE, San Francisco, May 2019. https://doi.org/10.1109/SP.2019.00031

26. Wolf, L., Hassner, T., Maoz, I.: Face recognition in unconstrained videos with matched background similarity. In: IEEE Conference on Computer Vision and Pattern Recognition, CVPR, IEEE, Colorado Springs, June 2011. https://doi.org/10.1109/CVPR.2011.5995566

27. Zhang, C., Gao, P.: Countering adversarial examples: combining input transformation and noisy training. In: IEEE/CVF International Conference on Computer Vision Workshops, ICCVW, IEEE, Montreal, October 2021. https://doi.org/10.1109/ICCVW54120.2021.00017

MCoM: A Semi-Supervised Method for Imbalanced Tabular Security Data

Xiaodi Li[✉][iD], Latifur Khan[iD], Mahmoud Zamani, Shamila Wickramasuriya, Kevin W. Hamlen[iD], and Bhavani Thuraisingham[iD]

The University of Texas at Dallas, Richardson, TX 75080, USA
{xiaodi.li,lkhan,mxz173130,scw130030,hamlen,bxt043000}@utdallas.edu

Abstract. MCoM (Mixup Contrastive Mixup) is a new semi-supervised learning methodology that innovates a *triplet mixup* data augmentation approach to address the imbalanced data problem in tabular security data sets. Tabular data sets in cybersecurity domains are widely known to pose challenges for machine learning because of their heavily imbalanced data (e.g., a small number of labeled attack samples buried in a sea of mostly benign, unlabeled data). Semi-supervised learning leverages a small subset of labeled data and a large subset of unlabeled data to train a learning model. While semi-supervised methods have been well studied in image and language domains, in security domains they remain under-utilized, especially on tabular security data sets which pose especially difficult contextual information loss and balance challenges for machine learning. Experiments applying MCoM to collected security data sets show promise for addressing these challenges, achieving state-of-the-art performance compared with other methods.

Keywords: Semi-Supervised Learning · Contrastive Learning · Tabular Data Sets · Security Data Sets

1 Introduction

Supervised learning [20, 22, 23, 28] has shown great success with large, labeled data sets collected and annotated by researchers in image, language, and many other domains. However, in real-world cybersecurity domains, the task of accurately labeling large data sets for supervised learning is often infeasible. For example, security-critical software products, such as operating systems, web servers, cloud computing architectures, and networking stacks, often consist of hundreds of millions of lines of code, and undergo hundreds or thousands of code changes per day (churn) as features are added, bugs are corrected, and hardware evolves. Accurately identifying and labeling even one security vulnerability in these large, mutating corpa often requires extremely high levels of expertise and many hundreds of person-hours of effort. As a result, previously undiscovered (zero-day) security vulnerabilities are so valuable and rare that some have sold for up to $2.5 million USD[1] to bug bounty programs and on the black market.

---

[1] https://zerodium.com.

Published by Springer Nature Switzerland AG 2022
S. Sural and H. Lu (Eds.): DBSec 2022, LNCS 13383, pp. 48–67, 2022.
https://doi.org/10.1007/978-3-031-10684-2_4

In order to aid defenders in analyzing such data sets before vulnerabilities become exploited, it is essential to efficiently leverage the small portion of the data set that has been labeled by experts, and train the model to handle the large amount of unlabeled data. Semi-supervised learning utilizes both labeled and unlabeled data to address this dilemma. In recent years, many semi-supervised methods [1,7,33,39] have emerged for different domains, bridging the gap between supervised learning and unsupervised learning. However, in security domains, semi-supervised methods on tabular security data sets remain relatively unexplored. This open problem has impeded cybersecurity research and practice, in that state-of-the-art software vulnerability detection approaches often suffer extremely high false positive rates (making them unusable), miss many vulnerabilities (making them unsafe), or cannot use machine learning approaches at all (posing scalability and automation problems).

Nevertheless, partially labeled data sets for this domain are widely available in the form of Common Vulnerabilities and Exposures (CVE)[2] and National Vulnerability Databases (NVDs)[3] accumulated by the security community for decades for large, widely used software products. These databases are not exhaustive—they represent only the small subset of software security vulnerabilities that have been discovered and documented for a relatively small subset of all software products. However, the vulnerability instances collected in these data sets are widely considered to be representative of the vast, unknown expanse of yet-to-be-discovered vulnerabilities. For example, Common Weakness Enumerations (CWEs)[4] represent informal efforts to document categories and patterns in these databases in order to document lessons learned and help programmers avoid mistakes conducive to software compromise. This data therefore constitutes a heavily imbalanced yet conceptually rich source of information about real-world software vulnerabilities.

There are many semi-supervised learning techniques in image and language domains due to the ease of data augmentation in these data sets. However, in security domains, data are usually in a tabular format. This impedes augmentation because the data lack context, causing significant information loss after augmentation. Tabular security data sets are also highly imbalanced. For example, the class ratio of the data set we use are 1:100 (positive : negative), where positive means vulnerable cases and negative means non-vulnerable cases. This huge imbalance issue is difficult to solve with traditional down sampling and up sampling methods (e.g., [3]). To address this problem, researchers have proposed a variety of approaches. For example, set convolution (SetConv) [13] and episodic training have been proposed to extract a single representative for each class, so that classifiers can later be trained on a balanced class distribution. Focal Loss [21] addresses this class imbalance by reshaping the standard cross entropy loss such that it down-weights the loss assigned to well-classified examples, focusing training on a sparse set of hard examples and preventing the vast number of easy negatives from overwhelming the detector during training.

---

[2] https://cve.mitre.org.

[3] https://nvd.nist.gov.

[4] https://cwe.mitre.org.

Class-balanced Loss [6] is a re-weighting method using the effective number of samples for each class to re-balance the loss.

As an alternative to these methods, we propose a novel *triplet mixup data augmentation* method to address the class imbalance problem by only augmenting the minority data. Triplet mixup goes beyond the traditional pairwise mixup, mixing three different data points from the same class, thereby joining the information from the features of the triple data to a larger extent. Experimental results demonstrate the effectiveness of our proposed data augmentation method over the prior approaches. In addition to doing mixup on the input, we also do manifold mixup in the hidden space on each pair of embeddings to create multiple views for our contrastive loss term. We further leverage the unlabeled subset by pre-training the encoder and using label propagation [17] to generate pseudo-labels for the unlabeled samples. Subsequently, the trained encoder and samples, for which we have generated pseudo-labels, are transferred to a downstream task where a simple predictor with Mixup [42] augmentation is trained.

The contributions of our work are fourfold: (1) We propose a novel triplet mixup data augmentation method that can reduce the data imbalance problem in large, sparsely labeled data sets. (2) Our work is the first semi-supervised learning framework on tabular security data sets. (3) We develop a tool to automatically extract source-level function features from sources processed by Joern [38] and binary-level function features from binaries produced by C compilers. (4) We achieve state-of-the-art performance on all the experiments, which demonstrate the superiority of our proposed method for cybersecurity data domains.

2   Background

2.1   Vulnerability Complexity

```
1 phar_set_inode(phar_entry_info *e)
2 {
3   char tmp[MAXPATHLEN];
4   int tmp_len;
5   tmp_len = e->filename_len + e->phar->fname_len;
6   memcpy(tmp, e->phar->fname, e->phar->fname_len);
7   memcpy(tmp + e->phar->fname_len, e->filename, e->>
      filename_len);
8   e->inode = (unsigned short)zend_get_hash_value(tmp,
      tmp_len);
9 }
```

Listing 1.1. An Example of A Vulnerable Function CVE 2015-3329

Software vulnerability detection is widely considered to be a difficult problem requiring high levels of human expertise and training. Listing 1.1 shows an example of a vulnerable function (CVE 2015-3329) in the Linux PHP interpreter. Despite having a small number of lines without loops or conditionals, this bug evaded auditors for over 2 years, leaving affected Linux machines susceptible to remote compromise until it was detected and patched in April 2015. The flaw

Table 1. Applications

Application	Description
Sudo	Enables users to run programs with the security privileges of another user
Poftpd	A simple ftp server that provide high configurable features
Libtiff	Library for reading and writing Tagged Image File Format (TIFF)
Libpng	Library for reading, creating and manipulating Portable Network Graphics (PNG)
Freetype	Library used to render text into bitmaps
TinTin	A console telnet client for playing MUD (Multi-User Dimension)
Tcpdump	Data network packet analyzer
Openssh	A secure networking utility works on Secure Shell protocol

involves unsafely copying a file name with attacker-controllable length into a buffer, potentially overflowing it and corrupting adjacent memory. When adjacent memory includes code pointers, the hijacker can take remote control of the program.

Providing defenders with more powerful tools to help them find these subtle but dangerous vulnerabilities in large bodies of complex code is an increasingly acute need in the software industry.

2.2   Data Set and Challenges

Previous work has considered the software vulnerability detection problem at various levels of granularity, including component-level granularity [14,41,45], source file-level granularity [9,25,31], and function-level granularity [40]. Finer granularities are more useful because they provide code programmers and auditors more precise information on where vulnerabilities might be located and how to patch them against exploitation; but they are often more difficult to achieve in practice because of the much greater level of human skill and time typically required to localize precise bug positions—especially for bugs that involve complex interactions between multiple components scattered throughout the code. This leads to greater data imbalance challenges, since finer-granularity labels are more difficult to produce. Accurately modeling software vulnerabilities therefore requires a suitably large data set. Moreover, the data set must usually consist of real-world applications and real-world bugs rather than synthetic data in order to yield a model that is effective for realistic vulnerability-finding tasks.

Building a large corpus of data using real-world applications is challenging. We used NVD archives to compile a labeled data set with a reasonable vulnerable-to-non-vulnerable ratio in records. The NVD database includes URLs with *patches* or *exploit* tags, but does not reveal which portions of each patch are relevant to the exploit, or which original code lines were exploited. Inferring the respective files, functions, and locations of the defective code is a manual effort requiring many person-hours. We collected a suitably large corpus by manually inspecting 8 real-world applications designed for variety of different purposes and whose known vulnerabilities are recorded within the NVD.

Table 1 shows the descriptions of the applications in our data set. Each is a large-scale open-source project written in C/C++ containing hundreds or thousands of functions, and tens or hundreds of thousands of lines of code. By manually studying all NVD records for these applications over the past decade, we assembled a data set of over 400 vulnerabilities, the exact bug locations that gave rise to each vulnerability, and the type of attack that exploited each vulnerability and that motivated the patch.

Table 2 summarizes the four different dimensions of features we studied associated with these vulnerabilities: structure-based, flow-based, binary-based, and pointer-based. These dimensions are inspired by prior works that have shown the effectiveness of using different aspects of software structures for modeling and discovering vulnerabilities [10,38]. In particular, the different dimensions are useful for detecting different types of vulnerabilities. For example, flow-based features tend to be associated with component interaction errors, wherein software components make inconsistent, conflicting assumptions about prerequisites or interfaces; whereas pointer-based features tend to be associated with incorrectly computed references to data or memory.

We collect source-level function features using Joern [38], which processes source files into code property graphs (CPGs) reflecting their syntax, control-flows, and dataflows. In addition to source level feature collection, we collect binary-based data in order to detect compiler-generated vulnerabilities that cannot be observed at the source code level. To our knowledge, ours is the first data set that combines detailed, fine-grained CVE data for both source and binary features. We developed a tool to automatically extract these features from sources processed by Joern and binaries produced by C compilers.

2.3   Data Augmentation

Data augmentation is a method to increase training data diversity without directly collecting more data [11]. It is often employed to address data insufficiency problems. In image and language domains, data augmentation has been well studied [16,18,19,30,32,34]. There are a variety of data augmentation methods available in these domains. For example, in image domains researchers use zoom, flip, contrast adjustment, etc., and in language domains researchers use language translation, next words and previous words predictions, interpolation, etc. Dating back to 2002, SMOTE (Synthetic Minority Over-sampling Technique) [3] is an efficient up-sampling method of the minority class. In recent years, Mixup [42] has emerged as a popular data augmentation method for alleviating memorization and sensitivity of adversarial examples of large deep neural networks. It regularizes the neural network to favor simple linear behavior between training examples by training a neural network on convex combinations of pairs of examples and their labels. RLCN [37] utilizes limited samples for training a model, and then applies it to classify normal instances and detect the emergence of novel classes over time. However, tabular data lacks context information, making it difficult to apply traditional data augmentation methods on tabular domains because it generates too much noise. To address this problem, we extend the idea of Mixup to a Triplet Mixup data augmentation

Table 2. Features

Dimension	Feature	Description
Structure-based	Parameters	number of parameters [45]
	Cyclomatic Complexity	number of linearly independent paths [24]
	Loop Number	number of loops [31]
	Nesting Degree	maximum nesting level of control structures in a function [29]
	SLOC	number of source lines [12]
	Variables	number of local variables [31]
Flow-based	In-degree	number of functions that call the corresponding function [27]
	Out-Degree	number of functions that called by the function [27]
	Height	distance to the closest external data input
Binary based	ALOC	number of assembly codes
	Conditions	number of binary conditions
	Cmps	number of cmp instructions
	Jmps	number of jmp instructions
Pointer based	Pointers	number of pointer variables
	Pointer Arguments	number of pointer arguments
	Pointer Assignments	number of pointer assignments

method and demonstrate the effectiveness of the proposed method with different experimental settings.

2.4 Semi-Supervised Learning and Contrastive Learning

Semi-supervised learning is a machine learning branch using both labeled and unlabeled data to perform certain learning tasks. Generally, semi-supervised methods can be partitioned into two categories: inductive methods and trans-ductive methods. Inductive methods aim to construct a classifier that can generate predictions for any object in the input space. A simple inductive approach called *wrapper methods* first trains classifiers on labeled data, and then uses the predictions of the resulting classifiers to generate additional labeled data [44]. The classifiers can then be re-trained on this pseudo-labeled data in addition to the existing labeled data. VIME [39] is a self- and semi-supervised learning framework that creates a novel pretext task of estimating mask vectors from corrupted tabular data in addition to the reconstruction pretext task for self-supervised learning. Contrastive Mixup [7] leverages mixup-based augmentation under the manifold assumption by mapping samples to a low-dimensional latent space, and encourages interpolated samples to have a high similarity within the same-labeled class. They cannot be directly used in the security domain because they cannot handle the imbalanced data problem. Our method MCoM can be regarded as a wrapper method derived from Contrastive Mixup with an optimized Triplet Mixup data augmentation method which is the main innovation compared to Contrastive Mixup. Our method can better work for minority classes and is superior on security data sets.

Contrastive learning aims to embed augmented versions of the same sample close to each other while separating embeddings from different samples. Recent methods such as SwAV [2], MoCo [15], and SimCLR [5] with modified approaches have produced results comparable to the state-of-the-art supervised method on the ImageNet [8] data set. Similarly, PIRL [26], Selfie [36], and the InfoMin principle [35] reflect the effectiveness of the pretext tasks being used and how they boost the performance of their models. In this work, we extend contrastive learning to tabular domains by computing a contrastive loss in the embedding space.

3   Preliminaries

In order to introduce our proposed method, we first provide some formulas of contrastive loss and semi-supervised loss (supervised and unsupervised loss). Provided with a data set with N examples, we define $D_L = (x_i, y_i)_{i=1}^{N_L}$ as the labeled data set and $D_U = (x_i)_{i=1}^{N_U}$ as the unlabeled data set, where x_i are the input features and y_i are the discrete labels. In our case, $y_i \in \{0,1\}$ where 1 indicates the sample is positive (vulnerable) and 0 indicates it is negative (non-vulnerable). In supervised learning, our goal is to learn a classifier f to minimize the corresponding loss function l.

3.1   Contrastive Loss

Contrastive learning is a popular method used in unsupervised learning. Data augmentation on the original data is usually the first step. The resulting model measures the similarity of the data pairs in an effort to make the data generated from the same data similar and the data generated from different data separated. In contrastive representation, a batch of N samples is generally augmentated through an augmentation function $Aug(\cdot)$ to create a multi-viewed batch with $2N$ pairs, $\{\tilde{x}_i, \tilde{y}_i\}_{i=1,\dots,2N}$ where $\tilde{x}_{2k}$ and $\tilde{x}_{2k-1}$ are two random augmentations of the same sample x_k for $k = 1,\dots,N$. The samples are fed to an encoder $e : x \to z$, which takes a sample $x \in X$ to obtain a latent representation $z = e(x)$. Typically when defining a pre-text task, a predictive model is trained jointly to minimize a contrastive loss function l.

$$\min_{e,h} \mathbb{E}_{(x,\tilde{y}) \sim P(X,\tilde{Y})}[l(\tilde{y}, h(e(x)))] \tag{1}$$

where h maps z to an embedding space $h : z \to v$. Within a multiviewed batch, $i \in I = \{1,\dots,2N\}$, the contrastive loss is defined as shown in Eq. 2:

$$l = \sum_{i \in I} -\log\left(\frac{\exp(sim(v_i, v_{j(i)})/\tau)}{\sum_{n \in I \setminus \{i\}} \exp(sim(v_i, v_n)/\tau)}\right) \tag{2}$$

where $sim(\cdot, \cdot) \in \mathbb{R}^+$ is a similarity function (e.g., dot product or cosine similarity), $\tau \in \mathbb{R}^+$ is a scalar temperature parameter, i is the anchor, $A(i)$ is the positive(s) and $I \backslash \{i\}$ are the negatives. The positive and negative samples refer to samples that are semantically similar and dissimilar, respectively. Intuitively, the objective of this function is to bring the positives and the anchor closer in the embedding space v than the anchor and the negatives (i.e., $sim(v^a, v^+) > sim(v^a, v^-)$, where v^a is the anchor and v^+, v^- are the positive and negative, respectively).

3.2 Semi-Supervised Loss

In semi-supervised learning, there are two disjoint data sets D_L, D_U in the whole data set D, where predictive model f is optimized to minimize the supervised loss, jointly with an unsupervised loss as shown in Eq. 3:

$$\min_f \mathbb{E}_{(x,y) \sim P(X,Y)}[l(y, f(x))] + \beta \mathbb{E}_{(x,y_{ps}) \sim P(X,Y_{ps})}[l_u(y_{ps}, f(x))] \quad (3)$$

The first term is estimated over the small labeled subset D_L, and the second unsupervised loss is estimated over the more significant unlabeled subset D_U. The unsupervised loss function l_u is defined to help the downstream prediction tasks like a supervised objective on pseudo-labeled samples in our case.

4 Methodology

Figure 1 illustrates our proposed MCoM framework, containing 4 parts: (1) triplet mixup data augmentation on the minority (vulnerable) class to address imbalance in the tabular security data set; (2) contrastive and feature reconstruction loss to train the encoder and the decoder; (3) pseudo-labeling of the subset of the unlabeled data using a label propagation technique; and (4) downstream tasks that train the predictor (e.g., MLP) with the fixed trained encoder.

4.1 Triplet Mixup Data Augmentation

This section proposes our novel data augmentation technique to generate more minority examples. Traditional Mixup [42] augments data between a data pair:

$$\hat{x} = \lambda x_i + (1 - \lambda)x_j \qquad \hat{y} = \lambda y_i + (1 - \lambda)y_j \quad (4)$$

where $\lambda \sim Beta(\alpha, \alpha)$ for $\alpha \in (0, \infty)$. In contrast, we propose a triplet mixup data augmentation to fit tabular domains:

$$\hat{x} = \lambda_i x_i + \lambda_j x_j + (1 - \lambda_i - \lambda_j)x_k \quad (5)$$

where $\lambda_i, \lambda_j \sim Uniform(0, \alpha)$ with $\alpha \in (0, 0.5]$. Data x_i, x_j, and x_k are from the same class. In our case, they are all from the minority (vulnerable) class (positive class) because our goal is to alleviate the data imbalance problem.

For example, if we have three data points $(1, 2, 1)$, $(2, 3, 4)$, and $(5, 2, 1)$ all from the minority class with $\lambda_1 = 0.2$, $\lambda_2 = 0.3$, and $1 - \lambda_1 - \lambda_2 = 0.5$, then the new generated data point is $(3.3, 2.3, 1.9)$. If we have more than two class labels, we do data augmentation on classes with less than 10% samples of other classes.

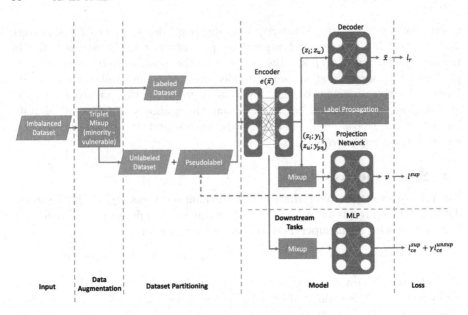

Fig. 1. Overview of MCoM

4.2   Contrastive and Feature Reconstruction Loss

In addition to the data augmentation to the input data, we also do mixup data augmentation in the hidden space. Given an encoder e, that is comprised of T layers f_t $(t \in 1, \dots, T)$, the samples are fed through to an intermediate representation h_t at layer t. We do interpolation in this intermediate layer:

$$\tilde{h}_{ij}^t = \lambda h_i^t + (1 - \lambda) h_j^t \tag{6}$$

where $\lambda \sim Uniform(0, \alpha)$ with $\alpha \in (0, 0.5]$, and h_i^t is the hidden representation of input x_i by feeding x_i to layer t of encoder e. We then feed the augmented samples $\tilde{h}_i^t$ and the original samples h_i^t, h_j^t to the rest of the encoder layers $t, \dots, T$ to obtain the latent representation z.

As shown in Fig. 1, we represent latent representation of labeled samples as z_l and unlabeled samples as z_u. We define the contrastive loss term to encourage samples created from pairs of the same class to have high similarity:

$$l_\tau^{sup} = \sum_{i \in I)} \frac{-1}{|P(i)|} \sum_{p \in P(i)} \log \left(\frac{\exp(sim(h_i^{proj}, h_p^{proj})/\tau)}{\sum_{n \in Ne(i)} \exp(sim(h_i^{proj}, h_n^{proj})/\tau)} \right) \tag{7}$$

where $P(i) = \{p \mid p \in A(i), y_i = \tilde{y}_p\}$ is the set of indices of positives with the same label as example i, $|P(i)|$ is its cardinality, and $Ne(i) = \{n \mid n \in I, y_i \neq y_n\}$. Function h^{proj} is a mapping of the latent representation to an embedding space via a projection network where the contrastive loss term is defined. This objective function will encourage mixed-upped labeled samples and anchors of the same sample to be close, leading to better clusterable representation.

In addition to the contrastive loss term, the encoder is trained to minimize the feature reconstruction loss via a decoder $f_\theta(e(x))$:

$$l_r(x_i) = \frac{|C|}{d} \sum_c^{|C|} \|f_\theta(e_\phi(x_i)^c) - x_i^c\|_2^2 + \frac{|D|}{d} \sum_j^{|D|} \sum_o^{d_{D_j}} \mathbf{1}[x_i^d = o] \log(f_\theta(e_\phi(x_i)^o)) \tag{8}$$

where C means continuous features and D means discrete features. We then combine the contrastive loss and feature reconstruction loss:

$$L = \mathbb{E}_{(x,y)\sim D_L}[l_\tau^{sup}(y, f(x))] + \beta \mathbb{E}_{x\sim D_U \cup D_L}[l_r(x)] \tag{9}$$

We first train the encoder using this loss term over K epochs to warm-start the representations in the latent space prior to pseudo-labeling, and leverage the unlabeled samples.

4.3 Pseudo-labeling

Until now we have only used the labeled set D_L in the contrastive loss term l_τ^{sup}. We next use label propagation [17,43] after K epochs of training with the supervised contrastive loss term L^{sup}. Given the encoder trained on D_L for K epochs, we map the small labeled set D_L and a subset of the unlabeled set $S_U \subset D_U$ to the latent space z and construct an affinity matrix G:

$$y = \begin{cases} sim(z_i, z_j) & \text{if } i \neq j \text{ and } z_j \in NN_k(i) \\ 0 & \text{otherwise} \end{cases} \tag{10}$$

where $NN_k(i)$ is the k nearest neighbor of sample z_i, and $sim(z_i, z_j)$ is the similarity measure (e.g. $z_i^T z_j$). We then obtain pseudo-labels for our unlabeled samples by computing the diffusion matrix C and setting $\tilde{y}_i := \arg\max_j c_{ij}$, where $(I - \alpha A)C = Y$. We use a conjugate method [17,44] to solve linear equations to obtain C, facilitating efficient computation of the pseudo-labels. Here $A = D^{-1/2}WD^{-1/2}$ is the adjacency matrix, $W = G^T + G$ and $D = diag(W1_n)$ is the degree matrix. Once we obtain the pseudo-labels for the unlabeled subset S_U, we train the encoder with unlabeled samples treating the generated labels as ground truth. Finally, the loss item combining contrastive loss and reconstruction loss with pseudo-labels is shown in Eq. 11:

$$L = \mathbb{E}_{(x,y)\sim D_L}[l^{sup}(y, f(x))] + \gamma \mathbb{E}_{x,y_{ps}\sim S_U}[l^{sup}(y_{ps}, f(x))] + \beta \mathbb{E}_{x\sim D_U}[l_r(x)] \tag{11}$$

We update the pseudo-labels every f epochs of training with the above loss term.

4.4 Downstream Tasks

After pre-training the encoder, the encoder is fixed and will be used for downstream tasks (see Fig. 1) with the generated pseudo-labels to train the predictor (e.g., MLP). We leverage Mixup augmentation [42] in the latent space and feed samples to a set of fully connected layers. The training loss for the downstream tasks is combined with cross-entropy loss for supervised (*sup*) for the labeled subset and unsupervised (*unsup*) for the unlabeled subset.

Algorithm 1: MCoM

---

1 **Given:** data set $(x, y) \in D_0$, positive and negative data sets $D_+, D_- \in D_0$, distribution parameter $\alpha \in (0, 0.5]$, pseudo-labeling weight parameter γ, unsupervised weight parameter β

/* Triplet Mixup Data Augmentation   */
2   $\tilde{D} \leftarrow []$
3   $\lambda_i \leftarrow$ random from $Uniform(0, \alpha)$
4   $\lambda_j \leftarrow$ random from $Uniform(0, \alpha)$
5   **for** $i \leftarrow 0, \ldots, |D_+| - 2$ **do**
6   **for** $j \leftarrow i + 1, \ldots, |D_+| - 1$ **do**
7   **for** $k \leftarrow j + 1, \ldots, |D_+|$ **do**
8                $\hat{x} \leftarrow \lambda_i x_i + \lambda_j x_j + (1 - \lambda_i - \lambda_j) x_k$
9   Append $\hat{x}$ to $\tilde{D}$
10 $D \leftarrow D_0 + \tilde{D}$
11 **repeat**
12       $t \leftarrow t + 1$ // update timestep
13       $x \leftarrow$ Selectbatch(D)
14       $h \leftarrow e^t(x)$

     /* Manifold Mixup   */
15       $\tilde{h} \leftarrow []$
16       $\lambda \leftarrow$ random from $Uniform(0, \alpha)$
17   **for** $i \leftarrow 0, \ldots, |D| - 1$ **do**
18   **for** $j \leftarrow i + 1, \ldots, |D|$ **do**
19               $\tilde{h} \leftarrow \lambda h_i + (1 - \lambda) h_j$
20   Append $\tilde{h}$ to $\tilde{h}$
21       $z \leftarrow$ Feed h and $\tilde{h}$ to $t, \ldots, T$ layers of encoder e

     /* Contrastive and Feature Reconstruction Loss   */
22       $l_\tau^{sup} \leftarrow$ Equation 7
23       $l_r \leftarrow$ Equation 8
24       $L \leftarrow \mathbb{E}_{(x,y) \sim D_L}[l_\tau^{sup}(y, f(x))] + \beta \mathbb{E}_{x \sim D_U \cup D_L}[l_r(x)]$
25   Optimize L using SGD over K epochs

     /* Pseudo-labeling   */
26   Compute affinity matrix G using Equation 10
27       $W \leftarrow G^T + G$
28       $D \leftarrow diag(W I_n)$
29       $A \leftarrow D^{-1/2} W D^{-1/2}$
30       $\tilde{y}_i \leftarrow \arg\max_j c_{ij}$, where $(I - \alpha A)C = Y$
31       $S_U \leftarrow$ subset of unlabeled subset D_u
32       $L \leftarrow \mathbb{E}_{(x,y) \sim D_L}[l^{sup}(y, f(x))] + \gamma \mathbb{E}_{x, y_{ps} \sim S_U}[l^{sup}(y_{ps}, f(x))] + \beta \mathbb{E}_{x \sim D_U}[l_r(x)]$
33   Optimize L using SGD
34 **until** stopping criterion is met
35 **return** encoder e_ϕ, decoder f_θ

     /* Downstream Tasks   */
36 **Given:** encoder e_ϕ, $D_U, D_L \in D$
37 **repeat**
38   Compute $l_{ce}^{sup}, l_{ce}^{unsup}$
39       $l \leftarrow l_{ce}^{sup} + \gamma l_{ce}^{unsup}$
40   Optimize l using SGD
41 **until** stopping criterion is met
42 **return** f_ψ^{mlp} // Predictor Training

4.5 Algorithm

Algorithm 1 integrates all four parts of our proposed MCoM method into a single pseudo-code. Triplet mixup data augmentation comprises lines 2–10, manifold mixup comprises lines 15–21, contrastive and feature reconstruction loss comprises lines 22–25, and pseudo-labeling comprises lines 26–30. Line 32 represents the total loss including pseudo-labeling. As mentioned in line 25, we first optimize the contrastive and feature reconstruction loss over K epochs, then add pseudo-labeling to the loss term. Lines 36–41 represent downstream tasks: the predictor training using the cross entropy loss with both of the supervised and unsupervised parts.

5 Experiments

This section demonstrates the superiority of our method on a large, imbalanced tabular security data set that we manually assembled from NVD and open source repositories (see Sect. 2.2). The data set contains 5692 records with 53 positive (vulnerable) cases and 5639 negative (non-vulnerable) cases, making data augmentation essential. We also do experiments on a less imbalanced data set with more positive cases (4491 records with 165 positive cases) and get similar results. Due to the page limit, we only report the results for the former data set.

We compare our method with 6 supervised methods (XGBoost [4], MLP, Logit Regression, SVM, Decision Tree, and KNN) and two state-of-the-art semi-supervised methods on tabular domains (VIME [39] and Contrastive Mixup [7]) with or without our proposed Triplet Mixup data augmentation. We compare our data augmentation method with existing down-sampling and SMOTE [3] up-sampling methods. We do experiments with different mixup strategies and demonstrate why triplet is superior. In addition, we compare with the pairwise mixup data augmentation with different loss functions, and show that our method with standard cross entropy loss function performs best among all the loss functions. We also do experiments with different labeled ratios and choose 0.1 as our labeled ratio for semi-supervised learning.

All the experimental results record accuracy, precision, recall, TPR (true positive rate), TNR (true negative rate), micro F1 score, macro F1 score, and weighted F1 score. Positive means vulnerable and negative means non-vulnerable. For the security data set, we assign more importance to the recall and TPR.

5.1 Results

Main Experimental Results. Table 3 shows the main experimental results of our method compared with 6 supervised methods and 2 semi-supervised methods (labeled ratio 0.1). We separate the experiments into 2 parts: (1) without triplet mixup data augmentation (upper part) and (2) with triplet mixup data augmentation (lower part). The upper part of Table 3 shows that without triplet mixup data augmentation, even the accuracy and TNR are near 100, and the precision, recall, and TPR are all 0, which means that all the methods can only predict negative data and not the positive (vulnerable) data sought by defenders. The results show all the methods perform poorly on imbalanced tabular security data without triplet data augmentation no matter how many labeled data the model utilizes.

The lower part of Table 3 applies triplet mixup data augmentation to the original positive data to obtain 17798 data with 4554 original data. The experimental results show that MCoM achieves the best recall and TPR (66.67) with only 0.1 labeled data (1779/17798). Although Logit Regression and VIME also achieve the same recall and TPR, they all exhibit worse performance according to the other metrics. In addition, Logit Regression is a supervised method utilizing all the labeled data, whereas our method uses only 0.1 labeled data. Thus, our method MCoM achieves the best performance among all the tested methods.

Experimental Results with Different Sampling Methods. Table 4 compares our triplet mixup data augmentation method with a down-sampling (reduce the data points) and an up-sampling method (SMOTE [3]). Compared with down-sampling and SMOTE, our method achieves the best recall, TPR (66.67), and precision (3.95), demonstrating that our method is better overall. Down-sampling reduces negative samples, losing information from the negative samples. In contrast, up-sampling generates more samples from the positive samples. SMOTE generates positive samples by adding small amounts to positive samples. However, our method leverages more information from positive samples by mixing-up triple data points.

Experimental Results with Different Mixup Strategies. Table 6 compares different mixup strategies: pairwise, quadruplet, pairwise + original (mixing a pair of data points including the output of pairwise mixup), pairwise + triplet (mix a pair of data points followed by triplet mixup, including the output of pairwise mixup). Triplet achieves the best recall and TPR (66.67). Although pairwise + original and pairwise + triplet achieve the same recall and TPR, Triplet achieves the best accuracy, precision, TNR, and F1 scores. Pairwise does not generate enough augmentations, while quadruplet generates too many. Triplet achieves the best results compared with mixed ones because it combines triple data with balanced weights.

Experimental Results with Different Loss Functions. Table 7 compares different loss functions aiming to deal with the data imbalance problem. We first apply pairwise mixup data augmentation on the original data and run experiments with different loss functions: Focal Loss [21], CB (Class Balanced) Loss [6], and Weighted CE (Cross Entropy) Loss. Weighted CE means cross entropy loss with weights 1 and 10 for the majority and minority classes, respectively. Our model uses the standard cross entropy loss. Our method achieves the highest TPR of 66.67 compared with only 44.44 by the others, while maintaining high levels for all other metrics.

Table 3. Main experimental results. Top two are shaded and best is bold.

Model	Accuracy	Precision	Recall	TPR	TNR	F1 Score Micro	Macro	Weighted
Without Triplet Mixup Data Augmentation								
Supervised (4554 labeled data)								
XGBoost	**99.21**	0	0	0	**100**	**99.21**	49.80	**98.82**
MLP	**99.21**	0	0	0	**100**	**99.21**	49.80	**98.82**
Logit Regression	**99.21**	0	0	0	**100**	**99.21**	49.80	**98.82**
SVM	**99.21**	0	0	0	**100**	**99.21**	49.80	**98.82**
Decision Tree	98.51	0	0	0	99.29	98.51	49.62	98.46
KNN	99.12	0	0	0	99.91	99.12	49.78	98.77
Semi-supervised (455 labeled data, 0.1 labeled ratio)								
VIME	**99.21**	0	0	0	**100**	**99.21**	49.80	**98.82**
Contrastive Mixup	**99.21**	0	0	0	**100**	**99.21**	49.80	**98.82**
With Triplet Mixup Data Augmentation								
Supervised (17798 labeled data)								
XGBoost	98.68	0	0	0	99.47	98.68	49.67	98.55
MLP	97.54	**4.76**	11.11	11.11	98.23	97.54	**52.71**	98.03
Logit Regression	81.02	2.74	**66.67**	**66.67**	81.13	81.02	47.36	88.79
SVM	89.37	4.10	55.56	55.56	89.64	89.37	51.00	93.67
Decision Tree	97.28	4.17	11.11	11.11	97.96	97.28	52.34	97.89
KNN	91.39	4.12	44.44	44.44	91.76	91.39	51.52	94.79
Semi-supervised (1779 labeled data and 0.1 labeled ratio)								
VIME	78.30	2.40	**66.67**	**66.67**	78.39	78.30	46.19	87.10
MCoM	86.91	3.95	**66.67**	**66.67**	87.07	86.91	50.20	92.28

Table 4. Experimental results with different sampling methods. Top two are shaded and best is bold.

Method	Accuracy	Precision	Recall	TPR	TNR	F1 Score Micro	Macro	Weighted
Supervised SVM								
Down Sampling	**92.53**	3.66	33.33	33.33	**93.00**	**92.53**	**51.35**	**95.40**
SMOTE	88.49	3.79	55.56	55.56	88.75	88.49	50.48	93.18
Semi-supervised (0.1 labeled ratio)								
MCoM	86.91	**3.95**	**66.67**	**66.67**	87.07	86.91	50.20	92.28

Table 5. Ablation study. Top two are shaded and best is bold.

Method	Accuracy	Precision	Recall	TPR	TNR	F1 Score Micro	Macro	Weighted
No Mixup	99.03	0	0	0	99.82	99.03	49.76	98.73
No Input Mixup	**99.21**	0	0	0	**100**	**99.21**	49.80	**98.82**
No Hidden Mixup	86.29	3.77	**66.67**	**66.67**	86.45	86.29	49.87	91.92
MCoM	86.91	**3.95**	**66.67**	**66.67**	87.07	86.91	**50.20**	92.28

Table 6. Experimental results with different mixup strategies. Top two are shaded and best is bold.

Method	Accuracy	Precision	Recall	TPR	TNR	F1 Score Micro	Macro	Weighted
Pairwise	**93.59**	**5.56**	44.44	44.44	**93.98**	**93.59**	53.28	**95.99**
Quadruplet	84.18	2.23	44.44	44.44	84.50	84.18	47.82	90.69
Pairwise+Original	78.21	2.39	**66.67**	**66.67**	78.30	78.21	46.16	87.04
Pairwise+Triplet	85.68	3.61	**66.67**	**66.67**	85.83	85.68	49.55	91.57
Triplet	86.91	3.95	**66.67**	**66.67**	87.07	86.91	50.20	92.28

Table 7. Experimental results with different loss functions. Top two are shaded and best is bold.

Method	Accuracy	Precision	Recall	TPR	TNR	F1 Score Micro	Macro	Weighted
With Pairwise Mixup Data Augmentation								
Focal Loss	93.23	5.26	44.44	44.44	93.62	93.23	52.95	95.80
CB Loss	93.06	5.13	44.44	44.44	93.45	93.06	52.79	95.70
Weighted CE	**93.59**	**5.56**	44.44	44.44	**93.98**	**93.59**	**53.28**	**95.99**
With Triplet Mixup Data Augmentation								
MCoM	86.91	3.95	**66.67**	**66.67**	87.07	86.91	50.20	92.28

Table 8. Experimental results with different labeled ratios

Labeled Ratio	Accuracy	Precision	Recall	TPR	TNR	F1 Score		
						Micro	Macro	Weighted
0.01	2.64	0.81	100	100	1.86	2.64	2.63	3.64
0.02	85.41	3.55	66.67	66.67	85.56	85.41	49.41	91.41
0.03	83.13	3.08	66.67	66.67	83.26	83.13	48.31	90.06
0.05	85.24	3.51	66.67	66.67	85.39	85.24	49.33	91.31
0.07	83.57	3.16	66.67	66.67	83.70	83.57	48.51	90.32
0.10	86.91	3.95	66.67	66.67	87.07	86.91	50.20	92.28
0.15	87.17	3.40	55.56	55.56	87.42	87.17	49.76	92.43
0.17	88.49	3.79	55.56	55.56	88.75	88.49	50.48	93.18
0.20	88.40	3.76	55.56	55.56	88.66	88.40	50.43	93.13
0.30	91.04	4.85	55.56	55.56	91.32	91.04	52.11	94.60
0.40	92.88	6.10	55.56	55.56	93.18	92.88	53.64	95.62
0.50	93.85	5.80	44.44	44.44	94.24	93.85	53.54	96.13
0.60	93.67	4.35	33.33	33.33	94.15	93.67	52.21	96.02
0.70	94.11	3.23	22.22	22.22	94.69	94.11	51.30	96.24
0.80	94.82	1.92	11.11	11.11	95.48	94.82	50.31	96.59
0.90	95.17	2.08	11.11	11.11	95.84	95.17	50.52	96.78

5.2 Ablation Study

We do ablation study with two important components: (1) Triplet Mixup Data Augmentation (Input Mixup), and (2) Mixup in Hidden Layers (Hidden Mixup). Table 5 shows the results after removing each mixup. From Table 5, we can see that without input mixup, the model cannot handle positive (vulnerable) cases. After adding the triplet mixup data augmentation, even without hidden mixup, the recall and TPR increase from 0 to 66.67. After adding the hidden mixup, other metrics except recall and TPR increase slightly.

5.3 Parameter Analysis

The most important parameter in our work is the labeled ratio. Table 8 examines ratios from 0.01 to 0.90. A ratio of 0.01 yields recall and TPR of 100 with accuracy of only 2.64 and TNR of only 1.86, which means the model performs very poorly on the security data set due to lack of labeled data. Setting the ratio from 0.02 to 0.10 achieves the best recall and TPR (66.67) among all the labeled ratios except 0.01. A ratio of 0.10 achieves the best accuracy, precision, TNR, and F1 scores; whereas increasing it from 0.15 to 0.90 decreases the recall and TPR to 11.11 with other metrics increasing slightly. This means the model overfits the data set. Thus, we choose 0.10 as the most appropriate labeled ratio.

6   Conclusion and Future Work

This paper proposed and evaluated MCoM, a novel semi-supervised machine learning method for analyzing highly imbalanced tabular security data sets. The method includes 4 components: (1) Triplet Mixup Data Augmentation, (2) Contrastive and Feature Reconstruction Loss, (3) Pseudo-labeling, and (4) Downstream Tasks. Comparison of MCoM with 6 supervised methods and 2 state-of-the-art semi-supervised methods in tabular domains shows that without the triplet mixup data augmentation, all the methods perform poorly (with 0 precision, recall, and TPR) on the data set. After adding our proposed triplet mixup data augmentation, the results improve substantially, with MCoM achieving the best recall and TPR (66.67). Future research should explore generalizing our technique to additional data sets in other domains. To enhance our proposed method, our plan is to work on graph data sets, such as CFGs, CPGs, and ASTs extracted from open-source applications to detect software vulnerabilities at the source and binary levels. Our proposed method will help the developers or experts to automatically label the graphs related to each function and component.

Acknowledgement. The research reported herein was supported in part by NSF awards DMS-1737978, DGE-2039542, OAC-1828467, OAC-1931541, and DGE-1906630, ONR awards N00014-17-1-2995 and N00014-20-1-2738, DARPA FA8750-19-C-0006, Army Research Office Contract No. W911NF2110032 and IBM faculty award (Research).

References

1. Berthelot, D., Carlini, N., Goodfellow, I., Papernot, N., Oliver, A., Raffel, C.A.: MixMatch: a holistic approach to semi-supervised learning. Advances in Neural Information Processing Systems (NeurIPS), vol. 32 (2019)
2. Caron, M., Misra, I., Mairal, J., Goyal, P., Bojanowski, P., Joulin, A.: Unsupervised learning of visual features by contrasting cluster assignments. In: Advances in Neural Information Processing Systems (NeurIPS), vol. 33, pp. 9912–9924 (2020)
3. Chawla, N.V., Bowyer, K.W., Hall, L.O., Kegelmeyer, W.P.: SMOTE: synthetic minority over-sampling technique. J. Artif. Intell. Res. (JAIR) **16**(1), 321–357 (2002)
4. Chen, T., Guestrin, C.: XGBoost: a scalable tree boosting system. In: Proceedings of the 22nd ACM SIGKDD International Conference on Knowledge Discovery and Data Mining (KDDM), pp. 785–794 (2016)
5. Chen, T., Kornblith, S., Norouzi, M., Hinton, G.: A simple framework for contrastive learning of visual representations. In: Proceedings of the 37th IEEE International Conference on Machine Learning (ICML), pp. 1597–1607 (2020)
6. Cui, Y., Jia, M., Lin, T.Y., Song, Y., Belongie, S.: Class-balanced loss based on effective number of samples. In: Proceedings of the 37th IEEE/CVF Conference on Computer Vision and Pattern Recognition (CVPR), pp. 9268–9277 (2019)
7. Darabi, S., Fazeli, S., Pazoki, A., Sankararaman, S., Sarrafzadeh, M.: Contrastive mixup: Self-and semi-supervised learning for tabular domain. arXiv Preprint arXiv:2108.12296 (2021)

8. Deng, J., Dong, W., Socher, R., Li, L.J., Li, K., Fei-Fei, L.: ImageNet: a large-scale hierarchical image database. In: Proceedings of the 27th IEEE/CVF Conference on Computer Vision and Pattern Recognition (CVPR), pp. 248–255 (2009)
9. Doyle, M., Walden, J.: An empirical study of the evolution of PHP web application security. In: Proceedings of the 3rd International Workshop on Security Measurements and Metrics, pp. 11–20 (2011)
10. Du, X., et al.: Leopard: identifying vulnerable code for vulnerability assessment through program metrics. In: Proceedings of the 41st International Conference on Software Engineering (ICSE), pp. 60–71 (2019)
11. Feng, S.Y., et al.: A survey of data augmentation approaches for NLP. arXiv Preprint arXiv:2105.03075 (2021)
12. Fenton, N., Bieman, J.: Software Metrics: A Rigorous and Practical Approach, 3rd edn. CRC Press, Boca Raton (2014)
13. Gao, Y., Li, Y.F., Lin, Y., Aggarwal, C., Khan, L.: SetConv: a new approach for learning from imbalanced data. In: Proceedings of the Conference on Empirical Methods in Natural Language Processing (EMNLP), pp. 1284–1294 (2021)
14. Gegick, M., Williams, L., Osborne, J., Vouk, M.: Prioritizing software security fortification through code-level metrics. In: Proceedings of the 4th ACM Workshop on Quality of Protection (QoP), pp. 31–38 (2008)
15. He, K., Fan, H., Wu, Y., Xie, S., Girshick, R.: Momentum contrast for unsupervised visual representation learning. In: Proceedings of the 38th IEEE/CVF Conference on Computer Vision and Pattern Recognition (CVPR), pp. 9729–9738 (2020)
16. Ioffe, S., Szegedy, C.: Batch normalization: accelerating deep network training by reducing internal covariate shift. In: Proceedings of the 32nd International Conference on Machine Learning (ICML), pp. 448–456 (2015)
17. Iscen, A., Tolias, G., Avrithis, Y., Chum, O.: Label propagation for deep semi-supervised learning. In: Proceedings of the 37th IEEE/CVF Conference on Computer Vision and Pattern Recognition (CVPR), pp. 5070–5079 (2019)
18. Kobayashi, S.: Contextual augmentation: data augmentation by words with paradigmatic relations. In: Proceedings of the Conference of the North American Chapter of the Association for Computational Linguistics: Human Language Technologies (NAACL-HLT), vol. 2, pp. 452–457 (2018)
19. Krizhevsky, A., Sutskever, I., Hinton, G.E.: ImageNet classification with deep convolutional neural networks. In: Advances in Neural Information Processing Systems (NeurIPS), vol. 25 (2012)
20. Lavee, G., Khan, L., Thuraisingham, B.: A framework for a video analysis tool for suspicious event detection. Multimedia Tools Appl. 35(1), 109–123 (2007)
21. Lin, T.Y., Goyal, P., Girshick, R., He, K., Dollár, P.: Focal loss for dense object detection. In: Proceedings of the IEEE International Conference on Computer Vision (ICCV), pp. 2980–2988 (2017)
22. Masud, M.M., Gao, J., Khan, L., Han, J., Thuraisingham, B.: Classification and novel class detection in data streams with active mining. In: Zaki, M.J., Yu, J.X., Ravindran, B., Pudi, V. (eds.) PAKDD 2010. LNCS (LNAI), vol. 6119, pp. 311–324. Springer, Heidelberg (2010). https://doi.org/10.1007/978-3-642-13672-6_31
23. Masud, M.M., Khan, L., Thuraisingham, B.: A hybrid model to detect malicious executables. In: 2007 IEEE International Conference on Communications, pp. 1443–1448. IEEE (2007)
24. McCabe, T.: A complexity measure. IEEE Trans. Softw. Eng. (TSE) **SE-2**(4), 308–320 (1976)

25. Meneely, A., Williams, L.: Strengthening the empirical analysis of the relationship between Linus' Law and software security. In: Proceedings of the 4th ACM International Symposium on Empirical Software Engineering and Measurement (ESEM) (2010)
26. Misra, I., van der Maaten, L.: Self-supervised learning of pretext-invariant representations. In: Proceedings of the 38th IEEE/CVF Conference on Computer Vision and Pattern Recognition (CVPR), pp. 6707–6717 (2020)
27. Nagappan, N., Ball, T., Zeller, A.: Mining metrics to predict component failures. In: Proceedings of the 28th International Conference on Software Engineering (ICSE), pp. 452–461 (2006)
28. Parveen, P., Weger, Z.R., Thuraisingham, B., Hamlen, K., Khan, L.: Supervised learning for insider threat detection using stream mining. In: 2011 IEEE 23rd International Conference on Tools with Artificial Intelligence, pp. 1032–1039. IEEE (2011)
29. Piwowarski, P.: A nesting level complexity measure. ACM SIGPLAN Notices 17(9), 44–50 (1982)
30. Sennrich, R., Haddow, B., Birch, A.: Improving neural machine translation models with monolingual data. In: Proceedings of the 54th Annual Meeting of the Association for Computational Linguistics (ACL) (2016)
31. Shin, Y., Williams, L.: Can traditional fault prediction models be used for vulnerability prediction? Empir. Softw. Eng. 18(1), 25–59 (2013)
32. Simonyan, K., Zisserman, A.: Very deep convolutional networks for large-scale image recognition. In: Proceedings of the 3rd International Conference on Learning Representations (ICLR) (2015)
33. Sohn, K., et al.: FixMatch: simplifying semi-supervised learning with consistency and confidence. In: Advances in Neural Information Processing Systems (NeurIPS), vol. 33, pp. 596–608 (2020)
34. Srivastava, N., Hinton, G., Krizhevsky, A., Sutskever, I., Salakhutdinov, R.: Dropout: a simple way to prevent neural networks from overfitting. J. Mach. Learn. Res. (JMLR) 15(1), 1929–1958 (2014)
35. Tian, Y., Sun, C., Poole, B., Krishnan, D., Schmid, C., Isola, P.: What makes for good views for contrastive learning? In: Advances in Neural Information Processing Systems (NeurIPS), vol. 33, pp. 6827–6839 (2020)
36. Trinh, T.H., Luong, M.T., Le, Q.V.: Selfie: Self-supervised pretraining for image embedding. arXiv Preprint arXiv:1906.02940 (2019)
37. Wang, Z., Dong, B., Lin, Y., Wang, Y., Islam, M.S., Khan, L.: Co-representation learning framework for the open-set data classification. In: IEEE International Conference on Big Data (BigData), pp. 239–244 (2019)
38. Yamaguchi, F., Golde, N., Arp, D., Rieck, K.: Modeling and discovering vulnerabilities with code property graphs. In: Proceedings of the 35th IEEE Symposium on Security and Privacy (S&P) (2014)
39. Yoon, J., Zhang, Y., Jordon, J., van der Schaar, M.: VIME: extending the success of self-and semi-supervised learning to tabular domain. In: Advances in Neural Information Processing Systems (NeurIPS), vol. 33, pp. 11033–11043 (2020)
40. Younis, A., Malaiya, Y., Anderson, C., Ray, I.: To fear or not to fear that is the question: code characteristics of a vulnerable function with an existing exploit. In: Proceedings of the 6th ACM Conference on Data and Application Security and Privacy (CODASPY), pp. 97–104 (2016)
41. Zeller, A., Zimmermann, T., Bird, C.: Failure is a four-letter word: a parody in empirical research. In: Proceedings of the 7th International Conference on Predictive Models in Software Engineering (Promise) (2011)

42. Zhang, H., Cisse, M., Dauphin, Y.N., Lopez-Paz, D.: Mixup: beyond empirical risk minimization. arXiv Preprint arXiv:1710.09412 (2017)

43. Zhou, D., Bousquet, O., Lal, T., Weston, J., Schölkopf, B.: Learning with local and global consistency. In: Advances in Neural Information Processing Systems (NeurIPS), vol. 16 (2003)

44. Zhu, X.J.: Semi-supervised learning literature survey. Technical report, University of Wisconsin-Madison (2008)

45. Zimmermann, T., Nagappan, N.: Predicting defects using network analysis on dependency graphs. In: Proceedings of the 30th ACM/IEEE International Conference on Software Engineering (ICSE), pp. 531–540 (2008)

Mitigating Privacy Vulnerability Caused by Map Asymmetry

Ryota Hiraishi[1]($\boxtimes$)(iD), Masatoshi Yoshikawa[1](iD), Shun Takagi[1](iD), Yang Cao[1](iD), Sumio Fujita[2](iD), and Hidehito Gomi[2](iD)

[1] Department of Social Informatics, Kyoto University, Kyoto, Japan
`hiraishi.ryouta.73m@st.kyoto-u.ac.jp`
[2] Yahoo Japan Corporation, Tokyo, Japan

Abstract. Geo-indistinguishability, an extension of differential privacy and thus, a mathematically rigorous privacy concept, has been researched extensively in recent years for protecting the location information in location-based services (LBSs). However the Laplace mechanism that satisfies GeoI outputs the location information equally in all directions considering the map is assumed to be symmetric. Therefore, when noise is added, the output can be directed to uninhabitable locations, such as the sea, To solve this problem, graph representation of the road network is used as a map and Geo-Graph-Indistinguishability (GeoI), which is differential privacy on the graph, and a graph-exponential mechanism (GEM), which satisfies GeoGI, were proposed. However, the problem that some vertices can be vulnerable in terms of privacy when measured using criteria based on adversary's error remains unresolved. In this paper, we first calculate the degree of privacy protection using the adversary's error when noise is added by GEM, and demonstrate that the privacy weakens at some vertices. We then propose two methods, the weight reduction method and the AE optimization method, to mitigate this problem. The experiments show these methods successfully mitigated the privacy vulnerability. Finally, we highlight the problems with these two methods and suggest possible solutions.

Keywords: Location Privacy · Geo-Indistinguishability · Road Network · Differential Privacy

1 Introduction

The importance of personal data has been constantly increasing in recent years, and the utilization of personal data has become essential for business and society, The possible usages of personal data include personalized services and data mining. However, considering the data can be abused, users should add random noises on their own terminals before providing their personal data to collectors. This idea is based on the method by Warner [15] and has been extended to a concept using differential privacy [7], called local differential privacy (LDP) [9]

© IFIP International Federation for Information Processing 2022
Published by Springer Nature Switzerland AG 2022
S. Sural and H. Lu (Eds.): DBSec 2022, LNCS 13383, pp. 68–86, 2022.
https://doi.org/10.1007/978-3-031-10684-2_5

[6]. This study focuses on generating personal location information based on the assumption that users add noise to their location information before providing it to the collector, who then use the data containing noise. Such data can be used for weather forecasting services and locate nearby stores. If large amounts of data can be collected and aggregated, it can help make business decisions such as opening new stores or expanding service areas. Furthermore it can be used in applications that provide information on traffic congestion and related conditions.

Geo-indistinguishability (hereinafter referred to as GeoI), first proposed by Andrés et al. [1] is widely known as a privacy protection standard for location information. They proposed the Laplace mechanism that adds noise following a two-dimensional Laplace distribution. However, Takagi et al. [14] point out the problem of such a mechanism satisfying GeoI and showed that the utility and the privacy protection level decrease when information on road networks is considered. They represent the road network as a graph, define Geo-Graph-Indistinguishability (GeoGI), which is a differential privacy criterion on graphs, and use the Graph-Exponential Mechanism (GEM) that satisfies it. In [14], the map is represented as a graph modeling the road network, with vertices and edges corresponding to locations and roads connected to those locations, respectively. However, considering the map is not symmetric and is affected by geographical features, the adversary's error (we define the adversary's error as the expected distance between the predicted location of the adversary observing the noise-added location and the actual user location. See Sect. 4 for details) is different for vertex to vertex, making the privacy of some vertices vulnerable. The similar issue occurs in GeoI. A naive way to avoid outputting seas in GeoI is to use remapping [3], a technique that maps the result of adding random noise to the user's true location (e.g. Laplace mechanism) to a utility-optimized location. In this case, the possible output locations around the user differ depending on her location, resulting in an asymmetric map.

This study addresses the issue of privacy vulnerability at some of these vertices. In this problem setting, we deal with privacy vulnerability that is represented by an adversary's error. Therefore, the value of the privacy parameter ϵ, which determines the specific privacy protection requirements, is unclear and cannot be determined by the designer of the mechanism. Chatzikokolakis et al. [4] argue that factors such as the number of regions indistinguishable from a region, population density, and the diversity of points of interests (POI) affect the degree of privacy protection. Furthermore, they use the concept of privacy mass, which reflects these factors, to estimate the degree of privacy protection required for each region. In [4], the graph is initially constructed by the representative points of regions that are made by splitting the map and adding edges whose length is a metric defined using privacy math and the privacy requirement function req. Therefore, the structure of the road network is considered lost given that the constructed graph has a different distance scale compared to the actual one. Moreover, it is difficult to define the privacy mass required for our privacy vulnerability problem. Although their research is not limited to location privacy, Gu et al. [8] define a privacy criterion, called the Input-Discriminative local differential privacy (ID-LDP), which considers the different privacy parameters ϵ required for each data, and proposed a method to determine a mechanism that satisfies ID-LDP by solving an optimization problem. However, to find the mechanism, it is necessary to set ϵ. Therefore, this method cannot be applied to the problem setting in this study, where ϵ, which is necessary to provide fair privacy in each region, is unknown. Therefore, to the best of our knowledge, our study is the first to deal with the problem that the degree of privacy protection decreases in different regions on a topography-aware map.

In this study, we first show that privacy becomes vulnerable at some vertices when noise is added by GEM. Then, we propose two methods to solve the privacy vulnerability problem. One is to change the weights assigned to vertices, and the other is to use an optimization problem. We demonstrate that the application of these methods improves the privacy vulnerability compared to when none of the methods are applied. Finally, we discuss the problems of these methods and future scope of research.

2   Preliminary

This section introduces the fundamentals of differential privacy used in this study.

2.1   Differential Privacy

Differential privacy, proposed by Dwork [7], is a mathematically rigorous privacy criterion, that intuitively indicates that the existence of one record has a small effect on the answer to a query on a database. Two databases D_1 and D_2 of the same size are said to be adjacent if they differ by a single record. In this case, differential privacy is defined as

Definition 1 (ϵ-differential privacy). *For $\epsilon \in \mathbb{R}^+$, a mechanism M for any adjacent database D_1, D_2 and $\forall S \subseteq range(M)$ satisfies ϵ-differential privacy if the following inequality holds.*

$$\Pr[M(D_1) \in S] \leq e^{\epsilon} \Pr[M(D_2) \in S]$$

where $\mathbb{R}^+$ is the whole set of positive real numbers and $range(M)$ is the output domain of M. ϵ is a parameter called privacy parameter or privacy budget. Generally, the smaller ϵ is, the closer the ratio of the probability that the outputs are contained in the same set is to 1. Therefore, it is difficult to distinguish two databases when only the outputs are observed. As a result, the degree of privacy protection increases; however, the utility ("accuracy") of the data decreases. Well-known mechanisms that satisfy ϵ-differential privacy include the Laplace mechanism [7], which adds random noise extracted from the Laplace distribution to the result of querying a database, and the exponential mechanism [11], which outputs a result with a probability that depends on a quality function representing the "quality" of the answer in numerical form.

2.2   Exponential Mechanism

The exponential mechanism was proposed by McSherry et al. [11] to satisfy the ϵ-differential privacy. The major difference between the exponential and Laplace mechanism is that the Laplace mechanism can be applied only to numerical data, whereas the exponential mechanism can be applied to non-numerical data as well. The exponential mechanism needs a quality function $q : (\mathcal{D} \times O) \to \mathbb{R}$ that expresses the "quality" of the output O of the mechanism numerically ($\mathcal{D}$ denotes the entire dataset, O denotes the set of possible outputs of the mechanism, and $\mathbb{R}$ denotes the entire set of real numbers, respectively). We define the sensitivity Δq of the quality function as follows,

$$\Delta q = \max_{\forall o, D_1 \simeq D_2} |q(D_1, o) - q(D_2, o)|$$

where $D_1 \simeq D_2$ indicates that D_1 and D_2 are adjacent. The sensitivity of the quality function represents the maximum change in the quality function between the result of a query on a database whose records differ by one record and the result of a query on the original database. Using this sensitivity, the exponential mechanism can be defined as follows:

Definition 2 (Exponential mechanism). *For the quality function* $q : (\mathcal{D} \times O) \to \mathbb{R}$ *and the privacy parameter* $\epsilon \in \mathbb{R}^+$, *the exponential mechanism* $\mathcal{M}_q^\epsilon(D)$ *outputs* $o \in O$ *with the probability proportional to* $\exp\left(\frac{\epsilon q(D,o)}{2\Delta q}\right)$. *In other words,*

$$\Pr[\mathcal{M}_q^\epsilon(D) = o] = \frac{\exp\left(\frac{\epsilon q(D,o)}{2\Delta q}\right)}{\sum_{o' \in O} \exp\left(\frac{\epsilon q(D,o')}{2\Delta q}\right)}$$

Therefore, the larger the sensitivity, the greater is the effect of a single record on the answer to the query, and the more noise is needed to ensure data privacy.

2.3 $d_\mathcal{X}$-privacy

Chatzikokolakis et al. [2] extend the definition of differential privacy to not only the databases but also data in general. Assuming the mechanism M on the domain $\mathcal{X}$ gives the probability distribution on the domain $\mathcal{Z}$, and $d_\mathcal{X}$ represents "distance" on $\mathcal{X}$, $d_\mathcal{X}$-privacy can be defined as follows

Definition 3 ($d_\mathcal{X}$-privacy). *for all* $x, x' \in \mathcal{X}, Z \subseteq \mathcal{Z}$, M *satisfies* ϵ-$d_\mathcal{X}$-*privacy if the following inequality holds*

$$\frac{\Pr(M(x) \in Z)}{\Pr(M(x') \in Z)} \leq \exp\left(\epsilon d_\mathcal{X}(x, x')\right)$$

In $d_\mathcal{X}$-privacy, the difficulty in discrimination depends on the distance between any two data. For data with small distances, the distribution of the outputs of the mechanism becomes closer, making it difficult to distinguish which of the two is the actual data by simply observing the outputs. Differential privacy on databases is equivalent to ϵ-$d_\mathcal{X}$-privacy, where $d_\mathcal{X}$ is the Hamming distance d_h and only databases with $d_h = 1$ are considered.

2.4 Differential Privacy over the Graph

Takagi et al. [14] propose ϵ-Geo-Graph-Indistinguishability (ϵ-GeoGI), a privacy criterion applying $d_\mathcal{X}$-privacy to data on an undirected connected graph. Let $\mathcal{V}$ be the vertex set of the graph, then, GeoGI is defined as

Definition 4 (ϵ-Geo-Graph-Indistinguishability(ϵ-GeoGI)). *A mechanism M satisfies ϵ-GeoGI if the following inequality holds*

$$\forall v, v' \in \mathcal{V}, \forall W \subseteq \mathcal{V}, \frac{\Pr(M(v) \subseteq W)}{\Pr(M(v') \subseteq W)} \leq \exp(\epsilon d_s(v, v')) \tag{1}$$

where d_s denotes the shortest distance between two vertices on the graph.

Graph-Exponential Mechanism (GEM), the exponential mechanism on graphs, is proposed as a mechanism that satisfies ϵ-GeoGI.

Definition 5 (Graph-Exponential   Mechanism(GEM))   *Graph-Exponential Mechanism $\mathcal{M}_{d_s}^{\epsilon}$ takes a vertex $v \in \mathcal{V}$ as input and outputs a vertex $v' \in \mathcal{V}$ with the following probability.*

$$\Pr(M(v) = v') = \alpha(v) \exp\left(-\frac{\epsilon}{2} d_s(v, v')\right)$$

where α is the normalization term and $\alpha(v) = \left(\sum_{v'' \in \mathcal{V}} \exp\left(-\frac{\epsilon}{2} d_s(v, v'')\right)\right)^{-1}$

3 Related Work

In this section, we introduce related work.

3.1 Application of Differential Privacy to Location Information

Extensive research has been conducted on the application of differential privacy to location information. The most widely known concept is the geo-indistinguishability (GeoI) [1] proposed by Andrés et al., which is regarded as a type of $d_\mathcal{X}$-privacy introduced in the previous section, where $\mathcal{X}$ is a location on a two-dimensional plane and $d_\mathcal{X}$ is the Euclidean distance. GeoI outputs the location information with noise extracted from a probability distribution, making it difficult to estimate the exact location information. The Laplace mechanism using the two-dimensional Laplace distribution satisfies GeoI. However, some studies have highlighted problems with GeoI. Simon et al. [12] analyze GeoI in terms of the error probability of an adversary that makes predictions by observing the noisy location information using a mechanism that satisfies GeoI. In their analysis, they assume that a user is evenly distributed in two locations, x and x', as the adversary's prior information. Furthermore the adversary makes a prediction based on the posterior probability when they observe the location z. The adversary's probability of error is defined as

$$p_e(x, x', z) = \frac{\Pr(M(x') = z)}{\Pr(M(x) = z) + \Pr(M(x') = z)}$$

This study shows that p_e can be used to express the definition of GeoI. Based on p_e, they also conclude that there is a difference in the value of p_e, which depends on the type of mechanism satisfying GeoI, and that the indistinguishability from distant locations is limited.

3.2   Local Differential Privacy

In differential privacy, which protects the privacy of data in a database, a trusted server collects the exact data of individuals and adds noise to the output of the answer to a query. However, servers are not always reliable considering that they may actually use the collected data illegally or sell them to third parties. Therefore, local differential privacy (LDP) [6,9] has attracted considerable attention. In LDP, users add noise to their data using a mechanism that satisfies differential privacy on their own terminals, such as smartphones, before sending the data to the server, who can only observe the data with noise and cannot know the exact data.

We present previous studies on data collection and aggregation using LDP and their relevance to this study.

Chatzikokolakis et al. [4] define cover(x), a set of points that are highly indistinguishable from x, and argue that the privacy of location information depends on the number of points in cover(x) and the "quality" (POI diversity, population density and so on) of each point in cover(x). [4] also proposes the concept of privacy mass to capture these factors numerically. Based on this mass, [4] constructs a graph by adding edges to ensure all locations satisfy the required privacy. Using the exponential mechanism on the graph, they construct a mechanism that consider the privacy properties of each location. Considering the algorithm proposed by [4] constructs an elastic metric different from the actual distance between discrete regions, such as a grid, it is possible that the information on the road network used by [14] could be lost using the exponential mechanism on the constructed graph.

Koufogiannis et al. [10] tackle the problem of differing degrees of privacy protection in regions with large and small populations. Based on the fact that the definition of differential privacy can be expressed in terms of the Lipschitz condition, they propose local Lipschitz privacy, a privacy criterion that allows the degree of privacy protection ϵ to vary for different regions. Furthermore, they propose a method to determine a mechanism that satisfy the local Lipschitz privacy by solving the eikonal equation. The problem we are considering is that the degree of privacy protection differs for different regions, especially near the boundary between land and sea; therefore this method can be applied by considering land and sea as regions with large and small population densities, respectively. However, as mentioned in [10], if the variation of ϵ by region is not sufficiently smooth, the solution of the eikonal equation cannot be determined, and the mechanism cannot be defined. Our problem, sea and land, is a situation where the "population density" can vary significantly. Therefore, it is considered difficult to apply the mechanism in practice.

Chen et al. [5] address the problem of adapting to situations wherein the same user has different requirements for privacy protection at different locations. Under LDP, they consider a safe region, wherein a user may disclose that she is in the region, but differential privacy must be satisfied at any two points in the region, and define personalized local differential privacy (PLDP). [5] also proposes a mechanism based on random responses satisfying PLDP and a method for counting the number of users in each region. However, the data obtained in [5] is limited to the distribution of users considering that the main objective is to obtain aggregate data. The objective of this research is to propose a method that can be used to provide services based on the location of individual users.

Gu et al. [8] define Input Discriminative LDP, a privacy criterion that considers the different degree of privacy protection requirements for each data, and find a mechanism to satisfy this privacy criterion by solving an optimization problem to minimize the MSE (mean squared error) using random responses. However, considering the data privacy parameters must be preconfigured in [8], it cannot be applied in our problem setting where the optimal privacy parameters are unknown. Therefore, we need to define a mechanism to mitigate privacy vulnerability.

4   Problem Definition

In this section, we describe the problems that arise when protecting location information with differential privacy and the detailed problem setup.

First, we present the symbols used in this paper and their meanings in Table 1.

4.1   Privacy Vulnerability in GeoI and GeoGI

In this section, we explain the privacy vulnerability caused by geographical features in detail. In this study, we assume a uniform distribution as a prior distribution of users to clarify that privacy is vulnerable depending on the terrain. This problem occurs for both vertices with many or few possible output vertices around them, but it is particularly noticeable for the latter vertices. Therefore, this vulnerability problem occurs even at the boundary of a map, which is constructed by cutting out the larger map for practical use. However, as this problem does not occur if another cut-out method (method to cut out a map such that the region is centered) is used, the privacy vulnerability in such regions should be separated from that occurring at the regions, like near the sea. Therefore, we consider a map slightly larger than the actual required area and apply the exponential mechanism within it.

Table 1. Meaning of symbols.

Symbols	Meaning
M	A mechanism for adding noise to data.
$\Pr(M(x) = x')$	Probability that mechanism M outputs x' when x is the input.
$\pi(x)$	Prior probability that the user is at location x.
v, v'	A vertex of a graph, usually identified by a positive integer.
$\hat{v}$	An adversary's prediction of the user location.
$\mathcal{V}$	The entire set of vertices of a graph.
$d_{\mathcal{G}}(v, v')$	Weight of the edge connecting the vertex v and vertex v'.
$((v, v'), d_{\mathcal{G}}(v, v'))$	An edge of the weight $d_{\mathcal{G}}(v, v')$ connecting vertices v and v'.
E	The entire set of edges of a graph.
d_s	The shortest distance on the graph between vertex v and vertex v'.
w_v	A weight assigned to vertex v.
$w_{\mathcal{G}}(v)$	A function that takes a vertex v as an argument.
	and returns the weight of that vertex.
$\mathcal{G}(\mathcal{V}, E, w_{\mathcal{G}})$	A graph with vertex set V, edge set E, and weight function $w_{\mathcal{G}}$.

The following adversarial error (AE) is calculated for each vertex as a measure of the degree of privacy protection.

Definition 6 (Adversarial Error per Vertex(AE_v)).

$$AE_v = \sum_{v', \hat{v}} \Pr(M(v) = v')\Pr(h(v') = \hat{v})d_s(\hat{v}, v)$$

where h is the probability distribution of the adversary's prediction and $\Pr(h(v') = \hat{v})$ is the probability that the adversary takes $\hat{v}$ as the prediction of the user's actual location when they observe the user's perturbed location v'. Intuitively, AE_v is the expected distance between the vertex of the adversary's prediction and the user's actual vertex v when noise is added to the location information using mechanism M. The smaller the value is, the more information about the user's location is revealed by the adversary, and hence, the degree of privacy protection is smaller.

In the experiment, we use the map of Enoshima in Kanagawa Prefecture, Japan[1] and the graph representation of it as shown in Figs. 1(a) and 1(b) respectively. Graph-Exponential Mechanism (GEM) [14] is applied to the graph of Fig. 1(b). The privacy parameter used in the exponential mechanism is $\epsilon = 0.015\,\mathrm{m}^{-1}$. We assume that Enoshima (corresponding to the lower half of the Fig. 1(b)) is an important location for data users and the other vertices are dummy vertices to avoid map boundaries. The adversary is assumed to make a naive attack, taking the user's output location as a prediction.

Figure 2 shows the result of calculating AE_v for each vertex v constituting Enoshima on the graph. The results showed that the value of AE_v is smaller for vertices with few and more vertices around them, which indicates that the degree of privacy protection in such vertices is deteriorating.

---

[1] This map is taken from OpenStreetMap https://www.openstreetmap.org/.

(a) Map of the Enoshima area.   **(b)** Graph representation of the Enoshima area used in the experiment.

Fig. 1. A map used in the experiment and result of the experiment.

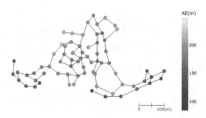

Fig. 2. AE_v for each vertex (only Enoshima area).

4.2 Exponential Mechanism Which Considers Weights

In this section, we propose a mechanism that considers vertex weights for a mechanism GEM that satisfies GeoGI, differential privacy criterion on graphs, and prove that this mechanism satisfies GeoGI. We treat undirected connected graphs $\mathcal{G}(\mathcal{V}, E)$ as in [14].

First, we assign a weight w_v to each vertex v on an undirected connected graph. In other words, the graph is represented by $\mathcal{G}(\mathcal{V}, E, w_\mathcal{G}))$. Then, we introduce the concept of weights into GEM proposed by [14]. Although the weight of every vertex is 1, it is necessary when applying the method to deal with the problem described in Sect. 4.1 when applying the method.

Definition 7 (Weighted-Graph-Exponential Mechanism(WGEM)).
Given a privacy parameter $\epsilon \in \mathbb{R}^+$, *the weighted-grid-exponential mechanism* $\mathcal{WM}_{d_s}^{\epsilon}(v)$ *outputs the vertex* $v' \in \mathcal{V}$ *whose weight is* $w_{v'}$ $(0 \le w_{v'} \le 1)$ *with a probability proportional to* $w_{v'} \exp\left(-\frac{\epsilon}{2} d_s(v, v')\right)$, *given as:*

$$\Pr(\mathcal{WM}_{d_s}^{\epsilon}(v) = v') = \alpha(v) w_{v'} \exp\left(-\frac{\epsilon}{2} d_s(v, v')\right)$$

where $\alpha(v)$ is the normalization term,

$$\alpha(v) = \frac{1}{\sum_{v'' \in \mathcal{V}} w_{v''} \exp\left(-\frac{\epsilon}{2} d_s(v, v'')\right)}$$

Suppose that $\forall v'' \in \mathcal{V}, 0 \leq w_{v''} \leq 1$, $\exists v'' \in \mathcal{V}, 0 < w_{v''}$. Additionally, in this definition $\frac{0}{0} = 1$.

Intuitively, the smaller the weight w_v set on a vertex v, the smaller is the probability that the vertex will be output. If $w_v = 0$, the vertex will never be output. Unlike GEM, WGEM does not necessarily maximize the probability of outputting the exact location of the user depending on the value of the weights.

In the following, we show that WGEM satisfies (1).

Proposition 1. *WGEM satisfies GeoGI.*

We refer the reader to the appendix for the proof.

5   Methods to Mitigate the Vulnerability Problem

In this section, we propose two methods to mitigate the vulnerability problem described in Sect. 4.1.

5.1   Weight Reduction Method

The Definition of the Algorithm. In the first method, called the "weight reduction method", we decrease the weights introduced in Sect. 4.2 to reduce the probability of the vertex being output and mitigate the privacy vulnerability at the vertex.

However, a non-convex programming problem must be solved to obtain optimal weights that minimize privacy vulnerability, which is computationally hard. Therefore, we use a greedy algorithm to obtain near-optimal weights.

We present a greedy algorithm in Algorithm 1 to successively decrease the weights of the vertices and obtain near-optimal weights. The algorithm takes a set of all vertices $\mathcal{V}$, a list of weights of each vertex W, an objective function f, a constraint function c, a criterion S that determines the order in which the vertices whose weights are to be reduced are selected in line 4, and a reduction amount of weights in one update δ as input, and outputs a near-optimal weight for each vertex. In line 1, the initial value of the objective function is calculated using $\mathcal{V}, W$. In lines 5–16, the weights of the vertices are reduced by δ (line 8), the value of the objective function is calculated with $\mathcal{V}, W'$ and whether the constraint is satisfied is judged (line 10). If the objective function is improved and the constraint is satisfied, the update is executed and we return to line 2. If the objective function does not improve, the change is discarded and the next ranked vertex is examined. In lines 17–19, if the objective function does not improve when the weights are reduced for all vertices, the algorithm is stopped and the final weights are output in line 21.

Algorithm 1. Weight reduction method.

Input: Set of all vertices $\mathcal{V}$, list of weights W, objective function f, constraint function c, selection criteria S, and decreasing amount δ.

Output: List of modified weights W.

1: $obj_{pre} \Leftarrow f(\mathcal{V}, W)$
2: **while** True **do**
3:    $W_0 \Leftarrow W$
4:    $\mathcal{V}_{list} \Leftarrow$ List of vertices in $\mathcal{V}$ stored in order of priority based on S.
5:    **for** v in $\mathcal{V}_{list}$ **do**
6:      $W' \Leftarrow W$
7:      **if** $W'[v] \geq \delta$ **then**
8:        $W'[v] \Leftarrow W[v] - \delta$
9:        $obj_{post} \Leftarrow f(\mathcal{V}, W')$, $cons \Leftarrow c(\mathcal{V}, W')$
10:        **if** $obj_{post} - obj_{pre} < 0$ **and** $cons$ **then**
11:          $W \Leftarrow W'$
12:          $obj_{pre} \Leftarrow obj_{post}$
13:          **break**
14:        **end if**
15:      **end if**
16:    **end for**
17:    **if** $W = W_0$ **then**
18:      **break**
19:    **end if**
20: **end while**
21: **return** W

Evaluation. In this section, we show the results of the actual application of the methods introduced in Sect. 5.1. The adversary predicts the user's location using the optimal attack [13], in which the adversary solves the following optimization problem to obtain a prediction function h that minimizes the user's AE.

$$\text{minimize} \quad \sum_{v,v',\hat{v}} \pi(v)\Pr(M(v) = v')\Pr(h(v') = \hat{v})d_p(v,\hat{v})$$

$$\text{subject to} \quad \Pr(h(v') = \hat{v}) \geq 0 \qquad \forall v', \hat{v} \in \mathcal{V}$$

$$\sum_{\hat{v}} \Pr(M(v') = \hat{v}) = 1 \qquad \forall v' \in \mathcal{V}$$

where $d_p(v, \hat{v})$ is the "distance" between the user's actual location v and the adversary's prediction $\hat{v}$. We can assume various adversaries by changing this. We use $d_{\mathcal{G}}$ throughout this paper. The objective function is to minimize the value of AE over the entire map, and the constraint is the condition for imposing it as a probability distribution. Although h is a probability distribution, the actual prediction is almost always deterministic in terms of the output $\hat{v}$ for the input v'. In our experiments, we solved this optimization problem using the Python library pulp.

We use the graph representation of Enoshima area from Sect. 4.1 as a map, and set $\epsilon = 0.015\,\mathrm{m}^{-1}$ as the value of the privacy parameter. The following is used as the objective function *obj*.

$$\sum_v \left(\sum_{v',\hat{v}} \Pr(M(v) = v')\Pr(h(v') = \hat{v})d_s(v,\hat{v}) - AE_{max} \right)^2 \qquad (2)$$

where

$$AE_{max} = \max_v AE_v$$

The expression (2) mitigates the vulnerability by keeping the value of AE in each region close to a constant. We use the order of decreasing values of AE as the selection criterion S of vertices, as the vertices with smaller values of AE have less privacy protection and their weights should be reduced preferentially. In this experiment, we do not specify any constraint c.

Figures 3(a) and 3(b) show AE_r per vertex using the optimal attack before and after applying the method, respectively. It can be seen that the vulnerability of the privacy of the southwest and southeast vertices is mitigated. Figure 3(c) plots the weights of each vertex after the algorithm is applied. It can be seen that the weights decrease around the vertices owing to the low degree of privacy protection.

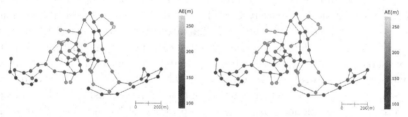

(a) AE per vertex before weights change.   **(b)** AE per vertex after weights change.

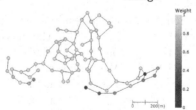

(c) Weight of each vertex after algorithm execution.

Fig. 3. Experimental results of applying the weight reduction method.

5.2 AE Optimization Method

Formularization. In this section, we describe the second method used to mitigate the privacy vulnerability problem. In this method, we calculate the mechanism by solving the following optimization problem and ensure that AE_v does not vary significantly from vertex to vertex.

$$\text{minimize} \quad \sum_v \left(\sum_{v', \hat{v}} \Pr(M(v) = v') \Pr(h(v') = \hat{v}) d_s(\hat{v}, v) - O \right)^2 \tag{3}$$

$$\text{subject to} \quad \Pr(M(v) = v') \geq 0, \ \forall v, v' \in \mathcal{V} \tag{4}$$

$$\sum_{v'} \Pr(M(v) = v') = 1, \ \forall v \in \mathcal{V} \tag{5}$$

$$\frac{\Pr(M(v) = v'')}{\Pr(M(v') = v'')} \leq \exp\left(\epsilon d(v, v') \right), \ \forall (v, v') \in E, \forall v'' \in \mathcal{V} \tag{6}$$

$$\Pr(M(v) = v') \leq \Pr(M(v) = v'') \ \ (if \ d_s(v, v') \geq d_s(v, v'')), \ \forall v, v', v'' \in \mathcal{V} \tag{7}$$

In the aforementioned definition of the optimization problem, (3) minimizes the squared error between AE_v of all vertices and some predetermined value of O, which eliminate the difference of AE_v from vertex to vertex. O is the target AE_v for each vertex, which may be set, for example, to the maximum value of AE_v with respect to the vertex when the exponential mechanism is used. (4) and (5) are the conditions that guarantee M is a probability distribution. (6) are conditional expressions to satisfy GeoGI. GeoGI is satisfied between all vertices if the conditions hold for two vertices that are directly connected by an edge. (7) are conditions for decreasing the output probability as the distance from the vertex increases. Although these are not necessary conditions for defining the mechanism, it is natural for the output probability to decrease as the distance increases, similar to the conventional exponential mechanism, Laplace mechanism, etc. For convenience purposes, this approach of solving the optimization problem is referred to as the AE optimization method in this study.

Evaluation. In this section, we show the results of calculating the mechanism by solving the optimization problem proposed in the previous section. Our environment is Python 3.8 and the solution of the optimization problem is obtained using the Python library CVXOPT. We computed the optimization problem in Sect. 5.2 using the map around Enoshima used in the Sect. 4.1. For simplicity, we assume that the adversary's prediction of the user's actual location is the observed location (naive attack). We use $\epsilon = 0.015 \, \text{m}^{-1}$ as the privacy parameter. Figure 4 plots AE_v when the optimal mechanism is used, cutting out only the Enoshima portion. As can be seen from the figure, AE_v is almost constant for all vertices, which indicates that the vulnerability reduces when AE_v is used as a privacy criterion.

Fig. 4. AE_v calculated using the optimized mechanism (naive attack).

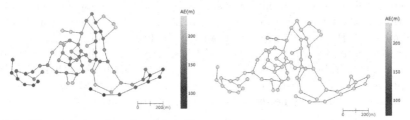

(a) AE_v calculated using the Exponential mechanism(optimal attack).

(b) AE_v calculated using the optimized mechanism(optimal attack).

Fig. 5. AE_v for each vertex assuming optimal attack.

In this section, we have assumed that the adversary performs only the naive attacks where the prediction is the vertex output from the user; however when we assume that the adversary performs an optimal attack [13] as mentioned in Sect. 5.1, the following results are obtained. The results of calculating AE_v for each vertex are shown in Fig. 5. Figure 5(a) shows the AE_v with the exponential mechanism before optimizing the mechanism whereas Fig. 5(b) shows the AE_v with the optimal mechanism. It can be seen that privacy vulnerability is mitigated even for adversaries that perform the optimal attack, partly due to the assumption of uniform prior distribution.

5.3   Comparison of the Two Methods

In this section, we compare the two methods proposed in Sects. 5.1 and 5.2. Table 2 shows the difference between the two methods in four perspectives. The contents of this table are described in detail here. First, regarding the accuracy, as the weight reduction method adjusts the weights based on the exponential mechanism, the degree of mitigation in privacy vulnerability is small as the mechanism cannot be changed freely. Considering the attack methods assumed when computing AE_v in constructing the mechanism, weight reduction methods can assume the arbitrary attack method, whereas the AE optimization method can only assume the naive attack method that predicts the same location as the observation to ensure the convexity of the objective and constraint functions.

Considering the amount of data required to actually add noise to the location information, the weight reduction method requires $|\mathcal{V}|$ weights for each vertex along with the map information, whereas the AE optimization method requires $|\mathcal{V}|^2$ probabilities for outputting each vertex. Lastly, we discuss whether fine tuning is possible or not based on whether or not it is possible to obtain a more ideal mechanism by specifying detailed conditions. In the weight reduction method, fine tuning is difficult considering the mechanism is an exponential mechanism. Conversely, the AE optimization method can be tuned easily by adding constraints, provided the constraints can be expressed using convex expressions.

The use of the two methods can thus be summarized as follows. The weight reduction method requires only the weight of each vertex to be stored in the terminal when the mechanism is actually applied. Therefore, it is appropriate to use this method when the amount of storage is severely limited, in order to reduce the vulnerability of privacy as much as possible. On the other hand, the AE optimization method should be used when the amount of storage is sufficient and privacy vulnerability needs to be significantly mitigated.

Table 2. Comparison of the weight reduction method and the AE optimization method.

	Weight reduction method	AE optimization method
Accuracy	low	**high**
Assumed attack method	**arbitrary**	only naive attack
Amount of data	$|\mathcal{V}|$	$|\mathcal{V}|^2$
Fine tuning	difficult	**relatively easy**

5.4 Performance Analysis

In this section, we analyze the performance of the two methods. For the weight reduction method, we discuss the computational complexity of the algorithm, whereas for the AE optimization method, we discuss the number of conditional expressions of the optimization problem.

The computational complexity of the weight reduction method depends on the outer loop count N_o in lines 2–20 and the inner loop count N_i in lines 5–16 of the algorithm, as well as on the computational complexity of the objective function. The objective function obj used in Sect. 5.1 requires $AE(O(|V|^2))$. Furthermore, it is necessary to compute the attack function h used by adversaries who conduct the optimal attack, which can be computed efficiently by [13]. Additionally, N_i is not so large in our observation. The smaller the AE is, the smaller will be the weight. Therefore, by selecting vertices in the ascending order of AE, N_i can be reduced. Considering the number of locations where the weights decrease tends to be small, N_o is also not so large.

The number of conditional expressions for the AE optimization method is as follows. (4) has $|V|^2$, (5) has $|V|$, (6) has $|E||V|$, and (7) has $O(|V|^2)$ conditional expressions. Considering the number of roads connecting to an intersection in a real road network is limited to 4 in most cases, the number of conditional expressions is $O(|V|^2)$.

6   Conclusion

In this study, we raise the issue that privacy protection based on AE is weak in some regions, even in the GEM proposed in [14], which focuses on the fact that a simple mechanism that satisfies GeoI does not consider road networks. Furthermore, We propose two methods to mitigate this problem and show that the problem can be mitigated through experiments. One method is by using an exponential mechanism based on a greedy algorithm to adjust the weights assigned to each vertex of the graph. The other is to compute the mechanism that minimizes an objective function that expresses the MSE between AE of each vertex and the target AE under differential privacy and customizable conditions. Lastly, we can obtain the mechanism by solving this optimization problem.

Finally, we discuss the problems and solutions of the two methods proposed in this study. As for the weight reduction method, the degree of improvement is found to be smaller than that of the AE optimization method, considering the basic mechanism is the exponential mechanism, which indicates that the number of variables that can be adjusted is small. This problem has a trade-off relationship with the amount of data required for using the mechanism, and hence, it is necessary to use the weight reduction method according to the situation.

As for the AE optimization method, we mentioned in Sect. 5.3 that the attack method can be assumed as the only naive attack that outputs the same location as the observed location. However, a rational adversary is expected to perform the optimal attack that minimizes the expected distance from the user's actual location. A possible way to address this problem is to optimize the objective function such that the attacker's attack function h does not change in the optimal attack.

One common challenge for the weight reduction method and AE optimization method is to consider factors other than topography that are related to privacy, such as population density and the number of POIs, which are considered in [4]. One way to address this issue is to vary O for each vertex when computing the MSE. In this way, we believe that we can obtain a mechanism that adjusts the expected value of AE_v for each vertex. Furthermore, we believe that adjusting the degree of privacy protection using an intuitive measure of expected distance from the adversary's prediction can be useful. These problems and their solutions will be discussed in future research.

Acknowledgements. This work was partially supported by JST CREST JPMJCR 21M2, JST SICORP JPMJSC2107, KAKENHI 21K19767, 19K20269.

A   Proof of Proposition 1

Proof. It is sufficient to show that for any two vertices $v, v' \in \mathcal{V}$ and any $V \subseteq \mathcal{V}$ the following holds.

$$\frac{\Pr(M(v) \in V)}{\Pr(M(v') \in V)} \le \epsilon d_s(v, v')$$

That is, for any two vertices $v, v' \in \mathcal{V}$, we find the maximum of the following ratio.

$$\frac{\Pr[\mathcal{WM}_{d_s}^{\epsilon}(v) = v'']}{\Pr[\mathcal{WM}_{d_s}^{\epsilon}(v') = v'']} = \frac{\alpha(v)w_{v''}\exp(-\frac{\epsilon}{2}d_s(v, v''))}{\alpha(v')w_{v''}\exp\left(-\frac{\epsilon}{2}d_s(v', v'')\right)}$$

First, when $w_{v''} = 0$, from Definition 7,

$$\frac{\alpha(v)w_{v''}\exp(-\frac{\epsilon}{2}d_s(v, v''))}{\alpha(v')w_{v''}\exp\left(-\frac{\epsilon}{2}d_s(v', v'')\right)} = \frac{0}{0} = 1 < e^{\epsilon}$$

Next, when $w_{v''} \ne 0$,

$$\frac{\alpha(v)w_{v''}\exp(-\frac{\epsilon}{2}d_s(v, v''))}{\alpha(v')w_{v''}\exp\left(-\frac{\epsilon}{2}d_s(v', v'')\right)}$$

$$= \frac{\alpha(v)}{\alpha(v')}\exp\left(\frac{\epsilon}{2}(d_s(v', v'') - d_s(v, v''))\right) \tag{8}$$

In this case, we consider the case where the expression (8) is maximum. That is, when $d_s(v', v'') - d_s(v, v'')$ takes the maximum value. As we are considering an undirected connected graph, it is possible to go through any vertex, so from the triangle inequality, $\forall v'' \in \mathcal{V}, d_s(v', v'') - d_s(v, v'') \le d_s(v, v')$ holds.

$$\frac{\Pr[\mathcal{WM}_{d_s}^{\epsilon}(v) = v'']}{\Pr[\mathcal{WM}_{d_s}^{\epsilon}(v') = v'']} \le \frac{\alpha(v)}{\alpha(v')}\exp\left(\frac{\epsilon}{2}d_s(v, v')\right)$$

Next, we show that $\frac{\alpha(v)}{\alpha(v')} \le \exp(\frac{\epsilon}{2}d_s(v, v'))$ holds, that is, the following expression holds.

$$\sum_{v''} \in \mathcal{V}w_{v''}\exp\left(-\frac{\epsilon}{2}d_s(v, v'')\right)\exp\left(\frac{\epsilon}{2}d_s(v, v')\right)$$

$$- \sum_{v'' \in \mathcal{V}} w_{v''}\exp\left(-\frac{\epsilon}{2}d_s(v', v'')\right) \ge 0$$

From the triangle inequality

$$\sum_{v'' \in \mathcal{V}} w_{v''} \exp\left(-\frac{\epsilon}{2} d_s(v, v'')\right) \exp\left(\frac{\epsilon}{2} d_s(v, v')\right) - \sum_{v'' \in \mathcal{V}} w_{v''} \exp\left(-\frac{\epsilon}{2} d_s(v', v'')\right)$$

$$= \sum_{v'' \in \mathcal{V}} w_{v''} \exp\left(\frac{\epsilon}{2}(d_s(v, v') - d_s(v, v''))\right) - \sum_{v'' \in \mathcal{V}} w_{v''} \exp\left(-\frac{\epsilon}{2} d_s(v', v'')\right)$$

$$\geq \sum_{v'' \in \mathcal{V}} w_{v''} \exp\left(-\frac{\epsilon}{2} d_s(v', v'')\right) - \sum_{v'' \in \mathcal{V}} w_{v''} \exp\left(-\frac{\epsilon}{2} d_s(v', v'')\right) = 0$$

Then,

$$\frac{\Pr[\mathcal{WM}^{\epsilon}_{d_s}(v) = v'']}{\Pr[\mathcal{WM}^{\epsilon}_{d_s}(v') = v'']} \leq \exp(\epsilon d_s(v, v'))$$

It is shown that WGEM satisfies expression (1).

References

1. Andrés, M.E., Bordenabe, N.E., Chatzikokolakis, K., Palamidessi, C.: Geo-indistinguishability: differential privacy for location-based systems. In: Proceedings of the 2013 ACM SIGSAC Conference on Computer and Communications Security, pp. 901–914. CCS 2013, Association for Computing Machinery, New York, NY, USA (2013)
2. Chatzikokolakis, K., Andrés, M.E., Bordenabe, N.E., Palamidessi, C.: Broadening the scope of differential privacy using metrics. In: De Cristofaro, E., Wright, M. (eds.) PETS 2013. LNCS, vol. 7981, pp. 82–102. Springer, Heidelberg (2013). https://doi.org/10.1007/978-3-642-39077-7_5
3. Chatzikokolakis, K., ElSalamouny, E., Palamidessi, C.: Practical Mechanisms for Location Privacy, p. 18 (2016)
4. Chatzikokolakis, K., Palamidessi, C., Stronati, M.: Constructing elastic distinguishability metrics for location privacy. In: Proceedings on Privacy Enhancing Technologies 2015, pp. 156–170, July 2015
5. Chen, R., Li, H., Qin, A.K., Kasiviswanathan, S.P., Jin, H.: Private spatial data aggregation in the local setting. In: 2016 IEEE 32nd International Conference on Data Engineering (ICDE), pp. 289–300 (2016)
6. Duchi, J.C., Jordan, M.I., Wainwright, M.J.: Local privacy and statistical minimax rates. In: 2013 IEEE 54th Annual Symposium on Foundations of Computer Science, pp. 429–438 (2013)
7. Dwork, C.: Differential privacy: a survey of results. In: Agrawal, M., Du, D., Duan, Z., Li, A. (eds.) TAMC 2008. LNCS, vol. 4978, pp. 1–19. Springer, Heidelberg (2008). https://doi.org/10.1007/978-3-540-79228-4_1
8. Gu, X., Li, M., Xiong, L., Cao, Y.: Providing input-discriminative protection for local differential privacy. In: 36th IEEE International Conference on Data Engineering, ICDE 2020, Dallas, TX, USA, April 20–24, 2020, pp. 505–516. IEEE (2020)
9. Kasiviswanathan, S.P., Lee, H.K., Nissim, K., Raskhodnikova, S., Smith, A.: What can we learn privately? In: 2008 49th Annual IEEE Symposium on Foundations of Computer Science, pp. 531–540 (2008)

10. Koufogiannis, F., Pappas, G.J.: Location-dependent privacy. In: 2016 IEEE 55th Conference on Decision and Control (CDC), pp. 7586–7591 (2016)
11. McSherry, F., Talwar, K.: Mechanism design via differential privacy. In: 48th Annual IEEE Symposium on Foundations of Computer Science (FOCS 2007), pp. 94–103 (2007)
12. Oya, S., Troncoso, C., Pérez-González, F.: Is geo-indistinguishability what you are looking for? In: Proceedings of the 2017 on Workshop on Privacy in the Electronic Society, pp. 137–140. WPES 2017, Association for Computing Machinery, New York, NY, USA (2017)
13. Shokri, R., Theodorakopoulos, G., Troncoso, C., Hubaux, J.P., Le Boudec, J.Y.: Protecting location privacy: optimal strategy against localization attacks. In: Proceedings of the 2012 ACM Conference on Computer and Communications Security, pp. 617–627. CCS 2012, Association for Computing Machinery, New York, NY, USA (2012)
14. Takagi, S., Cao, Y., Asano, Y., Yoshikawa, M.: Geo-graph-indistinguishability: protecting location privacy for LBS over road networks. In: DBSec (2019)
15. Warner, S.L.: Randomized response: a survey technique for eliminating evasive answer bias. J. Am. Statist. Assoc. **60**(309), 63–69 (1965)

Distributed Systems

Liberate Your Servers: A Decentralized Content Compliance Validation Protocol

Bowen Liu$^{(\boxtimes)}$ and Jianying Zhou

Singapore University of Technology and Design, Singapore, Singapore
bowen_liu@mymail.sutd.edu.sg

Abstract. Content compliance validation provides a formal and secure procedure for applications (like emails or social networks) to determine how an intended action can be carried out. By conducting the validation against predefined policies, only compliant content is allowed to be delivered. Unfortunately, current solutions suffer from multiple issues such as intensive server-side overheads, intransparency and centralization.

To address these drawbacks, we propose **DeCCV**, the first decentralized content compliance validation protocol for real-world applications. In our work, the application requires to transparently declare its validation policies (**Policy$_{VAL}^{Cont}$**) on the blockchain. Meanwhile, we outsource the resource-intensive validations to multiple decentralized off-chain *validation nodes*, which verify user's content locally and issue the proofs (signatures) accordingly. Therefore, the burden of server-end workloads is minimized to merely signature-based verification. Moreover, a dedicated incentive mechanism is proposed to motivate high accountability of validation participants. **DeCCV** is platform-friendly that can be compatible with most real-world applications. We fully implement **DeCCV** for Gmail, Twitter and Dropbox to show its versatility.

Keywords: Blockchain · Content Validation · Decentralization

1 Introduction

The process of compliance validation creates a strong guarantee for applications by filtering out the unsatisfied contents and provides a formal verification against the predefined policies. To avoid potential virus and transmission congestion, email providers (e.g., Gmail [11]) allow users to send email attachments up to 25 MB. The larger documents will be automatically added a Google Drive link. Meanwhile, the particular types (e.g., executable files and malicious macros) are disallowed [11] to be attached. Similarly, social networks [17] and cloud storage applications [22] usually utilize more complicated policies to censor the contents that are not appropriate for a diverse audience, such as racism and pornography.

The community has conducted research on the compliance validation of a given content. One direction is the methodologies for inspecting malware or recognizing potentially harmful behaviors of a content. The former [8,10] leverages

© IFIP International Federation for Information Processing 2022
Published by Springer Nature Switzerland AG 2022
S. Sural and H. Lu (Eds.): DBSec 2022, LNCS 13383, pp. 89–109, 2022.
https://doi.org/10.1007/978-3-031-10684-2_6

on automated dynamic malware analysis, reverse engineering and symbolic execution for detecting Trojans, viruses and malware, while the latter [3–5] employs machine learning techniques to discover the suspicious conducts with violence, pornography or racism. In practice, the companies may customize their content compliance policies, and integrate these tools for validation. However, current schemes suffer from multiple limitations. Firstly, they lack a transparent policy declaration, thereby the correctness and efficiency can not be examined. For instance, due to insufficient validation, a large number of tweets about child pornography existed on Twitter [18]. Secondly, current validations incur intense deployment cost and overlong performance delay (e.g., YouTube usually takes hours to censor the suspicious videos [13]) as the servers require to deal with a bulk of validation requests. Ideally, the burden of validations can be shifted to a public service or a cloud. Unfortunately, this might introduce centralization and censorship issues. Another direction is the multi-party validation framework deployed on a hybridized TEE-blockchain environment [32], which relies on multiple outsourced TEE environments to perform the necessary computations. However, most advanced validation tools cannot be ported into TEEs due to the limitations of programming languages [34]. Moreover, a dedicated incentive for computation nodes is absent [32], and hence their accountability can not be guaranteed.

In this paper, we propose **DeCCV**, the first (up to our best knowledge) decentralized content compliance validation protocol that aims at transparency, accountability and compatibility for real-world applications. In contrast to prior schemes, the applications transparentize the policy on the blockchain, indicating the categories and brief specifications. With multiple decentralized off-chain nodes which verify the content against policy and issue the proofs accordingly, the burden of server-side validations is minimized. Moreover, a crafted incentive is presented to motivate honest behaviors of validation participants. We show its feasibility and compatibility for Gmail, Twitter and Dropbox.

In summary, our work addresses several key technical challenges:

- **Transparent policy:** We transparentize the current ambiguous policy declaration by requiring applications to disclose the policy metadata (e.g., categories and corresponding validation mechanisms) on blockchains so that the correctness and efficiency can be inspected and improved.
- **Decentralized validation:** To remove centralized assumptions, we outsource the resource-intensive validations to multiple decentralized nodes, which issue the validation proofs as a token for users. Thus, **DeCCV** offloads the server's workloads to merely token (or signature) based verification yet resists against multiple adversarial behaviors, such as Sybil attacks, manipulation attacks, and substitution attacks.
- **Accountability and compatibility:** We present a dedicated incentive with financial rewards, penalties and dispute functionalities to motivate high availability and accountability of validation participants. Moreover, **DeCCV** is compatible with most real-world applications. We employ Gmail, Twitter and Dropbox as use cases to evaluate its efficiency and versatility.

2 Background

2.1 Blockchain and Smart Contract

A blockchain is an immutable distributed ledger that allows transactions (or data) to be securely stored among untrusted nodes who are mutually running over a consensus protocol. Ethereum was proposed [31] after Bitcoin which can execute self-enforcing programs (known as smart contracts) over an Ethereum Virtual Machine (EVM), which can implement nearly arbitrary logic of value due to the Turing completeness. From the perspective of implementation, Solidity [15] is the most popular language to develop the smart contracts. Ethereum has designed its native *gas* mechanism for charging transaction fees and paying the on-chain storage [39]. **DeCCV** employs the underlying smart contracts based blockchain platform as a place for transparentizing policies and enforcing the incentive logic.

2.2 Secure Communication Channels

In practice, a secure end-to-end communication channel between mutual parties is essential. Transport Layer Security (TLS) [35] protocol aims to establish an encrypted and safe transportation pipe between mutual parties, which can guarantee the integrity, confidentiality, and authenticity of transferred data [44]. TLS 1.3 [42] was proposed to improve the detected insecure underlying designs in TLS 1.2 [1] with an optimization reducing the previous two-step handshakes to only one (i.e., 1-RTT).

TLS 1.3 consists of two necessary stages: **handshake** and **channel encryption**. The **handshake** process is roughly divided into two distinct phases (i.e., *key exchanges* and *authentications*). The former allows the communicating parties to exchange hello messages and generate a shared key (e.g., Elliptic–curve Diffie–Hellman algorithm [36]), which is used as a symmetric key for channel's encryption. In contrast, the latter enables parties to validate the certificates. Upon a symmetric key is created in addition to the **handshake** is finalized, the parties start to communicate within this secured channel. Note that the mutual authentication is optional in TLS, but can be realized if both parties hold valid certificates for verification. In this paper, we employ TLS 1.3 as an efficient approach for transport protection among system participants.

2.3 Content Compliance Validation

Content compliance validation allows the application operators to filter out malicious behavior and control the content properly. Generally, many platforms have built up crafted policies for verifying the compliance of contents, which can be classified into three categories: (1) **Content property validation** ensures a file should conform particular specifications, such as file size and file types. This policy is widely adopted in most email applications; (2) **Content vulnerability validation** detects the presence of malware. The file that is intentionally developed to infiltrate or damage a system would be blocked; and (3) **Content behavior validation** prevents unsuitable conduct of contents, including hatred, racism, violence, and adult etc.

Unfortunately, the already-adopted schemes suffer from multiple limitations. Firstly, the policy metadata and deployed details are not transparent. Therefore, no entity can examine its correctness and robustness. The application users are even not aware how their contents are verified. Next, the storage utilization and computation are performed on the servers' side or a cloud, which are intuitively intense and may introduce regular downtime and centralized assumptions. Finally, current validation processes are always inadequate and usually take a long period of time. For instance, with insufficient validations, porn videos could be stealthily uploaded to YouTube and Twitter [2,12,18]. In **DeCCV**, we try to address these issues by presenting a transparent, lightweight and decentralized content validation protocol for real-world applications.

3   Protocol Overview

In this section, we sketch the insights of system model, and present our goals and requirements considered in **DeCCV**. In this work, we mainly focus on Ethereum as a natural place to transparentize policies and TLS for transport protection, but it can be easily extended to other blockchains and design choices of secure channel with comparable capabilities. Meanwhile, **DeCCV** is compatible with most applications that have content validation functionalities.

3.1   System Architecture

DeCCV involves three types of actors, as depicted in Fig. 1.

- **App:** is the **DeCCV**-compatible application that has a prototype of validation policies mechanism. Meanwhile, **App** requires to disclose its $\text{Policy}_{\text{VAL}}^{\text{Cont}}$ by deploying a smart contract $\text{Contr}_{\text{App}}$ on open blockchains and enforce incentive logic into $\text{Contr}_{\text{App}}$ for validation nodes. This declaration is updatable reflecting the requirements that user's content can be posted.
- **Node$_{\text{VAL}}$:** are multiple off-chain validation nodes. Each node receives the encrypted content from users via a secure communication channel (e.g., TLS), decrypts it, then validates against $\text{Policy}_{\text{VAL}}^{\text{Cont}}$ and issues the proof accordingly. The proof indicates whether a content is policy-compliant or policy-violated, and deviated proofs signed by ineligible nodes would be detected (we will discuss it in Sect. 5.1). **Node$_{\text{VAL}}$** can receive financial rewards for each honest behavior but should deposit crypto-assets ahead. Meanwhile, punishment and dispute functionalities are also devised to motivate their high accountability.
- **User:** is an **App** customer. She must obtain the proofs from **Node$_{\text{VAL}}$** before she can send her contents to the **App**.

Interactions. App first deploys a $\text{Contr}_{\text{App}}$ with policy metadata and incentive logic. This transparent declaration may enjoy several preferable properties.

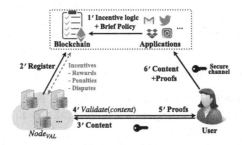

Fig. 1. Detailed architecture of **DeCCV**.

We will discuss it in Sect. 4.1. Next, **Node**$_{VAL}$ can fulfill registrations by specifying public keys and locking security deposits. A user requires to send her encrypted content to **Node**$_{VAL}$ before delivering it to **App**. Each node will decrypt the content, validate it against predefined **Policy**$_{VAL}^{Cont}$ and generate the proofs accordingly. This proof can act as the access credentials and only policy-compliant content bundled with valid proofs can pass the **App**-side verification. It seems to be counter-intuitive that each **Node**$_{VAL}$ is able to decrypt the user's content for validation, breaching the privacy nature. We emphasize that a feasible approach is to restrict the participation of **Node**$_{VAL}$ to reputable nodes[1] at registration phase, and hence the accountability of preserving the privacy of user's content can be held. Furthermore, a dedicated incentive mechanism is enforced on **Node**$_{VAL}$ with mandatory deposits, economic rewards and financial penalties to motivate honest behaviors. We will discuss more considerations on privacy protection in Sect. 4.3.

3.2   Threat Model

Blockchain. We assume the blockchain can function normally, and its consensus protocol cannot be compromised by the attackers. Meanwhile, we assume any party can interact with smart contracts normally (e.g., sending transactions or reading the blockchain state)

Threat Model. We assume that an adversary cannot compromise the underlying cryptographic primitives (e.g., hash function, signatures). The goal of an adversary is trying to bypass the validation and submit the non-compliant content to **App**. Under these assumptions, we assume that an adversary can compromise less than 1/3 of **Node**$_{VAL}$ to ensure the fault tolerance. To resist the misbehavior or ineligibility of **Node**$_{VAL}$, an incentive-based mechanism is utilized and enforced to motivate high accountability. Moreover, we assume that an adversary can breach the messages from a valid and compliant user, extract the valid proofs and replace a new content with the intercepted proofs. Alternatively,

---

[1] This consideration has been widely adopted in the trusted oracles [6,7,9] selection process in many Decentralized Finance (DeFi) platforms. As each reputable node is registered into **Contr**$_{App}$, the platform users can be aware of its identity.

he can even send over a *compliant* content for validation, replace a *non-compliant* one, and submit it to **App**. We will provide the security discussion in Sect. 7.

3.3 Protocol Requirements

Below, we summarize the design goals of **DeCCV**. Briefly, **DeCCV** aims at achieving the properties of transparency, decentralization, accountability, and efficiency.

Transparency. We pursue policy transparency that requires applications to explicitly reveal their policy specifications by deploying a smart contract.

Decentralization. To address the downsides of current centralized validations, the entire computation workloads are outsourced to multiple decentralized **Node**$_{VAL}$ operating off the chain securely and efficiently.

Accountability. All essential parties (i.e., validation nodes) should fulfill obligations as otherwise their security deposit would be slashed. Additionally, the applications reward the eligible nodes for each compliant behavior.

Efficiency. We shift resource-intensive validations to off-chain **Node**$_{VAL}$ and minimize the server-side overheads to only lightweight signature (or token) based verification. In terms of other necessary computation cost and blockchain-related fees, those are supposed to be minimized and optimized.

4   Protocol Details

In this section, we describe each sub-protocol of **DeCCV** in details, including initialization, content validation, proofs issuance, and access token. More detailed interactions among system actors are depicted in Appendix A.

4.1   Initialization

In the prior constructions, the content (e.g., an email with attachment or a tweet with selfie) is validated on **App**'s server side, which suffered several downsides like intransparency and heavy overhead. To mitigate it, **DeCCV** allows the **App** operators to deploy a **Contr**$_{App}$ with following fields hardcoded: (1) the brief description of content validation policies **Policy**$_{VAL}^{Cont}$ (cf. Policy$_i$ structure in Fig. 2), (2) the **Policy**$_{VAL}^{Cont}$ management interfaces operated by **App** owner only (cf. ManagePolicy method), and (3) the incentive logic with registration (cf. Register method), penalties and disputes functionalities (cf. Algorithm 2).

In general, **Policy**$_{VAL}^{Cont}$ blocks the potential malware or improper conducts and ensures the contents are strictly policy-compliant. In this work, we focus on three types of policy for real-world applications: content property checking, malware validation and misconduct detection. **App** owner just requires to declare the policy metadata on **Contr**$_{App}$, including policy categories and the particular open-sourced methodologies (e.g., by URLs) of each category.

Initialization Logic of **Contr$_{App}$**

Validation Nodes := [Node$_1$, Node$_2$..Node$_i$..]
Validation Policies := [Policy$_1$, Policy$_2$..Policy$_i$..]
let Node$_i$:= struct {Addr, \$bal, isValid, Flag := $\perp$}, Policy$_i$:= struct {Type, URL}
hardcode Nodes$_{Reputable}$ list, Incentive$_{Logic}$ (cf. Algorithm 2)
On receive ManagePolicy(args) from **App** owner:
    assert(msg.sender == **App** owner)
    //add(), delete(), update(), retrieve() operations on Policies := [Policy$_1$, Policy$_2$...]
    Code logic...
On receive Register(args) from Node$_i$:
    check(Eligibility of Node$_i$)//(1) if registered, and (2) if reputable
    set Node$_i$.Addr:= msg.sender//i.e., public key
    set Node$_i$.\$bal := msg.value//required security deposit
    set Node$_i$.isValid := **True**, .Flag := **OK**//used in future penalties and disputes

---

Fig. 2. Initialization logic of **Contr$_{App}$** in **DeCCV**.

Transparency Considerations. **App** operators are not always willing to disclose the policies, especially for those crafted tools that are only consumed internally. In such cases, we stress that the implementation details of validation tools do not have to be revealed. Instead, **App** could just provide the APIs that can be externally called by **Node$_{VAL}$**. Furthermore, this transparent declaration not only enjoys the preferable properties of underlying blockchain platforms and reduces the server's workloads, but also allows any party to inspect (or contribute to) the policies. In addition, the policy content can be managed by **App** easily.

Upon the **Contr$_{App}$** is deployed, multiple **Node$_{VAL}$** subsequently start to register by specifying their public keys and locking funds. In Fig. 2, the Register method first validates the identity of registering parties, then initializes the essential flags accordingly and stores the security deposit. We emphasize that, the locked assets aim to not simply motivate high accountability, but resist Sybil attacks. Moreover, this deposit can be freely withdrawn whenever an eligible party (no misbehaviors involved) wants to leave the protocol.

4.2 Content Validation

Before actual content validation, a secure communication channel between a user and each **Node$_{VAL}$** is supposed to be established (cf. Appendix A). Note that the addresses of valid registered nodes can be directly retrieved from **Contr$_{App}$** and every user holds a valid blockchain address, which allows for mutual authentication in channel's handshake stage. A user requires to submit her encrypted content to *each* **Node$_{VAL}$** over TLS for validation before it can be posted to **App** (cf. Step 3 in Fig. 1). Subsequently, every node will first decrypt the content, and validate it against **Policy$_{VAL}^{Cont}$**.

A validation proof is finally generated by each **Node**$_{VAL}$, which indicates the compliance of a user's content. In the next section, we will discuss the data objects of a proof, and the privacy considerations on the content.

4.3 Proofs Issuance

In general, modern applications can outsource their validation implementation to the cloud. Yet, we must fully trust this service. In contrast, **DeCCV** decentralizes such the workloads by leveraging multiple **Node**$_{VAL}$. Moreover, an incentive-based mechanism is enforced to motivate their high accountability and eliminate inferior ones. **Node**$_{VAL}$ can fulfill their duties by validating the content against policies. Technically, each node sets up a crafted local environment running all necessary tools defined in **Policy**$_{VAL}^{Cont}$, then performs the validation as per request, signs the result individually $\sigma_i = \text{Sign}_{sk_{\text{Node}_i}}(H(content)||res||cnt)$ over the hashed content, validation result and a monotonic counter (incremented for every validation for a given user) and sends a proof Proof$_i = [res, cnt, \sigma_i]$ to the requested user. This proof demonstrates whether the policy-violation conduct is detected or not. Since the public key of each **Node**$_{VAL}$ is registered and stored on **Contr**$_{App}$ (cf. Fig. 2), **App** can easily verify the signatures of corresponding nodes.

Privacy Considerations. Although it may be counter-intuitive that **Node**$_{VAL}$ can decrypt users' personal content for validation, there are essential discrepancies between "privacy-violation" statements and our approach. On the one hand, the registration of **Node**$_{VAL}$ can be limited to trusted and good-performance nodes (e.g., Chainlink [9] in the DeFi space) at registration phase, and hence the

Algorithm 1: App-side Token verification.

```
1  Inp = Encrypt([Content, Token = Proof_{1,2...N}])
2  Outp = The verification result
3  Content, Token ← Decrypt(Inp)
4  tk ← extract(Token), idx ← 0, size ← len(Nodes)
5  while idx++ < size do
6     // (1) Get Nodes_idx's pk
7     pk_Nodes_idx ← Nodes[idx].Addr
8     // (2) SigVerify(Proof_idx)
9     Proof_idx ← tk[idx]
10    msg ← H(Content) || True || Proof_idx.cnt
11    if !SigVerify_{pk_Nodes_idx}(msg, Proof_idx.σ_idx)
12       return False
13 return True
```

accountability of retaining the user's privacy can be held. This consideration has been widely adopted in DeFi ecosystem, where most DeFi platforms specify selected high-quality data providers [6,7,9] as their trusted oracles. Meanwhile, the platform users can check the identities of nodes easily as the addresses of nodes are registered into **Contr**$_{App}$. On the other hand, a dedicated incentive solution is further devised in our protocol with economic rewards, mandatory security deposits and financial punishment to motivate compliant behaviors. We stress that our approach does not downgrade the existing privacy assumptions of real-world applications (e.g., Twitter's validation nodes would have seen the pure plaintext of user's content). We will discuss the incentive design in Sect. 5.

Once the user receives a Proof_i from a $\mathbf{Node_{VAL}}$, a similar confirmation $\sigma_{\mathsf{User}} = \mathsf{Sign}_{sk_{\mathbf{User}}}(H(content)\|res\|cnt)$ is replied to the corresponding node, regarded as an evidence for future disputes. In contrast to current solutions, we significantly reduce the validation workloads to merely signature-based verification. The majority of compliance checking is offloaded to $\mathbf{Node_{VAL}}$'s local environment. We will discuss the practical cost in Sect. 6.

4.4 Deliver Content with Token

A user collects all the proofs from $\mathbf{Node_{VAL}}$, prepares them as a token, and posts it to **App** over a secure channel together with her content for verification. Note that the content has to be consistent with the data signed in σ_i. Any malicious replacement will be caught by **App**-side verification as each σ_i in a Proof_i has stuck to a valid node and a content.

In **DeCCV**, a token is implemented as a dynamical-size object, consisting of all proofs $\mathsf{Proof}_{\{1,2\cdots N\}}$, where N denotes the number of valid $\mathbf{Node_{VAL}}$ enrolled in our protocol. We sketch the logic of **App**-side token verification in Algorithm 1. By design, **App** first decrypts both the token and content, and then extracts the token. Subsequently, each signature $\mathsf{Proof}_i.\sigma_i$ in a token is verified by corresponding public keys [2] of $\mathbf{Node_{VAL}}$. Upon the verification is succeeded, the passed content by a user is allowed and authorized to be delivered in **App**.

4.5 Content Compliance Validation Policy

$\mathbf{Policy}_{\mathsf{VAL}}^{\mathsf{Cont}}$ defines a set of content compliance rules which can successfully pass the validation on $\mathbf{Node_{VAL}}$'s side. **App** owner is supposed to customize policies to regulate the compliance of delivered conduct. Now, we present the demonstrative policy types considered in **DeCCV**:

- **Property checking policy** enforces the specifications (e.g., file size or type) validation of a content. Emails and cloud storage platforms usually verify if the uploaded files exceed the size limits or contain malicious macros.
- **Malware validation policy** allows **App** to filter out the content with virus and malware (e.g., worms, Trojan, ransomware, and adware). In practice, a number of malware validation tools could be employed [10,25].
- **Behavior detection policy** is powerful for social networks or content sharing platform to block inappropriate conducts like hatred, violence, racism, and pornography. Normally, **App** relies on machine learning based tools to detect the misconducts of a content [5].

We stress that diversified policies with arbitrary complexity can be integrated into **DeCCV**. The potential policies can be validation tools for detecting or preventing particular misconducts from the platforms. Furthermore, this integration will not incur any server-end cost since all the computations and validations are conducted in the off-chain $\mathbf{Node_{VAL}}$.

---

[2] Every public key is registered and stored on $\mathbf{Contr_{App}}$ at initialization.

5   Incentives

The accountability of $\mathbf{Node}_{VAL}$ is essential that determines the security of our protocol. In this section, we introduce a dedicated incentive design for them.

5.1   Financial Penalties and Disputes

By design, an eligible $\mathbf{Node}_{VAL}$ is to validate the content and issue the proofs. As discussed in Sect. 3.2, an honest node may become malicious and interfere the functionality of our protocol. Intuitively, the requirement of security deposit is a feasible way to motivate high accountability, and **App** provides economic rewards for each honest behavior. However, no one scheme has been proposed and adopted [32] for fairness in blockchain-based multi-party validation systems.

Penalties. Apart from security deposits, we implement financial penalties allowing **App** to punish unaccountable nodes. Concretely, we punish $\mathbf{Node}_{VAL}$ in two ineligible behaviors: (1) wrong-answer, whose *res* field (cf. Sect. 4.3) of Proof_i deviates from others, and (2) responseless, which never issues Proof_i to users. To invoke a penalty, **App** calls $\mathtt{Punish()}$ method (cf. Algorithm 2) and submits the $\mathbf{Proof}_{Punish}$ including all Proof_i from validation nodes. As each proof is strictly related to the particular nodes, the invalid (or false) proof would be detected and the deposit of ineligible $\mathbf{Node}_{VAL}$ would be slashed. Upon all signatures are verified, $\mathbf{Contr}_{App}$ flips the state of punishing node to **Invalid**, transits its flag from $\bot$ to **Punish**, and emits the punishment event $\mathbf{Event}_{Punish}$. Subsequently, a dispute deadline $\mathbf{T}_{Dispute} := \mathbf{T}_{Punish} + \triangle_{Dispute}$ is triggered. This enables a punishing node to seek recourse before $\mathbf{T}_{Dispute}$. Meanwhile, we encourage nodes to dispute as fast as possible.

Disputes. Naturally, **App** has potential to trigger false penalties with outdated $\mathbf{Proof}_{Punish}$. Therefore, we further devise a $\mathtt{Dispute()}$ functionality that allows compliant nodes to arise self-justifications with $\mathbf{Proof}_{Dispute}$[3]. As discussed in Sect. 4.3, $\mathbf{Node}_{VAL}$ can employ the confirmation echo σ_{User} from user as the dispute proof, and submit it to $\mathbf{Contr}_{App}$ by $\mathbf{T}_{Dispute}$ for dispute. This proof σ_{User} acts as an acknowledgement signed by a user. Besides the corresponding flag and signature validation, $\mathtt{Dispute()}$ should further check if current timestamp is beyond the dispute deadline $\mathbf{T}_{Dispute}$. The successful dispute would prevent the deposit of eligible one from being slashed, as otherwise $\mathtt{Payout()}$ will be invoked by **App** operators to confiscate the locked funds of unaccountable nodes. With a fair penalty-dispute design, the forged or stale penalties can be prevented.

5.2   Reward Consideration

Each node requires to lock crypto-assets for countering Sybil attacks and motivating honest behaviors. This deposit can be freely withdrawn whenever an eligible node (no misbehaviors involved) wants to leave the protocol via $\mathtt{Withdraw()}$. Meanwhile, utilizing proper financial reward helps to boost the participation.

---

[3] $\mathbf{Proof}_{Dispute}$ includes *one single* signature of disputer.

Algorithm 2: Incentive Logic of **Contr$_{App}$**.

1   $\triangle_{Dispute}$ ← 1h, Event Punish(Party$_i$, **Addr**$_{Contra}$), Event Dispute(Party$_i$, **Addr**$_{Contra}$)

2   **function** *Punish (i, Party$_i$, Proof$_{Punish}$)*
3   require(msg.sender = owner & Party$_i$.isValid = Valid)
4   require(Verify(pk$_{Party}$, **Proof**$_{Punish}.\sigma$) = True)// Verify each σ in a **Proof**$_{Punish}$
5   detect(**Proof**$_{Punish}$[i] is null or non-compliant)// Find out the ineligible **Node**$_{VAL}$
6   T$_{Dispute}$ ← now + $\triangle_{Dispute}$
7   Party$_i$.isValid = Invalid, Party$_i$.Flag = Punish, Emit Punish(Party$_i$, **Addr**$_{Contra}$)

8   **function** *Dispute (Party$_i$, Proof$_{Dispute}$)*
9   assert(now ≤ T$_{Dispute}$), require(Party$_i$.Flag = Punish & Party$_i$.isValid = Invalid)
10   require(Verify(pk$_{Party_i}$, **Proof**$_{Dispute}.\sigma$) = True)
11   Party$_i$.isValid = Valid, Party$_i$.Flag = ⊥, Emit Dispute(Party$_i$, **Addr**$_{Contra}$)

12   **function** *Payout (Party$_i$)*
13   assert(now ≥ T$_{Dispute}$), require(msg.sender = owner & Party$_i$.Flag = Punish)
14   forfeit(Party$_i$.\$bal), Party$_i$.isValid = Invalid, Party$_i$.Flag = Forfeited

15   **function** *Withdraw (Party$_i$)*
16   require(Party$_i$.isValid = Valid & Party$_i$.Flag = ⊥)
17   withdraw(Party$_i$.\$bal), Party$_i$.isValid = Invalid, Party$_i$.Flag = Null

---

We enable **App** to reward *each* obligated behavior of **Node**$_{VAL}$ through marginal crypto-incentives (e.g., similar adoptions in many popular oracle-based blockchain platforms [6,7,9] with an amount of native tokens as rewards).

The entire system could benefit from this incentive scheme as more high-quality nodes would be incentivized to contribute. Interestingly, with more nodes registered, we could eliminate low-quality ones based on their performance, which in turn incentivizes them to provide better services. Moreover, the amount of reward should intuitively vary in content size and policy complexity. We will provide a brief discussion in Appendix C.2.

6   Implementation and Evaluation

We implement **DeCCV** based on Ethereum blockchain [24] testnet. The **Contr**$_{App}$ which includes brief **Policy**$_{VAL}^{Cont}$ and incentive logic is developed using the Solidity language [15] (compiler version v0.4.24) and deployed on Ethereum Truffle testnet [16] (version v4.1.15). We implement off-chain **Node**$_{VAL}$ with four nodes (the storage is leveraged by node-localStorage package of Node.js [14]) to perform validations in local environment. Each party is allocated to a valid Ethereum testnet address. The secure channel is implemented by TLS 1.3 protocol (AES-GCM-256 scheme [20] with the shared secret from the ECDH-exchange P256 curve [23]). The package of web3.js [19] is employed that allows for interactions with blockchains. Additionally, we use Ethereum's ECDSA signature scheme as the default one. Our experiments are performed on a MacBook laptop with an Intel Core i5 CPU, 8 GB RAM memory, and MacOS 10.15 [28].

6.1 Real-World Use Cases

DeCCV is compatible with general-purpose applications. **Contr**$_{App}$ is correctly deployed over Ethereum network and executed on Ethereum Virtual Machine. The **App** employing **DeCCV** should be able to enhance its content compliance validation architecture. Meanwhile, these **Apps** should have a deployed proto-type of validation policies mechanism. Within this model, we will discuss several real-world applications to show its versatility, applicability, and compatibility.

We consider email services (Gmail), social networks (Twitter) and cloud storage platforms (Dropbox) as use cases with dedicated **Policy**$_{VAL}^{Cont}$. Note that **DeCCV** aims to be compatible with any platform that has content validation capabilities.

Gmail. To demonstrate the perceptions, we enforce two demonstrative **Policy**$_{VAL}^{Cont}$ types for Gmail:

- *Email attachment policy* validates the attachments against system require-ment (i.e., size, extension, or malware). As the details of validation method-ology in Gmail are not transparently specified, we employ ClamAV [10] as a powerful tool for detecting Trojans, viruses, and malware in attachments.
- *Email content policy* detects if email context contains misconducts, such as pornography. We enforce an advanced tool [5] in **Policy**$_{VAL}^{Cont}$ of Gmail for checking the adult content.

Twitter. Social networkings pursue high availability in performance. Over-whelming validation may result in catastrophic downtime. Twitter can employ our protocol to mitigate the overhead by decentralizing the intense computation to multiple off-chain actors. As Twitter faces to the people with different values, we devise more complicated **Policy**$_{VAL}^{Cont}$ that limits the misconducts, including

- *Racism*: Users may not threaten racism against a person. The glorification of disrespect is also prohibited.
- *Abuse or Hatred*: Users may not engage in the harassment or promote violence against others on the basis of ethnicity.
- *Pornography*: Users may not post adult content or child sexual exploitation.

We employ crafted machine learning based tools [3,5] to detect the racism, hate-ful conducts and pornography.

Dropbox. Cloud storage platforms are infrastructure that are hosted by third-party providers and made available to users. Dropbox is another typical example that can be applied to our protocol. We customize the policies for Dropbox that forbid users to share malware, virus and the files with adult content.

6.2 Transaction Cost

The main blockchain cost is introduced due to the transaction computation of incentive-related transactions (i.e., registration, punishment, dispute) and smart

Table 1. Contr$_{App}$ deployment cost (in Gas).

Cost	Gmail	Twitter	Dropbox
Policy$_{VAL}^{Cont}$	229,418 (9%)	309,210 (12%)	230,017 (9%)
Incentives	1,297,372 (53%)	1,294,127 (51%)	1,296,746 (53%)
Misc	931,736 (38%)	940,446 (37%)	937,746 (38%)
Total (Gwei)	2,458,526	2,543,783	2,464,509
USD ($)	622.44	644.03	623.95

contract deployment cost. We perform experiments to measure the consumed gas and its monetary cost.

Contr$_{App}$ Deployment. Before the protocol execution, **App** owner deploys a smart contract specifying (1) brief policy statement, (2) incentive logic, and (3) other necessary operations. In Table 1, the overall costs of contract deployment are close in three platforms, and Twitter has highest cost ($644.03) since more policy types are enforced. The on-chain incentive logic is the dominant cost, with more than 50% in both three applications.

Incentives Cost. Each participant requires to deposit a substantial amount of crypto-assets into **Contr$_{App}$** during registration and specify public key (i.e., Ethereum address). We measure the registration cost for **Node$_{VAL}$**, and present the results in Table 2. A valid registration transaction takes **Contr$_{App}$** 20 bytes for identity storage, which is currently equivalent to $31.41 at the time we wrote the

Table 2. Incentive cost.

Incentive	Cost		
	Storage (B)	Gas (Gwei)	USD ($)
Register	20	124,082	31.41
Punish	65 × 4	377,525	95.58
Dispute	65	125,454	31.76
Payout	20	77,359	19.58
Withdraw	20	52,912	13.39

paper. To penalize an unaccountable **Node$_{VAL}$**, **App** should submit all Proof$_i$ (cf. Sect. 4.3) of nodes into **Contr$_{App}$**. Afterwards, the signatures will be verified on **Contr$_{App}$**'s side and the state of punishing party is flipped to **Punish**. The cost of Punish transaction (four Ethereum ECDSA signatures) is around $95.58. In contrast, to invoke a dispute transaction, an honest **Node$_{VAL}$** is expected to submit a self-justifying proof Proof$_{Dispute}$ (one single signature) to the blockchain. Intuitively, we found the Dispute cost is relatively cheaper ($31.76) as fewer (i.e., one) signature is performed. Meanwhile, due to minimal operations, on-chain Payout and Withdraw are just $19.58 and $13.39, respectively.

6.3   Performance

In this section, we evaluate the efficiency of our protocol by content validation cost, secure channel handshake performance, and access token verification cost.

Content Validation Cost. A user to access the **App** is supposed to first send the encrypted content to all $\mathbf{Node_{VAL}}$, each of which will check the validity against predefined $\mathbf{Policy_{VAL}^{Cont}}$. Table 3 indicates the validation of racism, hatred and pornography are the dominance due to machine learning based computations, while the content properties and virus detection are marginal (around 0.6 s). The overall validations are performed locally without incurring intensive efforts to their servers. Meanwhile, the actual cost naturally depends on the content size, policy

Table 3. Policy validation cost (content size $\approx$ 1 MB).

Time (s)	Applications		
	Gmail	Twitter	Dropbox
Size	0.01	0.01	0.01
Extension	0.01	0.01	0.01
Malware	0.51	0.50	0.51
Racism	N.A	35.57	N.A
Hatred	N.A	36.37	N.A
Porn	3.17	3.31	3.42
Total	3.70	75.77	3.95

complexity and the performance of validation tools. **App** owner could estimate the efficiency of tools and customize it based on the practical adoption considerations, which may also motivate the communities to craft more cost-effective tools.

Token Cost. Below, we will discuss the cost breakdown of token issuance and verification. A user is supposed to attach a token together with his content to **App**. As discussed in Sect. 4.4, a valid token is prepared as a dynamical-size object, consisting of multiple issued proofs $\mathsf{Proof}_{\{1,2...N\}}$, where N denotes the number of valid $\mathbf{Node_{VAL}}$ enrolled in our protocol. Each Proof_i follows the ECDSA signature signed by a valid $\mathbf{Node_{VAL}}$. In our experiment, we employ four $\mathbf{Node_{VAL}}$ to measure the average time cost of token issuance, which overall takes 0.52 s. Upon receiving the requests from users, as default actions, **App** decrypts the content and verifies the signatures extracted from token objects (cf. Algorithm 1). In contrast to prior schemes, the validation workloads are reduced to merely signature-based verification. Meanwhile, as each signature is bundled with a valid node, **App** can easily detect the ineligible parties and trigger penalty accordingly. The token verification cost is approximately 0.62 s.

As discussed, **DeCCV** aims at a confidentiality-preserving communication tunnel among system participants. We provide the time cost of secure channel handshake in Appendix B.

6.4   Efficiency and Features Comparisons

In Table 4, we compare the highlighted features of **DeCCV** with real-world applications. Firstly, we **transparentize** the validation policies and shift the server-end workloads to **off-chain decentralized** entities. Moreover,

Table 4. Comparison among legacy schemes and ours.

Comparison	Applications	DeCCV
	Gmail, Twitter, Dropbox	
$\mathbf{Policy_{VAL}^{Cont}}$ Validation	Ambiguous Server-side	Transparent Off-chain nodes
False positive	>0%	None

as discussed above, a large number of adult contents currently exist on Twitter [18]. In contrast, we reduce **false positive** (i.e., a non-compliant content is falsely regarded as a compliant one) to 0% due to the honest majority of Node_{VAL}.

7 Security Analysis and Discussion

In this section, we formalize our system by the following notations, and show the strategies that **DeCCV** can resist: **App** represents a real-world applications; $\mathcal{U}$ specifies an ordinary user; $\mathcal{A}$ indicates a potential attacker; Node_{VAL} refers to decentralized validation nodes; and $\text{Contr}_{\text{App}}$ denotes a smart contract deployed on blockchain.

Theorem 1 *(Sybil Attacks). Let us assume that $\mathcal{A}$ can prepare a large number of blockchain addresses to register as multiple malicious Node_{VAL}: he cannot make profit from launched Sybil attacks.*

Proof. To launch a Sybil attack, $\mathcal{A}$ registers numerous blockchain addresses, each of which subsequently acts as a valid validation node to interfere the process of proof issuance. However, we require each party to lock crypto-funds in $\text{Contr}_{\text{App}}$ and unaccountable behaviors would be detected by penalties so that Sybil attack is disincentivized. □

Theorem 2 *(Manipulation Attacks). Let us consider that $\mathcal{A}$ can manipulate several Node_{VAL}, or even he can be one (or several) peer of the parties: he cannot affect the issuance of validation proofs.*

Proof. $\mathcal{A}$ plays manipulation attacks by compromising several Node_{VAL}. Moreover, he could even act as one (or several) registered party. The goal of $\mathcal{A}$ is to generate the false validation proofs, and return to the user, which makes user's policy-compliant content invalid during **App**-side verification. However, in threat model (cf. Sect. 3.2) we assume the capability of $\mathcal{A}$ is to compromise a small proportion of Node_{VAL}. The honest majority would retain the fault tolerance. □

Theorem 3 *(Substitution Attacks). Let us assume that $\mathcal{A}$ can perform undesired substitutions: he is unable to bypass the **App**-side validation with any malicious replacement.*

Proof. We consider two scenarios of substitutions. Firstly, $\mathcal{A}$ breaches user's environment, maliciously gets all Proof_i, then prepares a "valid" token and replaces a new content with this intercepted token. One the other hand, $\mathcal{U}$ has potential to become malicious, who submits a *policy-compliant* content to Node_{VAL} yet replaces a *policy-violation* one, and finally posts it to **App**. We ensure that such the replacements will be reverted by **App**-side verification as the signature is signed by a particular valid node and sticks to a validated content. Any minor change or replacement won't bypass the verification by **App**. □

In Appendix C, we present the considerations on the design choices of transport protection, and a potential direction toward a more fine-grained reward mechanism. Meanwhile, we discuss the generalizability of **DeCCV**.

8   Related Work

Although content compliance validation is essential, we have not seen any decentralized framework to liberate server's workloads. To the best knowledge of ours, the most relevant academic researches are the secure multi-party computation systems for blockchains [32], the tools for detecting the misconducts, and the blockchain-based access control systems. Below, we discuss the works on the most related topics.

Content Validation. Currently, the communities mainly focus on developing the crafted tools for assessing the compliance of content. Several solutions [3–5,8,10] detecting virus or misconducts have been adopted. Moreover, **App** usually devises crafted mechanisms for internal consumption. However, the entire workloads are performed by servers and their specifications are not transparent to the platform users. **DeCCV** liberates this overhead in a decentralized fashion and transparentizes the policies in a publicly verifiable way.

Secure Multi-party Computations. Ekiden [32] is proposed by hybrid TEE-blockchain framework for fairness in multi-party computation. However, it lacks a design of fundamental incentive. Several researches [33,38,45] propose the improvement by slashing security deposits of parties under their unaccountability. In contrast, we present a more fine-grained incentive with penalties and disputes.

Blockchain-Based Access Control System. SMACS [39] presents an access control framework for blockchains by employing an off-chain token service to censor the access permission and grant the credentials. However, any participant should fully rely on this centralized service. **DeCCV** mitigates this assumption and utilizes multiple independent validation nodes to verify the compliance of a content and issue the access tokens accordingly.

9   Conclusion

In this paper, we presented **DeCCV**, the first decentralized content compliance validation protocol that achieved transparency, compatibility at low cost in addition to a fair incentive mechanism for protocol participants. **DeCCV** could offer following highlights. Firstly, **DeCCV** transparentized current policy declarations. Secondly, **DeCCV** largely minimized the server-side workloads by multiple decentralized validation nodes. Thirdly, with a dedicated incentive design, **DeCCV** motivated high accountability of participants and resisted attack vectors. Lastly, **DeCCV** was compatible with many practical applications. We would like to further investigate the possibility to deploy **DeCCV** into more real-world applications.

Acknowledgment. We thank the anonymous reviewers for their valuable comments. This work is supported by the Ministry of Education, Singapore, under the MOE AcRF Tier 2 grant (MOE2018-T2-1-111).

A   Detailed Interactions of DeCCV

The detailed interactions among system participants are shown in Fig. 3. The numbered procedures correspond with the high-level interactions (described in Fig. 1). Note that the transmitted data objects between protocol actors are encrypted over a secure channel. Meanwhile, the incentive interfaces, including penalties, disputes and payouts etc., are not depicted in Fig. 3 as these actions can be triggered whenever any misbehavior is detected.

B   Secure Communication Handshake Performance

DeCCV purses a confidentiality-preserving tunnel, and we utilize the latest version of TLS in our experiments. As discussed in Sect. 2.2, a full handshake process is divided into `key exchange` phase and `authentication` phase. In our experiment, the time consumption of these two procedures is 487ms and 671ms, respectively. Note that TLS is not the only design choice in practical for achieving transport protection. In Appendix C.1, we will discuss the considerations towards more design choices of communication protection.

C   Discussions

In this section, we provide the discussions with respect to transport protection, a future direction toward a more fine-grained economic reward mechanism, and the generalizability of our protocol.

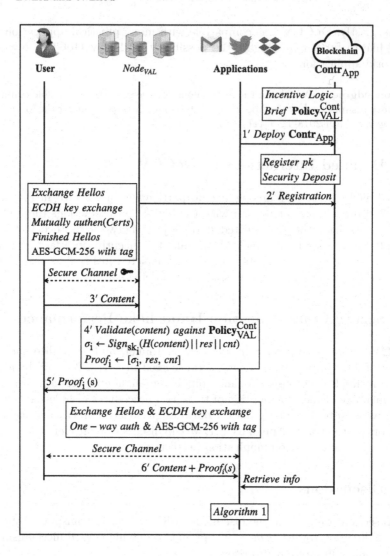

Fig. 3. The interactions of **DeCCV**.

C.1 Secure Communication Design Choices

In **DeCCV**, we adopt TLS protocol as a channel protection method among system parties. In practice, the feasible approaches are not limited to it. For instance, a dynamic secret sharing scheme [29,30,37,40,41,43] is regarded as an alternative that **DeCCV** can employ a recently proposed secret sharing scheme [40] for communication encryption. Concretely, with dynamical secret sharing, **App** can first generate a key pair (pk_{Apps}, sk_{Apps}), hardcode pk_{Apps} into the blockchain for an arbitrary user to encrypt his content, and distribute the associated sk_{Apps} to the key management committee members (i.e., a dedicated group of committee members to withhold the key). Once receiving an encrypted content from a user, each $\mathbf{Node}_{\mathsf{VAL}}$ will contact key management committees, then recover the sk_{Apps}, and decrypt the content for validation. We emphasize that secret sharing is seen as an *alternative* approach for transport protection. In particular, the proposed incentive mechanism could also applied to those key management members. In terms of performance, TLS is more resource-efficient when the number of key management members is beyond four. Moreover, since $\mathbf{Node}_{\mathsf{VAL}}$ and key management committees involve massive communications, TLS is deemed a more secure approach. We will keep track on the emergence of more effective transport protection schemes.

C.2 Towards A Fine-Grained Reward Design

Recall Sect. 5.2, with the increase in the number of registration, $\mathbf{Node}_{\mathsf{VAL}}$ would compete against each other to provide better validation services. Currently, we set the amount of rewards for each honest behavior as a fixed value. One possible improvement is making such the mechanism more fine-grained. For instance, as the computation consumption should vary in the size of user's contents and the complexity of $\mathbf{App}$'s policies, we could link the amount of reward to the size of requested content and the workloads of policy validations. More interestingly, $\mathbf{App}$ and $\mathbf{Node}_{\mathsf{VAL}}$ could transparentize their reward fees and service commissions, respectively, which would create a better service market. We will leave such the design direction as future work.

C.3 Generalizability

In Appendix C.1, different techniques for transport protection are able to be switched in our system based on the security and performance considerations. In addition, we stress that $\mathbf{DeCCV}$ is platform-agnostic with regards to blockchains and real-world applications. Although $\mathbf{Contr}_{\mathsf{App}}$ is deployed on Ethereum platform in our experiments, the policy declaration and incentive design can be easily implemented on other blockchains that have similar smart contract capabilities [21,26,27]. Meanwhile, any real-world application which requires regulating the delivered contents can take advantage of $\mathbf{DeCCV}$ to filter out non-compliant contents. All an $\mathbf{App}$ owner needs to do is policy declaration and smart contract deployment. We expect to see the possibility of collaboration with more real-world companies.

References

1. Vulnerability in TLS 1.2 (2014). https://cve.mitre.org/cgi-bin/cvename.cgi?name=cve-2014-3566
2. Youtube loophole (2017). https://www.bbc.com/news/technology-38652906
3. Detoxify (2020). https://github.com/unitaryai/detoxify
4. Machine learning based tools (2020). https://bit.ly/31fsn6K

5. Nsfw content detection (2020). https://github.com/GantMan/nsfw_model
6. Tellor network (2020). https://tellor.io/
7. Uniswap (2020). https://uniswap.org/
8. Virus detection tools (2020). https://bit.ly/3EYIrJl
9. Chainlink (2021). https://chain.link/
10. Clamav (2021). https://www.clamav.net/
11. Gmail rules (2021). https://support.google.com/a/answer/2364580?hl=en
12. Google YouTube validation process (2021). https://bit.ly/3Eya77E
13. How YouTube validates your video (2021). https://bit.ly/3CE6DPp
14. The node-localstorage package (2021). https://www.npmjs.com/package/node-localstorage
15. Solidity language (2021). https://docs.soliditylang.org/en/v0.4.24/
16. Truffle testnet (2021). https://www.trufflesuite.com/
17. Twitter (2021). https://twitter.com/home
18. Twitter's non-compliance (2021). https://bit.ly/3kLUhP3
19. Web3.js library (2021). https://web3js.readthedocs.io/en/v1.5.2/
20. Aes-gcm-256 (2022). https://en.wikipedia.org/wiki/Galois/Counter_Mode
21. Binance smart chain (2022). https://docs.binance.org/
22. Dropbox (2022). https://www.dropbox.com/
23. Ecdh key exchange (2022). https://en.wikipedia.org/wiki/Elliptic-curve_Diffie%E2%80%93Hellman
24. Ethereum (2022). https://ethereum.org/en/
25. Google detects email malware (2022). https://support.google.com/a/answer/9157861?hl=en
26. Polkadot (2022). https://polkadot.network/
27. Polygon (2022). https://polygon.technology/
28. Reference (2022). https://bit.ly/3NWMrPc
29. Baron, J., Defrawy, K.E., Lampkins, J., Ostrovsky, R.: Communication-optimal proactive secret sharing for dynamic groups. In: Malkin, T., Kolesnikov, V., Lewko, A.B., Polychronakis, M. (eds.) ACNS 2015. LNCS, vol. 9092, pp. 23–41. Springer, Cham (2015). https://doi.org/10.1007/978-3-319-28166-7_2
30. Bowers, K.D., Juels, A., et al.: HAIL: a high-availability and integrity layer for cloud storage. In: ACM Conference on Computer and Communications Security (2009)
31. Buterin, V.: Ethereum: a next-generation smart contract and decentralized application platform (2013)
32. Cheng, R., Zhang, F., Kos, J., He, W., Hynes, N., et al.: Ekiden: a platform for confidentiality-preserving, trustworthy, and performant smart contracts. In: IEEE European Symposium on Security and Privacy (2019)
33. Choudhuri, A.R., Green, M., Jain, A., Kaptchuk, G., Miers, I.: Fairness in an unfair world: fair multiparty computation from public bulletin boards. In: ACM Conference on Computer and Communications Security (2017)
34. Costan, V., Devadas, S.: Intel SGX explained. IACR Cryptology ePrint (2016)
35. Dierks, T., Rescorla, E.: The transport layer security (TLS) protocol version 1.2 (2008)
36. Haakegaard, R., Lang, J.: The elliptic curve Diffie-Hellman (ECDH) (2015). https://koclab.cs.ucsb.edu/teaching/ecc/project/2015Projects/Haakegaard+Lang.pdf
37. Herzberg, A., Jarecki, S., Krawczyk, H., Yung, M.: Proactive secret sharing or: how to cope with perpetual leakage. In: Coppersmith, D. (ed.) CRYPTO 1995. LNCS, vol. 963, pp. 339–352. Springer, Heidelberg (1995). https://doi.org/10.1007/3-540-44750-4_27

38. Kumaresan, R., Bentov, I.: Amortizing secure computation with penalties. In: ACM Conference on Computer and Communications Security (2016)
39. Liu, B., Sun, S., Szalachowski, P.: SMACS: smart contract access control service. In: IEEE/IFIP Conference on Dependable Systems and Networks (2020)
40. Maram, S.K.D., et al.: CHURP: dynamic-committee proactive secret sharing. In: ACM Conference on Computer and Communications Security (2019)
41. Ostrovsky, R., Yung, M.: How to withstand mobile virus attacks. In: ACM Symposium on Principles of Distributed Computing (1991)
42. Rescorla, E., Dierks, T.: The transport layer security (TLS) protocol version 1.3 (2018)
43. Schultz, D.A., Liskov, B., Liskov, M.: Mobile proactive secret sharing. In: ACM Symposium on Principles of Distributed Computing (2008)
44. Sikeridis, D., Kampanakis, P., Devetsikiotis, M.: Post-quantum authentication in TLS 1.3: a performance study. Cryptology ePrint Archive (2020)
45. Zyskind, G., Nathan, O., et al.: Decentralizing privacy: using blockchain to protect personal data. In: IEEE Security and Privacy Workshops (2015)

Knowledge Mining in Cybersecurity: From Attack to Defense

Khandakar Ashrafi Akbar[1]([✉]), Sadaf Md Halim[1], Yibo Hu[1], Anoop Singhal[2], Latifur Khan[1], and Bhavani Thuraisingham[1]

[1] The University of Texas at Dallas, 800 West Campbell Road, Richardson, TX 75080, USA
kxa190007@utdallas.edu
[2] National Institute of Standards and Technology, 100 Bureau Drive, Gaithersburg, MD 20899, USA

Abstract. In the fast-evolving world of Cybersecurity, an analyst often has the difficult task of responding to new threats and attack campaigns within a limited amount of time. If an analyst fails to do so, this can lead to severe consequences for the system under attack. In this work, we are motivated to aid the security analyst by introducing a tool which will help to produce a swift and effective response to incoming threats. If an analyst identifies the nature of an incoming attack, our system can produce a ranked list of solutions for the analyst to quickly try out, saving both effort and time. Currently, the security analyst is typically left to manually produce a solution by consulting existing frameworks and knowledge bases, such as the ATT&CK and D3FEND frameworks by the MITRE Corporation. To solve these challenges, our tool leverages state-of-the-art machine learning frameworks to provide a comprehensive solution for security analysts. Our tool uses advanced natural language processing techniques, including a large language model (RoBERTa), to derive meaningful semantic associations between descriptions of offensive techniques and defensive countermeasures. Experimental results confirm that our proposed method can provide useful suggestions to the security analyst with good accuracy, especially in comparison to baseline approaches which fail to exhibit the semantic and contextual understanding necessary to make such associations.

Keywords: Cyber Threat Intelligence · Natural Language Processing · Semantic Association

1   Introduction

In the event of an attack, a security analyst has a small window within which to react and produce an effective counter-response. In this setting, time is of the essence. However, the entire process of analyzing the threat and determining the type of offense, and then coming up with the correct measure is often tedious and time consuming. This is compounded by the fact that knowledge in the

© IFIP International Federation for Information Processing 2022
Published by Springer Nature Switzerland AG 2022
S. Sural and H. Lu (Eds.): DBSec 2022, LNCS 13383, pp. 110–122, 2022.
https://doi.org/10.1007/978-3-031-10684-2_7

cybersecurity domain is very scattered, and all the required information can rarely be found in one place. Furthermore, the array of attack techniques is rapidly expanding so it becomes even more difficult to process and respond in real-time. It is therefore imperative that we are able to speed up this process and assist the security analyst to minimize the harm as much as possible.

A security analyst has various resources at their disposal. One example is the National Vulnerability Database (NVD) [4], which provides detailed analysis of CVE [16] vulnerabilities, as well as exploitability and impact scores for those vulnerabilities. This tool is useful for understanding what kind of vulnerabilities might be exploited in the event of an attack. However, should an attack occur, the analyst needs to not only understand the vulnerabilities being exploited, but also be ready to produce an effective counter-response to that attack. Cyber attacks like SolarWinds [11] are inevitable in certain situations when supply chain compromises cannot be handled well. In these cases, root-level system analytics or countermeasures are necessary to find out and solve particular attack tactics or techniques which are possibly being performed behind the scenes, in order to prevent any significant aftermath. Another existing resource for security analysts is a knowledge-base built by the MITRE corporation. In fact, MITRE offers two different frameworks: ATT&CK [17] and D3FEND [18]. ATT&CK is a framework that offers knowledge regarding certain offensive techniques, and D3FEND offers defensive techniques and countermeasures. Both of these offensive and defensive frameworks are hierarchically structured almost the same way: they consist of tactics at the top level and of techniques and sub-techniques at the bottom level. Techniques are composed of sub-techniques (if any) and each technique belongs to a tactic or multiple tactics in the hierarchy. All these tactics, techniques, and sub-techniques have their respective textual descriptions which are presented either from the behavioral or the technical perspective. D3FEND was generated based only on patent information in combination with a few other external resources such as the Cyber Analytic Repository (CAR).

In the current scenario, a security analyst would have to look up resources such as the knowledge bases offered by MITRE, in order to figure out both the nature of the attack being conducted, as well as a potential solution for the attack. This is evidently slow, and given the vast possibilities for attack types and countermeasures, this entire process is akin to finding a needle in a haystack, under severe time constraints. This inevitably increases the chance of extensive harm being done. Furthermore, existing frameworks such as D3FEND [18] provide associations of defensive techniques and offensive techniques, but these knowledge bases are manually generated, with enormous human effort involved. Thus, if new defensive techniques are to be associated with already existing attack techniques or zero-day attack techniques (and vice versa) we will need to manually perform associations in the absence of any automated solutions.

It is thus clear that the security analysts' toolkit is presently missing an important tool - a comprehensive and automated system which can quickly provide the analyst with relevant solutions in the event of an attack. We are therefore motivated to fill this gap and create this tool. In this paper, we present a tool that aids the security analyst and automatically identifies potential counter-measures and makes recommendations to the analyst. The recommendations are made by identifying meaningful associations between the ongoing attack tactic or technique and the candidate countermeasure(s). These associations are found through the aid of advanced machine learning and natural language processing techniques. We use the language model called RoBERTa (Robustly Optimized BERT Pre-training Approach) [12], which we show to be similarly effective to classical techniques such as bag of words or word2vec [14].

Typical topic modeling might fail in establishing such associations since the dataset in this particular task is limited and unstructured. Moreover, capturing semantics from textual descriptions can be tricky with traditional models. Instead, we use the RoBERTa model which is pre-trained efficiently with a large number of tokens (leading to a bigger vocabulary size) and which can aid zero-shot learning [19], since this model is trained with a large amount of data nearing 160 GB of uncompressed text. Zero-shot learning is a type of machine learning technique where the model is used without fine-tuning on a particular task. Thus, models like RoBERTa which are ready-to-use can generate effective representations of texts in order to find semantic similarities among them.

We now present an example use-case for our tool. Our tool works as follows: Suppose the security analyst identifies an offensive technique used to perform an attack, such as "Spearphishing Link". The security analyst can query our tool to find recommendations on what defensive techniques or countermeasures to take. Our tool will provide a ranked list of defensive techniques and countermeasures such as "Homoglyph Detection, File-Hashing, File Carving, Process Spawn Analysis". In this hypothetical list, the recommendations are ranked in descending order of priority. The analyst can then quickly attempt these solutions in that order. We can thus see how this system can largely relieve the security analyst of the tedium as well as the stress of having to manually figure out how to respond to a critical system attack. This in turn minimizes the harm to the system by producing a solution faster.

In this work, our contributions can be summarized by the following:

- The creation of a tool which recommends appropriate countermeasures and defensive techniques to the security analyst when queried with an attack technique.
- The automation of associations between offensive and defensive techniques and countermeasures using language models.

This paper is organized as follows: In Sect. 2, we formally present the problem statement. In Sect. 3, we describe our approach in detail. Experimental results are presented in Sect. 4. In Sect. 5, we provide a study on related works. Lastly, Sect. 6 provides the conclusion for this study.

2   Problem Statement

2.1   A Dive into Statistics: Offense and Defense

A security analyst needs to have the appropriate knowledge or a framework handy in the event of an attack, so that they can quickly respond with defensive measures before any persistent damage is done. The D3FEND framework is generated manually (knowledge extraction with human intervention). Plenty of offensive and defensive techniques evolve everyday, and so it is quite impossible to associate them quickly and effectively (to form meaningful associations). Existing cybersecurity solutions cannot be used effectively if a security analyst doesn't know when and how to use them.

To remedy these drawbacks of manual knowledge association, we want to semi-automate this process. We will have to investigate some statistics and other facts to emphasize on the necessity of building a language model for associating defensive countermeasures to offensive techniques. These statistics mainly shed light on why we need to semi-automate this process. These statistics are given in the following two Tables: 1a and 1b.

There are at least 259 offensive techniques or sub-techniques which do have at least a single associated defensive countermeasure. On average, a single offensive technique or sub-technique has 3–4 defensive techniques or sub-techniques as countermeasures. In Table 1, max and min count indicates the maximum and minimum number of associations that a single offensive or defensive technique or sub-technique has. A count of zero for the number of associations indicates that an offensive technique or sub-technique have no associated countermeasure(s) within the 'D3FEND' framework, and we discovered that there are many such cases. Specifically, there are 287 offensive techniques or sub-techniques have no association as of now which is more than half of the whole set. This tells us that the D3FEND framework is clearly not comprehensive enough. Eventually, to fill this gap, more resources will be appended, so that effective countermeasures can be well-associated with the offensive techniques or sub-techniques. This large expansion will require semi-automated or fully automated associations between offensive and defensive techniques or sub-techniques.

Table 1. A Dive into Statistics

Total Offensive Techniques	546
Max Count	28
Min Count	0
Average	3.341
Count of Zero	287

(a) Statistic for Offensive Techniques

Total Defensive Techniques	123
Max Count	173
Min Count	0
Average	23.195
Count of Zero	50

(b) Statistic for Defensive Techniques

2.2   Challenges for Recommendation

A security analyst needs to be directed towards the right path of either performing some kind of analytics or taking any defensive measures which stops an ongoing adversarial campaign. But this sort of initiative requires prompt attention so that proper action can be taken before any permanent damage can take place. Thus, proper attack information should be associated with proper defensive countermeasures so that the exhaustive search for the security analyst can be reduced significantly. For example, if a security analyst has to iterate over a bunch of solutions to find the solution to a particular problem, the damage will be done long before the security analyst engages in the actual work. And it is almost impossible for a security analyst to know the solution to every problem right away given the fast expansion of attack techniques. Thus, if security analysts are given recommendations on which solutions to try and in which order, quick responses can be ensured. But associating meaningful defensive countermeasures is challenging as the textual descriptions for the defensive countermeasures are not always technically sound. A particular offensive technique can have multiple solutions, each of them being effective in different degrees. A security analyst should know in which order he should try out those countermeasures so that he can stop the ongoing adversarial campaign as early as possible. Structural knowledge is required for such ranked associations. It is also challenging to always have structural knowledge available for such associations as knowledge-graphs are often constructed manually. Thus, the structural knowledge can be missing due to the tedious processing required, or it can also take a lot of time to be built.

3   Approach

There are a number of ways to find matches among textual descriptions. We have used some of the most widely used techniques as baselines and masked-language modeling based pre-trained model as our primary model. We discuss the baselines and language model in detail in the next few subsections and afterwards, we discuss our proposed method in detail.

3.1   Common Techniques

TF-IDF. Term Frequency-Inverse Document Frequency, commonly known as TF-IDF, can be used to represent documents as vectors and then the similarity between the two documents can be calculated. Similar to Bag-of-Words, TF-IDF operates based on the counts of words. This means that learning is often "shallow", with little understanding of actual semantics or context. This limits the utility of TF-IDF in applications like ours, where understanding the semantics of the textual descriptions is of paramount importance.

Word2Vec. Word2Vec [14], developed at Google, is one of the most popular methods for learning high quality word embeddings. It does so by employing a shallow neural network. Essentially, Word2Vec learns word associations from a large corpus of text. While Word2Vec has proved effective for a number of tasks, Word2Vec does not handle out-of-vocabulary words well, which can happen in many cases. Furthermore, Word2Vec embeddings are *context independent*. A word can have multiple meanings depending on the context in which it is used. However, Word2Vec combines all of these different *senses* of the word into one overall embedding. This is a clear limitation which is not present in newer transformer based language models like BERT [6], which can have multiple vector representations of the same word, depending on the context. Lastly, large scale language models, which we will discuss next, are simply known for being able to capture a deeper understanding of the semantics in text.

Language Models. Transformer-based language models have revolutionized many areas of natural language processing. BERT, released by Google, is one such model which achieved state of the art performance on a variety of natural understanding tasks when it was published. Since then, BERT has become a ubiquitous baseline for many natural language tasks. An important enhancement on BERT, called RoBERTa [12], was released by Facebook AI. RoBERTa made adjustments to the pretraining objective and the hyperparameters, both of which contributed to state of the art performance in a wide range of tasks. RoBERTa is trained on a huge corpus (measured at 160 gigabytes) and it is known for its ability to understand semantics and context at a level that was previously not possible. This is what motivated us to apply RoBERTa to our specific problem.

3.2 Proposed Method

Our approach is summarized in Fig. 1. The major task at hand is that of matching attack techniques with defensive techniques and countermeasures. To do this, we take advantage of the ATT&CK and D3FEND frameworks that we have described earlier. In Fig. 1, this part of the approach is represented by the boxes with green text. First, from the ATT&CK framework, we extract the textual descriptions of our attack techniques and tactics. At the same time, we extract textual descriptions of the defensive techniques from the D3FEND framework. Once we have both sets of textual descriptions, we then proceed to the next step where we use RoBERTa. As discussed earlier, RoBERTa is already pretrained on an enormous dataset, and we leverage the deep semantic knowledge present inside the standard RoBERTa model to derive meaningful associations between attack techniques and defensive countermeasures. RoBERTa investigates the textual descriptions of the attack and defense techniques, and provides us a ranked list of D3FEND-based countermeasures for each attack technique in ATT&CK. Note that we do not fine-tune RoBERTa on our dataset of textual descriptions. This is because our dataset is much too small for the model to meaningfully learn from, and it might in fact affect the original RoBERTa model's ability to understand semantics and context. Instead, we directly leverage the deep semantic understanding that the standard RoBERTa model is equipped with, to give us meaningful associations between the descriptions that we have extracted.

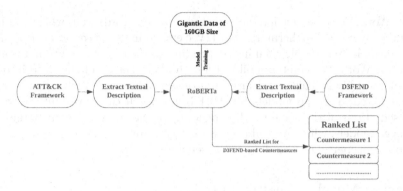

Fig. 1. Work Flow Diagram

4   Experimental Results

4.1   Experimental Setup

We have used the textual descriptions of the offensive and defensive techniques and sub-techniques from the ATT&CK and D3FEND framework as part of our dataset. The RoBERTa model is used from hugging face [7] along with the tokenizer. For Word2Vec, which is a baseline in our study, the glove (Global Vectors for Word Representation) [8, 21] vectors are used for word representations. Pre-trained word vectors with the following characteristics are used: 6B tokens, 400K vocab, uncased, 300 dimensional vectors. The embedding for a whole textual description is calculated by taking the average of the embeddings of all the words belonging to that description. For TF-IDF based experimentation, we have considered each of the textual description as a document and have generated the vectors considering all those descriptions (documents) as the corpus.

4.2   Results

The experimentation is done in two phases. The results of the first phase are tabulated in Table 2a and 2b.

Precision, recall, and f1-score are reported for RoBERTa-base along with the other baselines. All these three metrics are measured in two different settings, one while considering all possible offensive techniques and sub-techniques and the other while considering the techniques only (excluding the sub-techniques). RoBERTa-base outperforms the baseline in both these settings. As baselines, we have used Word2Vec [15] and TF-IDF [22] models. Precision, recall and f1-score are reported for the following criteria: top_3, top_5, top_7, and top_10. For all the models including the baselines, it is clear that the RoBERTa base model performs the best in terms of all three metrics.

These results are significant since this is not merely a binary classification where a random guess (50% accuracy, precision or recall) might be enough. The association of offensive techniques to defensive techniques is one to many ranging from 3 (min count) to 28 (max count). There are in total 73 defensive techniques which are associated with the offensive techniques. There are 259 techniques and sub-techniques which are associated with at least a single defensive technique among which 88 of them are techniques only.

Table 2. Precision, Recall, and F1-score for the whole ontology

		Precision	Recall	F1-Score
RoBERTa Base	top_3	0.39	0.13	0.20
	top_5	0.35	0.20	0.26
	top_7	0.35	0.28	0.31
	top_10	0.30	0.34	0.32
		Precision	Recall	F1-Score
Word2Vec	top_3	0.10	0.03	0.05
	top_5	0.10	0.06	0.07
	top_7	0.12	0.09	0.10
	top_10	0.12	0.14	0.13
		Precision	Recall	F1-Score
TF-IDF	top_3	0.25	0.08	0.13
	top_5	0.22	0.12	0.16
	top_7	0.20	0.16	0.18
	top_10	0.17	0.19	0.18

(a) Precision, Recall and F1-Score - For Techniques Only

		Precision	Recall	F1-Score
RoBERTa Base	top_3	0.31	0.13	0.18
	top_5	0.29	0.21	0.24
	top_7	0.28	0.28	0.28
	top_10	0.25	0.35	0.29
		Precision	Recall	F1-Score
Word2Vec	top_3	0.09	0.04	0.05
	top_5	0.08	0.06	0.07
	top_7	0.09	0.09	0.09
	top_10	0.08	0.12	0.10
		Precision	Recall	F1-Score
TF-IDF	top_3	0.19	0.08	0.11
	top_5	0.17	0.12	0.14
	top_7	0.16	0.16	0.16
	top_10	0.14	0.2	0.17

(b) Precision, Recall and F1-Score - For Techniques and Sub-Techniques

4.3 Results with Pruned Ontology

We have done another set of experiments with a pruned ontology of the D3FEND framework. In this special experimental setup, we have considered only the relevant defensive tactics from the D3FEND framework. This narrows down the associated techniques for an offensive technique or sub-technique which fall under the relevant defensive tactics only. For any offensive technique or sub-technique the possible list of associations are brought down from the count of 73 (all existing defensive techniques in D3FEND framework) to a certain number depending on the defensive tactics which they can be associated to. For example, the offensive technique "Spearphishing Attachment" can only have associations under the hood of the following defensive tactics according to the D3FEND framework: Network Traffic Analysis, File Analysis, Network Isolation, Message Analysis, Identifier Analysis, User Behavior Analysis, Decoy Object instead of all the 17 different defensive tactics in the D3FEND framework. This way we narrow down the search scope which eventually leads to better suggestions by producing an improved and more relevant ranked list. This is validated through the tabulated results listed in Tables 3a and 3b.

Table 3. Precision, Recall, and F1-score for pruned ontology

		Precision	Recall	F1-Score
RoBERTa Base	top_3	0.60	0.26	0.36
	top_5	0.54	0.38	0.45
	top_7	0.47	0.47	0.47
	top_10	0.41	0.59	0.48
		Precision	Recall	F1-Score
Word2Vec	top_3	0.28	0.12	0.17
	top_5	0.27	0.19	0.22
	top_7	0.28	0.27	0.27
	top_10	0.28	0.38	0.32
		Precision	Recall	F1-Score
TF-IDF	top_3	0.39	0.17	0.24
	top_5	0.36	0.26	0.30
	top_7	0.35	0.35	0.35
	top_10	0.32	0.45	0.37

(a) Precision, Recall, and F1-Score -
For Techniques and Sub-Techniques

		Precision	Recall	F1-Score
RoBERTa Base	top_3	0.65	0.22	0.33
	top_5	0.56	0.32	0.41
	top_7	0.50	0.40	0.44
	top_10	0.46	0.52	0.49
		Precision	Recall	F1-Score
Word2Vec	top_3	0.31	0.10	0.15
	top_5	0.28	0.16	0.20
	top_7	0.29	0.23	0.26
	top_10	0.30	0.34	0.32
		Precision	Recall	F1-Score
TF-IDF	top_3	0.44	0.15	0.22
	top_5	0.4	0.23	0.29
	top_7	0.39	0.31	0.35
	top_10	0.36	0.41	0.38

(a) Precision, Recall, and F1-Score -
For Techniques Only

4.4 Use Case

Certain iterative projects, e.g. [24], exist for finding cyber threats with
ATT&CK-based analytics. Behavioral identification, or the detection of anomalies and outliers, is the key part to identifying cyber-threats within a system
or network according to this analytics method. Methodologies based on system
telemetry or network data inspection [1,2,26] can identify certain ongoing offensive campaigns within a system and define the tactics or techniques [9,13] which
are being used to execute the campaign. But as soon as an anomalous behavior
or particular vulnerability is spotted, a prompt and proper reaction is necessary
from the defensive end. If appropriate actions are suggested, relevant measures
can be taken in time to battle the cyber-threat. The use-case of our contribution
in this paper applies to a scenario such as the following:

A security analyst might find that a vulnerability has been detected, or they
may want to identify an ongoing attack campaign within a system. To do so, the
analyst has to perform certain analytics. Knowing what analytics needs to be
performed for a specific scenario requires a lot of domain knowledge or iterative
search. For example, an adversary might communicate using the Domain Name
System (DNS) application layer protocol to avoid detection or being filtered at
the network level by blending in with existing traffic. Commands sent to a remote
system and the results of those commands can be embedded with the protocol
traffic between the client and server. This sort of technique can be used to maintain an established Command and Control (C&C) server. This phenomenon can
be identified using certain analytics based approaches such as: protocol metadata
anomaly detection, remote terminal session detection, client-server payload profiling, etc. The analyst can use such tools to identify the nature of the attack.
Next, in this context, our tool helps the security analyst specifically because
of the following: the particular offensive technique we are concerned with, i.e.,
'Domain Name System (DNS)' is associated with 18 different defensive countermeasures of the D3FEND framework. Using our tool, when we sort the ranked
list of all possible defensive solutions (a count of 73), the top 10 from that sorted
list contains 5 of those 18 associated defensive measures. So, a security analyst

can search for solutions among all the possible cybersecurity solutions and can still find problem-specific suggestions using our tool, quickly and efficiently.

Depending on what vulnerability has been detected or what attack campaign is ongoing, the analyst might have to perform a different and specific set of actions to mitigate the situation. For example, if an analyst comes to know that a compromise has taken place in a software supply chain, then he needs to update the software as soon as possible with the necessary security update. To direct him towards this decision-making, a ranked list of counteractions can be suggested to him so that he can try them out in an ordered fashion. As another instance, if some server is facing denial of service at network level, the security analyst might have to perform inbound traffic filtering or outbound traffic filtering or user geolocation logon pattern analysis. These solutions can be suggested to the security analyst in a ranked fashion to be tried out irrespective of the security or domain knowledge of the security analyst, which can aid and speed up the decision-making process to produce a quick reaction.

5 Related Works

In D3FEND, the offensive techniques are associated with defensive technique based on some digital artifact relationships using some digital artifact objects (DAO). These associations are inferred, i.e., they are experimentally established from the DAOs. When security analysts are searching for countermeasures to particular problems, the D3FEND framework can be handy in terms of analytics. But as per as the discussion section in 1, this framework is not comprehensive. If a novel attack is happening, relevant countermeasures cannot be found easily, and thus we need a dynamic or robust framework. This can motivate us to also crawl the web. However, crawling the web to associate defensive knowledge with offensive techniques leads to a lot of junk, and so the data needs to be cleaned.

Various industry efforts have sought to provide threat sharing formats that can be applied by security professionals to share threat informatics. They include the Open Indicator of Compromise format (openIOC) [20], Structured Threat Information eXpression (STIX) [23], Trusted Automated Exchange of Intelligence Information (TAXII) [25], CVEs, and CWE. These formats leverage machine-readable formats to exchange threat indicators like the skill level of attackers involved in an attack, the tools used, the attack phases, and the attack tactics used. MITRE ATT&CK covers why and how attackers perform advanced persistent attacks. Attackers use various approaches to achieve their goal including deploying CVE vulnerabilities.

Some valuable resources have been built based on CVE vulnerabilities. One such example is the National Vulnerability Database (NVD) [4]. This was developed by the National Institute of Standards and Technology (NIST). Once a CVE is published to the list of CVEs, NVD is tasked with analyzing each CVE. The vulnerabilities are then categorized with a common weakness identifier (CWE). They are also given CVSS scores, which are metrics that characterize the exploitability and the impact of the vulnerability. When a malicious entity tries to launch an attack campaign against a system, they will often try to exploit vulnerabilities in the system such as those identified in CVE. Therefore, resources such as NVD can be used to establish associations between the CVE vulnerabilities and the type of offenses that exploit them. This is out of scope for our paper because we focus on associating the offenses to countermeasures. However, if the links between CVE vulnerabilities and the offense techniques existed, it could be used in conjunction with our system to create associations between the CVE vulnerabilities and the countermeasures themselves, by using the offensive techniques as an intermediary. This is an area for future work.

Recently, researchers have worked on techniques to automatically extract useful threat information from data available online in blogs and threat report websites. Hutchins et al. [10] provided a technique to categorize advanced persistent threat attacks to kill chain phases. By classifying the attacker's actions into phases [5], defenders can comprehend an attacker's steps and their motives.

Lastly, we have also previously worked [3] on leveraging NLP techniques to extract attacker actions from threat report documents generated by different organizations and automatically classifying them into standardized tactics and techniques. This was based on MITRE data. All of the related work described here seeks to extract information or classify based on these information sources, but our proposed method is the first that attempts to establish connections without any preliminary knowledge (i.e. labeled data) between offensive and defensive techniques. To the best of our knowledge, there is no comprehensive study that attempts to establish these links across such varying types of data at all levels. Furthermore, the unstructured nature of the data includes new challenges that we will aim to tackle with advanced machine learning models.

6   Conclusion

Our study shows the effectiveness of language models in suggesting the right set of solutions to the security analyst. It is clear that traditional models cannot be used effectively for this task as those models cannot understand the context as well as the language models. Along with better natural language processing techniques, quality data is also required for making this knowledge association more comprehensive. Filling out the gaps within the framework to associate each of the offensive techniques with some countermeasures can be done if proper counteractive solutions and their descriptions exist in a structured way. To extend this work, we plan to build a large corpus of our own to accommodate all possible in-the-wild counteractive solutions. We also plan to automate the collection of such counteractive solutions for further association and automatically extract the part of text which talks about 'mitigation'.

Disclaimer. Commercial products are identified in order to adequately specify certain procedures. In no case does such identification imply recommendation or endorsement by the National Institute of Standards and Technology, nor does it imply that the identified products are necessarily the best available for the purpose.

Acknowledgement. The research reported herein was supported in part by NSF awards DMS-1737978, DGE-2039542, OAC-1828467, OAC-1931541, and DGE-1906630, ONR awards N00014-17-1-2995 and N00014-20-1-2738, Army Research Office Contract No. W911NF2110032, DARPA FA8750-19-C-0006, and IBM faculty award (Research).

References

1. Akbar, K.A., Wang, Y., Islam, M.S., Singhal, A., Khan, L., Thuraisingham, B.: Identifying tactics of advanced persistent threats with limited attack traces. In: Tripathy, S., Shyamasundar, R.K., Ranjan, R. (eds.) ICISS 2021. LNCS, vol. 13146, pp. 3–25. Springer, Cham (2021). https://doi.org/10.1007/978-3-030-92571-0_1
2. Ayoade, G., et al.: Evolving advanced persistent threat detection using provenance graph and metric learning. In: 2020 IEEE Conference on Communications and Network Security (CNS), pp. 1–9 (2020). https://doi.org/10.1109/CNS48642.2020.9162264
3. Ayoade, G., Chandra, S., Khan, L., Hamlen, K., Thuraisingham, B.: Automated threat report classification over multi-source data. In: 2018 IEEE 4th International Conference on Collaboration and Internet Computing (CIC), pp. 236–245 (2018). https://doi.org/10.1109/CIC.2018.00040
4. Booth, H., Rike, D., Witte, G.: The national vulnerability database (NVD): Overview (2013-12-18 2013). https://tsapps.nist.gov/publication/get_pdf.cfm?pub_id=915172
5. Debnath, B., et al.: Loglens: a real-time log analysis system. In: 2018 IEEE 38th International Conference on Distributed Computing Systems (ICDCS), pp. 1052–1062 (2018). https://doi.org/10.1109/ICDCS.2018.00105
6. Devlin, J., Chang, M.W., Lee, K., Toutanova, K.: BERT: pre-training of deep bidirectional transformers for language understanding. In: NAACL (2019)
7. Face, H.: RoBERTae (2019). https://huggingface.co/docs/transformers/model_doc/roberta. Accessed 26 Mar 2022
8. GloVe: Global vectors for word representation (2014). https://nlp.stanford.edu/projects/glove/. Accessed 21 Mar 2022
9. Han, J., Khan, L., Masud, M., Gao, J., Thuraisingham, B.: Systems and methods for detecting a novel data class, October 2015, 9165051
10. Hutchins, E.M., Cloppert, M.J., Amin, R.M.: Intelligence-driven computer network defense informed by analysis of adversary campaigns and intrusion kill chains. Lead. Issues Inf. Warfare Secur. Res. **1**, 80 (2011)
11. Jibilian, I., Canales, K.: The US is readying sanctions against Russia over the SolarWinds cyber attack. Here's a simple explanation of how the massive hack happened and why it's such a big deal (2021). https://www.businessinsider.com/solarwinds-hack-explained-government-agencies-cyber-security-2020-12. Accessed 13-April 2022
12. Liu, Y., et al.: RoBERTa: a robustly optimized BERT pretraining approach. arXiv:abs/1907.11692 (2019)
13. Masud, M.M., Gao, J., Khan, L., Han, J., Thuraisingham, B.: Classification and novel class detection in data streams with active mining. In: Zaki, M.J., Yu, J.X., Ravindran, B., Pudi, V. (eds.) PAKDD 2010. LNCS (LNAI), vol. 6119, pp. 311–324. Springer, Heidelberg (2010). https://doi.org/10.1007/978-3-642-13672-6_31
14. Mikolov, T., Chen, K., Corrado, G., Dean, J.: Efficient estimation of word representations in vector space (2013)

15. Mikolov, T., Sutskever, I., Chen, K., Corrado, G., Dean, J.: Distributed representations of words and phrases and their compositionality. CoRR abs/1310.4546 (2013). http://arxiv.org/abs/1310.4546
16. MITRE: CVE. https://cve.mitre.org/
17. MITRE: Enterprise matrix (2015–2021). https://attack.mitre.org/matrices/enterprise/. Accessed 10 Mar 2022
18. MITRE: D3fend (2021). https://d3fend.mitre.org. Accessed 10 Mar 2022
19. OpenCV: Zero-shot learning : An introduction (2020). https://learnopencv.com/zero-shot-learning-an-introduction/. Accessed 13 Mar 2022
20. OpenIOC: Open indicator of compromise (2013). https://www.fireeye.com/blog/threat-research/2013/10/openioc-basics.html. Accessed 18 June 2021
21. Pennington, J., Socher, R., Manning, C.D.: Glove: Global vectors for word representation. In: Empirical Methods in Natural Language Processing (EMNLP), pp. 1532–1543 (2014). http://www.aclweb.org/anthology/D14-1162
22. Sammut, C., Webb, G.I. (eds.): TF-IDF, pp. 986–987. Springer, US, Boston, MA (2010). https://doi.org/10.1007/978-0-387-30164-8_832
23. STIX: Structured threat information expression (2021). https://oasis-open.github.io/cti-documentation. Accessed 18 June 2021
24. Strom, B.E., et al.: Finding cyber threats with ATT&CK - based analytics, June 2017. https://www.mitre.org/publications/technical-papers/finding-cyber-threats-with-attck-based-analytics
25. TAXII: Trusted automated exchange of intelligence information (2021). https://oasis-open.github.io/cti-documentation. Accessed 18 June 2021
26. Zou, Q., Singhal, A., Sun, X., Liu, P.: Deep learning for detecting network attacks: an end to end approach. No. 12840, DBSec 2021: Data and Applications Security and Privacy XXXV, Virtual, US (2021-07-19 04:07:00 2021). https://doi.org/10.1007/978-3-030-81242-3_13, https://tsapps.nist.gov/publication/get_pdf.cfm?pub_id=930878

Attack-Resilient Blockchain-Based Decentralized Timed Data Release

Jingzhe Wang$^{(\boxtimes)}$ and Balaji Palanisamy

University of Pittsburgh, Pittsburgh, PA, USA
{jiw148,bpalan}@pitt.edu

Abstract. Timed data release refers to protecting sensitive data that can be accessed only after a pre-determined amount of time has passed. While blockchain-based solutions for timed data release provide a promising approach for decentralizing the process, designing a reliable and attack-resilient timed-release service that is resilient to malicious adversaries in a blockchain network is inherently challenging. A timed-release service on a blockchain network is inevitably exposed to the risk of *post-facto attacks* where adversaries may launch attacks after the data is released in the blockchain network. Existing incentive-based solutions for timed data release in Ethereum blockchains guarantee protection under the assumption of a fully rational adversarial environment in which every peer acts rationally. However, these schemes fail invariably when even a single participating peer node in the protocol starts acting maliciously and deviates from the rational behavior.

In this paper, we propose an attack-resilient and practical blockchain-based solution for timed data release in a mixed adversarial environment, where both malicious adversaries and rational adversaries exist. The proposed mechanism incorporates an effective decentralized reputation model to evaluate the behaviors of the peer in the network. Based on the reputation model, we design a suite of novel reputation-aware timed-release protocols that effectively handles the mixed adversarial environment consisting of both malicious adversaries and rational adversaries. We implement a prototype of the proposed approach using Smart Contracts and deploy it on the Ethereum official test network, *Rinkeby*. For extensively evaluating the proposed techniques at scale, we perform simulation experiments to validate the effectiveness of the reputation-aware timed data release protocols. The results demonstrate the effectiveness and strong attack resilience of the proposed mechanisms and incurs only a modest gas cost.

Keywords: Timed Release · Blockchain · Smart Contract

1 Introduction

Timed data release refers to protecting sensitive data that can be accessed only after a pre-determined amount of time has passed. Examples of application using

© IFIP International Federation for Information Processing 2022
Published by Springer Nature Switzerland AG 2022
S. Sural and H. Lu (Eds.): DBSec 2022, LNCS 13383, pp. 123–140, 2022.
https://doi.org/10.1007/978-3-031-10684-2_8

timed data release include secure auction systems where important bidding information needs protection until arrivals of all bids and secure voting mechanisms where votes are not permitted to be accessed until the close of the polling process. Since the early research effort on timed information release [16], there has been several efforts focusing on providing effective protection of timed release of data. In the past few decades, a number of rigorous cryptographic constructions [5,6,8,9,21] have enriched the theoretic foundation of the timed-release paradigm to provide provable security guarantees. Even though the theoretic constructions in cryptography provide strong foundations for the development of the timed data release, designing a scalable and attack resilient infrastructure support for timed release of data is a practical necessity to support emerging real-world applications, especially decentralized applications that require timed data release. Recently, a category of network structures, namely self-emerging data infrastructures [19], have been proposed to provide a practical infrastructure support for supporting the timed data release paradigm. Such a self-emerging data infrastructure aims at protecting the data until a prescribed release time and automatically releasing it to the recipient. In such data infrastructures, participating entities of a decentralized peer-to-peer network (e.g., an Ethereum Blockchain network) take charge of protecting and transferring the data. This approach provides an alternate decentralized management of the timed release in contrast to traditional solutions (e.g., cloud storage platforms) that may provide a centralized view to support timed data release. A centralized construction completely relies on a single point of trust that becomes a key barrier to security and privacy, especially in emerging decentralized applications.

Decentralized design of self-emerging data infrastructures [13] has been gaining attention recently with the proliferation of blockchains and blockchain-based decentralized applications. A blockchain provides a public decentralized ledger system operated by global volunteers connected through a *peer-to-peer* network. Powerful consensus protocols such as *Proof-of-Work* guarantee the correctness of operations in a blockchain. Such attractive features of blockchains provide a flexible and reliable design platform for developing decentralized self-emerging infrastructures. While blockchains enable a promising platform for building decentralized infrastructures, several inherent risks have been exposed. In this paper, we particularly focus on two major risks of blockchain-based infrastructures: *First*, the open and public environment in blockchains, where a large number of mutually distrusted participants jointly engage in some services, is full of uncertainty. Such an environment may consist of peers with heterogeneous unpredictable behaviors. One can imagine a scenario where some participants with misbehavior always seek opportunities to sabotage a decentralized service while some other peers may perform actions for seeking maximum profit. *Second*, the blockchain-based infrastructure is inevitably under the threats of *post-facto attacks*, where adversaries may launch potential attacks after the data is released in the blockchain network and control some of the participating peer nodes. In this paper, we materialize such a type of attack with two representative examples, namely *drop attack* and *release-ahead attack*. In a drop attack, an adversary may successfully launch such an attack by destroying the data at any time before the prescribed release time, which results in the failure of the release of the data. For instance, in a secure biding system, such an attack may destruct the protected biding information before the arrival of all bids. A release-ahead attack may be launched by an adversary who covertly interacts with some participating nodes to intercept the data and perform premature release of such data before the prescribed release time. For example, adversaries may maliciously disclose the protected biding information before the prescribed release time. With such concerns in mind, designing a reliable and attack-resilient timed release service is significantly challenging. Existing blockchain-based protection for timed data release focus on two aspects. *First*, grounded on the game theory, incentive-based solutions [12–14] protect the timed data release from peers with a fully rational context in the Ethereum network. *Second*, a cryptography-based solution [18] is proposed to handle the malicious adversaries who launch incentive-based attacks. However, existing solutions either disregard the heterogeneous marketplace in blockchains or ignore the damage of *post-facto* attacks, which makes blockchain-based timed-release service less practical and secure.

In this paper, we carefully consider a mixed adversarial environment in blockchains where both rational peers and malicious peers exist. Specifically, a rational peer only performs attacks when s/he receives higher profit. A malicious peer always deviates from the timed-release protocol without being concerned of any monetary loss. Designing a strong timed-release protocol that survives in such contexts consisting of heterogeneous unpredictable behaviors incurs multiple challenges. First, the incentive-only mechanism in blockchain-based timed release is not sufficient for evaluating peers with malicious behaviors and it is important to design a metric that is able to effectively capture the behaviors of each peer. Second, it is crucial to measure and quantify attack resilience and designing an attack-resilient timed-release scheme to mitigate the impact of mixed adversarial environment is inherently challenging. Finally, evaluating peers' dynamic behaviors in a decentralized environment is essential to identifying and rewarding honest peer behavior in the system. For addressing these challenges, we first propose an uncertainty-aware reputation measure to evaluate the behavior of each peer. Such a measure captures how likely a peer may perform honest actions or malicious actions in an incoming timed-release request. Based on the uncertainty-based reputation model, we propose a suite of reputation-aware timed-release protocol consisting of two key ingredients: *First*, a reputation-time-aware peer recruitment policy is designed to achieve better drop attack resilience and release-ahead attack resilience while the selected peers' working time windows cover the entire lifecycle of the timed-release service. *Second,* a suite of decentralized on-chain protocols are proposed to guarantee the normal operations of the timed-release protocol. For extensively evaluating our proposed timed-release protocol, we first perform simulation studies using a synthetic dataset to evaluate the techniques at scale. We then implement a proof-of-concept prototype through real-world smart contracts using *Solidity* programming language, and deploy the smart contracts on the *Ethereum* official test net, *Rinkeby*. The results demonstrate that, compared with the existing solutions, the proposed techniques achieve significantly higher attack resilience while incurring only a modest on-chain gas cost.

In summary, our key contributions of this paper are as follows:

(1) We carefully design an effective uncertainty-based reputation mechanism for blockchain-based timed-release services.
(2) We propose a suite of novel reputation-aware timed-release protocol to construct the expected timed-release scheme that achieves better attack resilience.
(3) We perform extensive evaluations for our proposed protocol in terms of scalable simulations as well as proof-of-concept prototype implementation on official Ethereum test network *Rinkeby*.

The rest of this paper is organized as follows. In Sect. 2, we provide an overview of the framework as well as the adversary model. Then, we highlight the limitations in the existing works with motivating examples. In Sect. 3, we first build our reputation model with formal descriptions. Then, using the proposed reputation model, the full view of the construction of our reputation-aware timed-release protocol is unfolded. In Sect. 4, we perform our simulation studies and show the numerical results, and we implement our proposed techniques through real-world smart contracts in *Solidity*, and we deploy them on the *Ethereum* official testnet *Rinkeby*. The detailed on-chain gas evaluations are also shown in this section. In Sect. 5, we show the current positions of the timed-release research as well as the related work. In Sect. 6, we conclude the paper.

2   Background and Motivation

In this section, we first introduce blockchain-based self-emerging data infrastructures. Then, the adversary models, analysis of the limitations as well as motivations are demonstrated with examples.

2.1   Decentralized Timed-release of Self-emerging Data Using Ethereum Blockchain

There are four key components for supporting a timed-release service, namely *Data Sender*, *Data Recipient*, *Cloud*, and *Blockchain Infrastructure* respectively. Without loss of generality, we denote multiple timed-release service requests as $Req = \{req_1, ..., req_m\}$, where $m \in \mathbb{Z}^+$. A pair of data sender and data recipient as well as a group of peers over the Ethereum network are responsible for each request. We formally describe the four key components below.

Data Sender: A new timed-release service is initialized by a data sender S_i, S_i encrypts the private data that needs to be transferred with a secret key, and sends the encrypted private data to a trusted cloud storage platform. Then, at the start time T_s^i of the service req_i, S_i sends the encrypted secret key to the blockchain network and such a key will be released at a prescribed release time T_r^i. By taking into consideration multiple service requests, we denote $\mathcal{S} = \{S_1, ..., S_m\}$ as the data sender set for different timed-release service requests.

Data Recipient: For each timed-release service req_i, the corresponding data recipient R_i is responsible for receiving and decrypting the encrypted secret key sent by the data sender S_i at the prescribed release time T_r^i, and decrypting the encrypted private data from the cloud storage to obtain the original private data. We assume that S_i and R_i can perform negotiation before a new req_i in terms of off-chain interactions. We denote $\mathcal{R} = \{R_1, \ldots, R_m\}$ as the data recipient set for different timed-release service requests.

Cloud: A cloud storage infrastructure acts as a trusted third-party storage platform between a pair of data sender and data recipient to store the encrypted private data.

Blockchain Infrastructure: In our framework, we use the Ethereum network as the core infrastructure for supporting a decentralized service. Specifically, the smart contract is owned by a *Contract Account (CA)*, and each registered peer as well as data senders and data recipients are represented by multiple *Externally Owned Accounts(EOAs)* in the Ethereum account network. Without loss of generality, we denote $\mathcal{SC}$ as the smart contract and $\mathcal{P} = \{P_1, ..., P_j\}$ as the registered peers in $\mathcal{SC}$ for participating the timed-release service.

2.2 Adversary Model

2.2.1 Mixed Adversarial Environment

We consider three different types of peer accounts[1], namely *honest peer*, *rational peer*, and *malicious peer*, existing in the *Ethereum* account network. Specifically, every *honest peer* always participates in timed-release service protocols with absolutely honest actions. This type of peer never performs any malicious actions. Every *rational peer* acts with economic rationality. Such a type of peer is driven by self-interest and only chooses to violate timed-release service protocol when doing so let him earn a higher profit. Every *malicious peer* always maliciously launches attacks and deviates arbitrarily from the prescribed timed-release service in an attempt to violate security.

To concretely capture such a mixed adversarial environment, we assume that there always exists a malicious adversary M holding an EOA as well as a global view of our protocol to aggressively break normal operations of our timed-release service. Such an adversary may adopt two potential approaches to corrupt heterogeneous peers. One is bribery [13], where the rational peers are the chief victims. The other one is malicious peer injection, where M intentionally creates a set of peer accounts acting as the malicious peers and controls them to register themselves with the timed-release smart contract, $\mathcal{SC}$, at any time. Once such malicious peers are selected as participants for a timed-release service, potential attacks will occur. We formally define the attacks next.

---

[1] In this paper, we use the terms peer and peer account interchangeably. We also highlight that a peer may represent an individual holding *Ethereum* account and not a miner node.

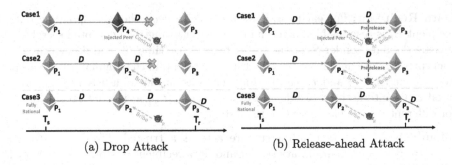

(a) Drop Attack   (b) Release-ahead Attack

Fig. 1. *Post-facto* Attack Examples

2.2.2 Post-facto Attacks

We consider two concrete *post-facto attacks* in our framework. One is *drop attack*, which aims at destroying the data before the prescribed release time and results in a failing data release at the prescribed release time. Such an attack may be launched by M who controls one or more injected malicious peers engaging in the timed-release service. For example, in Case 1 of Fig. 1a, M controls the injected malicious peer P_4 to drop the data D^2, and after T_r, D is missing. In addition, M also can adopt bribery to corrupt rational peers. As an example, in Case 2, in another service, M could let the rational peer P_2 drop D by bribing P_2 through off-chain interactions to make P_2 earn more profit. As a consequence, after T_r, nothing will be released.

The other form of attack is the *release-ahead attack*. A successful release-ahead attack results in a premature release of the data D. It can be launched by M by corrupting a fraction of peers engaging in the timed-release service to get the data before the prescribed release time and disclose it. For example, in Fig. 1b Case 1, M may control P_4 and bribe P_3 to successfully launch a release-ahead attack. Specifically, we note that in our protocol, the data D will be encrypted using the public keys of P_1, P_4, and P_3. If M wants to pre-release D, he/she must control P_4 to acquire the encrypted data and bribe P_3 to get the private key of P_3 to decrypt the encrypted data and pre-release at that time point which is earlier than T_r. Additionally, by adopting bribery, in Case 2, M must bribe P_2 and P_3 to successfully launch the *release-ahead attack*.

2.3 Limitations of Existing Solutions

We present an example to illustrate the fully rational environment [13], described in Case 3 in Fig. 1a and Fig. 1b, in which the global-view adversary M also acts rationally. The incentive-only solution [13] can regulate each rational peer's behavior based on the existence of *Nash Equilibrium* [17], and D will be normally released at T_r as expected. However, by comparing Case 3 with Case 2 as well as Case 1 in Fig. 1a and Fig. 1b, it is easy to find that if we still apply the incentive-only solution in Case 1 and Case 2, the protection of D will inevitably suffer

---

[2] We generalize D as any data transmitted over the *Ethereum* account network. In this paper, specifically, D refers to the secret key generated by the sender.

from a striking degradation even if there are only a few malicious peers. This limitation motivates us to design an attack-resilient protocol to protect the data during a timed-release service in our practical mixed adversarial environment.

3   Reputation-Aware Timed-Release Protocol

In this section, we demystify the detail of our reputation-aware timed-release service protocol. We first build an uncertainty-aware reputation mechanism to evaluate the behavior of each peer. Then, incorporated with such a mechanism, four tightly coupled components, namely **Peer Registration**, **Service Setup**, **Service Enforcement**, and **Service Summary** are elaborately described with examples.

3.1   Uncertainty-Aware Reputation Measure

In our protocol, after each service, $\mathcal{SC}$ judges peers' on-chain behaviors with two distinct types. One is honestly following the protocol, denoted by FL, and the other is dishonestly deviating the protocol, denoted by DV. Such evaluations of behaviors are governed by our *Service Enforcement* and *Service Summary* protocols, which we will describe in detail in Sect. 3.2.3 and Sect. 3.2.4 respectively. Since there are multiple request demands of timed-release services, each registered peer may be recruited by different senders to engage in more than one service. Inspired by the binary assessments of behaviors as well as the engagement within multiple requests, we borrow the ideas from *Beta* distribution [7] to measure the reputation of each engaged peer from an uncertainty perspective. Next, we detail the establishment of our reputation measure. We start with the sketch of the *Beta* distribution, which is a two-parameter family of functions represented by α and β, defined as $f(Pr|\alpha,\beta) = \frac{\Gamma(\alpha+\beta)}{\Gamma(\alpha)\Gamma(\beta)}Pr^{\alpha-1}(1-Pr)^{\beta-1}$, where $0 \leq Pr \leq 1, \alpha > 0, \beta > 0$ with the constraint that the probability variable $Pr \neq 0$ if $\alpha < 1$, and $Pr \neq 1$ if $\beta < 1$. Given α and β, the expectation of Pr is described as $E[Pr] = \frac{\alpha}{\alpha+\beta}$. Our reputation measure can be expressed as follows: For each peer P_j who participates in a timed-release service, an on-chain post-service evaluation for P_j within the i-th timed-release service $e(j,i)$ falls in $\mathcal{S} = \{FL, DV\}$. If P_j honestly follows the i-th timed-release protocol, $e(j,i) = FL$, otherwise, $e(j,i) = DV$. For counting the evaluations and recording in $\mathcal{SC}$, we denote $I(j,i,FL) = 1$ if $e(j,i) = FL$. Otherwise, $I(j,i,DV) = 1$, where $I(j,i,FL) + I(j,i,DV) = 1$ for each $req_i \in Req$. Then for each peer, we define $\alpha(j,i) = I(j,i,FL)+1$, and $\beta(j,i) = I(j,i,DV)+1$. Since P_j may engage in multiple timed-release services, we have $\alpha(j) = \sum_{i=1}^{m} I(j,i,FL)+1$, and $\beta(j) = \sum_{i=1}^{m} I(j,i,DV) + 1$, where $\alpha(j)$ captures the total observations of honest evaluations of P_j among m requests, and $\beta(j)$ captures the total observations of deviation evaluations for P_j among m requests. Then, based on the above definitions, we have $E[Pr(j)]$ for P_j, where $E[Pr(j)] = \frac{\alpha(j)}{\alpha(j)+\beta(j)}$ denotes the likelihood that P_j honestly follows the protocol when participating in the future service, given the observations of honest evaluations $\alpha(j)$ and the observations of deviating evaluations $\beta(j)$. Based on $E[Pr(j)]$, we define the reputation measure of P_j as follows:

$$Rep(j) = \frac{\alpha(j)}{\alpha(j) + 1 + \xi \cdot [\beta(j) - 1]} \tag{1}$$

where $\xi \geq 1$ is a predetermined penalty factor which is designed to penalize any dishonest behaviors of P_j. The design objectives of this measure are two-fold: first, given that the historical evaluations, $Rep(j)$ reflect the likelihood that P_j honestly follows future engaged services, it measures the reputation with uncertainty. Second, adjusted by ξ, for P_j, $Rep(j)$ is gradually built up when P_j honestly contributes in the protocol and it is rapidly reduced when P_j dishonestly deviates the protocol. For instance, if P_j has been engaged in 12 timed-release services, wherein he/she honestly follows the protocol 8 times and dishonestly deviates the protocol 4 times, the reputation is measured by $Rep(j) = \frac{(8+1)}{(8+1)+1+3*4} = 0.41$, which indicates that for the incoming service engagement, P_j holds 0.41 likelihood to follow such service. In particular, for a peer who does not hold any past observations, the reputation score is initialized with $\frac{1}{2}$.

3.2   Reputation-Aware Timed-Release Protocol

We now describe the detailed design of our reputation-aware timed-release protocol.

3.2.1   Peer Registration

At any time, each voluntary peer $P_j \in \mathcal{P}$ can register himself with $\mathcal{SC}$. The detailed design is described as follows: 1. Each voluntary peer $P_j \in \mathcal{P}$ can submit his/her personal information $I_j := \{pk_j, w_j, d_j\}$ to the smart contract $\mathcal{SC}$. 2. After receiving the registration request from P_j, $\mathcal{SC}$ performs the following operations: $\mathcal{SC}$ first updates w_j with $\mathcal{SC}.WITree$ (an *Interval Tree* [2] structure to store working windows). Then, $\mathcal{SC}$ initializes an account, namely, $Peer(j)$ for P_j to store the on-chain profile, which consists of the content as follows: the account balance of P_j, the public key pk_j of P_j, the history of service evaluations of P_j, and the initial reputation score $Rep(j) = 0.5$. In parallel, $\mathcal{SC}$ constructs IP, a map that indexes $Peer(j)$ with the key w_j. After the transactions corresponding to the registration procedure are confirmed, the information regarding P_j is stored on the public on-chain, which can be observed by any peer within the network.

3.2.2   Service Setup

Before initializing a new timed-release service, the sender S_i and recipient R_i first negotiate through off-chain connections to achieve an agreement for a new timed-release service. Such an agreement consists of the following configurations of the incoming timed release service: a prescribed release time T_r^i and minimum deposit needed. After negotiating, the responsible sender S_i makes provision for the incoming service with $\mathcal{SC}$ by means of the *Service Setup* protocol. The logic behind the *Service Setup* in our protocol is similar to one presented in [13]. The novel feature that differentiate our protocol from the one in [13] is the newly designed reputation-aware peer recruitment policy which we describe next.

(i) **Reputation-Aware Peer Recruitment:** For a specific timed-release service request req_i, the sender S_i first interacts with $\mathcal{SC}$ to observe the available peer windows. Then, S_i will make a decision to select a number of peers such that the set union of the working windows of such peers must cover $[T_s^i, T_r^i]$. The set of selected peers forms a routing-like path to store the data and perform the data hand-off between each peer. In parallel, the sender S_i is also concerned with the performance of data protection provided by such a set of peers. Such a protection can be specifically represented as follows: given a set of selected peers, what is the likelihood that the data is prevented from *drop attack* as well as *release-ahead attack*?

We formally quantify such likelihood with two distinct attack resilience metrics, namely *drop attack resilience* and *release-ahead attack resilience* respectively. With the help of our uncertainty-aware reputation measure $Rep(\cdot)$, given a peer recruitment scheme E that consists of l peers, we define such metrics as follows: The *drop attack resilience* of E, denoted as F_d^E, captures the failure likelihood of the adversary M when he/she intends to launch a drop attack, quantified as $F_d^E = \prod_{k=1}^{l} [Rep(k)]$, which reflects that M must control or bribe at least one peer in E to successfully launch a drop attack. The *release-ahead attack resilience* of E, denoted as F_r^E, captures the failure likelihood of M when he/she intends to launch release-ahead attacks. It is quantified as $F_r^E = 1 - \prod_{k=1}^{l} [1 - Rep(k)]$. Since the scheme E is protected with the *Onion Routing* [20] scheme, an adversary must control all peers to prematurely release the data at the start time. We discuss this later in the *Service Enforcement* protocol.

Our peer recruitment for the timed-release service consists of multiple rounds. In each round of selection, the sender will take a time point as the input. By retrieving all the available registered peers whose working window covers the input time point in terms of $WITree$, the sender will pick the one having the highest reputation score as the responsible peer for the current round. Then, the start time of the selected peer and the hand-off time zone will be taken as the input of the next round selection. In particular, two conditions will end the recruitment. When the $WITree$ finds that no available peers are in a selection round or when the start time of the selected peer is earlier than T_s.

We illustrate our design approach using an example in Fig. 2a. In the example, there are totally 7 peers P_1–P_7 who have already registered with $\mathcal{SC}$ as well as available within $[T_s, T_r]$. The numerical value associated with each peer represents the current reputation measure, which is publicly known. The different numerical measures associated with the peers indicate their historical behaviors when they engaged in timed-release requests in the past. The blue color represents rational peers, the red color represents the malicious peers, and the green color represents the honest peers. T_h denotes a predefined hand-off timezone. The sender S first takes $T_r + T_h$ as the input of the first-round selection. There are totally 3 peers, P_6, P_7, and P_8, who are available at this time point. Then, S picks the highest reputation one, P_7, whose reputation is $Rep(P_7) = 0.98$, as one of the peer candidates. Then, S performs the second-round selection, which takes $T_s(P_7) + T_h$, where $T_s(P_7)$ represents the start time of the working window of P_7, as the input time point. The working windows of two peers, P_5 and P_6, cover such a time point. The one holding a higher reputation P_5, $Rep(P_5) = 0.94$, is selected. Followed by the third-round selection, P_3 is selected. Finally, the last-round selection picks P_1 as well as checks that the start time of P_1 is prior to the start time of the timed-release service, T_s, which ends the reputation-aware recruitment procedure. The order of peers, $P_1{\to}P_3{\to}P_5{\to}P_7$, jointly take charge of the incoming timed-release service. We denote this scheme as E^1.

(ii) Resilience Analysis: We provide a concrete example to show the resilience analysis of our proposed reputation-aware peer recruitment policy as well as the time-aware recruitment proposed in [13] as the baseline for comparison. To analyze its resilience, we independently consider the drop attack and the release-ahead attack. The release-ahead attack resilience of E^1 from our proposed reputation-aware peer recruitment is derived from $F_r^{E^1} = 1 - (1 - 0.98) \cdot (1 - 0.94) \cdot (1 - 0.97) \cdot (1 - 0.95) = 0.999$, and the drop attack resilience is calculated as $F_d^{E^1} = 0.98 \cdot 0.94 \cdot 0.97 \cdot 0.95 = 0.85$. For the reputation-unaware recruitment in Fig. 2b, in each round of selection, only the peer who has the longest working time is selected. The peers $P_2{\to}P_4{\to}P_6$ take charge of the service. We denote this scheme as E^2. The release-ahead attack resilience is $F_r^{E^2} = 1 - (1 - 0.2) \cdot (1 - 0.3) \cdot (1 - 0.6) = 0.77$, and the drop attack resilience is $F_d^{E^2} = 0.2 \cdot 0.3 \cdot 0.6 = 0.036$. Compared with our reputation-aware recruitment, both $F_r^{E^2}$ and $F_d^{E^2}$ show significant degradation. After providing all information mentioned above, S_i and R_i deposit d and register the information with $\mathcal{SC}$.

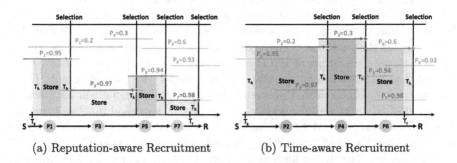

(a) Reputation-aware Recruitment   (b) Time-aware Recruitment

Fig. 2. Peer Recruitment Example

3.2.3 Service Enforcement

After completing *Service Setup*, a timed-release service moves into execution. *Service Enforcement* takes charge of monitoring the correctness and timeliness of the executions after the data is released into the blockchain network. Moreover, with the help of the *Service Enforcement* protocol, $\mathcal{SC}$ can abort the service in time if any misbehavior is detected. We adopt the basic procedures of the *Service Enforcement* protocol described in [13]. We describe it next.

We denote $E^i = \{P_k\}_{k \in [1,l]}$ as the selected peers from the reputation-aware recruitment policy from S_i, and S_i generates an *onion* by encrypting the original data with the public keys of the peers in E^i and transfer it to P_1 to initialize the *Service Enforcement* protocol. Without loss of generality, under the scope of the timed-release service, we capture the action space of each peer with $\mathcal{A} = \{cs, ws, tr, vr, rp\}$, where cs represents that P_k verifies the received certification from the P_{k-1}. The certification is used to detect drop attacks. ws indicates that P_k builds private channel using the *Whisper Key* protocol [13] with the subsequent peer P_{k+1} to transfer the *onion*, and tr represents that P_k transfers the onion to P_{k+1}, vr aims at verifying the on-time results of cs and ws, and rp captures the possible misbehavior actions. In order to detect misbehavior in time, we bound the major actions within $\mathcal{A}$ with corresponding deadlines, which enables our protocol to be aborted timely if any misbehavior is detected. Concretely, we associate each peer with a series of pre-determined hard deadlines. For example, for the peer $P_k \in E^i$, before T_1, P_k must perform cs. Then, P_k must perform vr for the verification of cs, and perform ws before T_2. The verification of ws, and the delivery of the *onion* to the subsequent peer P_{k+1} must be executed before T_3. Such deadlines follow the ordering: $T_1 < T_2 < T_3$. In particular, if P_{k+1} does not receive the corresponding *onion* from P_k, he/she must report the issue (rp) before performing cs, otherwise, if a failed submission of the certification is detected from P_{k+1}, P_{k+1} will be judged as launching the *drop attack*. Our *Misbehavior Detection* protocol is similar to the one described in [13]. Corresponding to the results from the verification mentioned above, we denote the finite state space of each $P_k \in E^i$ as $\mathcal{B}_k^i = \{INIT, VF, WS, TR, FAIL\}$. It is described as follows: all peers within E^i start with the $INIT$ state when engaged in req_i. For P_k, if he/she passes the verification for cs, then the state of P_k will be updated to VF from $INIT$. Then, if P_k passes the verification for ws, the state will be updated to WS from VF. If P_{k+1} does not report any misbehavior of P_k, the state of P_k will be updated to TR from VF. If any previous verification fails or a drop report is emitted, the state of P_k will be moved to $FAIL$ and the current service will be aborted. If all peers in E^i honestly follow the protocol, R_i will get the original data and close the current service by following *Service Summary* which is described next.

3.2.4   Service Summary

There are two scenarios that trigger *Service Summary*: (1) A timed-release service is successfully finished. Under this scenario, R_i is responsible for the final evaluations of each peer as well as updating the on-chain reputation. (2) A timed-release service is aborted at a time point before the prescribed release time T_r^i. We adopt a remuneration policy similar to one described in [13] for the incentive refund. For the behavior evaluation as well as for updating the reputation, $\mathcal{SC}$ follows the rules to perform evaluations: $\mathcal{SC}$ checks the state of each peer within E^i. If the final state of a peer is TR, the binary assessment for the peer is FL, and if the final state of a peer is $FAIL$, the assessment is DV. Otherwise, if a peer has $INIT$ state, $\mathcal{SC}$ does not perform any evaluations. Finally, the reputation measure of each peer in E^i will be updated using by following Eq. 1.

4   Evaluations

4.1   Simulation Evaluations

We first perform extensive simulation experiments to show the benefits and effectiveness of our reputation measure as well as the reputation-aware peer recruitment policy. We evaluate our protocol, namely _RS_, on two metrics, F_r and F_d. Specifically, we expect the protocol to demonstrate high F_r as well as F_d. For comparisons, we also implement the timed-aware peer recruitment proposed in [13], namely _NRS_, as a baseline, which does not consider peer reputation when performing peer recruitment. We implement a simulator in JAVA, and the generated synthetic data as well as default experimental settings in our evaluations are described below:

Synthetic Peer Profile: The default number of registered peers in the simulation is set to 1000. In the simulator, we first randomly select 5 registered peers as the honest peers. Then, given a malicious peer percentage, we randomly select malicious peers based on that percentage. The remaining peers are all rational peers. For each peer, the duration of his/her working window is drawn from a _normal_ distribution with the mean of 50 h and 5-h standard deviation.

Protocol Configurations: Following the assumptions in Sect. 2.2, in our simulated protocol, the malicious peers in the registered pool 100% deviate from the protocol, and the honest peers 100% follow the protocol. The rational peers only launch attack with respective of the bribery value from the malicious adversaries. The penalty factor $\xi = 10$.

Experimental Evaluation Settings: We evaluate the resilience by varying the percentage of malicious peers from 15% to 95%. In each percentage setting, the simulator first generates a new peer account network (registered peers) based on the descriptions mentioned above. Then 500 requests are executed for the evaluation, where 70% of them are training requests, and 30% of them are validation requests. We calculate the average resilience as the result of each peer malicious percentage setting. Each experiment is executed 10 times and the average resilience is obtained.

Effectiveness Under Different Scales of Registered Peer: The first set of experiments demonstrates effectiveness of our proposed reputation-aware peer selection protocol under three different scales of peer accounts network, namely 100 peers, 1000 peers and 10000 peers. We set the number of honest peers as 5 in each setting. The time duration of each service is set to 300 h, and the hand-off time zone is set to 4 h. When there are 100 peers, compared with _NRS_, under each setting of malicious peer percentage, _RS_ shows significantly higher release-ahead attack resilience (Fig. 3a) and drop attack resilience (Fig. 3d). We increase the size of the registered list towards 1000 peers in Fig. 3b. Under each setting of malicious peer percentage, our proposed _RS_ achieves a higher release-ahead attack resilience than _NRS_. Also in Fig. 3e, compared with _NRS_, our proposed _RS_ achieves a significantly higher drop attack resilience. Finally, under

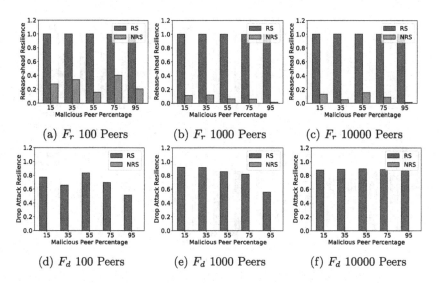

(a) F_r 100 Peers   (b) F_r 1000 Peers   (c) F_r 10000 Peers

(d) F_d 100 Peers   (e) F_d 1000 Peers   (f) F_d 10000 Peers

Fig. 3. Different Scales of Registered Peers

a relatively large scale peer network with 10000 peers in Fig. 3c and Fig. 3f, our proposed RS scheme achieves a higher release-ahead attack resilience and drop attack resilience. In summary, under different scale of peer network, the proposed approach RS can effectively protect the data with higher attack resilience.

Effectiveness Under Different Duration of Service: In this set of experiments, we learn the effectiveness of our proposed protocol under different duration of service time. Apart from the default 300 h service time, in this set of experiments, we set a short duration, 100 h, a moderate length duration 600 h, and a longer duration 1200 h. We fix the number of registered peers as 1000, and the hand-off time zone is set to 4 h. In Fig. 4a and Fig. 4d, we observe that compared with NRS, RS significantly improves the release-ahead attack resilience and drop attack resilience under different percentage of malicious peers. Then, from the results of 600-h service time, compared with NRS, RS achieves a significantly higher release-ahead attack resilience and drop attack resilience under different malicious peer percentage. Finally, the results corresponding to the 1200-h setting also shows similar benefits for RS. In summary, RS can achieve significantly better resistance for both the release-ahead attacks as well as the drop attacks under different duration of service.

4.2   Prototype Implementation

4.2.1   Implementation Description

In this section, we present our prototype implementation. We implement our smart contract in the official programming language *Solidity* [4]. We deploy our smart contract on Ethereum official test network *Rinkeby* [3] through the interface, *Infura* [1]. We use the data from our simulation studies as the input for

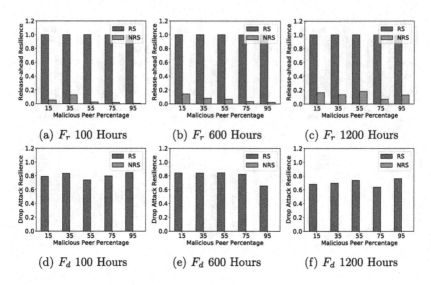

(a) F_r 100 Hours   (b) F_r 600 Hours   (c) F_r 1200 Hours

(d) F_d 100 Hours   (e) F_d 600 Hours   (f) F_d 1200 Hours

Fig. 4. Different Duration of Timed-release Service

on-chain validations. We have 7 selected peers in total taking charge of 1200 h-service. The results from Table 1 show the detailed information of our implementations. The implementation of our reputation-aware timed-release protocol consist of five different modules. ① **Registration:** this module provides interfaces for every peer to register with $\mathcal{SC}$ as well as to manage their own information. *peerRegister* is invoked by any peers to register with $\mathcal{SC}$. *deposit* and *withdraw*, are invoked by the registered peers to manage the account balance. *updatePubKey* and *updateWindow* are invoked by the registered peers to manage the information regarding the timed-release service. ② **Setup:** this module provides interfaces for senders and recipients to perform service provisioning for timed-release requests. *senderSign* is invoked by senders to register with $\mathcal{SC}$. The second function *recipientSign* is invoked by the corresponding recipients. The third function *setup* is invoked by senders to finish the provisioning of a service. ③ **Enforce:** this module guarantees the normal executions of a timed-release service. *setCertificate* is invoked by senders to submit the certification. *submitCertificate* is invoked by any engaged peers or the recipients to verify the correctness of the certification. *setWhisperKey* is invoked by the engaged peers or the senders to build private channels. The fourth function *verification* is invoked by any peers to actively verify the behaviors of each peer. ④ **Detection:** This module consists of four functions to detect and reward the reporting of behaviors. *releaseReport* is invoked by any peer to report the evidence of the release-ahead attack, and after verification by $\mathcal{SC}$, *releaseReward* is invoked by the reporter to receive rewards. *dropReport* is invoked by any peer to report the drop attack evidences. After the verification, the reporter invokes the function *dropReward* to get rewards. ⑤ **Summary:** The last module consists of two functions. The first one, *peerEvaluation*, is invoked by the last responsible peer of each service to assess peers' behaviors, and the second function *reputationUpdate* is invoked by the same peer to finally update the peers' reputation measure, which is publicly recorded on-chain.

4.2.2 Cost Analysis

From Table 1, we have two significant observations regarding the cost: first, there are four functions incurring relatively higher cost namely *peerRegister (229669)*, *senderSign (355534)*, *setup (122682)*, and *peerEvaluation (139363)*. Specifically, *peerRegister* is invoked by any peers, *senderSign* and *setup* are both invoked by a sender. *peerRegister* is invoked by the last peer in the routing scheme. We note that those four functions are only invoked once per request and therefore it is an one-time cost. Second, our proposed on-chain reputation mechanisms only incurs a modest gas cost from the summary module where *peerEvaluation* incurs 139363 and *reputationUpdate* incurs 48620.

Table 1. Gas Cost

Module	Function	Gas Cost
Registration	*peerRegister*	229669
	deposit	42349
	withdraw	29283
	updatePubKey	43556
	updateWindow	83884
Setup	*senderSign*	355534
	recipientSign	62292
	setup	122682
Enforce	*setCertificate*	70539
	submitCertificate	44460
	setWhisperKey	64585
	verification	26036
Detection	*releaseReport*	69541
	releaseReward	29596
	dropReport	65362
	dropReward	29662
Summary	*peerEvaluation*	139363
	reputationUpdate	48620

5 Related Work

Practically constructing decentralized timed-release services has gained attention recently. *Self-emerging infrastructure* [19] provides a promising solution.

Two representative constructions were developed using this design philosophy. Based on *Distributed Hash Table (DHT)*, the first set of solutions, [10,11], design a set of mechanisms within *DHT* to statistically resist potential attacks launched by adversaries. The second type of solution [13,14] suggests the use of blockchain technologies to support timed release of data by using the Ethereum network. Besides timed release of data, there are several other practical contributions. The decentralized protocol presented in [12] schedules a transaction that is executed at a future point of time while protecting the information regarding the transaction before the release time. Ning et al. [18] proposed a carrot-and-stick mechanism using smart contracts to tackle premature release issues when developing timed-release applications. While such practical constructions advance the development of timed-release applications in real world, aggressive adversarial impacts on such paradigm inevitably exist and raise major concerns.

A preliminary discussion about the importance of protecting timed-release services in mixed adversarial environments is recently introduced by the authors in [23]. In this research paper, we focus on developing a comprehensive solution to the problem by designing a reputation-aware scheme for protecting against attackers in mixed adversarial settings consisting of both malicious and rational peers. The reputation-based scheme is designed to detect dishonest behaviors and reward and incentivize honest behavior in the context of supporting timed release of data. The transparent nature of blockchains provides a convenient context to build reputation measure. There are several representative blockchain-based reputation mechanism in the literature. Based on social norm, Li et al. [15] builds a reputation model on *Ethereum*-based crowdsourcing framework to regulate the worker's behaviors. Zhou et al. [25] leverages a simple reputation measure to block the witnesses with misbehaviors in a blockchain-based witness model. RTChain [22] integrates a reputation system into the blockchains that focus on e-commerce to achieve a transaction incentives and distributed consensus. Repu-Coin [24] designs *proof-of-reputation* in a permissionless blockchain to achieve a strong deterministic consensus, which is robust to attacks. Unlike the reputation scheme developed in this work, these existing schemes primarily focus on blocking the participants with misbehaviors and are not designed to directly provide quantitative analysis to aid peer selection in mixed adversarial settings.

6   Conclusion

In this paper, we develop techniques to protect blockchain-based timed data release in mixed adversarial environments where both malicious adversaries and rational adversaries exist. An uncertainty-aware reputation measure is developed to quantitatively capture the behavior of peers engaging in timed release service. Based on the reputation measure, a novel reputation-aware timed-release protocol is designed to handle such mixed adversarial settings. First, an off-chain reputation-aware peer recruitment is performed by carefully considering the impact on attack resilience. Then, a suite of on-chain mechanisms jointly take charge of monitoring the states of the proposed protocol and evaluate the behavior of each engaged peer. Our extensive simulations demonstrate the effectiveness of our proposed protocol. Compared with the existing solutions, the approach achieves significantly higher attack resilience. We develop a prototype of the proposed protocol using smart contracts and we deploy it on the *Ethereum* official test net, *Rinkeby*. The on-chain evaluations show that our protocol incurs only a moderate amount of gas cost and demonstrates its cost-effectiveness.

Acknowledgement. This material is based upon work supported by the National Science Foundation under Grant #2020071. Any opinions, findings, and conclusions or recommendations expressed in this material are those of the author(s) and do not necessarily reflect the views of the National Science Foundation.

References

1. Infura. https://infura.io/
2. Interval tree. https://github.com/gnidan/interval-trees-solidity
3. Rinkeby. https://www.rinkeby.io/#stats
4. Solidity. https://docs.soliditylang.org/en/v0.8.10/
5. Bitansky, N., Goldwasser, S., Jain, A., Paneth, O., Vaikuntanathan, V., Waters, B.: Time-lock puzzles from randomized encodings. In: Proceedings of the 2016 ACM Conference on Innovations in Theoretical Computer Science, pp. 345–356 (2016)
6. Boneh, D., Naor, M.: Timed commitments. In: Bellare, M. (ed.) CRYPTO 2000. LNCS, vol. 1880, pp. 236–254. Springer, Heidelberg (2000). https://doi.org/10.1007/3-540-44598-6_15
7. Josang, A., Ismail, R.: The beta reputation system. In: Proceedings of the 15th Bled Electronic Commerce Conference, vol. 5, pp. 2502–2511 (2002)
8. Kasamatsu, K., Matsuda, T., Emura, K., Attrapadung, N., Hanaoka, G., Imai, H.: Time-specific encryption from forward-secure encryption. In: Visconti, I., De Prisco, R. (eds.) SCN 2012. LNCS, vol. 7485, pp. 184–204. Springer, Heidelberg (2012). https://doi.org/10.1007/978-3-642-32928-9_11
9. Kikuchi, R., Fujioka, A., Okamoto, Y., Saito, T.: Strong security notions for timed-release public-key encryption revisited. In: Kim, H. (ed.) ICISC 2011. LNCS, vol. 7259, pp. 88–108. Springer, Heidelberg (2012). https://doi.org/10.1007/978-3-642-31912-9_7
10. Li, C., Palanisamy, B.: Emerge: self-emerging data release using cloud data storage. In: 2017 IEEE 10th International Conference on Cloud Computing (CLOUD), pp. 26–33. IEEE (2017)
11. Li, C., Palanisamy, B.: Timed-release of self-emerging data using distributed hash tables. In: 2017 IEEE 37th International Conference on Distributed Computing Systems (ICDCS), pp. 2344–2351. IEEE (2017)
12. Li, C., Palanisamy, B.: Decentralized privacy-preserving timed execution in blockchain-based smart contract platforms. In: 2018 IEEE 25th International Conference on High Performance Computing (HiPC), pp. 265–274. IEEE (2018)
13. Li, C., Palanisamy, B.: Decentralized release of self-emerging data using smart contracts. In: 2018 IEEE 37th Symposium on Reliable Distributed Systems (SRDS), pp. 213–220. IEEE (2018)
14. Li, C., Palanisamy, B.: SilentDelivery: practical timed-delivery of private information using smart contracts. IEEE Trans. Serv. Comput. (to appear)

15. Li, M., et al.: CrowdBC: a blockchain-based decentralized framework for crowd-sourcing. IEEE Trans. Parallel Distrib. Syst. **30**(6), 1251–1266 (2018)
16. May, T.C.: Timed-release crypto (1993). http://www.hks.net/cpunks/cpunks-0/1460.html
17. Nash, J.F., Jr.: Equilibrium points in n-person games. Proc. Natl. Acad. Sci. **36**(1), 48–49 (1950)
18. Ning, J., Dang, H., Hou, R., Chang, E.-C.: Keeping time-release secrets through smart contracts. IACR Cryptology ePrint Archive, p. 1166 (2018)
19. Palanisamy, B., Li, C.: Self-emerging data infrastructures. In: 2019 IEEE 5th International Conference on Collaboration and Internet Computing (CIC), pp. 256–265 (2019)
20. Reed, M.G., Syverson, P.F., Goldschlag, D.M.: Anonymous connections and onion routing. IEEE J. Sel. Areas Commun. **16**(4), 482–494 (1998)
21. Rivest, R.L., Shamir, A., Wagner, D.A.: Time-lock puzzles and timed-release crypto
22. Sun, Y., Xue, R., Zhang, R., Qianqian, S., Gao, S.: RTChain: a reputation system with transaction and consensus incentives for e-commerce blockchain. ACM Trans. Internet Technol. (TOIT) **21**(1), 1–24 (2020)
23. Wang, J., Palanisamy, B.: Protecting blockchain-based decentralized timed release of data from malicious adversaries. In: 2022 IEEE International Conference on Blockchain and Cryptocurrency (2022)
24. Jiangshan, Yu., Kozhaya, D., Decouchant, J., Esteves-Verissimo, P.: RepuCoin: your reputation is your power. IEEE Trans. Comput. **68**(8), 1225–1237 (2019)
25. Zhou, H., Ouyang, X., Ren, Z., Su, J., de Laat, C., Zhao, Z.: A blockchain based witness model for trustworthy cloud service level agreement enforcement. In: IEEE INFOCOM 2019-IEEE Conference on Computer Communications, pp. 1567–1575. IEEE (2019)

IoT Security

Local Intrinsic Dimensionality of IoT Networks for Unsupervised Intrusion Detection

Matt Gorbett$^{(\boxtimes)}$, Hossein Shirazi, and Indrakshi Ray

Colorado State University, Fort Collins, CO 80523, USA
{Matt.Gorbett,Hossein.Shirazi,Indrakshi.Ray}@colostate.edu

Abstract. The Internet of Things (IoT) is revolutionizing society by connecting people, devices, and environments seamlessly and providing enhanced user experience and functionalities. Security and privacy issues remain mostly ignored. Attackers can compromise devices, inject spurious packets into an IoT network, and cause severe damage. Machine learning-based Network Intrusion Detection Systems (NIDS) are often designed to detect such attacks. Most algorithms use labeled data for training the classifiers, which is difficult to obtain in a real-world setting.

In this work, we propose a novel unsupervised machine learning approach that uses properties of the IoT dataset for anomaly detection. Specifically, we propose the use of Local Intrinsic Dimensionality (LID), a theoretical complexity measurement that assesses the local manifold surrounding a point. We use LID to evaluate three modern IoT network datasets empirically, showing that for network data generated using IoT methodologies, the LID estimates of benign network packets fit into low LID estimations. Further, we find that malicious examples exhibit higher LID estimates. We use this finding to propose a new unsupervised anomaly detection algorithm, the *Weighted Hamming Distance LID Estimator*, which incorporates an entropy weighted Hamming distance into the LID Maximum Likelihood Estimator algorithm. We show that our proposed approach performs better on IoT network datasets than the Autoencoder, KNN, and Isolation Forests. We test the algorithm on ToN IoT, NetFlow Bot-IoT (NF Bot-IoT), and Aposemat IoT-23 (IoT-23) datasets, using leave-one-out validation to compare results.

Keywords: Intrusion detection systems · IoT · Anomaly detection

1 Introduction

The proliferation of IoT systems has introduced new, and emerging security vulnerabilities [2,5,13,49] which can be readily exploited to cause harm.

This work was supported in part by funding from NSF under Award Number CNS 1822118, NIST, ARL, Statnett, AMI, Cyber Risk Research, NewPush, and State of Colorado Cybersecurity Center.

© IFIP International Federation for Information Processing 2022
Published by Springer Nature Switzerland AG 2022
S. Sural and H. Lu (Eds.): DBSec 2022, LNCS 13383, pp. 143–161, 2022.
https://doi.org/10.1007/978-3-031-10684-2_9

Network Intrusion Detection Systems (NIDS) play a critical role in security of IoT networks [14]. Modern-day NIDS' depend in part on machine learning algorithms' ability to detect malicious actors. However, heterogeneity and non-standardized protocol of IoT networks have been posited as critical challenges for enhancing the security of IoT systems [11,23,37] – networks with diverse devices ranging from single-purpose machines to robust servers, each with varied communication structures, are cumbersome to protect.

1.1 Limitations of Prior Attempts

Various machine learning solutions have been proposed for NIDS in IoT networks. Such solutions incorporate deep learning such as autoencoders and classifiers [10,38,44,45], as well traditional machine learning algorithms [32]. While these solutions are each impactful in their own right, most are supervised learning solutions requiring a fully annotated dataset to train – a costly, time-intensive task. Moreover, with constantly evolving attack vectors (malicious actors acting in novel ways), supervised NIDS solutions trained on datasets with particular attack types become vulnerable [33,47]. Further, IoT networks are fundamentally different from standard networks – devices will be added to the network, and existing devices may have software/firmware updates with greater frequency. Supervised algorithms are unable to detect new devices or updates in these situations without expensive retraining or reconfiguration [9].

To mitigate the problems of supervised learning algorithms in IoT, Haefner and Ray [19] take the novel approach to intrusion detection in IoT from the perspective of device traffic complexity. The authors measure the complexity of network traffic on a per device basis to tune an (unsupervised) Isolation Forest algorithm. They find that several single-purpose IoT devices contain simple (non-malicious) network traffic, enabling us to assume trust of the device based on its low network packet variability. However, the tuning procedure used for the Isolation Forest assumes a particular contamination rate: for more complex devices, they assume a more significant and fixed percentage of network packets are anomalies, an assumption that could lead to false positives and not perform well in real-world scenarios.

1.2 Proposed Approach

We take a different approach by using complexity measurements to detect malicious data. Gorbett et al. [17] showed that heterogeneous IoT networks have a lower complexity than regular non-IoT datasets using Intrinsic Dimensionality (ID). ID is a property that has been proposed to measure the complexity of a data set as a whole [50]. Gorbett et al. [17] measured IoT datasets at the network level and device level. We instead show that at the sample-level (network packets), IoT traffic can be categorized as benign or malicious using a device-independent unsupervised model. We do this using LID, which estimates the intrinsic dimension around an individual data point, and show that malicious activity exhibits higher LID values than benign samples.

1.3   Problem Statement

We focus on the question of heterogeneity and complexity in IoT networks and their effects on detecting malicious activity via NIDS. Specifically, we ask the following questions:

1. Do the properties of multi-device heterogeneous IoT networks exhibit fundamentally more complex behavior?
2. Can we detect malicious activity at the IoT network level in an unsupervised manner, without the need to label each device and attack?
3. Which attacks are networks more susceptible to?

In this work, we measure the complexity of IoT network traffic using the novel perspective of LID. Using this metric, we focus on the problem of detecting malicious actors in IoT networks. We measure the complexity of network packets by formulating an entropy-weighted Hamming distance calculation on top of the LID measurement to construct a novel anomaly detection algorithm. The results of the algorithm show that benign network data in IoT datasets exhibit a lower LID measurement compared to malicious actors, which provides us the opportunity to threshold this measurement during test time. The unsupervised algorithm uses benign IoT network data as a training set and assumes any test sample under threshold τ is benign network behavior. If the LID estimate is above this threshold, we can flag the example as malicious.

Contributions

- We propose a novel algorithm for unsupervised anomaly detection using a combination of Hamming distance and the Hill Maximum Likelihood Estimator (MLE) LID, and show that the algorithm performs competitively with several state-of-the-art algorithms.
- To the best of our knowledge, this is the first work that uses LID to measure IoT datasets. We show the potential utility of this measurement in security by outlining the theoretical basis for the approach.
- We measure the complexity of IoT traffic at the network level, and show that, even for networks with several devices, benign data generally fits into low LID estimates. In contrast, malicious data exhibits higher LID values.

2   Related Work

2.1   Intrusion Detection Systems

Intrusion Detection Systems (IDS) can broadly be classified based on 1) where the detection is placed (network or host) and 2) the detection method that is employed (Machine Learning (ML) anomaly-detection algorithms or traditional signature-based detection where attack patterns are defined in a database). In this work, we concentrate on network-based intrusion detection where anomalies are classified based on an ML algorithm. ML based NIDS are employed in production into a key point within a network to monitor traffic to and from all devices connected to the network. Network features are extracted from the entire subnet about the passing traffic and scored by the ML detection algorithm. NIDS can operate on-line (real-time detection) or off-line (batch detection). Real-time detection offers more robust security and beneficial results as long as it does not impair the overall speed of the network. Our study aims to characterize network data in real-time.

2.2   IoT

IoT is a rapidly evolving field, with research being done at dozens of institutions across industry and academia [11,23,25,37]. It is postulated that IoT increases the vulnerability of networks because the *attack surface* has increased, with many new entry and exit points with new devices available on networks [30,39]. A heterogeneous IoT network is typically made of various sub-devices within a distributed network. It includes resource-constrained devices, such as a smart light bulb or garage door opener, and more powerful devices such as embedded and regular computers.

Existing research notes that IoT networks and devices have multiple intrusion sources: IoT backends, cloud services supporting an IoT device, and other hubs within the IoT system [1,35], which makes it difficult to implement traditional intrusion detection approaches such as rule-based and signature-based methods.

2.3   State-of-the-Art Network Intrusion Models

Several works propose new and existing algorithms for intrusion detection on commonly used datasets. Nour [32] released dataset *TON_IoT* (*TON_IoT*), as a baseline result that uses many supervised learning algorithms. Sahu et al. [41] proposed a hybrid deep learning model which uses a CNN/LSTM framework to achieve 96% accuracy on the IoT-23 dataset generated by [15] and outperformed several proposed deep learning-based attack detection. Kozik et al. [26] use hybrid time window embeddings with a transformer neural network to classify IoT-23 data. This model achieves between 93% and 95% accuracy on attacks in IoT-23 and does better than three other proposed deep learning models: HaddadPajouh et al. [18] use an LSTM trained on IoT devices execution operation codes (OpCodes), Roy and Cheung [40] use a bi-directional LSTM for detecting attacks on UNSW-NB15, and Azmoodeh et al. [7] use OpCodes to train a deep Eigenspace model to detect attacks. Moustafa and Slay released UNSW-NB15 dataset [33] that was generated using IXIA PerfectStorm. The dataset has been widely used as a benchmark for comparison. MStream [10] is an online neural network-based anomaly detection algorithm. It uses multi-aspect streams, such as multiple features, continuous, categorical. This tool achieves 0.90 AUROC on UNSW-NB15 and is considered state-of-the-art according to PapersWithCode.com[1]. The Edge-detect model [45] is another neural network-based framework that proposes a lightweight model to detect anomalies on edge and was

---

[1] https://paperswithcode.com/dataset/unsw-nb15.

tested on UNSW-15 and is also considered state-of-the-art. Meftah et al. [29] performed a similar approach to [22], using Recursive Feature Elimination and Random Forests to select features, achieving up to 86% F1 accuracy. It should be noted that UNSW-NB15 is only used in this paper to measure dataset complexity, not anomaly detection. We specifically concentrate our anomaly detection on IoT datasets, especially since the high complexity of UNSW-NB15 makes it a poor choice for our algorithm.

Several other papers are published using alternative datasets that propose different machine learning models for intrusion detection. Rezvy et al. [38] proposed a deep learning framework for intrusion classification and prediction in 5G and IoT networks. They propose an autoencoder neural network for detecting intrusion or attacks in 5G and IoT networks, evaluating the model on the Aegean Wi-Fi Intrusion dataset. Their results showed an overall detection accuracy of 99.9% for different types of attacks. Kasongo and Sun [22] argue that feature selection is essential for the performance of ML models in intrusion detection since model accuracy decreases with more high-dimensional datasets. They apply a filtering technique on features and train several ML models using this technique, showing strong performance. They relate the feature selection to IoT devices with limited capacity, showing that less robust modeling techniques are favorable in limited-capacity systems such as small IoT devices.

2.4   Complexity and Anomaly Detection in Deep Learning

Neural networks trained with back propagation provide diverse structures and objectives to learn from high-dimensional data. Despite their incredible power, anomaly detection remains an open research problem, even in state-of-the-art models. Notably, several works in computer vision have shown that classification, generative, and unsupervised deep neural networks are all susceptible to anomalous data [16,20,31,34,43]. For example, one common computer vision experiment involves training a deep learning model on CIFAR-10, a dataset with 60,000 images labeled into ten classes. It is expected that the likelihood of a CIFAR-10 test image will be higher than images from other datasets during test time. However, several papers have shown that the examples from the dataset SVHN produces a higher likelihood when passed through the model trained on CIFAR-10 [31,34,43]. Recently, Serra et al. showed that anomalous high-likelihood data could be linked to complexity [43]. They find that the simplicity of SVHN data compared to CIFAR-10 data causes the deep learning model to exercise a higher likelihood on SVHN examples than the complex CIFAR-10 data. They use image compression scores as a complexity metric (likelihood ratio) to determine whether the high likelihood can be attributed to lower complexity.

2.5   Complexity and Anomaly Detection in Security

Interestingly, a similar complexity finding to [43] was found in a recent security paper [19]. Using data from various IoT devices, they find that each device has varying complexity. They formalize a complexity measure (IP Spread/IP

Depth) per device in order to fine-tune an Isolation Forest anomaly detection algorithm. Their architecture, ComplexIoT, measures network traffic on a device level, which can be used in Host Intrusion Detection Systems. This work is similar to ComplexIoT [19] in that we propose a complexity measurement; however, there are several key differences: (i) We analyze IoT datasets both from the point of view of network-level and the device level, while ComplexIoT only looks at device level complexity. (ii) ComplexIoT proposes a device complexity score to moderate the contamination rate of an Isolation Forest. This is problematic as it assumes $x\%$ of a device's traffic will be malicious given a complexity score and lead to false positives. (iii) The ComplexIoT complexity score is based on IP spread and IP depth and does not consider other network features to compute its complexity estimate. (iv) The efficacy of the ComplexIoT approach has not been measured via binary classification metrics on benign and malicious examples. In this paper, we measure the results of the weighted Hamming LID estimator on common IoT network Intrusion datasets.

3   Proposed Approach

We begin by explaining concepts and mathematics behind ID, in order to gain an intuitive understanding of the approach. We will then use this to detail LID. Next, we describe our approach to measuring LID in IoT datasets. Finally, we summarize the Weighted Hamming Distance LID Estimator, including the algorithm details, baseline models we compare against, and our experimental protocol.

3.1   Intrinsic Dimensionality

The ID of a dataset can be thought of as the minimum number of variables needed to retain a full approximation of the data [8]. It is based on the observation that high-dimensional data can often be described by a lower number of variables. The utility of lower dimensional representations is apparent throughout ML research, from data compression (such as autoencoders [21]) to dimensionality reduction (PCA). ID is akin to autoencoders and PCA, however quite distinct in that its an estimate of the lowest possible dimension of a dataset (e.g. the lowest possible bottleneck size in an autoencoder), and not a reduction technique in itself. ID can be thought of as a geometric property to measure complexity of a dataset as a whole [50].

Formally, the ID of dataset $\mathcal{X} \in \mathbb{R}^{m \times n}$, with m samples and n features, lies on a lower dimensional manifold $\mathcal{M}$, where $ID = dim(\mathcal{M})$, i.e. ID is the dimension of the manifold $\mathcal{M}$ of the data. Usually, the ID measurement is significantly less than extrinsic dimension n, or number of features.

The main approach to estimate ID involves examining the neighborhood around a reference point x_i for each x in $\mathcal{X}$. A common equation used in existing research was proposed by Levina and Bickel [27]:

$$ID(\mathcal{X}) = \left(\frac{1}{m(k-1)} \sum_{i=1}^{m} \sum_{j=1}^{k-1} log \frac{T_k(x_i)}{T_j(x_i)} \right)^{-1} \tag{1}$$

where m is the number of samples, x_i is a sample in the dataset, and k and j are integer values representing the kth and j^{th} nearest neighbors from x_i. $T_k(x_i)$ is the distance between x_i and x_k, similarly, $T_j(x_i)$ is the distance between x_i and x_j. Intuitively, Eq. 1 measures the rate that new neighbors are encountered as we move out from the reference point x_i.

Recently, ID has been gaining relevance in the machine learning community [4,6,36]. Pope et al. [36] showed that common computer vision datasets exhibit very low intrinsic dimension relative to their number of pixels. They also showed that the intrinsic dimension greatly impacts learning: the higher the intrinsic dimension of a dataset, the harder it is to learn from it. In addition, they showed that the extrinsic dimension of the dataset, *i.e.* the total number of pixels per image in a dataset, did not effect learning and generalization, indicating that sample complexity only depends on the intrinsic dimension rather than the total dimension of the dataset. Ansuini et al. [6] showed that neural networks exhibit low intrinsic dimensionality at deep layers of the models. Outside of deep learning, intrinsic dimensionality has been used in applications such as anomaly detection[46], clustering, similarity search, and deformation in complex materials.

3.2 Local Intrinsic Dimensionality

In contrast to ID, LID estimates individual data samples, rather than the full dataset. It is based on the observation that individual data points in a dataset often fit within a specific lower-dimensional structure when only considering a subset of the nearby data. As a result, these values can vary greatly within a dataset. Intuitively, the LID measurement can be interpreted as the dimension immediately surrounding a data point.

LID has been proposed for anomaly/out-of-distribution detection [48] as well as detection of adversarial examples in deep neural nets [28]. Theoretically, examples within a dataset should have lower LID values than anomalous examples generated from an alternative source.

Amsaleg et al. [4] propose several estimators for the LID, though they note that these are theoretical quantities and only estimates of the true local dimension. We use their Maximum Likelihood Estimator in Sect. 3.3. Their equation provides a strong balance between efficiency and complexity:

$$\widehat{LID}(x) = - \left(\frac{1}{k} \sum_{i=1}^{k} log \frac{r_i(x)}{r_k(x)} \right)^{-1} \tag{2}$$

where r_i is the distance of data point x to the ith closest neighbor and r_k is the distance to the kth neighbor. Additionally, it has been shown that hyperparameter k is sensitive and must be experimentally tuned. Equation 2 is a theoretical quantity, and it should be noted that $\widehat{LID}(x)$ is an *estimation*. Further, the dimension estimate is usually not an integer value, except in idealized distributions and datasets.

Ma et al. [28] used LID estimates to characterize adversarial subspaces in deep learning. They showed how traditional density measures can fail to detect adversarial examples in the final layers of deep learning models, while LID measurements can better characterize these subspaces. This is because traditional measures only measure the density of neighboring points surrounding an example, whereas LID measures the rate at which new neighbors occur.

Algorithm 1. Weighted Hamming Distance LID Estimator

Require: $\mathcal{X}_{train}, \mathcal{X}_{test}$, nearest neighbors k, threshold τ
Require: $\mathcal{X}_{train}$ contains only benign examples
  for x_i in $\mathcal{X}_{test}$ **do**
    $\{\mathcal{H}_1...\mathcal{H}_m\} \leftarrow \mathcal{H}(x_i, \{\mathcal{X}_{train}\})$
    $\{\mathcal{H}_1...\mathcal{H}_n\} \leftarrow$for all distinct $\mathcal{H}_i \in \{\mathcal{H}_1...\mathcal{H}_m\}$
    if 0 is in $\{\mathcal{H}_1...\mathcal{H}_n\}$ **then**
      x_i is benign (exact match)
    else
      $LID(x_i) \leftarrow LID(\{\mathcal{H}_1...\mathcal{H}_m\}, k)(Eq.2)$
      if $LID(x_i) \leq \tau$ **then**
        x_i is benign
      else
        x_i is malicious
      end if
    end if
  end for

3.3 Weighted Hamming Distance LID Estimator

LID is typically measured on a sample using distances from its neighbors in a dataset, and can be thought of as the *rate of growth* between a point and its neighbors. In this work, we use Eq. 2 for LID estimation, using the training data $\mathcal{X}_{train}$ as neighboring points.

Distance Metric. For the distance metric required in Eq. 2, we use Hamming Distance to compute similarity between both categorical and continuous feature points. Hamming distance is computed for continuous features by setting them to mismatching if they don't match exactly. While Euclidean Distance is typically used in Eq. 2 to measure LID, Ma et al. [28] suggested not using Euclidean Distance as the underlying distance metric. Choosing the Hamming Distance metric over Euclidean Distance for continuous variables showed better experimental results. Effectively, this turns each pairwise feature distance into a binary metric: 0 for same, 1 for different. We compute Hamming Distance using the Python SciPy library as:

$$\mathcal{H}(x_i, x_j) = \frac{\text{Number of mismatching features}}{\text{Total Features}} \tag{3}$$

Entropy. We calculate entropy of each feature and set it as the weight. In a dataset with n features, we set weight w_i for feature i to $n/Entropy(i)$, where the entropy of a feature i is:

$$-\sum_{j=1}^{m} p_j log_2(p_j) \tag{4}$$

and n is the total number of features and j are specific classes in the feature. p_j is calculated by getting the counts of each class within feature i. For example, the protocol feature may have TCP and UDP classes, we compute the counts for each to calculate entropy. We find that features with low entropy should be weighted more since they are stable properties of benign samples. For example, if benign examples come from TCP protocol 99% of the time, we can theorize that new examples matching the TCP protocol may be similar to a benign example.

After computing Hamming distance between x_i and the set of $\mathcal{X}_{train}$, we have a set of $\mathcal{H}_1...\mathcal{H}_m$ Hamming distances the size of $\mathcal{X}_{train}$. We filter all duplicate distances where $\mathcal{H}_i = \mathcal{H}_j$, to include only a single distance value for each cluster of distances, leaving a set of $\mathcal{H}_1...\mathcal{H}_n$ distances where $n \leq m$. In other words, when examples have the same distance $\mathcal{H}$ to a reference point x_i, we filter them into a single distance in order to gather a unique set of distances. From here, we are able to compute the final LID score using Eq. 2.

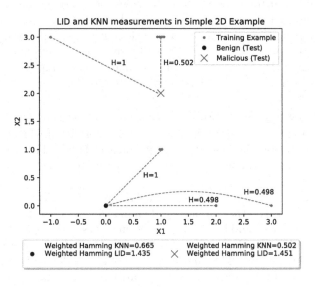

Fig. 1. A visual explanation of how the Weighted Hamming Distance LID estimator can detect anomalous examples where the traditional KNN algorithm will fail. See the end of Sect. 3.3 for more details.

Figure 1 depicts a visual example of how the Weighted Hamming LID Estimator can classify an anomalous example where the KNN algorithm will fail.
For example, the traditional KNN algorithm can discriminate test examples
as benign or malicious by measuring a samples average distance to K training
samples, where lower average distances indicate a benign example and higher
distances indicate a malicious example. Figure 1 shows how KNN can fail on a
simple two dimensional problem: the red X is closer to several training examples, however, the black dot matches the more relevant feature, X2. We show
how the LID estimate corrects this issue, yielding a lower value for the benign
example compared to the malicious example. We weight the Hamming distances
in the KNN and LID estimates with 2/Entropy of each feature. Entropy for X1
is 1.99 and 2.01 for X2. In the image, results are presented with a weighted
Hamming distance, however Euclidean distance yields the same results on KNN
when K = 3. Here, the LID is calculated as $-1/ln(0.502)$ and $-1/ln(0.498)$.

3.4 Baseline Models

In the previous section, we explain our proposed Weighted Hamming Distance
LID Estimator model. We compare our proposed model with several models as
baselines in the tasks of detecting attacks in the IoT networks. These models
include include several modern and classic algorithms: KNN, Isolation Forest,
and Autoencoder. In the following, we briefly explain each of these models.

KNN Algorithm. K-Nearest Neighbors (KNN) classification is an unsupervised machine learning model that measures the distance between a sample point
and its neighbors. It takes an arbitrary distance measurement and measures the
average distance between a reference point and its neighbors using this distance.
In our experiments, we take the average of these nearest neighbor distances and
use them to threshold scores. Theoretically, reference points with lower KNN
averages should belong to the normal, non-malicious examples in the dataset,
and malicious examples should have higher KNN averages.

Isolation Forest. Isolation Forest is an efficient algorithm to determine anomalies in an unsupervised manner. It does not need a profile of what is normal and
not normal and identifies anomalies independent of labels. The algorithm relies
on the tendency of anomalies to be easier to separate from the rest of the sample
compared to normal points.

Notably, an Isolation Forest was used in [19], where they tune the contamination parameter based on the complexity of an IoT device. They argue that devices
with low complexity should have contamination values close to zero because their
expected network traffic should fit certain patterns, hence the device should never
receive anomalous traffic. This means that, should the device be compromised,
the algorithm would likely not classify the attack as anomalous because of the
low expected contamination. As a result, the algorithms assumption that a certain percentage of examples are contaminated makes it vulnerable to changes in
the number of contaminated records.

Autoencoder. Autoencoder is a neural network based model commonly used for unsupervised anomaly detection, such as in [38]. The model compresses the training set into a bottleneck representation before reconstructing it. We train the autoencoder on benign examples, and in theory, the reconstruction loss should be smaller for all benign examples compared to malicious examples.

The objective function is the reconstruction loss: given example x and continuous feature x_c we use mean-squared error:

$$\mathcal{L}(x_c, x'_c) = ||x_c - x'_c||^2 \tag{5}$$

where x' is the reconstructed output of the neural network. For discrete categorical features, we encode the categories into embedding layers to input them into the model. The outputs of the autoencoder for categorical variables are one-hot vectors, denoted x_d, and we use cross entropy for the objective function:

$$\mathcal{L}(x_d, x'_d) = x_d log(x'_d) + (1 - x_d)log(1 - x'_d) \tag{6}$$

We sum the loss of the continuous and categorical variables to obtain the full reconstruction loss. We use Adam optimization with the default learning rate.

3.5   Experimental Setup

To train each model in an unsupervised manner, we first take all clean examples ($\mathcal{X}_{benign}$). For each experiment, we run the algorithm on $\mathcal{X}_{benign}$ using leave-one-out cross validation, *i.e.*, calculate distances $\mathcal{H}$ from x_i on each member of the training set but x_i. We also pass it the entire set of malicious data, $\mathcal{X}_{malicious}$. The result of each sample is either 0 distance, exact match, or a weighted Hamming LID estimate. Zero's are automatically classified as benign, while lower LID estimates are also classified as benign.

A proper threshold τ can be determined based on the desired accuracy rate. In other words, if its important to classify all malicious samples, we can set a lower τ for higher detection, though this may lead to some benign examples being classified as malicious (false positive).

To measure results, we use Receiver Operating Characteristic curve (ROC) and Precision-Recall curve (PR). ROC plots the True Positive Rate (TPR) against False Positive Rate (FPR). PR plots the precision versus the recall calculated by following formulas:

$$precision = \frac{True\ Positive}{True\ Positive + False\ Positive} \tag{7}$$

$$recall = \frac{True\ Positive}{True\ Positive + False\ Negative} \tag{8}$$

4   Datasets

This section summarizes the datasets we use in our experiments. We use three IoT related datasets: (*TON_IoT*, NF Bot-IoT, IoT-23,).

4.1 TON IoT

TON_IoT [3,32], published in 2020, comprises heterogeneous IoT data across several devices. The work uses several data source types, including sensor, raw, and log data. Additionally, it includes several infrastructure layers in the testbed architecture, such as the edge, fog, and cloud layers with nine types of generated attacks: Distributed Denial-of-Service (DDoS), Scanning, Ransomware, Backdoor, and Injection attacks. The dataset has 41 total features; however, the authors recommend not to use source IP/port and destination IP/port. The dataset simulates traffic from seven IoT sensors: weather, smart garage door, smart fridge, smart TCP/IP Modbus, GPS tracker, motion-enabled light, and a smart thermostat.

4.2 NF Bot-IoT

NF Bot-IoT [42] is a dataset based on the BotNet IoT dataset [24,25]. Botnets are an important attack vector to protect against as they have been the source of several breaches over the past few years [24]. NF Bot-IoT converts four common network NIDS datasets into network flow datasets using the commonly deployed NetFlow [12] protocol for network traffic collection. Authors argue NetFlow's features are easier to extract compared to the complex features used in the original NIDS datasets since NetFlow's features are usually extracted from packet headers. The dataset includes several attacks, including DDoS, Denial-of-Service (DoS), OS and Service Scan, Keylogging, and Data exfiltration attacks.

4.3 IoT-23

IoT-23 [15] was released in 2020. The dataset has 23 different scenarios, of which three are benign traffic scenarios captured on real IoT devices. The dataset contains almost 11 million total records; however, with the difficulty of modeling this much data, we sample a million records with the following logic: From the entire dataset, we sample 500K malicious records and 500K benign examples from simulated files that contain a source IP or destination IP with an internal IP address and have at least 50 samples belonging to that specific IP address. We find that 99.99% of internal IPs have at least 50 samples. We also included all samples from three real devices (Philips HUE smart LED lamp, Amazon Echo, and a Somfy smart door lock) with 1,634 total packets.

We categorize these devices similar to IoT-Sense as a light (Philips HUE smart LED lamp), Smart Controller (Amazon Echo), and Appliance (Somfy smart door lock). Philips HUE light is in both datasets so that it can be used for comparison device-specific ID measurements.

This dataset also captures 20 simulated scenarios of both benign and malicious traffic. It offers several attack examples: DDoS, FileDownload (to infected device), HeartBeat (indicates packets sent on the connection are used to keep track of infected host by CC server), Mirai, Torii, and Okiru BotNets (new common attacks), and HorizontalPortScan (used to gather information for further attacks).

Table 1. Dataset summaries including total number of samples, percentage of benign samples, percentage of malicious samples, percent duplicates, number of features, and number of attacks.

Name	Samples	Ben(%)	Mal(%)	Dup (%)	Feats(#)	Attk(#)
UNSW-NB15	82K	45%	55%	12.5%	42	-
KDD Cup	24K	45.8%	54.2%	0%	41	-
TON_IoT	461K	65%	35%	62%	38	9
IoT-23	1M	50%	50%	2%	19	7
IoT Sense	54K	100%	0	63%	21	-
NF Bot-IoT	599K	21.7%	78.3	0%	12	4

4.4 IoT Dataset Features

We use the available features for each dataset, except we exclude source and destination IP and port as well as any ID or timestamp columns for *TON_IoT* and IoT-23. We include IPs and ports in NF Bot-IoT because of its small number of available features to provide more discriminability. Features among the datasets include protocol, source, and destination bytes, connection state, service, duration, missed bytes, number of packets, window size, payload, entropy, DNS, SSL, and HTTP properties.

5 Anomaly Detection Results

In this section, we summarize our findings of LID measurements on IoT networks, showing that we can use the localized complexity measurement of LID to detect anomalous behavior.

5.1 Algorithm Comparison Results

Gorbett et al. [17] showed that benign IoT network datasets and devices exhibit low ID measurements. In this section, we extend this finding to the sample level, showing that malicious examples have higher LID. We use this finding for the task of anomaly detection, using three public IoT datasets with benign and malicious examples. Results are compared against each other in Table 2.

Table 2 reports results of our proposed Weighted Hamming LID versus other baseline models of KNN and Weighted Hamming KNN, Isolation Forest, and the Autoencoder. We run experiments with four different K values of 3, 5, 10, and 20 for the KNN and Weighted Hamming algorihtms, and report the best findings of each. In all three cases, the same K value performed the best between KNN, Weighted KNN, and Weighted Hamming LID algorithms for the given dataset. For NF Bot-IoT K = 5, *TON_IoT* K = 10, and IoT-23 K = 3.

Our algorithm outperforms baseline models in all but one case (*TON_IoT* PR performs best with the Autoencoder). The most notable results were with the IoT-23 and NF Bot-IoT datasets, where the algorithm outperformed other unsupervised learning algorithms in both ROC and PR scores.

Table 2. Results of the Weighted Hamming LID algorithm on 3 datasets, plus the results of four baseline models. We experiment with K values of 3, 5, 10, and 20 for the KNN, KNN (Weighted Hamming), and Weighted Hamming LID estimators. We choose the K with the best result for each experiment, with K = 5, 10, and 3 for NF Bot-IoT, *TON_IoT*, and IoT-23 respectively. The best ROC and PR for each dataset is in bold.

	NF Bot-IoT		Ton-IoT		IoT-23	
Test Type	ROC	PR	ROC	PR	ROC	PR
Isolation Forest	0.957	0.999	0.567	0.364	0.492	0.594
KNN	0.961	0.999	0.973	0.943	0.990	0.970
Weighted Hamming KNN	0.955	0.998	0.973	0.944	0.990	0.918
Autoencoder	0.944	0.998	0.981	**0.985**	0.981	.972
Weighted Hamming LID (Ours)	**0.970**	**0.999**	**0.985**	0.983	**0.998**	**0.994**

Table 3. Anomaly Detection Results specific attack type available in each dataset. Varied results indicate networks may be more prone specific attacks in IoT networks.

Dataset	Attack	Sample Size	ROC	PR
IoT-23	Horiz.PortScan	199,283	0.998	0.989
	DDoS	54,750	0.999	0.892
	Okiru	53,959	0.999	0.701
	C&C	271	0.999	0.632
NF Bot-IoT	Theft	1,909	0.990	0.902
	DDoS	56,844	0.999	0.999
	DoS	56,833	0.998	0.999
	Recon.	470,655	0.963	0.999
TON_IoT	Scanning	19,995	0.993	0.812
	DoS	19,994	0.987	0.755
	Injection	19,930	0.995	0.932
	DDoS	19,790	0.966	0.838
	Password	17,428	0.970	0.746
	XSS	8,914	0.952	0.727
	Ransomware	7,221	0.983	0.511
	Backdoor	19,908	0.983	0.621
	MITM	1,041	0.988	0.523

Notably, algorithms that performed distance computations to their closest neighbors exhibited the best results (KNN, weighted Hamming KNN, and LID algorithms). Isolation Forest had low results for both *TON_IoT* and IoT-23. The Autoencoder did well on two out of the three datasets, but did not perform as well on NF Bot-IoT.

The Weighted Hamming LID algorithm showed the most consistent results across all three datasets, highlighting its efficacy and promise as a robust approach.

These results indicate it is a strong alternative to classic anomaly detection algorithms such as the Autoencoder, Isolation Forest, and K-nearest neighbors. The algorithm shows promising results across three unique IoT datasets, indicating it generalizes well to several types of attacks and network datasets.

5.2 Attacks Specific Results

In this experiment, we break down our results by attack in each IoT dataset using the Weighted Hamming Distance LID estimator. We group some IoT-23 attacks based on their broad category; for example, we group File Download and Heartbeat attacks as C&C, because these attacks both come from a known C&C server and they have a small overall sample size. The results of this experiment is reported in Table 3,

Results are varied for IoT-23 and *TON_IoT*; stronger results for NF Bot-IoT. While some attacks are easily recognizable by our algorithm, such Distributed Denial-of-Service (DDoS) and DoS attacks, others do very poorly, such *TON_IoT*'s Ransomware, Backdoor, and Man-in-the-middle attack (MITM) attacks.

The first two datasets in Table 3, IoT-23 and NF Bot-IoT, performed well on all ROC metrics for each attack. Precision-Recall metrics performed slightly worse than ROC in IoT-23, with lower values for Okiru and C&C attacks. We found that both attacks had network packets that were largely indistinguishable from benign network. For example, Okiru attacks were generally TCP protocol with packet count of 1 and low byte count, similar to many benign network packets.

While the results of attack detection using the Weighted Hamming Distance LID estimator are stronger than other algorithms, results on specific attack types show that IoT networks may still be vulnerable in certain cases. In particular, *TON_IoT* did not perform as well, leading us to further analyze the data. We found that of 300K benign examples, 61.8% were packets with an exact match with another benign packet, *i.e.*, all 38 features had the same value. Further, more than 26K malicious examples had an exact match with at least one benign sample. These factors indicate that the data generated for *TON_IoT* has low discriminability when excluding source and destination IPs and ports, as we did. We note in Sect. 4.4 that the authors of the original papers [3,32] performed supervised classification on *TON_IoT*, yielding high accuracy using both source and destination IPs and ports. They recommended removing source and destination IPs and ports for further experimentation, however, the remaining 38 features contained identical or close to identical values for benign and malicious examples.

6 Conclusion

In this work, we view several network datasets through the lens of complexity and show that IoT datasets exhibit a lower ID complexity estimate than standard network collections. This finding extends to the point-wise estimation of complexity, where individual samples in (benign) IoT datasets contain low LID measures. We show that benign examples can be identified by either 1) exactly matching the features of a training set sample or 2) by a low LID estimate. We propose a novel algorithm for detecting malicious actors in an unsupervised manner, providing the ability to deploy a model into production with only two hyperparameters needed (k value for distance measurements and threshold value τ). The algorithm is based on the theoretical LID estimation using the Hill MLE estimator, using an entropy weighted Hamming distance for measuring distances between points and features.

Future Work. Several avenues can be explored to extend this work in future research. First, evaluating our model with a broader set of attacks would enable a more robust picture of LID's strengths and weaknesses. Second, this work focused on regular IoT networks. In the future, we want to investigate the applicability of our approach on specialized IoT networks, such as industrial IoT. Lastly, evaluating the LID metric in more complex domains, such as more complex network architectures, would provide a broader picture of the algorithms capabilities.

References

1. Ahmad, R., Alsmadi, I.: Machine learning approaches to IoT security: a systematic literature review. Internet Things. **14**, 100365 (2021). https://doi.org/10.1016/j.iot.2021.100365, https://www.sciencedirect.com/science/article/pii/S2542660521000093
2. Alaba, F.A., Othman, M., Hashem, I.A.T., Alotaibi, F.: Internet of Things security: a survey. J. Netw. Comput. App. **88**, 10–28 (2017). https://doi.org/10.1016/j.jnca.2017.04.002, https://www.sciencedirect.com/science/article/pii/S1084804517301455
3. Alsaedi, A., Moustafa, N., Tari, Z., Mahmood, A., Anwar, A.: TON_IoT telemetry dataset: a new generation dataset of IoT and IIoT for data-driven intrusion detection systems. IEEE Access **8**, 165130–165150 (2020). https://doi.org/10.1109/ACCESS.2020.3022862
4. Amsaleg, L., et al.: Estimating local intrinsic dimensionality. In: Proceedings of the 21th ACM SIGKDD International Conference on Knowledge Discovery and Data Mining, pp. 29–38. KDD 2015, Association for Computing Machinery (2015). https://doi.org/10.1145/2783258.2783405
5. Andrea, I., Chrysostomou, C., Hadjichristofi, G.: Internet of things: security vulnerabilities and challenges. In: IEEE Symposium on Computers and Communication (ISCC), pp. 180–187 (2015). https://doi.org/10.1109/ISCC.2015.7405513
6. Ansuini, A., Laio, A., Macke, J.H., Zoccolan, D.: Intrinsic dimension of data representations in deep neural networks. arXiv:1905.12784 [cs, stat] (2019)
7. Azmoodeh, A., Dehghantanha, A., Choo, K.K.R.: Robust malware detection for internet of (battlefield) things devices using deep eigenspace learning. IEEE Trans. Sustain. Comput. **4**(1), 88–95 (2019). https://doi.org/10.1109/TSUSC.2018.2809665
8. Bernal, D.: 3 - Analytical techniques for damage detection and localization for assessing and monitoring civil infrastructures. In: Wang, M.L., Lynch, J.P., Sohn, H. (eds.) Sensor Technologies for Civil Infrastructures, vol. 56, pp. 67–92. Woodhead Publishing (2014). https://doi.org/10.1533/9781782422433.1.67, https://www.sciencedirect.com/science/article/pii/B978178242242650003X

9. Bezawada, B., Bachani, M., Peterson, J., Shirazi, H., Ray, I., Ray, I.: IoTSense: behavioral fingerprinting of IoT devices. arXiv:1804.03852 [cs] (2018)

10. Bhatia, S., Jain, A., Li, P., Kumar, R., Hooi, B.: MSTREAM: fast anomaly detection in multi-aspect streams.In: Proceedings of the Web Conference 2021, pp. 3371–3382 (2021). https://doi.org/10.1145/3442381.3450023, http://arxiv.org/abs/2009.08451

11. Choudhary, D.: Security challenges and countermeasures for the heterogeneity of IoT applications. J. Autonom. Intell. 1, 16 (2019). https://doi.org/10.32629/jai.v1i2.25, http://en.front-sci.com/index.php/JAI/article/view/25

12. Claise, B.: Cisco Systems NetFlow Services Export Version 9. Request for Comments RFC 3954, Internet Engineering Task Force (2004). https://doi.org/10.17487/RFC3954, https://datatracker.ietf.org/doc/rfc3954

13. Conti, M., Dehghantanha, A., Franke, K., Watson, S.: Internet of Things security and forensics: challenges and opportunities. Future Gener. Comput. Syst. 78, 544–546 (2018). https://doi.org/10.1016/j.future.2017.07.060, http://arxiv.org/abs/1807.10438

14. Elrawy, M.F., Awad, A.I., Hamed, H.F.A.: Intrusion detection systems for IoT-based smart environments: a survey. J. Cloud Comput. 7(1), 21 (2018). https://doi.org/10.1186/s13677-018-0123-6

15. Garcia, S., Parmisano, A., Erquiaga, M.J.: IoT-23 dataset: a labeled dataset of malware and benign IoT traffic. (version 1.0.0) [data set] zenodo. https://www.stratosphereips.org/datasets-iot23

16. Gorbett, M., Blanchard, N.: Utilizing network properties to detect erroneous inputs. arXiv:2002.12520 [cs] (2020)

17. Gorbett, M., Shirazi, H., Ray, I.: The intrinsic dimensionality of IoT networks. In: Proceedings of the 2022 ACM Symposium on Access Control Models and Technologies (SACMAT) (2022)

18. HaddadPajouh, H., Dehghantanha, A., Khayami, R., Choo, K.K.R.: A deep Recurrent Neural Network based approach for Internet of Things malware threat hunting. Future Gener. Comput. Syst. 85, 1-9 (2018). https://doi.org/10.1016/j.future.2018.03.007, https://www.sciencedirect.com/science/article/pii/S0167739X1732486X

19. Haefner, K., Ray, I.: ComplexIoT: Behavior-based trust for IoT networks. In: 2019 First IEEE International Conference on Trust, Privacy and Security in Intelligent Systems and Applications (TPS-ISA), pp. 56–65 (2019). https://doi.org/10.1109/TPS-ISA48467.2019.00016

20. Hendrycks, D., Gimpel, K.: A Baseline for detecting misclassified and out-of-distribution examples in neural networks. arXiv:1610.02136 [cs] (2018)

21. Hinton, G.E., Salakhutdinov, R.R.: Reducing the dimensionality of data with neural networks. Science 313(5786), 504–507 (Jul 2006). https://doi.org/10.1126/science.1127647, https://www.science.org/doi/10.1126/science.1127647

22. Kasongo, S.M., Sun, Y.: Performance analysis of intrusion detection systems using a feature selection method on the UNSW-NB15 dataset. J. Big Data 7, 105 (2020). https://doi.org/10.1186/s40537-020-00379-6

23. Kollolu, R.: A Review on wide variety and heterogeneity of IoT platforms. SSRN Scholarly Paper ID 3912454, Social Science Research Network, Rochester, NY (2020). https://doi.org/10.2139/ssrn.3912454, https://papers.ssrn.com/abstract=3912454

24. Koroniotis, N., Moustafa, N., Sitnikova, E., Slay, J.: towards developing network forensic mechanism for botnet activities in the IoT based on machine learning techniques. In: Mobile Networks and Management. pp. 30–44. Springer International Publishing, Cham (2018). https://doi.org/10.1007/978-3-319-90775-83

25. Koroniotis, N., Moustafa, N., Sitnikova, E., Turnbull, B.: Towards the development of realistic botnet dataset in the Internet of Things for network forensic analytics: Bot-IoT dataset. Future Gener. Comput. Syst. **100**, 779–796 (2019). https://doi.org/10.1016/j.future.2019.05.041, https://www.sciencedirect.com/science/article/pii/S0167739X18327687

26. Kozik, R., Pawlicki, M., Choraś, M.: A new method of hybrid time window embedding with transformer-based traffic data classification in IoT-networked environment. Pattern Anal. Appl. **24**(4), 1441–1449 (2021). https://doi.org/10.1007/s10044-021-00980-2, https://www.mendeley.com/catalogue/92cc3e51-9dc9-3c8e-9e05-aeea7382b93c/

27. Levina, E., Bickel, P.J.: Maximum Likelihood estimation of intrinsic dimension. In: Proceedings of the 17th International Conference on Neural Information Processing Systems, pp. 777–784. NIPS 2004, MIT Press, Cambridge, MA, USA (2004)

28. Ma, X.,et al.: Characterizing Adversarial Subspaces Using Local Intrinsic Dimensionality. arXiv:1801.02613 [cs] (2018)

29. Meftah, S., Rachidi, T., Assem, N.: Network based intrusion detection using the UNSW-NB15 dataset. Int. J. Comput. Digital Syst. **8**, 478–487 (2019). https://doi.org/10.12785/ijcds/080505, https://journal.uob.edu.bh:443/handle/123456789/3580

30. Mohsin, M., Anwar, Z., Husari, G., Al-Shaer, E., Rahman, M.A.: IoTSAT: a formal framework for security analysis of the internet of things (IoT). In: 2016 IEEE Conference on Communications and Network Security (CNS), pp. 180–188 (2016). https://doi.org/10.1109/CNS.2016.7860484

31. Morningstar, W., Ham, C., Gallagher, A., Lakshminarayanan, B., Alemi, A., Dillon, J.: Density of states estimation for out of distribution detection. In: Proceedings of The 24th International Conference on Artificial Intelligence and Statistics, pp. 3232–3240. PMLR (2021). https://proceedings.mlr.press/v130/morningstar21a.html

32. Moustafa, N.: A new distributed architecture for evaluating AI-based security systems at the edge: network TON_iot datasets. Sustain. Cities Soc. **72**, 102994 (2021). https://doi.org/10.1016/j.scs.2021.102994, https://www.sciencedirect.com/science/article/pii/S2210670721002808

33. Moustafa, N., Slay, J.: UNSW-NB15: a comprehensive data set for network intrusion detection systems (UNSW-NB15 network data set). In: 2015 Military Communications and Information Systems Conference (MilCIS), pp. 1–6 (2015). https://doi.org/10.1109/MilCIS.2015.7348942

34. Nalisnick, E., Matsukawa, A., Teh, Y.W., Gorur, D., Lakshminarayanan, B.: Do Deep Generative Models Know What They Don't Know? (2018). https://openreview.net/forum?id=H1xwNhCcYm

35. Tapping AI for Intrusion Detection Systems, October 2021. https://www.iotworldtoday.com/2021/10/18/tapping-ai-for-intrusion-detection-systems/

36. Pope, P., Zhu, C., Abdelkader, A., Goldblum, M., Goldstein, T.: The Intrinsic Dimension of Images and Its Impact on Learning (2020). https://openreview.net/forum?id=XJk19XzGq2J

37. Rashma, B.M., Macherla, S., Jaiswal, A., Poornima, G.: Handling heterogeneity in an IoT infrastructure. In: Patnaik, S., Yang, X.-S., Sethi, I.K. (eds.) Advances in Machine Learning and Computational Intelligence. AIS, pp. 635–643. Springer, Singapore (2021). https://doi.org/10.1007/978-981-15-5243-4_60
38. Rezvy, S., Luo, Y., Petridis, M., Lasebae, A., Zebin, T.: An efficient deep learning model for intrusion classification and prediction in 5G and IoT networks. In: 2019 53rd Annual Conference on Information Sciences and Systems (CISS), pp. 1–6 (2019). https://doi.org/10.1109/CISS.2019.8693059
39. Rizvi, S., Orr, R., Cox, A., Ashokkumar, P., Rizvi, M.R.: Identifying the attack surface for IoT network. Internet Things. **9**, 100162 (2020). https://doi.org/10.1016/j.iot.2020.100162, https://www.sciencedirect.com/science/article/pii/S2542660520300056
40. Roy, B., Cheung, H.: A Deep Learning Approach for Intrusion Detection in Internet of Things using Bi-Directional Long Short-Term Memory Recurrent Neural Network, pp. 1–6 (2018). https://doi.org/10.1109/ATNAC.2018.8615294. ISSN: 2474-154X
41. Sahu, A.K., Sharma, S., Tanveer, M., Raja, R.: Internet of Things attack detection using hybrid Deep Learning Model. Comput. Commun. **176**, 146–154 (2021). https://doi.org/10.1016/j.comcom.2021.05.024, https://www.sciencedirect.com/science/article/pii/S0140366421002164
42. Sarhan, M., Layeghy, S., Moustafa, N., Portmann, M.: NetFlow datasets for machine learning-based network intrusion detection systems. In: Deze, Z., Huang, H., Hou, R., Rho, S., Chilamkurti, N. (eds.) BDTA/WiCON -2020. LNICST, vol. 371, pp. 117–135. Springer, Cham (2021). https://doi.org/10.1007/978-3-030-72802-1_9
43. Serrà, J., Álvarez, D., Gómez, V., Slizovskaia, O., Núñez, J.F., Luque, J.: Input Complexity and Out-of-distribution Detection with Likelihood-based Generative Models (2019). https://openreview.net/forum?id=SyxIWpVYvr
44. Shone, N., Ngoc, T.N., Phai, V.D., Shi, Q.: A deep learning approach to network intrusion detection. IEEE Trans. Emerg. Topics Comput. Intell. **2**, 41–50 (2018). https://doi.org/10.1109/TETCI.2017.2772792
45. Singh, P., Jaykumar, J., Pankaj, A., Mitra, R.: Edge-Detect: Edge-centric Network Intrusion Detection using Deep Neural Network. arXiv:2102.01873 [cs], February 2021
46. Stolz, B.J., Tanner, J., Harrington, H.A., Nanda, V.: Geometric anomaly detection in data. Proc. Natl. Acad. Sci. **117**(33), 19664–19669 (2020). https://doi.org/10.1073/pnas.2001741117, https://www.pnas.org/content/117/33/19664
47. Vasudevan, A., Harshini, E., Selvakumar, S.: SSENet-2011: a network intrusion detection system dataset and its comparison with KDD CUP 99 dataset. In: 2011 Second Asian Himalayas International Conference on Internet (AH-ICI), pp. 1–5 (2011). https://doi.org/10.1109/AHICI.2011.6113948
48. Wang, Q., Erfani, S.M., Leckie, C., Houle, M.E.: A Dimensionality-Driven Approach for Unsupervised Out-of-distribution Detection, p. 9 (2021)
49. Zhao, K., Ge, L.: A Survey on the Internet of Things Security, pp. 663–667 (2013). DOI: https://doi.org/10.1109/CIS.2013.145
50. Zhou, S., Tordesillas, A., Pouragha, M., Bailey, J., Bondell, H.: On local intrinsic dimensionality of deformation in complex materials. Sci. Rep. **11**(1), 10216 (2021). https://doi.org/10.1038/s41598-021-89328-8, https://www.nature.com/articles/s41598-021-89328-8

On the Data Privacy, Security, and Risk Postures of IoT Mobile Companion Apps

Shradha Neupane[1], Faiza Tazi[2], Upakar Paudel[3], Freddy Veloz Baez[1],
Merzia Adamjee[1], Lorenzo De Carli[1(✉)], Sanchari Das[2], and Indrakshi Ray[3]

[1] Worcester Polytechnic Institute, Worcester, MA 01609, USA
{sneupane,fevelozbaez,madamjee,ldecarli}@wpi.edu
[2] University of Denver, Denver, CO 80208, USA
{Faiza.Tazi,Sanchari.Das}@du.edu
[3] Colorado State University, Fort Collins, CO 80523, USA
{Upakar.Paudel,Indrakshi.Ray}@colostate.edu

Abstract. Most Internet of Things (IoT) devices provide access through mobile companion apps to configure, update, and control the devices. In many cases, these apps handle all user data moving in and out of devices and cloud endpoints. Thus, they constitute a critical component in the IoT ecosystem from a privacy standpoint, but they have historically been understudied. In this paper, we perform a latitudinal study and analysis of a sample of 455 IoT companion apps to understand their privacy posture using various methods and evaluate whether apps follow best practices. Specifically, we focus on three aspects: data privacy, securityOur findings indicate: (i) apps may over-request permissions, particularly for tasks that are not related to their functioning; and (ii) there is widespread use of programming and configuration practices which may reduce security, with the concerning extreme of two apps transmitting credentials in unencrypted form.

Keywords: IoT security · IoT privacy · Mobile security

1 Introduction

The Internet of Things (IoT) has become an integral part of our everyday lives, for convenience, entertainment [32], health monitoring [23], online education [46], and other daily activities [62]. However, with increasing interactions of IoT devices with users through their companion mobile apps, inadequate privacy and security has caused several breaches [15,24]. Prior research on the privacy and security of IoT devices mostly focuses on the devices themselves. Thus, it leaves out a crucial component: the mobile apps through which users configure and control

Shradha Neupane and Faiza Tazi contributed equally as first authors. This work was supported in part by funding from NSF under Award Number CNS 1822118, NIST, ARL, Statnett, AMI, Cyber Risk Research, NewPush, State of Colorado Cybersecurity Center, and a gift from Google.

S. Sural and H. Lu (Eds.): DBSec 2022, LNCS 13383, pp. 162–182, 2022.
https://doi.org/10.1007/978-3-031-10684-2_10

IoT devices. Such IoT companion apps have visibility on the information flowing through devices (e.g., camera streams, network details) [41,58], and retain their potentially sensitive operations (e.g., smart locks, children toys) [16,59]. Thus, from a privacy, security, and risk standpoint they are a critical gateway; programming and design bugs, and deliberate leaking of personal data, can have a critical negative impact on users.

Our goal is to generate an understanding of privacy-related behavior and issues in IoT companion apps. We explicitly design our effort as a latitudinal study, i.e., we aim at carrying a selected number of privacy-related analyses on a large number of apps. We limit ourselves to analyzing companion apps in isolation, because analyzing each app as it interacts with its specific IoT device is not practical for a large scale study. We collect apps (N = **455**) from the Google Play Store [7] using a hybrid method that combines automatic scraping with manual review. We inspect the collected apps using a number of relevant analyses leveraging, where possible, existing industry-standard tools. The tools measure app posture in terms of three different aspects: data privacy, security (e.g. absence of privacy-sensitive vulnerability), and risk (i.e., app trustworthiness). The data privacy and security analyses focus on issues that can be specifically identified; whereas the risk analysis attempts to estimate the potential for latent issues that cannot yet be discovered.

We aim to answer the following research questions with regards to IoT apps:

RQ1: How do companion apps fare with respect to the measured security- and privacy-related aspects? Are there significant general concerns broadly affecting companion apps? Furthermore, the use of heterogeneous analyses covering multiple app aspects also allows us to answer an additional important empirical question: *RQ2: Is there evidence of positive or negative correlation between metrics measuring different aspects of app privacy (e.g., sensitive permissions and presence of vulnerabilities)?*

Our analysis finds that many apps over-request permissions that appear to be unrelated to their core functionality. Moreover, there are many apps which deploy insecure programming or configuration practices, with the extreme of two apps transmitting user credentials in cleartext. **Our work makes the following contributions:** (i) We propose a *threat model* informed by domain expertise, and derive broad analysis categories from the model. (ii) We propose a method to identify and scrape IoT companion apps from the Google Play Store. (iii) We define methods to quantitatively and reproducibly assess aspects of companion app privacy along the dimension of data privacy, security, and risk as it correlates with the privacy and security of the IoT device itself. (iv) We perform a large-scale measurement study of the properties[1]. (v) We investigate whether privacy aspects correlate among multiple measured dimensions.

2   Threat Model

We adopt a holistic definition of IoT apps: *An IoT device is one which senses/ actuates the physical world and is able to exchange sensing/actuation data with*

---

[1] Our raw metrics are anonymously available at https://osf.io/gf7cs/?view_only=c70 1039702f648849e32ecd4c2e1fd54.

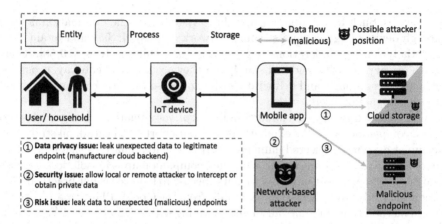

Fig. 1. IoT ecosystem and threat model of IoT companion apps

another networked node [33,47]. In practice, this style of definition is typically and implicitly extended to exclude non-embedded computing devices such as laptops and smartphones; we follow the same approach in our work. We define a companion app as follows: *a companion app is an app which connects to an IoT device over a network, to rely actuation commands or receive sensing data.*

Our ecosystem consists of a user, an IoT device, a companion IoT app, and the cloud backend. Our model is adapted from the LINNDUN threat modeling system [66]: in Fig. 1 the system is depicted as a dataflow diagram, where nodes can be *entities, processes,* and *data stores.* Flows of sensitive user data are represented as arrows. We also represent attacker-related entities. We make some simplifying assumptions. First, we define as "sensitive user data" any data existing on the user phone, for which the user has a reasonable expectation of privacy. Second, we assume the user is in agreement with IoT device data being transmitted/received to/from the IoT device and a cloud backend managed by the device manufacture that is needed for its core functionality. Furthermore, we define as *privacy leak* any companion app-mediated unwanted access to sensitive user data, where "unwanted" may mean: (i) the app accesses/transmits data which are not necessary to carry out its function *(data privacy issue)*; (ii) app is vulnerable/misconfigured allowing an attacker to access data *(security issue)*; (iii) app transmit data to unexpected endpoints and/or perform malicious actions *(risk issue)*.

3   Data Collection and Analysis

We adapt the data collection methodology proposed by Wang et al. [64] and follow up with manual removal of all non-IoT apps. The procedure includes:

[Step 1: Manual Search] We manually downloaded IoT apps from the Google Play Store based on definition of IoT apps (ref. Sect. 1). This entailed searching for apps used in the context of smart home/IoT. This forms our *Seed App Set.*

Table 1. Details of privacy categories and their associated permissions.

Category	Permissions
Network	INTERNET, ACCESS_NETWORK_STATE, CHANGE_NETWORK_STATE, ACCESS_WIFI_STATE, CHANGE_WIFI_STATE, CHANGE_WIFI_MULTICAST_STATE
Content	WRITE_MEDIA_STORAGE, READ_EXTERNAL_STORAGE, WRITE_EXTERNAL_STORAGE, MANAGE_EXTERNAL_STORAGE, MANAGE_MEDIA, MOUNT_FORMAT_FILESYSTEMS
Location	ACCESS_FINE_LOCATION, ACCESS_COARSE_LOCATION ACCESS_BACKGROUND_LOCATION, ACCESS_MEDIA_LOCATION ACCESS_LOCATION_EXTRA_COMMANDS
Device Id	READ_PHONE_STATE, READ_BASIC_PHONE_STATE READ_PRECISE_PHONE_STATE, MODIFY_PHONE_STATE
Contact	WRITE_CONTACTS, ACCOUNT_MANAGER,READ_CONTACTS
Telephony Services	CALL_PHONE, PROCESS_OUTGOING_CALLS, READ_SMS, SEND_SMS READ_PHONE_NUMBERS, USE_SIP, MANAGE_ONGOING_CALLS CALL_PRIVILEGED, ANSWER_PHONE_CALLS, WRITE_CALL_LOG READ_CALL_LOG, RECEIVE_SMS
Calendar	WRITE_CALENDAR, READ_CALENDAR

[Step 2: App Scraping] We scraped more related IoT apps, starting from our seed set and following the "Similar Apps" suggestions presented by the Play Store. We used play-scraper [44] to collect app names and descriptions.

[Step 3: Keyword-based Filtering] We found a high number of false positives (i.e. apps that do not match our definition of IoT companion apps) in Step 2. Therefore, we first removed apps matching specific keywords (e.g., *currency, compiler, etc.*). We generated the set of keywords empirically, by identifying keywords highly correlated with false positives.

[Step 4: Naïve-Bayes Classification] We refined the candidate set by using machine learning to classify IoT and non-IoT apps. We first attempted to apply the BERT algorithm [26] to leverage context for better classification and Logistic Regression Model in conjunction with the TF-IDF vectorizer. However, these algorithms performed poorly on our dataset. Using a Naïve-Bayes classifier lead to better, but still suboptimal accuracy (64.6%) on a small set of manually labeled data.

[Step 5: Manual Filtering] We manually reviewed all apps classified by Naïve Bayes as IoT-related and we retained only those which unambiguously match our definition of companion app (given in Sect. 2).

Data collection results: We downloaded the app packages (APKs) using Play-storeDownloader [11]. Our initial set of **2000** scraped apps was reduced to **1596** by keyword-based and Naïve Bayes filtering (a **20%** reduction). Manual inspection determined that only **484 (30%)** were matching our definition and thus relevant to our analysis. We retained only **455** APKS as the remaining apps could not be downloaded, or were in a format incompatible with our tooling.

Table 2. Data privacy categories relevant to our analysis, and respective tools

Category	Tool
1. Requests for privacy-sensitive permissions	Manifest permission analysis
2. Evidence of permission-related data leaks	FlowDroid
3. Analysis of privacy policies	Polisis

4   Data Privacy Posture

4.1   Methods

Our privacy evaluation is an extension of Kang et al.'s work on *privacy meter* which helps visualize privacy risks [38]. The app manifest provides detailed information [53,60] including measurements the app does to obtain user data, i.e. the permissions required, details, and how it is collected, thus analysis of the app manifests is critical [35,52]. The first relevant issue is whether an app exhibits *requests for privacy-sensitive permissions*. However, the presence of sensitive permission does not imply data leaks; thus we also consider *evidence of permission-related data leaks*. The app privacy policy, when available, also provides important context. Thus we perform an *analysis of privacy policy*.

4.2   Tools and Analyses

Mapping between analysis categories and tools is summarized in Table 2. Details of individual analyses are provided below.

*Manifest Permission Analysis (**Cat. 1**).* We identify the privacy-sensitive permissions requested by each app as classified by Google [10]. These permissions provide access to resources that manage privacy sensitive data such as personally identifiable information, location data, contact books and so on [19]. Thereafter, we identify the user data categories accessed by the mobile apps. This classification is necessary as these categories can reveal sensitive user and device information regardless of the app type. The permission categories included: *Contacts, Content, Location, Calendar, Network, Device ID*, and *Phone State* [63]. We then map privacy-sensitive permissions to these categories according to the type of data to which each permission grants access.

From the declaration of the app permissions, we calculate privacy scores for the categories using $S_c = p_c / \sum_i p_i$ where S_c is the score for category c, p_c is the number of permission pertaining to c, and $\sum_i p_i$ is the sum of all permissions pertaining to c. Each category can request several permission accesses as mentioned in Table 1. For each permission, we have considered a binary 0 or 1 depending on whether the app requests the permission. Thereafter, we follow a hierarchical permission model. In the case of higher privilege access which encompasses lower privileges, we considered the higher privileges to avoid double counting. For example, *Full Network Access* encompasses all the other network-related permissions. Thus, for our privacy score calculations, if an app only requests

Table 3. Mean, min and max for each privacy category

Perms	Mean	Min	Max
Network	0.75	0	1
Content	0.26	0.5	0
Location	0.44	0	1
Device Id	0.08	0	0.5
Contact	0.12	0	1
Telephony Services	0.01	0	0.75
Calendar	0.01	0	1

this permission, it will get a score $S_{network} = 1$. Similarly, if an app is requesting fine-grained location, it is considered as $p_{location} = 2$ since coarse-grained location data is covered by fine-grained. Furthermore, permission to write storage implies permission to read. Thus, write storage is considered as two permissions. This also applies to read/write contacts, call logs, and calendar events.

FlowDroid (Cat. 2). We use FlowDroid to analyze each app's privacy leaks and map these leaks to permissions that are necessary for the app to have access to that type of data. FlowDroid investigates data flows between *sources* (locations where sensitive information could be created) and *sinks* (locations where such information could leave the app). Sources and sinks are specified as Java function signatures. FlowDroid parses the app binaries and produces an analysis of the application call graph as the output, including the existence of paths from source to sink. These represent situations where leakage of sensitive data is possible. In this analysis, we only consider the sources, since leaking personal data is a breach of privacy, no matter the destination.

Analysis of Privacy Policy (Cat. 3). We conduct automated analysis of app privacy policies using the Polisis framework [30]. It breaks down the privacy policy into self-contained, semantically coherent segments and passes each into a set of neural network classifiers to designate labels depicting the privacy practices described in the policy, the labels include 10 high-level and 122 fine-grained classes. These classifiers are trained on the OPP-115 dataset by Wilson et al. [65].

Concretely, we collect policies linked by each app and pass them to Polisis. The output is a classification result by category level for the segment classifier and attribute levels where applicable for each segment. In this analysis we were mainly interested by the following classification labels at the category level for segment classification: *First Party Collection, Third Party Sharing, Access, Edit, Delete.* As for the attributes we were interested in: *personal-information-type, third-party-entity, access-type, action-first-party* and *identifiability.*

Limitations: We considered Android-defined permissions for our permission analysis. Although custom permissions are prevalent in our corpus, we did not take into consideration these permissions—developer-defined permissions that allow them to set restrictions and share resources and capabilities with other

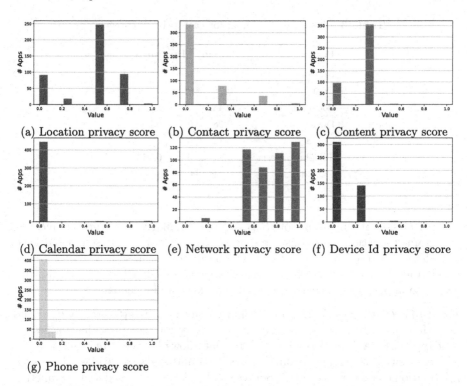

(a) Location privacy score   (b) Contact privacy score   (c) Content privacy score

(d) Calendar privacy score   (e) Network privacy score   (f) Device Id privacy score

(g) Phone privacy score

Fig. 2. Individual distributions of privacy scores for the IoT applications

apps—due to tool limitations. Li et al. acknowledge that the use of custom permissions is commonplace, and note that malicious applications try to exploit the flaws of custom permissions by getting dangerous system permissions without user consent and thus gaining illegal access to platform resources [43]. We were unable to extract the application manifest for **3** apps. The privacy policy analysis was carried out for **402** apps (the remaining apps had non-English policies unsupported by tooling, or did not provide a policy.)

4.3   Results

Manifest Permissions Analysis. **129** of the **448** apps got a network permission score of **1**, which means that these apps either requested the whole set of network permissions or opted to request the highest privilege permissions. A high score is expected as companion apps need to be linked with a device through the network. The mean network permission score was **0.75**. The mean location permission score was the second-highest (**0.44**) (Table 3). The most requested permissions for location are ACCESS_COARSE_LOCATION and ACCESS_MEDIA_LOCATION which allows apps to access locations saved within the user's media.

The content permission score mean was not as high (**0.26**), with the majority of applications (**353**) requesting the permission to write to external storage. Only

Table 4. r_s Between privacy categories (Loc = Location; Ctc = Contacts; Con = Content; Cal = Calendar; DId = Device Id; TeS = Telephony Service.)

	Net	Con	Loc	Did	Ctc	TeS	Cal
Net	1.00	-	-	-	-	-	-
Con	0.325	1.00	-	-	-	-	-
Loc	0.388	0.296	1.00	-	-	-	-
Did	0.119	0.216	0.182	1.00	-	-	-
Ctc	0.195	0.195	0.222	0.293	1.00	-	-
TeS	0.065	0.062	0.114	0.305	0.374	1.00	-
Cal	−0.062	−0.002	0.0	0.090	0.195	0.310	1.00

92 out of 448 apps did not request any content permission. The rest of the categories had lower mean scores. It should be mentioned, however, that none of those permission categories is necessary to implement the core functionality of a companion app. Figures 2a–g detail the privacy score for each category. Table 4 presents Spearman's rank correlation coefficient r_s values between each pair of privacy categories (for all reported values, $p < 0.01$). We use Spearman as score distributions are non-normal. The most relevant finding is that a number of categories exhibit weak (>0.3) correlation with each other.

FlowDroid Permissions Analysis. FlowDroid detected leaks in **315 (69.23%)** apps. **96** applications presented privacy leaks that were caused by custom permissions, not included in this analysis. **219** applications presented leaks caused by a set of **8** permissions: ACCESS_FINE_LOCATION, ACCESS_WIFI_ STATE, READ_PRIVILEGED_PHONE_ STATE, RECORD_ AUDIO, READ_SMS, READ_ PHONE_STATE, READ_PHONE_NUMBERS, BLUETOOTH_CONNECT. Six of these permissions were identified in privacy categories from Table 1.

The permission which provided data for the most number of leaks was ACCESS_FINE_LOCATION, with **214** apps leaking information related to fine-grained geographical location. Note, only **20** apps declared this specific permission in their manifest. A less significant issue concerned **20** apps leaking privileged phone state data. Moreover, **4** apps leaked audio recording data. Similarly, SMS, phone numbers, and phone state data were leaked by 3 apps each. These results are shown in Fig. 3.

Privacy Policy Analysis: Polisis. We analyzed personal information type labels (as categorized by Polisis) declared in app privacy policies. Polisis uses the following 15 personal information type labels: *Computer information (CI), Contact (CON), Cookies and tracking elements (C&TE), Demographic (DEM), Financial (FIN), Generic personal information (GPI), Health (HLT), IP address and device IDs (IP&ID), Location (LOC), Personal identifier (PI), Social media data (SMD), Survey data (SURV), User online activities (UOA), User profile (UP)* and *Other Data (OD)*. Polisis predicts attributes' labels with an average

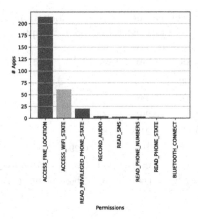

Fig. 3. Permissions responsible for the data leaks found through FlowDroid

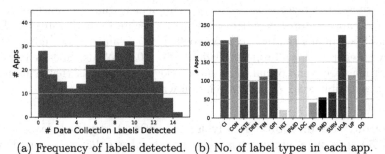

(a) Frequency of labels detected.   (b) No. of label types in each app.

Fig. 4. Personal Information Type Labels Statistics

precision of **0.84**, and only considered a prediction of over **0.5**. The distribution of number of labels per app is presented in Fig. 4a. The maximum number of labels detected in a privacy policy was **14** which was observed in two apps, and the average number of labels per privacy policy was **6.76**. The *Other Data* label was the most recurrent label, predicted in **277** privacy policies. The least frequent label was *Location* which was predicted in **41** of the policies. **28** privacy policies stated that they did not collect personal information on users (Fig. 4b).

Take-aways.   Significant number of apps request permissions (e.g., *phone state*) not directly related to their typical functions; although the privacy score for such categories is low. Many apps leaked information requested through ACCESS_FINE_LOCATION, without declaring this permission. Many app providers did not describe all the types of collected data in their privacy policy.

5   Security Posture

5.1   Methods

Many app security analysis techniques exist (e.g., [2,3,39,57]). For an technique to be used in our analysis, we require the following: tooling must be (i) available;

Table 5. Security categories relevant to our analysis

Category	Tool
1. Presence of known vulnerabilities	MobSF static analysis
2. Evidence of lack of maintenance	Days since update
3. Lack of in-transit data protection	MobSF static analysis
	MobSF dynamic analysis
	Manual inspection

(ii) not abandoned (we used a fixed threshold of two years w/o updates to determine abandonment); and (iii) executable on a modern machine/OS. We restrict our search to techniques measuring one of three different categories. The first is the *presence of known vulnerabilities*, as vulnerable software is at higher risk of facilitating accidental or attacker-driven information leaks. However, an app may also suffer from latent, undiscovered security issues that cannot be directly fingerprinted. Thus, we also measure *evidence of lack of maintenance*, as lack of updates may cause the presence of such latent issues [48]. The third security category is lack of *in-transit data protection*. Most apps encrypts in-transit data with Transport Layer Security (TLS). A misconfigured TLS stack, or lack of TLS, may result in an attacker being able to read in-transit user data.

5.2   Tools and Analyses

We decided to perform the bulk of the analysis using the Mobile Security Framework (MobSF) [3] which is a mature Open-Source pen-testing tool for Android. It takes an APK as input and produces a parseable vulnerability report as output. We also implemented a measurement of software abandonment (category 2 - *Evidence of lack of maintenance*). Table 5 summarizes tools used for each category. We discuss individual analyses below.

MobSF CVSS Score (Cat. 1). We use MobSF to statically fingerprint common, generic security-adverse patterns (e.g., logging sensitive information in plain text). MobSF further assigns a severity score between 0 and 10 to each issue, using the CVSS scoring system [1]. The tool also outputs the average CVSS scores across all detected issues. MobSF also generates information about the high-level category associated with each problem, according to CWE (Common Weakness Enumeration) categorization [4].

Days Since Update (Cat. 2). Modern apps tend to make use of many third-party libraries. Every software needs to be updated and patched regularly as new vulnerabilities get discovered. We use Days Since Last Released Update (scraped using the `play-scraper` Python package) as an analysis to investigate abandonment issues. This is consistent with previous work [28], which has used "failure to release" as a proxy symptom of abandonment for software projects.

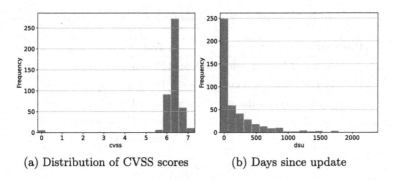

(a) Distribution of CVSS scores   (b) Days since update

Fig. 5. Security Metrics

*Transport Layer Misconfigurations (**Cat. 3**)*. HTTPS (Secure HTTP) is used for encrypted and secure transfer of data. HTTPS uses the TLS (Transport-Layer Security) standard to provide this functionality. We use MobSF static analyzer to identify app misconfigurations which may allow data to be transmitted in not properly encrypted form. Even if TLS is configured correctly, the use of invalid TLS certificates may still create risks. Thus we also use MobSF's static analyzer to identify invalid/expired TLS certificates.

*Transport Layer Secrecy Issues (**Cat. 3**)*. We complement static TLS analysis with dynamic analysis of app-generated network connections. We perform four MobSF-driven tests: TLS misconfiguration, TLS Pinning/Certificate transparency, TLS Pinning/Certificate transparency Bypass, and Cleartext Traffic. The TLS misconfiguration test involved enabling an HTTPS Man-in-the-middle Proxy and removing the root CA. It uncovers insecure configurations allowing HTTPS connections bypassing certificate errors or SSL/TLS errors in WebViews. The TLS certificate transparency bypasses test attempts to bypass the certificate or public key pinning and certificate transparency controls. The ClearText Traffic test inspects whether an app exchanges any non-TLS-encrypted traffic.

*Manual User Flow (**Cat. 3**)*. We manually performed the following operations: user creation, password recovery, login, and single sign-on (if allowed by the manufacturer), while recording traffic generated by the app. Subsequently, we inspected the traffic for issues. We limited this test to a small set of apps that were found to transmit unencrypted data by other tests. Inspection involved determining the nature and sensitivity of such unencrypted data if any.

Limitations: The MobSF static analyzer failed on **3** apps. **20%** of apps we run through the *Transport Layer Secrecy Issues* analysis crashed due to incompatibility with test environment (Android Studio) and other issues. *Manual User Flow* requires manual analysis of app network traces, which is complex and time-consuming. Due to the combination of these factors, we limited the latter two analyses to a smaller set of **15** apps.

5.3   Results

Presence of Known Vulnerabilities. Measurements of the aggregate MobSF CVSS score resulted in an average score of **6.45**, with a minimum of **0** and a maximum of **7.5**. The distribution is presented in Fig. 5a. Scores exhibits a fairly concentrated distribution, with only **5** apps showing a score of **0** and **417** having a score of **4.0** to **6.9**, which is considered medium severity according to the CVSS qualitative severity scale [1]. While the data may appear to be close to normally distributed, it fails the Shapiro-Wilk normality test ($W = 0.37$, $p = 1.68e^{-36}$). Upon further analysis, we determined that MobSF captures several discouraged but common programming practices; the fact that a small set of issues recurs across a large number of apps causes the consolidation of scores observed in the data.

Table 6 lists the top-10 CWEs associated with the vulnerabilities in the apps. Several common CWEs identify behaviors that might pose relatively minor threats. CWE-532 was found in almost every application because they were creating files in the system or logging operation results. Although this practice is discouraged, not all exposed information may be critical, and reading it requires physical access to the device. Other common CWE such as CWE-312, -330, and -327 are concerning as they indicate deviation from best data secrecy practices.

Evidence of Lack of Maintenance. The average number of days since an update is   **237** (min: **0**; max: **2462**). The distribution, reported in Fig. 5b, is concentrated around low values, which implies most companion apps are frequently updated (more than **238** received an update within the last **100** days). This metric is however uncorrelated to *CVSS score* (as discussed in Sect. 7.1), so a high frequency of updates does not imply absence of vulnerabilities.

Table 6. Most common CWEs found by MobSF Issue Analysis

CWE	Name	Apps
CWE-532	Insertion of Sensitive Information into Log File	445
CWE-276	Incorrect Default Permissions	411
CWE-312	Cleartext Storage of Sensitive Information	403
CWE-330	Use of Insufficiently Random Values	390
CWE-327	Use of a Broken or Risky Cryptographic Algorithm	381
CWE-200	Information Exposure	349
CWE-89	Improper Neutralization of Special Elements used in an SQL Command ('SQL Injection')	347
CWE-649	Reliance on Obfuscation or Encryption of Security-Relevant Inputs without Integrity Checking	208
CWE-749	Exposed Dangerous Method or Function	185
CWE-295	Improper Certificate Validation	123

Table 7. Network security configuration issues detected across the app dataset

Description	Apps
Base cfg is insecurely configured to permit clear text traffic to all domains	99
Domain cfg is insecurely configured to permit clear text traffic to these domains	71
Base cfg is configured to trust system certificates	65
Base cfg is configured to trust user installed certificates	16
Base cfg is configured to bypass certificate pinning	12
Domain cfg is configured to trust system certificates	5
Domain cfg is configured to trust user installed certificates	2

Lack of In-transit Data Protection. Transport-layer misconfigurations:
Table 7 summarizes network-related vulnerabilities in an app's network security
configuration, which centralizes network security settings in a standardized file.
Enforcing directives in the configuration is up to individual network libraries, and
indeed not all libraries respect the configuration [67]. The top-two issues allow
unencrypted communications to all or some domains. The others generally violate various best practices concerning the choice of TLS certificates that should
be trusted. We also measured the use of invalid/expired TLS certificates, which
appears to be quite widespread: it affects **96 out of 452 (21.2%)** applications.

Transport-layer secrecy issues: For this dynamic analysis, we selected **15**
apps for which other analyses had identified potentially concerning issues based
on high risk index values given by RiskInDroid (detailed in Sect. 6.2). The results
of the dynamic TLS tests on the 15 apps are summarized in Table 8. While the
app sample is too small to extract general conclusions, this test identified significant TLS deployment issues. Note that, differently from our static analysis
results reported in the "Transport layer misconfigurations" test—which represent configuration issues potentially leading to security problems—the dynamic
test identifies issues concerning the actual network traffic generated by apps.

Table 8. Dynamic analysis results for the selected 15 apps

TLS Test	Percent passing
Cleartext traffic Test	60%
TLS Misconfiguration Test	46.7%
TLS Pinning/Cert. Transparency Bypass Test	73.3%
TLS Pinning/Cert. Transparency Test	53.3%

Manual user flow analysis: In order to further investigate the results above,
we manually analyzed app-generated traffic. This analysis revealed that, in practice, most apps were using TLS to send critical information and only used cleartext traffic to access public data. Two apps, however, had concerning behavior:

(i) *XVRView (com.xvrview)* is an app developed by 杭州韬视 that allows users to monitor home cameras from their cell phones. The app has > 100,000 downloads and receives active support from its developers, as the last update took place in February 2022. However, it failed every TLS test except "TLS Pining/Certificate Transparency Bypass". Our manual analysis found that all the user credentials are sent in clear text, which is an extremely risky practice. An on-path attacker could obtain credentials and get direct access to users' home cameras. (ii) *Vss Mobile*, by ZenoTech, has > 500,000 downloads. It is a remote monitoring client that allows users to view videos over the network. At the time of testing, the application had not been updated in over a year . Manual traffic analysis revealed that the app transmits login credentials over unencrypted TCP connections. This is a critical issue that could breach data privacy and allow snooping on user data. We disclosed the issues to the app maintainers.

Take-aways. Results show that many apps are plagued by noncritical but concerning poor programming patterns (e.g., logging sensitive information in cleartext); and configuration issues affecting secrecy of in-transit data (e.g., use of expired certificates). An in-depth dive into apps with particularly concerning flags revealed isolated cases of sensitive credentials being sent in cleartext.

6   Risk Posture

6.1   Methods

By risk posture, we refer to the likelihood that an app may purposely mishandle user data. There exist a variety of risk profiling techniques [17, 36, 37, 50, 55, 61]. For selection, we used the same criterion discussed in Sect. 5. Most techniques have the goal of assessing the similarity of an app to given malware; therefore, we further used published results to exclude older techniques that are generally outperformed by more recent ones. *Similarity to known malware* is an indirect measure, as an app could perform malicious operations which do not resemble known patterns. Thus we also include a limited but direct measure of risk, *presence of malicious URLs*, which considers whether an app contains URLs associated with known malicious domains. Tool selection is summarized in Table 9 and discussed below (Fig. 6).

Table 9. Risk categories relevant to our analysis

Category	Tool
1. Similarity to known malware	RiskInDroid score
2. Presence of malicious URLs	URL analysis pipeline

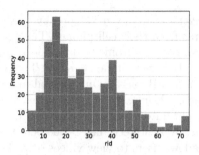

Fig. 6. RiskInDroid score

6.2 Tools and Analyses

RiskInDroid (Cat. 1) distinguishes risky applications from non-risky ones based on permissions, using machine learning-based classifiers (multiple techniques are supported, including SVM, Multinomial Naive Bayes, Grading Boosting, and Logistic Regression). The tool produces a risk index value (RIV) as output; RIV estimates the similarity of the permission set to those commonly seen in malware. Higher RIVs correspond to risky applications and possibly malware. The value of RIVs ranges from 0 to 100, where values above 75 suggests potential malware. *URL Analysis (Cat. 2)* uses MobSF static analyzer to extract URLs within an app APK. It then uses three different blocklists [6,12,13]) to identify risky and/or malicious URLs.

Limitations: RiskInDroid failed on **9 out of 455** apps, thus the results are for **446** apps only. The blocklists we used for URL analysis will flag an entire CDN/content provider hostname (e.g., *gw.alicdn.com*) when one of their customers performs malicious actions, thus resulting in potential false positives. We manage this issue by manually post-processing the URL analysis results.

6.3 Results

Similarity to Known Malware. The minimum RiskInDroid score in our apps was **4.9** and the maximum was **75.59**. Only **3** apps have a RIV higher than 75: *XVRView*, *blurams*, and *Verisure Cameras*. According to their descriptions, all three apps are used to remotely stream home smart cameras. A cursory app review did not find evidence of malicious behavior, so it is simply possible that the combination of permissions required by this class of apps is close to RiskInDroid's internal malware model. We remark that in our security analysis (Sect. 5.3) we also found that *XVRView* transmits credentials in cleartext.

Presence of Malicious URLs. Overall, we extracted and analyzed **5722** URLs from our corpus of apps. **14** hostnames appear on security blocklists, and **3** belong to a domain which suffered a recent breach. However, upon manual inspection we determined that all hostnames either belonged to CDN platforms/backends (e.g., *ytimg.com*), appeared related to the device manufacturers (e.g., *xiaoyi.pl*), or were popular content hosting platforms (e.g., *imgur.com*). In all these cases, it is impossible, without further knowledge, to unambiguously determine that the URL is malicious. We note, however, that **345** apps (**76.3%**) were found to use backend services provided by *firebase.io*, which has been in the past the subject of large-scale data leaks [5].

Take-aways. Most apps do not exhibit characteristics commonly associated with malicious software and data misuse. This may be the result of selection bias: as the Play Store screens uploaded apps for malware, there may exist malicious apps which however do not exhibit easily detectable malware behavior. Reliable mobile malware detection is a complex task in itself, and orthogonal to our work.

7 Discussion

Our main research question (ref. Sect. 1) was: *How do companion apps fare in respect to the measured privacy-related aspects? Are there significant general concerns broadly affecting companion apps?* Overall, the privacy picture painted by our analysis is not critical, but certainly sub-optimal. While no app was found to carry overtly malicious behavior (Sect. 6), apps routinely request permissions that do not appear necessary (Sect. 4). Poor app programming and configuration practices, likely to increase the risk of compromise and data leaks, were also common (Sect. 5).

Given these considerations, we believe it would be important for users evaluating the purchase of a device and related app, to have access to understandable insights about the app privacy posture. Such information would enable users to prefer security-robust apps, which in turn may incentivize manufacturers to improve their privacy practices.

In other communities, visibility into the security of software packages via online aggregators is rapidly becoming popular. Examples from the Open Source Software community include the OpenSSF Security Metrics project [9] and the LFX insights project [8]. We believe a similar resource focused on IoT app privacy would be beneficial to the Android IoT user community.

7.1 Cross-Dimension Analysis

We now evaluate the relationships between the results of different analyses (*RQ2: Is there evidence of positive or negative correlation between metrics measuring different aspects of app privacy?* in Sect. 1.) We only consider measures that result in a non-boolean numerical score: Privacy Score (Sect. 4.3, averaged across all categories), CVSS score (Sect. 5.3), Days since update (Sect. 5.3), RiskInDroid score (Sect. 6.3). We additionally generate a score from the FlowDroid analysis of Sect. 4, by counting all paths between FlowDroid sources and sinks. As the value distribution of many measures deviates from normal, we used non-parametric Spearman's rank correlation (r_s). According to accepted practice [31], we interpret r_s values < 0.3 as representing no correlation.

Table 10. Spearman's rank correlation coefficients between measured characteristics ("Priv" stands for "Average Privacy Score"; "DSU" for "Days Since Update"; "RID" for "RiskInDroid Score")

	Priv	FlowDroid	CVSS	DSU	RID
Priv	1.00	-	-	-	-
FlowDroid	0.147	1.00	-	-	-
CVSS	0.003	0.075	1.00	-	-
DSU	−.197	0.028	0.049	1.00	-
RID	0.149	0.027	0.104	0.007	1.00

Results: The correlation matrix is shown in Table 10; no significant correlation is evidenced between any pair of measures. Based on our results, thus **privacy issues do not appear to propagate along with multiple aspects**: the posture of each app according to one aspect is uncorrelated to the same along with other aspects. For the same reason, **we did not find evidence of tradeoffs between app quality in different aspects**.

7.2 State of Measuring Tools

FlowDroid [18], MobSF [3], and RiskInDroid [50] are mature and well-maintained tools, and we found them easy to integrate into an automated analysis workflow. MobSF and FlowDroid are backed by robust developer communities; while FlowDroid is backed by a mobile security startup. Polisis [30] works on textual privacy policies and we did not run into significant issues while using it. We considered Axplorer [21], Arcade [14] and IccTA [42] for computing app permissions without relying on the manifest. Unfortunately, none worked and we implemented our manifest analysis. We considered CryptoGuard [57] and CryLogger [56] for detecting incorrect use of crypto primitives. We found them to be less applicable to a broad set of apps. Both exhibited a high failure rate.

8 Related Work

Related Work on Metrics: Kang et al. [38] calculate Android app privacy scores based on a list of 30 permissions commonly used by malware. Biswas et al. [22] developed a method to measure privacy across Location, Content, and Contacts. In our paper, we extended and combined these two methods to calculate privacy for different categories. Recently, Babun et al. [20] proposed IoT-WATCH, a methodology for matching user privacy preferences to app-transmitted data. Integrating IoTWATCH in our work is an interesting future direction.

Jansen [34] highlighted limitations of popular security metrics, such as the reliance on human judgment and inherent subjectivity. Similarly, Krutz et al. found that user ratings weakly correlate with security [40]. Consequently, we mostly focus on security analyses rooted in objective properties of each app (e.g., score of CVSS issues). RiskMon [37] assesses the risk incurred by app sensitive operations relative to user-provided expectations. As we require an assessment to be automated, this approach is outside the scope of our work. WHYPER [54] flags unexplained app permissions in app descriptions. We do not include this approach as lack of explanation, while suspicious, does not represent a security issue per se. Peng et al. [55] proposed probabilistic generative models to attribute a risk score to Android apps based on the combination of permissions requested. Later work [50] has shown that ML-driven analysis of permission sets leads to superior results; therefore we prefer the latter approach.

Related Work on IoT-Based Studies: Liu et al. [45] defined the notion of *app-in-the-middle* IoTs, which illustrates the increasingly popular setup where constrained IoT devices rely on mobile apps for connectivity. They then proposed a formalization of the security of such setups. Ding and Hu [27] proposed a framework for identifying security-relevant hidden integration between IoT apps.

Wang et al. [64] and Mauro Junior et al. [49] analyzed mobile companion apps [64] to infer vulnerabilities in their devices and backends. Both works focus mainly on devices and not apps. Chatzoglou et al. [25] performed an in-depth security analysis of a small (41) number of IoT apps. We focus on large-scale lightweight automated analysis, thus maximizing external validity. Fernandes et al. [29] performed an analysis of smart home apps on the Samsung SmartThings platform, revealing numerous issues due to over-privileging. Our analysis focuses on mobile IoT apps rather than third-party smart-home apps. Mohanty and Sridhar conducted a review of the security of 102 IoT companion apps [51]. This paper focused specifically on identifying 9 pre-determined security issues in apps built using hybrid frameworks; our work has broader scope both in terms of types of apps, and issues of interest.

9   Conclusions

We analyzed the privacy posture of 455 Android mobile companion apps by evaluating three pillars of it including data privacy, security, and risk. Our study shows that overall app data privacy, security, and risk posture are reasonable. However, it also evidences some ecosystem-level shortcomings; such as over-requesting permissions; and the widespread use of programming and configuration practices negatively affecting security. We hope our work can act as the starting point for further investigations in this domain, and facilitate the design of software quality metrics and guidelines that can lead to better app design.

References

1. Common vulnerability scoring system version 3.1: Specification document (2019). https://www.first.org/cvss/specification-document
2. GitHub - linkedin/qark: Tool to look for several security related Android application vulnerabilities (2019). https://github.com/linkedin/qark

3. Mobile security framework (2020). https://github.com/MobSF/Mobile-Security-Framework-MobSF
4. Cwe list version 4.6 (2021). https://cwe.mitre.org/data/index.html
5. Popular android apps with 142.5 million collective installs leak user data (2021). https://cybernews.com/security/research-popular-android-apps-with-142-5-million-collective-downloads-are-leaking-user-data/
6. Bulk domain blacklist checker (2022). https://www.bulkblacklist.com
7. Google play (2022). https://play.google.com/store
8. LFX insights (2022). https://insights.lfx.linuxfoundation.org/projects
9. Metrics - open source security foundation (2022). https://metrics.openssf.org
10. Permissions on android (2022). https://developer.android.com/guide/topics/permissions/overview
11. Play store downloader (2022). https://github.com/ClaudiuGeorgiu/PlaystoreDownloader
12. Url/ip lookup—webroot brightcloud (2022). https://www.brightcloud.com
13. Website reputation checker (2022). https://www.urlvoid.com
14. Aafer, Y., Tao, G., Huang, J., Zhang, X., Li, N.: Precise android API protection mapping derivation and reasoning. In: ACM CCS (2018)
15. Alhirabi, N., Rana, O., Perera, C.: Security and privacy requirements for the internet of things: a survey. ACM Trans. Internet Things 2(1), 1–37 (2021)
16. Allhoff, F., Henschke, A.: The internet of things: foundational ethical issues. Internet Things 1, 55–66 (2018)
17. Alshehri, A., Marcinek, P., Alzahrani, A., Alshahrani, H., Fu, H.: PUREDroid: permission usage and risk estimation for android applications. In: ICISDM (2019)
18. Arzt, S., et al.: Flowdroid: Precise context, flow, field, object-sensitive and lifecycle-aware taint analysis for android apps. In: PLDI (2014)
19. Baalous, R., Poet, R.: How dangerous permissions are described in android apps' privacy policies? In: SIN (2018)
20. Babun, L., Celik, Z.B., McDaniel, P., Uluagac, A.S.: Real-time analysis of privacy-(UN) aware IoT applications. In: PETS (2021)
21. Backes, M., Bugiel, S., Derr, E., McDaniel, P., Octeau, D., Weisgerber, S.: On demystifying the android application framework: re-visiting android permission specification analysis. In: USENIX Security Symposium (2016)
22. Biswas, D., Aad, I., Perrucci, G.P.: Privacy panel: usable and quantifiable mobile privacy. In: ARES (2013)
23. Catarinucci, L., et al.: An IoT-aware architecture for smart healthcare systems. IEEE Internet Things J. 2(6), 515–526 (2015)
24. Celik, Z.B., Fernandes, E., Pauley, E., Tan, G., McDaniel, P.: Program analysis of commodity IoT applications for security and privacy: challenges and opportunities. ACM Comput. Surv. (CSUR) 52(4), 1–30 (2019)
25. Chatzoglou, E., Kambourakis, G., Smiliotopoulos, C.: Let the cat out of the bag: popular android IoT apps under security scrutiny. Sensors 22(2), 513 (2022)
26. Devlin, J., Chang, M.W., Lee, K., Toutanova, K.: Bert: pre-training of deep bidirectional transformers for language understanding. arXiv preprint arXiv:1810.04805 (2018)
27. Ding, W., Hu, H.: On the safety of IoT device physical interaction control. In: ACM CCS (2018)
28. English, R., Schweik, C.M.: Identifying success and tragedy of floss commons: a preliminary classification of sourceforge.net projects. In: FLOSS ICSE Workshops (2007)

29. Fernandes, E., Jung, J., Prakash, A.: Security analysis of emerging smart home applications. In: IEEE S&P (2016)
30. Harkous, H., Fawaz, K., Lebret, R., Schaub, F., Shin, K.G., Aberer, K.: Polisis: automated analysis and presentation of privacy policies using deep learning. In: USENIX Security Symposium (2018)
31. Hinkle, D.E., Wiersma, W., Jurs, S.G.: Applied statistics for the behavioral sciences, vol. 663. Houghton Mifflin College Division (2003)
32. Holloway, D., Green, L.: The Internet of toys. Commun. Res. Pract. **2**(4), 506–519 (2016)
33. ISO/IEC: ISO/IEC 20924:2018(EN), Information technology - Internet of Things (IoT) - Vocabulary. https://www.iso.org/obp/ui/#iso:std:iso-iec:20924:ed-1:v1:en
34. Jansen, W.: Research Directions in Security Metrics. Technical report 7564, NIST (2009)
35. Jha, A.K., Lee, S., Lee, W.J.: Developer mistakes in writing android manifests: an empirical study of configuration errors. In: IEEE/ACM MSR (2017)
36. Jiang, J., Li, S., Yu, M., Chen, K., Liu, C., Huang, W., Li, G.: MRDroid: a multi-act classification model for android malware risk assessment. In: IEEE MASS (2018)
37. Jing, Y., Ahn, G.J., Zhao, Z., Hu, H.: RiskMon: continuous and automated risk assessment of mobile applications. In: CODASPY (2014)
38. Kang, J., Kim, H., Cheong, Y.G., Huh, J.H.: Visualizing privacy risks of mobile applications through a privacy meter. In: ISPEC (2015)
39. Kapitsaki, G., Ioannou, M.: Examining the privacy vulnerability level of android applications. In: WEBIST (2019)
40. Krutz, D.E., Munaiah, N., Meneely, A., Malachowsky, S.A.: Examining the relationship between security metrics and user ratings of mobile apps: a case study. In: WAMA (2016)
41. Kumar, D., et al.: All things considered: an analysis of IoT devices on home networks. In: USENIX Security Symposium (2019)
42. Li, L., et al.: ICCTA: detecting inter-component privacy leaks in android apps. In: IEEE/ACM ICSE (2015)
43. Li, R., Diao, W., Li, Z., Du, J., Guo, S.: Android custom permissions demystified: from privilege escalation to design shortcomings. In: 2021 IEEE Symposium on Security and Privacy (SP), pp. 70–86. IEEE (2021)
44. Liu, D.: play-scraper. https://pypi.org/project/play-scraper/
45. Liu, H., Li, J., Gu, D.: Understanding the security of app-in-the-middle IoT. Comput. Secur. **97**, 102000 (2020)
46. Marquez, J., Villanueva, J., Solarte, Z., Garcia, A.: IoT in education: integration of objects with virtual academic communities. In: New Advances in Information Systems and Technologies. AISC, vol. 444, pp. 201–212. Springer, Cham (2016). https://doi.org/10.1007/978-3-319-31232-3_19
47. Matheu, S.N., Hernández-Ramos, J.L., Skarmeta, A.F., Baldini, G.: A survey of cybersecurity certification for the Internet of Things. ACM Comput. Surv. **53**(6), 1–36 (2021)
48. Mathur, A., Malkin, N., Harbach, M., Peer, E., Egelman, S.: Quantifying users' beliefs about software updates. In: Proceedings 2018 Workshop on Usable Security (2018)
49. Mauro Junior, D., Melo, L., Lu, H., d'Amorim, M., Prakash, A.: A study of vulnerability analysis of popular smart devices through their companion apps. In: IEEE SPW (2019)

50. Merlo, A., Georgiu, G.C.: RiskInDroid: machine learning-based risk analysis on android. In: De Capitani di Vimercati, S., Martinelli, F. (eds.) SEC 2017. IAICT, vol. 502, pp. 538–552. Springer, Cham (2017). https://doi.org/10.1007/978-3-319-58469-0_36

51. Mohanty, A., Sridhar, M.: HybriDiagnostics: evaluating security issues in hybrid smarthome companion apps. In: IEEE SPW (2021)

52. Momen, N., Hatamian, M., Fritsch, L.: Did app privacy improve after the GDPR? IEEE Secur. Priv. **17**(6), 10–20 (2019)

53. Mylonas, A., Theoharidou, M., Gritzalis, D.: Assessing privacy risks in android: a user-centric approach. In: Bauer, T., Großmann, J., Seehusen, F., Stølen, K., Wendland, M.-F. (eds.) RISK 2013. LNCS, vol. 8418, pp. 21–37. Springer, Cham (2014). https://doi.org/10.1007/978-3-319-07076-6_2

54. Pandita, R., Xiao, X., Yang, W., Enck, W., Xie, T.: Whyper: towards automating risk assessment of mobile applications. In: USENIX Security (2013)

55. Peng, H., et al.: Using probabilistic generative models for ranking risks of android apps. In: ACM CCS (2012)

56. Piccolboni, L., Di Guglielmo, G., Carloni, L., Sethumadhavan, S.: Crylogger: detecting crypto misuses dynamically. In: IEEE S&P (2021)

57. Rahaman, S., et al.: Cryptoguard: high precision detection of cryptographic vulnerabilities in massive-sized java projects. In: ACM CCS (2019)

58. Ren, J., Dubois, D.J., Choffnes, D., Mandalari, A.M., Kolcun, R., Haddadi, H.: Information exposure from consumer IoT devices: a multidimensional, network-informed measurement approach. In: ACM IMC (2019)

59. Rivera, D., et al.: Secure communications and protected data for a internet of things smart toy platform. IEEE Internet Things J. **6**(2), 3785–3795 (2019)

60. Tandel, S., Jamadar, A.: Impact of progressive web apps on web app development. Int. J. Innov. Res. Sci. Eng. Technol. **7**(9), 9439–9444 (2018)

61. Utama, R.A., Sukarno, P., Jadied, E.M.: Analysis and classification of danger level in android applications using Naive Bayes algorithm. In: ICoICT (2018)

62. Vashi, S., Ram, J., Modi, J., Verma, S., Prakash, C.: Internet of Things (IoT): a vision, architectural elements, and security issues. In: I-SMAC (2017)

63. Wader, S.S.: How android application permissions impact user's data privacy? Int. J. Res. Publ. Rev. **2**(3), 498–502 (2021)

64. Wang, X., Sun, Y., Nanda, S., Wang, X.: Looking from the mirror: evaluating IoT device security through mobile companion apps. In: USENIX Security (2019)

65. Wilson, S., et al.: The creation and analysis of a website privacy policy corpus. In: Proceedings of the 54th Annual Meeting of the Association for Computational Linguistics (Volume 1: Long Papers), pp. 1330–1340 (2016)

66. Wuyts, K., Joosen, W.: LINDDUN privacy threat modeling: a tutorial. CW Reports (2015)

67. Yermakov, M.: Understanding the android cleartexttrafficpermitted flag (2020). https://appsec-labs.com/portal/understanding-the-android-cleartexttrafficpermitted-flag/

Verification and Validation Methods for a Trust-by-Design Framework for the IoT

Davide Ferraris$^{(\boxtimes)}$, Carmen Fernandez-Gago, and Javier Lopez

Network, Information and Computer Security Lab, University of Malaga,
29071 Malaga, Spain
{ferraris,mcgago,jlm}@lcc.uma.es

Abstract. The development of an Internet of Things (IoT) entity is a difficult process that can be performed following a System Development Life Cycle (SDLC). Two important phases of a SDLC process are verification and validation (V&V). Moreover, if we want to guarantee that trust is considered through the SDLC we have to implement it since the first phases and verify and validate its implementation during V&V. Verification usually is defined as "the system has been built right", on the other hand validation refers to the fact that "the right system has been built". Concerning trust, following our methodologies we can state that we can verify that "the trusted IoT entity has been built" and validate that "the right trusted IoT entity has been built". In this paper, we propose a methodology to verify and validate requirements related to a trusted IoT entity. Following the methodology, it is possible to check if the requirements elicited in the early phases of the SDLC have been implemented in the developed functionalities. These final phases will be fundamental in order to achieve trust in the developed IoT entity.

Keywords: Trust · SysML · UML · Internet of Things (IoT) · System Development Life Cycle (SDLC)

1 Introduction

The Internet of Things (IoT) allows humans and smart entities to cooperate among them anyhow and anywhere [23]. The IoT entities are growing each year and "there are expected to be more than 64B IoT devices worldwide by 2025"[1]. This prediction states that that the IoT paradigm will define how the world will be connected. For this reason, even if there will be more opportunities to be connected, also many issues will arise. We believe that security and trust can help to solve these issues implementing them in the IoT during the System Development Life Cycle (SDLC) [12]. Usually, the SDLC is composed of different

---

[1] https://techjury.net/blog/internet-of-things-statistics/.

© IFIP International Federation for Information Processing 2022
Published by Springer Nature Switzerland AG 2022
S. Sural and H. Lu (Eds.): DBSec 2022, LNCS 13383, pp. 183–194, 2022.
https://doi.org/10.1007/978-3-031-10684-2_11

phases. In the earliest ones, the requirements are elicited. This phase will lead to the development of the entity, but in order to conclude the process it is fundamental to verify and validate the requirements. In fact, through verification is possible to say that *the entity has been built in the right way* that means that the functionalities are working as expected. On the other hand, validation means that *the right entity has been built*. In this case, we can say that the IoT entity has been developed as it was intended for the originated need. Moreover, in the SDLC of an IoT entity, the developers must tackle other challenging tasks. One is how to consider the dynamic environment where the IoT device will interact with other devices. We believe that trust can help overcome this issue, because a trusted device will ensure that the interaction can be performed in a secure way. Moreover, considering trust during the whole SDLC will prevent later issues and as demonstrate by [15], when a task is conducted early in the SDLC, it will save money for the whole project instead of consider it later [19]. However, trust is hard to define because it is strongly dependent on the topic in which is considered [9]. Moreover, trust is connected to the context, in fact it "means many things to many people" [7]. Nevertheless, usually at least two actors must be involved in a trust relationship: the trustor and the trustee. The trustor is the one that needs the trustee in order to fulfill an action or a service. For example, in an IoT environment the trustor can be the user and the trustee can be the IoT device. In this paper, we will propose a method that help developers in verifying and validating requirements related to a trusted IoT entity.

The structure of the paper is as follows. In Sect. 2, we explain the previous work connected to this paper. Then, in Sect. 3, we describe the related work about verification and validation. Then, the core of this paper concerning requirements verification and validation phases are presented in Sect. 4 and 5. The implementation of these phases are explained in Sect. 6 and 7. Finally, in Sect. 8, we conclude and discuss the future work.

2   Background

IoT allows smart entities to be connected through the Internet. This configuration brings many possibilities (i.e., to connect entities even if they are far). On the other hand, the connection among them can trust or security issues. Another difficulty that is strongly dependent on the IoT paradigm is that the smart entities are usually produced by different vendors and they cover different topics [20]. This variety increase the issues but also the potentialities of the IoT [5].

In our previous works, we have developed a framework that considers trust holistically during the whole SDLC of a smart IoT entity [12]. The framework is composed of a K-Model shown in Fig. 1 and several transversal activities (i.e., Traceability, Risk Analysis). Moreover, it is fundamental to take the context into consideration during each phase of the SDLC. This aspect is very important for IoT due to the dynamicity and heterogeneity of this paradigm. The context can depend on several aspects such as the environment or the functionalities of an entity.

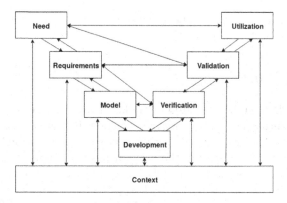

Fig. 1. K-Model: with the *Transversal Activities* it compounds the framework [12]

In the K-Model, we can see different phases covering all the SDLC of the IoT entity under development: from cradle to grave. The first phase is related to the needs phase, where it is proposed the purpose of the new IoT product. All the stakeholders related to the entity have a key role on it. The second phase considers the requirements elicitation process. In this phase, the developers must elicit the requirements according to the needs considered in the previous phase. About this part, we proposed TrUStAPIS [11]. This methodology consider trust according to other domains such as security, usability, privacy, availability, safety, identity. We believe that considering other domains according to trust is necessary to guarantee it in a virtuous circle that enhance the protection of the IoT entity under development. To state this assumption, we have followed and expanded Hoffman and Pavlidis' works [16, 21].

The output of the requirements elicitation process must be taken into consideration when developers will perform verification and validation in latter phases of the K-Model. In the middle, there is the third phase which considers the model definition [22]. In fact, it is fundamental to refine the requirements turning them into models useful for the developers in order to realize the IoT entity in the following and central phase of the K-Model that is the development phase. Thus, before the entity is delivered two important phases, the core of this paper, must be performed: verification and validation. Verification phase is connected to Requirements and Model phase as shown in Fig. 1. On the other hand, Validation is connected to Requirements and Need phase. This difference is very important in order to perform these activities. For both the phases, we will use JSON code developed in the second phase (i.e., Requirements) of the K-Model, in order to help the developers to perform both the verification and validation process.

JSON has been chosen because "it is easily readable by humans and machines" and as stated in [2] this aspect allows developers to share it among either stakeholders and applications. JSON is also useful to connect the requirements and the needs in the validation phase as we will show in Sect. 5. However,

Verification and Validation has been considered during the years. In the next section, we will briefly introduce them.

3   Related Work

Verification and, later in the SDLC, validation are two phases performed to prove that the entity has been properly developed. If validation is related to the final product, on the other hand, verification can be performed in any phase in order to find errors or modify the original plan. Anyhow, it is important to consider verification also as a separate phase, in order to check completely that the functionalities of the IoT entity work as planned. A definition of verification appears in the Project Management Body of Knowledge (PMBOK) [6] where verification is considered as "the evaluation of whether or not a product, service, or system complies with a regulation, requirement, specification, or imposed condition. It is often an internal process. Contrast with validation". This phase is fundamental in order to verify that *the entity has been built in the right way*. This means that all the specifications have been followed in a correct way. In the verification phase the functionalities of the entity are tested as well as its correct implementation. However, tests are performed both in verification and validation. In fact, Linhares et al. [18] stated that "test is realized on the implemented system". It involves a set of possible inputs executing the functionalities in order to check if something wrong occurs. Another element that is used during verification processes are the inspections. Fagan et al. [8] described for the first time the inspection processes which were lately considered by Ackerman et al. [1] that described the inspection processes as fundamental for the verification phase. However, it is possible that the developed entity has passed the verification phase, but it fails when validated. This situation can happen when the entity has been built for the specifications, but the specifications themselves fail to address the user's needs. Validation is defined by the PMBOK [6] as "the assurance that a product, service, or system meets the needs of the customer and other identified stakeholders. It often involves acceptance and suitability with external customers. Contrast with verification". By validation we state that *the right entity has been built* [15]. This means that the desired entity has been developed as the users and vendors wanted to be. In addition, this phase checks that the entity works properly in a real system's environment. In order to understand the problem, there can be different categories of validations. Process validation has been analyzed in [17]. This guidance promotes a "lifecycle" approach. Then, retrospective validation is executed for a product that is already distributed or sold to the customers [14]. Next, partial validation is often used for research purposes or prototypal studies if the time before the utilization phase is constrained. Finally, a powerful tool that can be used is called *Independent Verification and Validation* (IV&V), as stated by Arthur et al. [4]. This is a tool that can be exploited in order to mitigate the growing complexity related to the expansion of modeling and simulation problems. Moreover, in a later work [3], the author showed an important issue with IV&V according to agile development. One of them was related to traceability and documentation. However, with our work, we have implemented traceability that allows developers to solve the aforementioned issues.

4   Verification

In this paper, we expand and explore the fifth and sixth phases of the K-Model [12] where we have only proposed them without any further explanation. Thus, the verification process is keen to analyze the requirements according to the models and to test the functionalities in order to prove that the requirements are well formed and the "system has been built right". At the end of this phase we can state that "the trusted IoT entity has been built right". The verification process is the following. The steps are shown in Fig. 2.

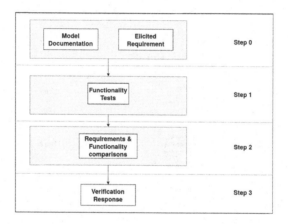

Fig. 2. Verification Process: step-by-step methodology

The output of each step is the input for the following steps.

1. The step zero is related to the comparison of the originating model documentation (collected during the third phase of the K-Model) and the elicited requirements. In fact, we need to compare the requirements and the models in order to verify the functionalities of the developed IoT entity as they have been modeled and planned.
2. The first step is performed in order to execute tests on the functionalities.
3. In order to check that the requirements have been respected, the functionalities tested in the previous step must be connected to the originating requirements to certify that they have been designed in a correct way.
4. The response of the comparison performed in step 2 is the output of the final step. If the functionality follows the requirements, then, the verification test is successful, otherwise the functionality must be modified according to the elicited requirements. This feedback is represented in the K-Model and it is necessary in order to develop the correct IoT entity.

5   Validation

The validation process is based on the fact that "the right system has been built". In order to clarify this, we need to check that the IoT entity and its functionalities match the initial stakeholder's need. Each need is delineated by a statement and it is represented by one or more stakeholders. The stakeholders are the "persons" which have an interest in the system. These needs must be collected by the developers in the first phase of the K-Model. Then, in the requirements phase, the needs are analyzed and transformed in requirements. We resumed these two phases because they are considered also in the validation phase to check if the IoT entity represents the original needs. At the end of this phase, we can state that "the right trusted IoT entity has been built". The validation process is the following. The steps are shown in Fig. 3.

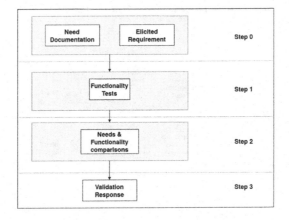

Fig. 3. Validation process: step-by-step methodology

The output of each step is important in the following steps.

1. The step zero is related to the comparison of the originating needs and the elicited requirements. In this phase, the needs and the connected requirements are compared, this step is helpful to discover if there are some missing or wrong requirements.
2. The first step is performed in order to execute tests related to the functionalities developed following the elicited requirements satisfying the needs.
3. The comparisons between needs and requirements is performed in the second step, where the output of the test is compared to the originating need.
4. The response of the comparison performed in the previous step is considered in the last step of the methodology. If the functionality satisfies the need, the validation test is successful, otherwise the functionality must be modified. This means that the developers must go back in the K-Model to the previous phases in order to perform the correct modifications. Anyway, all the previous phases, if correctly performed, reduce this possibility.

6   Verification Scenario: Smart Cake Machine

In this section, we will present how to verify the requirements presented in [11] concerning a use case scenario regarding a Smart Cake Machine (SCM) previously introduced in [12]. We briefly describe here the scenario for the readers. Let us assume that, after a market analysis, the stakeholders have had the idea to produce a SCM. It should tell the users which ingredients are needed for a particular cake where the recipes can be downloadable from a website or inserted by the users. Moreover, it is supposed that this device can communicate with other IoT entities. In this case, let us assume that the SCM can check the Smart Fridge (SF) for an ingredient or it can send a request to the trusted nearest supermarket (SM) in order to buy missing ingredients. This operation must be performed through a Smart Hub (SH) in order to preserve the SCM from possible external attacks [10]. According to the users, the SCM must check the trusted users allowed to interact with. From these needs and considering the context, the requirements are elicited following TrUStAPIS methodology [11] and the models following [13], Then, the functionalities have been developed in the central phase of the K-Model. Now, there are verification and validation phases to be performed. In this section, we present the verification.

Step 0. The elicited requirements related to [11] are shown in Table 1. Then, in the third column, we can see the model connected to the requirement. These models have been presented in [13]. In this step, we compare the model documentation and the elicited requirements.

Table 1. Requirements and model connections.

Domain	Requirement	Model
Usability	**USAB01** - The user shall be able to insert new recipes	**State Machine Diagram 1 (SMD1)**: Upload a recipe into the SCM
Privacy	**PRIV03** - User data shall be kept private	**Activity Diagram 1 (AD1)**: Securing user data
Security	**SEC02** - The SCM shall delegate the Smart Hub to order the missing ingredients	**Sequence Diagram 1 (SD1)**: User, SCM, SF, SH and SM interaction
Identity	**IDNT02** - The user shall provide his/her data in order to be registered	**Use Case Diagram 1 (UCD1)**: User data
Trust	**TRST01** - The SCM shall trust a Smart Supermarket with a trust level above 0.5	**Class Diagram 1 (CD1)**: SCM and SM service classes

In this example, we will show only how to verify requirement USAB01 according to SMD1 diagram. Thus, in Fig. 4, we show the JSON related to USAB01. In fact, it is useful to speed up the verification process by checking if the goal and the characteristics are met.

```
17 ▾    "IoT_requirement_USAB01" : {
18 ▾      "Context" : {
19 ▾        "Domain" : [{
20 ▾          "Usability" : {
21              "Characteristic" : ["Simplicity, Understandability"] } }],
22          "Environment" : "Smart Home",
23          "Scope" : "User Interface" } ,
24 ▾      "Actor" : {
25          "Role" : "User",
26          "Type" : ["Human User"] },
27 ▾      "Action" : {
28          "Type" : ["Fulfill"] ,
29          "Measure" : [" "]},
30        "Goal" : "Let the user insert new recipes"
31    },
```

Fig. 4. JSON code for USAB01

Step 1. After the collection of the requirements and the models performed in the previous steps, the developers must perform the functionality tests. In this case, it is necessary to verify different aspects. In first instance, that only a trusted user can access the SCM. In fact, only after this important step, it is possible to insert a new recipe. Then, if the first control is positive, the functionality tests must check if the recipes are correctly uploaded. SMD1 was designed in the following way. Firstly, for any new recipe, it was mandatory to insert a new title. Secondly, the items and their quantity. The recipe upload ends when all the items have been inserted. Thus, the test must check if all the items are correctly inserted. If not, the test fails, and the code must be checked in order to find the error. Otherwise, the functionality test passes, and it is possible to proceed to the following step.

Step 2. This step is a second check that guarantees that the requirements are met, and the functionalities have been correctly implemented. Traceability guarantees this aspect as we have seen in Table 1. In the case the previous step has ended correctly, it is possible to confirm that the requirement USAB01 and its derived functionalities have been corrected implemented. On the other hand, it will be raised an issue that will be checked in order to adjust the wrong functionality. After all the functionalities have been checked positively or negatively, it is possible to proceed to the final step of the verification process.

Step 3. The verification response is positive if all the previous steps have been correctly performed. Thus, a document certifying which tests have been positively or negatively performed will be the output of this phase. In the case some tests have been negatively performed, there will be a modification of the functionalities, and a new verification process will be performed after the needed modifications.

7   Validation Scenario: Smart Cake Machine

In this section, we will present how to validate the SCM. In the validation phase, the tests are performed in the environment, in order to check if the needs are met and the cooperation with other IoT entities is fulfilled. In Fig. 5, it is possible to see the connections among the SCM and other IoT entities.

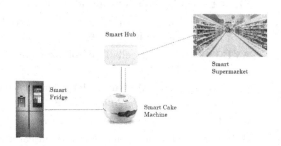

Fig. 5. Smart Cake Machine and its relationships with the other IoT entities

Step 0. In this step, it is performed the comparison of the *Need* documentation and elicited requirements. According to [11], we have identified the following subset of originating needs:

1. **Need 1**: The temperature of the SCM must be checked and it could not overcome 250 °C.
2. **Need 2**: The recipes must be downloadable from the vendor website or inserted by authenticated users. Authentication must be performed by code.
3. **Need 3**: The SCM could interact with a SF to check if a particular ingredient is present. If not, the SCM can interact with a trusted SM through the home SH and order the missing ingredient.
4. **Need 4**: The communication among the smart home entities must be guaranteed and encrypted.

In the third column of Table 2, we can see the need connected to requirements. Needs X are not strictly connected to the requirements, but to the context.

For the validation test, we consider requirement TRST01 and Need 3.

Step 1. As we will present in the following and final phase of the K-Model, an algorithm is needed to introduce the new IoT entity in a smart home context. Anyhow, in this case, we need to focus only on the functionalities that must be validated. In this case, it is related to the interaction between the SCM and a trusted SM. The trust value is provided by the SH or from the user (i.e., because the user has a direct past relationship with an SM). The value can be computed after considering multiple parameters (i.e., cost, distance, quality), and the service is satisfied if any interaction among SCM and the SM is performed if and

Table 2. Requirements elicited using TrUStAPIS from [11]

Requirement	Statement of the Requirement	Need
Trust Req.	**TRST01** - The SCM shall trust a Smart Supermarket with a trust level above 0.5	Need 3
Usability Req.	**USAB01** - The user shall be able to insert new recipes	Need 2
Security Req.	**SEC01** - The user shall be authenticated	Need 2
Security Req.	**SEC02** - The SCM shall delegate the Smart Hub to order the missing ingredients	Need X
Availability Req.	**AVBT01** - The SCM shall be able to connect to the Smart Hub	Need X
Privacy Req.	**PRIV01** - The SCM shall perform an encrypted communication with the Smart Fridge	Need 4
Identity Req.	**IDNT01** - The user shall be authenticated	Need 2
Identity Req.	**IDNT01**.2 - The user shall be authenticated by code	Need 2
Safety Req.	**SFT01** - The SCM shall be able to check its temperature level	Need 1
Safety Req.	**SFT01**.1 - The SCM temperature level shall be lower than 250 °C	Need 1

only if the computed trust value is more than 0.5. If the interaction is performed at a lower level, the validation test fails. Otherwise, it succeeds.

Step 2. This step is fundamental in order to certify that the tested functionalities satisfy the requirements and fulfil the originating need. If the previous step ends correctly, it confirms that the originating need is met. Otherwise, an issue is raised, and the developers will need to check and correct it. After all the functionalities have been checked in their environment and compared with the needs, it is possible to continue to the final step of the validation process.

Step 3. The validation response is positive if all the previous steps have been positively performed. Thus, documentation is produced to certify that stakeholders' needs have been met and it is possible to proceed to K-Model's final phase: Utilization. However, if validation tests have failed, it will be produced documentation about the failed functionalities to discuss and fix the raised issues.

8   Conclusion and Future Work

Trust is important in the IoT environment. In order to guarantee trust in the IoT, we believe that it is useful to consider it during the whole SDLC. In this paper, we focused on two phases of the SDLC: verification and validation. In the verification phase, developers analyze the previously elicited requirements.

Then, the functionalities are tested to prove that the entity has been built in the right way. Finally, during the validation process, the developers must check that the complete IoT entity matches its originating needs. Thus, if the validation process is correctly performed, it is possible to assert that the right IoT entity has been built. As a future work, we will perform the tests in a complex scenario.

Acknowledgement. This work has been supported by the Spanish Ministry of Science and Innovation Project SecureEDGE (PID2019-110565RB-I00), by the Regional Ministry of Economic Transformation, Industry, Knowledge and Universities of Andalusia SAVE (P18-TP-3724) and by the EU H2020-SU-ICT-03-2018 Project No. 830929 CyberSec4Europe (cybersec4europe.eu). Moreover, we thank Huawei Technology for their support. This work reflects only the authors view and the Research Executive Agency is not responsible for any use that may be made of the information it contains.

References

1. Ackerman, A.F., Buchwald, L.S., Lewski, F.H.: Software inspections: an effective verification process. IEEE Softw. **6**(3), 31–36 (1989)
2. Alonso-Nogueira, A., Estévez-Fernández, H., García, I.: JREM: an approach for formalising models in the requirements phase with JSON and NoSQL databases. Int. J. Comput. Inf. Eng. **11**(3), 353–358 (2017)
3. Arthur, J.D., Dabney, J.B.: Applying standard independent verification and validation (IV&V) techniques within an agile framework: is there a compatibility issue? In: 2017 Annual IEEE International Systems Conference (SysCon), pp. 1–5. IEEE (2017)
4. Arthur, J.D., Nance, R.E.: Independent verification and validation: a missing link in simulation methodology? In: Proceedings Winter Simulation Conference, pp. 230–236. IEEE (1996)
5. Čolaković, A., Hadžialić, M.: Internet of things (IoT): a review of enabling technologies, challenges, and open research issues. Comput. Netw. **144**, 17–39 (2018)
6. Edition, F.: Ieee guide-adoption of the project management institute (pmi®) standard a guide to the project management body of knowledge (pmbok® guide) (2011)
7. Erickson, J.: Trust metrics. In: International Symposium on Collaborative Technologies and Systems, CTS 2009, pp. 93–97. IEEE (2009)
8. Fagan, M.: Design and code inspections to reduce errors in program development. In: Broy, M., Denert, E. (eds.) Software Pioneers, pp. 575–607. Springer, Heidelberg (2002). https://doi.org/10.1007/978-3-642-59412-0_35
9. Fernandez-Gago, C., Moyano, F., Lopez, J.: Modelling trust dynamics in the internet of things. Infor. Sci. **396**, 72–82 (2017)
10. Ferraris, D., Daniel, J., Fernandez-Gago, C., Lopez, J.: A segregated architecture for a trust-based network of internet of things. In: 2019 16th IEEE Annual Consumer Communications & Networking Conference (CCNC) (CCNC 2019). Las Vegas, USA, January 2019
11. Ferraris, D., Fernandez-Gago, C.: TrUStAPIS: a trust requirements elicitation method for IoT. Int. J. Inf. Securi. **19**, 1–17 (2019)
12. Ferraris, D., Fernandez-Gago, C., Lopez, J.: A trust by design framework for the internet of things. In: NTMS'2018 - Security Track (NTMS 2018 Security Track). Paris, France, February 2018

13. Ferraris, D., Fernandez-Gago, C., Lopez, J.: A model-driven approach to ensure trust in the IoT. Hum.-Cent. Comput. Inf. Sci. **10**(1), 1–33 (2020)
14. Food, U., Administration, D., et al.: Guideline on general principles of process validation. US FDA, Rockville (1987)
15. Haskins, C., Forsberg, K., Krueger, M., Walden, D., Hamelin, D.: Systems engineering handbook. In: INCOSE (2006)
16. Hoffman, L.J., Lawson-Jenkins, K., Blum, J.: Trust beyond security: an expanded trust model. Commun. ACM **49**(7), 94–101 (2006)
17. Katz, P., Campbell, C.: FDA 2011 process validation guidance: process validation revisited. J. GXP Compliance **16**(4), 18 (2012)
18. Linhares, M.V., de Oliveira, R.S., Farines, J.M., Vernadat, F.: Introducing the modeling and verification process in SysML. In: 2007 IEEE Conference on Emerging Technologies and Factory Automation (EFTA 2007), pp. 344–351. IEEE (2007)
19. Marche, C., Nitti, M.: Can we trust trust management systems? IoT **3**(2), 262–272 (2022)
20. Nkuba, C.K., Kim, S., Dietrich, S., Lee, H.: Riding the IoT wave with VFuzz: discovering security flaws in smart homes. IEEE Access **10**, 1775–1789 (2021)
21. Pavlidis, M.: Designing for trust. In: CAiSE (Doctoral Consortium), pp. 3–14 (2011)
22. Ponsard, C., Ramon, V.: Survey of automation practices in model-driven development and operations. Tech. rep, EasyChair (2022)
23. Roman, R., Najera, P., Lopez, J.: Securing the internet of things. Computer **44**(9), 51–58 (2011)

Privacy-Preserving Access
and Computation

Robust and Provably Secure Attribute-Based Encryption Supporting Access Revocation and Outsourced Decryption

Anis Bkakria[✉]

IRT SystemX, Palaiseau, France
`Anis.Bkakria@irt-systemx.fr`

Abstract. Attribute based encryption (ABE) is a cryptographic technique allowing fine-grained access control by enabling one-to-many encryption. Existing ABE constructions suffer from at least one of the following limitations. First, single point of failure on security meaning that, once an authority is compromised, an adversary can either easily break the confidentiality of the encrypted data or effortlessly prevent legitimate users from accessing data; second, the lack of user and/or attribute revocation mechanism achieving forward secrecy; third, a heavy computation workload is placed on data user; last but not least, the lack of adaptive security in standard models. In this paper, we propose the first single-point-of-failure free multi-authority ciphertext-policy ABE that simultaneously (1) ensures robustness for both decryption key issuing and access revocation while achieving forward secrecy; (2) enables outsourced decryption to reduce the decryption overhead for data users that have limited computational resources; and (3) achieves adaptive (full) security in standard models. The provided theoretical complexity comparison shows that our construction introduces linear storage and computation overheads that occurs only once during its setup phase, which we believe to be a reasonable price to pay to achieve all previous features.

Keywords: ABE · Threshold Cryptography · Adaptive Security

1 Introduction

Cloud computing enables the on-demand provision of various resources, such as computing power and storage over the Internet, freeing companies from maintaining IT infrastructure and managing data centers so they can focus on their core business. In addition, cloud computing enables users to take advantage of a variety of powerful resources on a pay-as-you-go basis. Nevertheless, security and privacy issues have become the main obstacle to the wider adoption of cloud computing. According to Techfunnel's top five cloud computing predictions for 2020 [26], security tops the list of the biggest cloud challenges. Hence,

© IFIP International Federation for Information Processing 2022
Published by Springer Nature Switzerland AG 2022
S. Sural and H. Lu (Eds.): DBSec 2022, LNCS 13383, pp. 197–214, 2022.
https://doi.org/10.1007/978-3-031-10684-2_12

users/companies are reluctant to outsource their important data to non fully-trusted Cloud servers.

In a non fully trusted cloud environment, preserving data confidentiality, making appropriate decisions about data access, and enforcing fine-grained access policies are major challenges. Hence, many cryptography-based system models and techniques have been proposed to enable efficient and secure cloud access control. Among the previous, ABE [23] allows simultaneous confidentiality preservation and fine-grained access control. ABE has succeeded in attracting considerable research efforts [2,32] which allows defining additional cryptographically functional features, such as access revocation, accountability, and robustness to the basic construction. Unfortunately, all the proposed ABE constructions suffer from at least one of the following limitations. First, the lack of robustness meaning that once the authority responsible for issuing decryption keys to data users is compromised, an adversary can either easily break the confidentiality of the encrypted data or effortlessly prevent legitimate users from accessing data. Second, the lack of access revocation making the concerned approaches inflexible. Third, most of the proposed ABE constructions require heavy computation workload to be performed by data users at access time. Last but not least, the lack of security in standard models. We provide a full comparison with related literature in Sect. 2.

In this paper, we propose a new multi-authority ciphertext-policy ABE (CP-ABE) scheme with some interesting features. First, it ensures robustness for both decryption key issuing and access revocation processes. That is, an adversary needs to compromise several authorities to be able either to break the confidentiality of the outsourced data or to prevent authorized users from accessing outsourced data. Second, our construction enables attribute revocation while achieving forward secrecy. Third, it enables to outsource most part of the decryption process to the cloud server while ensuring that the latter learns nothing about the partially decrypted data. Fourth, our construction achieves adaptive security in standard models. The construction we propose in this paper is – to our knowledge – the first to provide all previously mentioned features. Finally, we conduct a theoretical comparison with similar constructions to show that ours introduces linear storage and computation overheads that occur only once during its setup phase.

The paper is organized as follows. Section 2 reviews related work and provides a comprehensive comparison with our construction. Sections 3 and 4 present the assumptions and the adversary model we are considering to achieve provable security. Section 5 formalizes our primitive. Then, in Sect. 6, we provide the security results. In Sect. 7, we discuss the complexity of our construction. Finally, Sect. 8 concludes.

2   Related Work

Revocable ABE. Several researchers have been devoted to build ABE constructions allowing access revocation. Liang et al. [15] introduce a provably selectively secure CP-ABE construction that enables access revocation through proxy re-encryption. Using the latter technique, Luo et al. [19] designed a selectively secure and small attribute universe based CP-ABE supporting policy updating. Always relying on proxy re-encryption, Yu et al. [31] propose an AND-gate policy based ABE construction enabling attribute and user revocation. The proposed construction is proved to be selectively secure under the decisional bilinear Diffie-Hellman (DBDH) assumption. To allow the enforcement of non-monotonic access structures, Lewko et al. [10] propose a selectively secure in the standard model ABE construction that enables attribute revocation. Hur and Noh [8] rely on a stateless group key distribution method based on binary trees to define a CP-ABE solution enabling attribute revocation. The authors claimed that the proposed scheme achieves backward secrecy and forward secrecy without providing formal security analysis. Yang et al. [28] propose a CP-ABE construction enabling attribute and user revocation based on a ciphertext re-encryption mechanism performed by a third-party honest-but-curious server. The proposed construction is proved to be selectively secure under the q-type assumption. In [29], Yang et al. propose a multi-authority CP-ABE supporting revocation process. The latter is performed mainly by attribute authorities which are responsible for computing an updated decryption key for each non-revoked user. Relying on binary trees, Cui et al. [6] propose a CP-ABE scheme that enables attribute revocation where most of the computations are delegated to an untrusted server. Similarly to [8], the authors of [6] claim that their construction is both backward and forward secure without providing any formal proofs. Liu et al. [18] propose a large universe CP-ABE construction enabling both user revocation and accountability. The authors show that the proposed construction is selectively secure in standard models. Li et al. [13] propose a new multi-authority CP-ABE scheme enabling attribute revocation while being adaptively secure in the setting of bilinear groups with composite order. Relying on an untrusted server, Qin et al. [22] design an adaptively secure CP-ABE scheme enabling attribute revocation. In the proposed scheme, the untrusted server is used to help non-revoked users to decrypt ciphertexts. Very recently, Xiong et al. [27] propose an adaptively secure CP-ABE scheme allowing attribute revocation. It uses monotonic span program [9] as an access structure to reduce the number of pairing and exponentiation operations required for encryption and decryption.

Outsourced Decryption-Based ABE. To mitigate the burden of decryption for data users, Yang et al. [29] propose a construction that outsources most part of the computations to the cloud server. The same idea was later used in [6,22,27,30].

Robust ABE. A common weakness of the previously mentioned ABE constructions is that they all include a single point of failure on security. That is, as soon as an attribute authority is compromised by an adversary, the latter can easily break the confidentiality of the outsourced data by issuing valid secret decryption keys. To mitigate the previous threat, Li et al. [14] propose a multi-authority CP-ABE called TMACS. In contrast to previously mentioned approaches, in TMACS, the set of attribute authorities are collaboratively managing the whole set of attributes and no one of them can have full control over any specific attribute. The construction relies on a (t, n) threshold secret sharing protocol (see Section 3.2 of the extended version of this paper [4]) to require the collaboration of at least t attribute authorities to issue a valid decryption key, which allows to prove that the proposed construction is selectively secure even when $t-1$ authorities are compromised. Unfortunately, neither the access revocation, nor the outsourced decryption has been addressed in this work.

Table 1 presents a comprehensive feature comparison of the (most) related CP-ABE schemes. According to it, the construction we propose in this paper is the only one that achieves simultaneously robustness, access revocation, outsourced decryption, and adaptive security.

Table 1. Feature comparaison of (most) related CP-ABE constructions

Approaches	Robustness	Revocation	Security Model	Outsourced Decryption
[7, 16, 20, 21, 23, 25]	✗	✗	Selective	✗
[8, 10, 12, 15, 19, 28, 31]	✗	✓	Selective	✗
[6, 29, 30]	✗	✓	Selective	✓
[14]	✓	✗	Selective	✗
[3, 11, 24]	✗	✗	Fully	✗
[13, 18]	✗	✓	Fully	✗
[22, 27]	✗	✓	Fully	✓
This work	✓	✓	Fully	✓

3   Preliminaries

Definition 1 (Bilinear Maps). *Let $\mathbb{G}_1$, $\mathbb{G}_2$, and $\mathbb{G}_T$ be three multiplicative cyclic groups of prime order p. Let $e : \mathbb{G}_1 \times \mathbb{G}_2 \to \mathbb{G}_T$ be a bilinear map having the following properties:*

- *Symmetric bilinearity: $\forall g_1 \in \mathbb{G}_1, \forall g_2 \in \mathbb{G}_2$ and $\forall a, b \in \mathbb{Z}_p$, we have $e(g_1^a, g_2^b) = e(g_1^b, g_2^a) = e(g_1, g_2)^{a \cdot b}$.*
- *Non-degeneracy: $e(g_1, g_2) \neq 1$.*
- *The group operations in $\mathbb{G}_1$, $\mathbb{G}_2$ and $e(\cdot, \cdot)$ are efficiently computable.*

The security of our construction holds as long as $\mathbb{G}_1 \neq \mathbb{G}_2$ and no efficiently computable homomorphism exists between $\mathbb{G}_1$ and $\mathbb{G}_2$ in either directions. In the sequel, the we refer to $(\mathbb{G}_1, \mathbb{G}_2, \mathbb{G}_T, p, e(\cdot, \cdot))$ as a bilinear environment.

Definition 2 (independence [5]). *Let p be some large prime, r, s, t, and c be positive integers. Let $R = \langle r_1, \cdots, r_r \rangle \in \mathbb{F}_p[X_1, \cdots, X_c]^r$, $S = \langle s_1, \cdots, s_s \rangle \in \mathbb{F}_p[X_1, \cdots, X_c]^s$, and $T = \langle t_1, \cdots, t_t \rangle \in \mathbb{F}_p[X_1, \cdots, X_c]^t$ be three tuples of* multivariate polynomials over the field $\mathbb{F}_p$. We say that polynomial $f \in$ $\mathbb{F}_p[X_1, \cdots, X_c]$ is dependant on the triple $\langle R, S, T \rangle$ if there exists $r \cdot s + t$ constants $\{\vartheta_{i,j}^{(a)}\}_{i,j=1}^{i=r, j=s}$, $\{\vartheta_k^{(b)}\}_{k=1}^t$ such that

$$f = \sum_{i,j} \vartheta_{i,j}^{(a)} \cdot r_i \cdot s_j + \sum_k \vartheta_k^{(b)} \cdot t_k$$

We say that f is independent of $\langle R, S, T \rangle$ if f is not dependent on $\langle R, S, T \rangle$.

Definition 3 (GDHE assumption [5]**).** Let $(\mathbb{G}_1, \mathbb{G}_2, \mathbb{G}_T, p, e(\cdot, \cdot))$ be a bilinear environment and r, s, t, and c be positive integers. Let $R = \langle r_1, \cdots, r_r \rangle$ $\in \mathbb{F}_p[X_1, \cdots, X_c]^r$, $S = \langle s_1, \cdots, s_s \rangle \in \mathbb{F}_p[X_1, \cdots, X_c]^s$, and $T = \langle t_1, \cdots, t_r \rangle$ $\in \mathbb{F}_p[X_1, \cdots, X_c]^t$ be three tuples of multivariate polynomials over the field $\mathbb{F}_p$. The GDHE assumption states that, given the vector

$$H(x_1, \cdots, x_c) = (g_1^{R(x_1, \cdots, x_c)}, g_2^{S(x_1, \cdots, x_c)}, e(g_1, g_2)^{T(x_1, \cdots, x_c)}) \in \mathbb{G}_1^r \times \mathbb{G}_2^s \times \mathbb{G}_T^t$$

it is hard to decide whether $U = e(g_1, g_2)^{f(x_1, \cdots, x_c)}$ or U is random if f is independent of (R, S, T).

4 System and Security Models

In this section, we introduce the system model we are considering. Then, we define the scheme we are proposing, the considered threat model, and the security requirements we aim to ensure.

4.1 System Model

The system we consider to build our scheme is composed of five entities: A decentralized certificate authority, multiple attribute authorities, data providers, data users, and a cloud server provider.

- The decentralized certificate authority (DCA) is a consortium blockchain-based PKI management system (e.g., [1]) which is responsible of setting up of the system by choosing its parameters such as, the set of attributes as well as the bilinear environment to be used. It is also in charge of registering data users and attribute authorities. Finally, DCA is responsible for choosing the robustness level that should be satisfied, i.e., the number of attribute authorities that should be compromised to break the confidentiality of the shared data. DCA is not involved in decryption key issuing and access revocation.
- Attribute authorities (AAs) are a set of entities that collaboratively control the access to the shared data by cooperatively issuing decryption keys to data users.
- Cloud storage provider (CSP) provides data storage and computation capabilities such as outsourced decryption and ciphertext re-encryption.

- The data provider (DP) is the entity that aims to share its data. It encrypts his/her data using a chosen access policy that specifies who can get access to his/her data.
- The data user (DU) represents an entity that aims to access and use the shared data. A DU is labeled by a set of attributes. It is supposed to be able to download any encrypted data from the CSP. However, only DUs with proper attributes can successfully decrypt the retrieved encrypted data.

4.2 Definition of Our Construction

Our construction consists of eight algorithms: `GlobalSetup`, `CAKeyGen`, `AAKeyGen`, `Encrypt`, `DecKeyGen`, `PartialDecrypt`, `Decrypt`, and `Revoke`. The algorithms `GlobalSetup` and `CAKeyGen` are performed by DCA. `AAKeyGen` is performed by AAs. `DecKeyGen` is performed collaboratively between a DU and AAs. `Revoke` is collaboratively performed by AAs and CSP. `Encrypt` is performed by DP. `PartialDecrypt` algorithm involves DU and CSP. Finally, `Decrypt` is performed by DU.

- `GlobalSetup`$(\lambda, t, \Sigma) \rightarrow env$ is a probabilistic algorithm that takes as input the security parameter λ, a robustness level t, and a set of attributes Σ. It outputs the public parameters of the system env. The latter will be implicitly used by all the following algorithms and so will be omitted.
- `AAKeygen`$() \rightarrow (SK, PK)$ is a probabilistic algorithm that returns a secret key share SK and a master public key share PK.
- `CAKeyGen`$(\{PK_i\}) \rightarrow MPK$ is a probabilistic algorithm that takes as input the set of master public key shares $\{PK_i\}$ of the involved AAs and outputs a master public key MPK.
- `Encrypt`$(M, \mathbb{M}, MPK) \rightarrow \chi$ is a probabilistic algorithm that takes a message M and an access structure $\mathbb{M}$ and outputs an encrypted bundle χ.
- `DecKeyGen`$(MPK, AA) \rightarrow \mathcal{K}$ is a probabilistic algorithm that takes as input the master public key MPK and the set of registered attribute authorities AA and outputs a secret decryption key $\mathcal{K}$.
- `Revoke`$(u, \{\sigma_i\}) \rightarrow (MPK, ReK)$ is a probabilistic algorithm that takes as input a data user u and a set of attributes $\{\sigma_i\}$ and returns an updated master public key MPK and an updated re-encryption key ReK.
- `PartialDecrypt`$(\mathcal{SK}_{csp}, \overline{\mathcal{K}}, ind) \rightarrow \overline{\chi}$ is a deterministic algorithm that takes as input the secret key $\mathcal{SK}_{csp}$ of the CSP, a randomized decryption key $\overline{\mathcal{K}}$, and the index ind of the data item to decrypt χ and returns a partially decrypted data item $\overline{\chi}$.
- `Decrypt`$(\mathcal{K}, \overline{\chi}) \rightarrow M$ is a deterministic algorithm that takes as input a DU's secret decryption key $\mathcal{K}$ and a partially decrypted data item $\overline{\chi}$ and outputs a plaintext data item M.

4.3 Threat Model

In our scheme, as the DCA capabilities are supposed to be provided by a blockchain-based PKI management system, then we fairly assume that the DCA is a trusted, single point of failure-free, entity. Hence, DCA is supposed to issue correct signed certificates to the different registered entities involved in the system. Attribute authorities involved in the system are considered as *honest-but-curious* entities. They are honest in the sense that they are supposed to correctly perform the different operations of our construction, but we suppose that some of them can be corrupted by an adversary who aims to learn as much information as possible about the data. Similarly, we assume that the CSP is also *honest-but-curious* as it will correctly follow the proposed protocol, yet may try to learn information about the shared data. Data consumers are considered to be malicious entities that can collude with each other and/or with compromised attribute authorities. Finally, we suppose that the CSP will not collude with data users to infer more information about the shared data. We believe that this last assumption is fairly reasonable since, in a free market environment, an open dishonest behavior will result in considerable damages for the involved entities.

4.4   Security Requirements

Three security requirements are considered in our construction: collusion resistance, robustness, as well as forward secrecy. The formalization of the following requirements is given in the full version of the paper [4].

Collusion Resistance. Since we suppose that multiple malicious data users may collude to gain access to an encrypted data that none of them can access alone, we require our construction to be secure against such collusion attacks.

Robustness. According to the threat model we are considering, we suppose that a subset of attribute authorities can be compromised by an adversary. Hence, we require our construction to be robust. That is, any encrypted data item remains fully protected against unauthorized entities as long as no more than $t-1$ attribute authorities are compromised, with t denoting the robustness level.

Forward Secrecy. Forward secrecy is a mandatory property for enabling secure revocation. Forward secrecy requires that it should not be feasible for a data user to decrypt previous (non downloaded) and subsequent ciphertexts, if a subset of his/her attributes required for decryption are revoked.

5   Our Proposed Scheme

We now present the details of our construction. Since DCA capabilities are provided by a consortium blockchain-based PKI management system, we use the same blockchain as a trusted shared storage to store the different public elements exchanged between the different parties that compose our system. Hence, the consortium blockchain is supposed to be accessible to all the entities involved in the system. In the sequel, we refer to the former as $\mathcal{B}$.

5.1 System Initialization

GlobalSetup. Let $(\mathbb{G}_1, \mathbb{G}_2, \mathbb{G}_T, p, e(\cdot, \cdot))$ be a bilinear environment, g_1 and g_2 be two random elements of $\mathbb{G}_1$ and $\mathbb{G}_2$ respectively. Let $H : \mathbb{G}_T \to \{0, 1\}^m$ be a cryptographic hash function for some $m(\geq 256)$ and $\varXi$ be an unforgeable under adaptive chosen message attacks signature system. The DCA generates a signature key SMK and a verification key VMK and sends the pubic parameters $env = (\mathbb{G}_1, \mathbb{G}_2, \mathbb{G}_T, p, e(\cdot, \cdot), g_1, g_2, H, \varXi, VMK)$ to $\mathcal{B}$ for storage.

System Initialization. The system is initialized using the following steps.

- **AA registration:** Each attribute authority AA_i uses $\varXi$ to generate a private key $\mathcal{SK}_{AA_i}$ and a public key $\mathcal{PK}_{AA_i}$ and sends a registration request to DCA. If AA_i is a legal authority, the DCA generates a random global identity $aid \in Z_p$, issues a signed certificate $Cert_{aid}$, and submits the couple $(aid, Cert_{aid})$ for storage in $\mathcal{B}$.
- **CSP registration:** This step is triggered when CSP sends a registration query to DCA. Then, the latter assigns a random identifier $cspid \in \mathbb{Z}_p$, issues a certificates $Cert_{cspid}$, and submits the couple $(cspid, Cert_{cspid})$ for storage in $\mathcal{B}$. Finally, CSP initializes its secret key as $\mathcal{SK}_{csp} = \emptyset$. The latter will be used to enforce access revocation by updating encrypted data items.
- **Robustness level selection:** Let us suppose that n attribute authorities $AA = \{A_1, \cdots, A_n\}$ are registered in the system. Using this process, DCA chooses the robustness level t $(t < n)$ that should be satisfied and sends the master public key $MPK = (env, n, t)$ for storage in $\mathcal{B}$.
- **AA key generation:** This process is performed by each one of the n attribute authorities. The process requires the cooperation of the attribute authorities with each other to call the trusted third party free threshold secret sharing (see [4], Section 3.2). Each A_i performs the following steps:
  - Select three random scalars $a_i, \alpha_i, \overline{\alpha}_i \in \mathbb{Z}_p$ as sub-secrets and generate three random polynomials $f_i(x)$, $h_i(x)$, and $\overline{h}_i(x)$ of degree $t-1$ such that $f_i(0) = a_i$, $h_i(0) = \alpha_i$, and $\overline{h}_i(0) = \overline{\alpha}_i$. Then for all $j \in \{1, 2, \cdots, n\}\setminus\{i\}$, calculate $s_{i,j}^{\{a\}} = f_i(aid_j)$, $s_{i,j}^{\{\alpha\}} = h_i(aid_j)$, and $s_{i,j}^{\{\overline{\alpha}\}} = \overline{h}_i(aid_j)$, and send $s_{i,j}^{\{a\}}$, $s_{i,j}^{\{\alpha\}}$, and $s_{i,j}^{\{\overline{\alpha}\}}$ securely to A_j.
  - After receiving $s_{j,i}^{\{a\}}$, $s_{j,i}^{\{\alpha\}}$ and $s_{j,i}^{\{\overline{\alpha}\}}$ from all other $n-1$ AAs, each A_i calculates for $k \in \{a, \alpha, \overline{\alpha}\}$: $sk_i^{\{k\}} = \sum_{j=1}^{n} s_{j,i}^{\{k\}}$, $pka_i = g_1^{sk_i^{\{a\}}}$, $\overline{pka}_i = g_2^{sk_i^{\{a\}}}$, $pke_i = e(g_1, g_2)^{sk_i^{\{\alpha\}}}$, and $pkr_i = g_2^{sk_i^{\{\overline{\alpha}\}}}$. Finally, each A_i sends its master public key share $PK_i = \{pka_i, \overline{pka}_i, pke_i, pkr_i\}$ to $\mathcal{B}$ for storage. The secret key share of A_i is set as $SK_i = \{sk_i^{\{k\}}\}_{k \in \{a, \alpha, \overline{\alpha}\}}$.
  - For each attribute $\sigma \in \Sigma$, choose a random scalar $\theta_{\sigma,i} \in \mathbb{Z}_p$, compute $\Theta_{\sigma,i} = g_1^{\theta_{\sigma,i}}$ and $\overline{\Theta}_{\sigma,i} = g_2^{\theta_{\sigma,i}}$ and send them to the $\mathcal{B}$ for storage.
  - For each attribute $\sigma \in \Sigma$, store an initially empty list of users $\mathcal{U}_{r,\sigma}$ denoting the users to whom the attribute σ is revoked.

- **Master public key generation**: This step is performed by DCA which randomly selects t out of the n AAs master public key shares $\{PK_1, \cdots, PK_n\}$. Let us denote by $\mathcal{I}$ the set of indices of the t chosen master public key shares. The global public key of the system is then computed as follows.

$$pka = \prod_{i \in \mathcal{I}} (pka_i)^{\prod_{j \in \mathcal{I}, j \neq i} \frac{aid_i}{aid_j - aid_i}} = g_1^a$$

$$\overline{pka} = \prod_{i \in \mathcal{I}} (\overline{pka}_i)^{\prod_{j \in \mathcal{I}, j \neq i} \frac{aid_i}{aid_j - aid_i}} = g_2^a$$

$$pke = \prod_{i \in \mathcal{I}} (pke_i)^{\prod_{j \in \mathcal{I}, j \neq i} \frac{aid_i}{aid_j - aid_i}} = e(g_1, g_2)^\alpha$$

$$pkr = \prod_{i \in \mathcal{I}} (pkr_i)^{\prod_{j \in \mathcal{I}, j \neq i} \frac{aid_i}{aid_j - aid_i}} = g_2^{\overline{\alpha}}$$

with $a = \sum_{i=1}^n a_i$, $\alpha = \sum_{i=1}^n \alpha_i$, and $\overline{\alpha} = \sum_{i=1}^n \overline{\alpha}_i$. Then, DCA computes Θ_σ and $\overline{\Theta}_\sigma$ for all $\sigma \in \Sigma$ as $\Theta_\sigma = \prod_{i=1}^n \Theta_{\sigma,i}$ and $\overline{\Theta}_\sigma = \prod_{i=1}^n \overline{\Theta}_{\sigma,i}$. Finally, DCA sends the master public key $MPK = \{env, pka, \overline{pka}, pke, pkr, \Theta_\sigma, \overline{\Theta}_\sigma, \pi_p = 0\}_{\sigma \in \Sigma}$ to $\mathcal{B}$ for storage. The scalar π_p represents the timestep on which the public key is created/updated.

We emphasize here that the master key $MK = \{a, \alpha, \overline{\alpha}\}$ is implicitly shared among the different AAs. However, it does not need to be obtained by any entity in the system.

5.2 Data Sharing

The data encryption operation Encrypt is performed by the data provider independently. Before outsourcing the data item to CSP, similarly to most ABE schemes, the data to be shared M is firstly encrypted using a secure symmetric key algorithm (e.g., AES). The used symmetric key is generated then encrypted as we describe in the following steps.

- The data provider starts by defining a monotone boolean formula involving a subset of attributes $\Sigma^* \subseteq \Sigma$ as the access policy that should be enforced on the data to be outsourced/shared. Then he/she executes the Encrypt algorithm which picks a random scalar $s \in \mathbb{Z}_p$ and uses the component pke of the master public key MPK to generate the symmetric key $\kappa = H(pke^s) = H\left(e(g_1, g_2)^{\alpha \cdot s}\right)$. κ is then used to encrypt the data item to be shared M to get $E_\kappa(M)$.
- The data provider chooses the access policy to be enforced and transforms it into a Linear Secret Sharing Scheme (LSSS) access structure $(\mathbb{M}, \rho)$ as described in [17], where $\mathbb{M}$ is an $l \times k$ LSSS matrix and $\rho(x)$ maps each row of $\mathbb{M}$ to an attribute $\sigma \in \Sigma$. Next, to make sure that only the keys that satisfy $(\mathbb{M}, \rho)$ will be able to compute κ, we hide the random element s used

to generate κ by choosing a random vector $\boldsymbol{v} = \{s, v_2, \cdots, v_k\} \in \mathbb{Z}_p^k$. For each row vector M_i of M, $\lambda_i = \mathrm{M}_i \cdot \boldsymbol{v}^\top$ is calculated and a random scalar $r_i \in \mathbb{Z}_p$ is chosen. The ciphertext encrypting the symmetric encryption key κ is computed as $\mathcal{C} = \{C' = g_2^s, \; C_i = \overline{pka}^{\lambda_i} \cdot \overline{\Theta}_{\rho(i)}^{-r_i}, \; D_i = g_2^{r_i}\}_{i \in [1,l]}$. Finally, the data owner sends the encrypted data item bundle $\chi = (E_\kappa(M), \mathcal{C}, \pi_c = \pi_p)$ to CSP. Similarly, π_c is used to denote the timestep on which the data item has been encrypted. At encryption, the timestep π_c is the same as the timestep associated to the master public key MPK.

5.3   User Registration and Key Generation

When a user u_i joins the system, he/she sends a registration query to the DCA to get a unique uid and a signed certificate $Cert_{uid}$. Let us denote by Σ_{u_i} the set of attributes that has to be assigned to u_i according to the role he/she plays in the system. Thus, to generate a secret decryption key, u_i performs the following steps:

- First, u_i selects t out of the n registered attribute authorities according to his/her own preferences. Then, u_i separately queries each of the selected t attribute authorities to request a secret decryption key share. We emphasis here that a data user will be able to generate a valid secret decryption key if and only if he/she gets t secret decryption key shares from t different attribute authorities. To request a secret decryption key share from an attribute authority A_j, u_i sends a secret decryption issuance query containing the identifier uid of u_i signed using $Cert_{uid}$ to A_j. Once the query is recieved by A_j, the latter starts by checking the signature of DCA on $Cert_{uid}$ then authenticates the request content by verifying the signature of u_i on the request. If u_i is authorized to access the shared data, then A_j assigns the set of attributes $\Sigma_{u_i}^{(j)} = \Sigma_{u_i} \setminus \{\sigma | u_i \in \mathcal{U}_{r,\sigma}\}$ to u_i where $\{\sigma | u_i \in \mathcal{U}_{r,\sigma}\}$ is the set of attributes that has been revoked from u_i. Then, A_j chooses a random scalar $b_j \in \mathbb{Z}_p$ and uses the MPK to generate a secret decryption key share for u_i as $\mathcal{K}_{u_i,j} = \{K_j = g_1^{sk_j^{\{\alpha\}}} \cdot pka^{b_j}, \; L_j = g_1^{b_j}, \; K_{\sigma,j} = \Theta_\sigma^{b_j}\}_{\sigma \in \Sigma_{u_i}^{(j)}}$.
- Once u_i gains t secret decryption key shares from t different attribute authorities, he/she computes his/her secret decryption key as following.

$$K = \prod_{i=1}^{t} K_i^{\prod_{j=1, j \neq i}^{t} \frac{aid_j}{aid_j - aid_i}}$$

$$= g_1^\alpha \cdot g_1^{a \cdot \sum_{i=1}^{t} (b_i \cdot \prod_{j=1, j \neq i}^{t} \frac{aid_j}{aid_j - aid_i})}$$

$$L = g_1^{\sum_{i=1}^{t} (b_i \cdot \prod_{j=1, j \neq i}^{t} \frac{aid_j}{aid_j - aid_i})}$$

$$K_\sigma = \Theta_\sigma^{\sum_{i=1}^{t} (b_i \cdot \prod_{j=1, j \neq i}^{t} \frac{aid_j}{aid_j - aid_i})}, \quad \sigma \in \Sigma_{u_i}$$

For sake of simplicity, let us introduce the parameter d:

$$d = \sum_{i=1}^{t} \left(b_i \cdot \prod_{j=1, j \neq i}^{} \frac{aid_j}{aid_j - aid_i} \right)$$

Therefore, the user's secret key can be simplified as $\mathcal{K}_u = \{K = g_1^{\alpha} \cdot g_1^{a \cdot d}, L = g_1^{d}, K_{\sigma} = \Theta_{\sigma}^{d}, \pi_u = \pi_p\}_{\sigma \in \Sigma_{u_i}}$ where π_u is used to denote the timestep on which $\mathcal{K}_u$ is issued.

We note here that the queried attribute authorities may assign different attributes $\Sigma_{u_i}^{(j)}$ to u_i. If it is the case, $\mathcal{K}_u$ will involve only the set of attributes $\Sigma_{u_i} = \cap_{j=0}^{t} \Sigma_{u_i}^{(j)}$ that are assigned by all t attribute authorities.

5.4   Access Revocation

Our construction aims to achieve robust fine-grained and on-demand access revocation. That is, to prevent a compromised AA from prohibiting authorized users from accessing the outsourced data by revoking their attributes, our construction requires the collaboration of t out of the n $(t > n/2)$ registered attribute authorities to perform an access revocation. The revocation process is performed according to the following three steps.

Step 1: Collaborative Revocation Request. The access revocation process is triggered by an attribute authority A_i that wants to revoke the access granted by specific set of attributes $\Sigma_r \subset \Sigma$ to a specific set of data users $\mathcal{U}_r$. A_i generates a random scalar $t \in \mathbb{Z}_p$ and computes $\mathcal{R}_i = \{R_i = g_2^{t \cdot sk_i^{\overline{\alpha}}}, R_v = pkr^t, R_b = g_2^t, \Sigma_r, \mathcal{U}_r\}$ Then, A_i signs $\mathcal{R}_i$ using $Cert_{aid_i}$, sends it to $\mathcal{B}$ for storage, and broadcasts the revocation request to other registered attribute authorities. Once the revocation request is received by the attribute authorities, each A_j, $j \in [1,n] \backslash \{i\}$ authenticates then processes the access revocation request. If it is legitimate, it computes the revocation request share as following $\mathcal{R}_j = \{R_j = R_b^{sk_j^{\overline{\alpha}}}, R_v = pkr^t, \Sigma_r, \mathcal{U}_r\}$ then, signs $\mathcal{R}_j$ and sends it to $\mathcal{B}$ for storage. Afterwards, each of the attribute authorities that participates to the previous collaborative revocation request updates locally the list of revoked user for each attribute as $\forall \sigma \in \Sigma_r : \mathcal{U}_{r,\sigma} = \mathcal{U}_{r,\sigma} \cup \mathcal{U}_r$.

Step 2: Revocation Enforcement. Once more than $t - 1$ shares for a revocation request are committed to $\mathcal{B}$, CSP computes

$$\prod_{i=1}^{t} R_i^{\Pi_{j=1, j \neq i}^{t} \frac{aid_j}{aid_j - aid_i}} \tag{1}$$

Thanks to the usage of the trusted third party free threshold secret sharing, the collaboration of t attribute authorities are required to compute the shared secret scalar $\overline{\alpha}$. Hence, if Formula (1) is equal to R_v, CSP will be sure that the access revocation is requested by at least t out of the n registered attribute authorities.

Then, CSP generates a random scalar $z \in \mathbb{Z}_p$ and updates the master public key MPK as $\forall \sigma \in \Sigma_r : \Theta_\sigma \leftarrow \Theta_\sigma^z, \overline{\Theta}_\sigma \leftarrow \overline{\Theta}_\sigma^z$, and $\pi_p \leftarrow \pi_p + 1$ and updates its secret key $\mathcal{SK}_{csp}$ as $\mathcal{SK}_{csp} \leftarrow \mathcal{SK}_{csp} \cup \{\mu_{\pi_p} = z\}$ Finally, CSP sends the updated MPK for updation in $\mathcal{B}$.

Step 3: Secret Decryption Key Updating. Once an access revocation request is performed, each data user needs to request a fresh secret decryption key as described in Sect. 5.3.

5.5   Outsourced Pre-decryption and User Decryption

Our construction enables data users to shift expensive computations, i.e., pairing operations to CSP without disclosing any information about the encrypted data to CSP. Outsourced pre-decryption is performed according to the following steps.

Input: $\mathcal{SK}_{csp}, \overline{\mathcal{K}_u}, MPK, ind$
Output: $\overline{\kappa}, E_\kappa(M)$

1 $(E_\kappa(M), \mathcal{C}, \pi_c) = $ get_item(ind)
2 $\mathbb{I} = \{i : \rho(i) \in \Sigma_u\}$
3 if $\pi_u < \pi_p$ then
4 $\quad$ | return exception(``outdated secret decryption key")
5 end
6 $\{C', C_i, D_i\}_{i \in [1,l]} = \mathcal{C}$
7 if $\pi_c < \pi_p$ then
8 $\quad$ $z = 1$
9 $\quad$ for $i \in]\pi_c, \pi_p]$ do
10 $\quad$ $\quad$ | $z = z * \mu_i$
11 $\quad$ end
12 $\quad$ foreach $i \in [1,l]$ do
13 $\quad$ $\quad$ | $D_i = D_i^z$
14 $\quad$ end
15 $\quad$ update_data_item(ind,$\mathcal{C}$, π_p))
16 end
17 $\overline{\kappa} = \dfrac{e(K', C')}{\prod_{i \in \mathbb{I}}\big(e(L', C_i) \cdot e(K_i', D_i)\big)^{w_i}}$
18 return $(\overline{\kappa}, E_\kappa(M))$

Algorithm 1: Outsourced pre-decryption. $\mathbb{M}_u$ is used to denote the submatrix of $\mathbb{M}$, where each row of $\mathbb{M}_u$ corresponds to an attribute in Σ_u, $\mathbb{I}$ is a subset of $\{1, 2, \cdots, l\}$, and $\mathbb{M}_i$ is used to denote the ith row of $\mathbb{M}$. Finally, let $\{w_i\}_{i \in \mathbb{I}}$ be constants such that $\sum_{i \in \mathbb{I}} w_i \cdot \mathbb{M}_i = (1, 0, \cdots, 0)$.

Step 1: Secret Decryption Key Randomization. A DU u starts by randomizing its secret decryption key as follows. He/She picks a random scalar $x \in \mathbb{Z}_p$ and computes $\overline{\mathcal{K}_u} = \{K' = K^x, L' = L^x, K'_\sigma = K^x_\sigma, \pi_u\}$. Then, u sends $\overline{\mathcal{K}_u}$ and the index ind of the item to be pre-decrypted to CSP.

Step 2: Outsourced Pre-decryption. After receiving $(\overline{\mathcal{K}_u}, ind)$, CSP performs the `PartialDecrypt` algorithm which we detail in Algorithm 1. To be useful for pre-decrypting the data item, $\overline{\mathcal{K}_u}$ should include a set of attributes in Σ_u that satisfies the access structure $(\mathbb{M}, \rho)$ used to encrypt the requested data item. As detailed in Algorithm 1, the `PartialDecrypt` algorithm takes as input the secret key $\mathcal{SK}_{csp}$ of the CSP, a randomized secret decryption key $\overline{\mathcal{K}_u}$, the master public key MPK, and the index ind of the data item to encrypt. It outputs a pre-decrypted symmetric key $\overline{\kappa}$ and the data item ciphertext $E_\kappa(M)$.

Step 3: User Decryption. Once the user retrieves the pre-decrypted symmetric key $\overline{\kappa}$ and the ciphertext $E_\kappa(M)$, he/she recovers the symmetric key κ by computing $\kappa = H\left(\overline{\kappa}^{1/x}\right)$ which can be used to decrypt the data item.

6   Security Results

This section presents the security results of our construction. First, in Theorem 1, we show that our construction provides a correct revocable fine-grained access control capabilities. Then, we prove the collusion resistance, the robustness and the forward secrecy properties in Theorems 2, 3, and 4 respectively. The proofs of the following theorems are provided in the full version of this paper [4].

Theorem 1 (Correctness). *Given a data user u to whom a set of attributes Σ_u is assigned and a ciphertext $\mathcal{C}$ encrypted using an access structure $\mathbb{M}$. Let us denote by $\Sigma_r \subset \Sigma_u$ the revoked attributes for u. As long as $\Sigma_u \backslash \Sigma_r$ satisfies $\mathbb{M}$, then the secret decryption key issued to u allows recovering the plaintext of $\mathcal{C}$.*

Theorem 2. *Our construction is collusion resistant under the GDHE assumption.*

Theorem 3. *Our construction is (t, n)-robust under the GDHE assumption.*

Theorem 4. *Our construction is forward secure under the GDHE assumption.*

7   The Complexity

In this section, we analyze the practicability of our construction regarding several properties. We evaluate the storage and communication overheads, as well as the computation cost of the different operations used by our construction. We also evaluate the sizes of the different cryptographic keys to be used by the

Table 2. Notations used in the conducted evaluation

Notation	Description
n	The number of AAs
t	Robustness level ($\leq n$)
N_Σ	The number of attributes in the system
N_u	The number of attributes held by a user
$N_\mathcal{U}$	The number of users in the system
$N_\mathcal{O}$	The number of data owners in the system
$N_\mathcal{I}$	Average data item size
l	The number of rows of the access matrix
$S_{\mathbb{G}_*}$	The size of an element in $\mathbb{G}_*$, $* \in \{0, 1, t\}$
$S_{\mathbb{Z}_p}$	The size of an element in $\mathbb{Z}_p$
π	Number of performed access revocations
$\mathcal{X}$	Set of data encrypted items
$N_{\mathcal{U},R}$	Number of users concerned by a revocation request
$N_{\Sigma,R}$	Number of attributes concerned by a revocation request
$\mathcal{M}$	A group exponentiation operation
$\mathcal{E}$	A pairing operation

entities involved in our construction. For a better understanding of the evaluation results, we conduct a comparative analysis between our construction and TMACS [14]. Both schemes are achieving robustness while providing ABE-based fine-grained access control. The notations we used in the complexity evaluation are described in Table 2. In the sequel, we used (-) to indicate that no storage (resp. communication, resp. computation) is required by an entity, and (N/A) to indicate that a process is not supported by a scheme.

7.1 Storage Complexity

In Table 3, we compare the storage complexity of our construction and TMACS on the different involved entities. Specifically, we quantify the storage complexity in terms of the size of elements (e.g., group elements, certificates, etc.) that are

Table 3. Comparison of the storage complexity

Entity		This work	TMACS
DCA		$(N_\mathcal{U} + n)S_{\mathbb{Z}_p}$	$(2N_\Sigma + 10)S_{\mathbb{G}_1} + (2N_\mathcal{U} + n)S_{\mathbb{Z}_p}$
AA		$(3 + 2N_\Sigma)S_{\mathbb{Z}_p}$	$(6 + 2N_\Sigma)S_{\mathbb{Z}_p}$
DP		-	-
DU		$(2 + N_u)S_{\mathbb{G}_1}$	$(2 + N_u)S_{\mathbb{G}_1}$
CSP	**Keys**	$\max_{c \in \mathcal{X}}(\pi - \pi_c)S_{\mathbb{Z}_p}$	-
	Data	$(1 + 2l)S_{\mathbb{G}_2}$	$(1 + 2l)S_{\mathbb{G}_2} + S_{\mathbb{G}_t}$

to be stored by each entity. Compared to TMACS, our construction requires less information to be stored by DCA and AA. In addition the size of an encrypted data item in our scheme is smaller than the one of TMACS. On the DU side, no more information needs to be stored compared to TMACS. When it comes to CSP, our construction requires the CSP to store a revocation key that grows linearly with the number of performed revocation operations. While the latter can be large in some use cases, we stress that the CSP is supposed to have unlimited storage space. Note that the TMACS scheme does not require the CSP to store any revocation key as it does not enable access revocation.

7.2   Communication Complexity

In Table 4, we provide a comparison of the theoretical communication complexities incurred by the different processes involved in our construction and TMACS. Specifically, we quantify the amount of information (in terms of the sizes of used group elements) exchanged by each entity during the different processes. As illustrated in the table, our construction does not include any communication overhead compared to TMACS, except for (i) AA during the setup process and (ii) DU during the data decryption process. However, we stress that both (linear) overheads can be tolerated since the first occurs only once during the setup phase, while the second permits the DU to considerably reduce the amount of computations required for data decryption (Table 5) by using the outsourced pre-decryption. Besides, our construction slightly reduces the communication complexity for DCA and CSP during the setup and the data decryption processes respectively.

Table 4. Comparison of the communication complexity

Process	Entities	This work	TMACS
Setup	DCA	$(2n + 2N_{\mathcal{U}} + 2)S_{\mathbb{Z}_p}$	$4N_{\mathcal{U}} + 4N_{\mathcal{O}} + 2nN_{\Sigma}$
	AA	$(5n + 3)S_{\mathbb{Z}_p} + (N_{\Sigma} + 1)S_{\mathbb{G}_1} + (N_{\Sigma} + 2)S_{\mathbb{G}_2} + S_{\mathbb{G}_t}$	$(2n + 1)S_{\mathbb{Z}_p} + S_{\mathbb{G}_1}$
	DU	$4S_{\mathbb{Z}_p}$	$4S_{\mathbb{Z}_p}$
	DO	$(2N_{\mathbb{U}} + 1)S_{\mathbb{G}_2}$	$(2N_{\mathbb{U}} + 1)S_{\mathbb{G}_2}$
Decryption Key	AA	$(2 + N_u)S_{\mathbb{G}_1}$	$(2 + N_u)S_{\mathbb{G}_1}$
Generation	DU	$(2 + N_u)tS_{\mathbb{G}_1}$	$(2 + N_u)tS_{\mathbb{G}_1}$
Data	DU	$(2 + N_u)S_{\mathbb{G}_1}$	-
Decryption	CSP	$S_{\mathbb{G}_t} + N_{\mathcal{I}}$	$(2 + N_u)S_{\mathbb{G}_2} + N_{\mathcal{I}}$
Revocation	CSP	$(t + 1)S_{\mathbb{G}_2} + N_{\Sigma, R}(S_{\mathbb{G}_1} + S_{\mathbb{G}_2})$	N/A
	AA	$3S_{\mathbb{G}_2} + (2 + N_u)(N_{\mathcal{U}} - N_{\mathcal{U}, R})S_{\mathbb{G}_1}$	N/A
	DU	$(2 + N_u)tS_{\mathbb{G}_1}$	

7.3   Computation Complexity

In this section, we give a comparative analysis of the computational complexity of our scheme and TMACS. Table 5 shows, for the two constructions, the computational complexities for the different entities of the system when performing the different processes. The processes' complexities are expressed mainly in terms of the number of group exponentiations and pairings. We note here that we ignore computations related to certificate generation and signature as they are performed by most existing ABE schemes.

Table 5. Comparison of the computation complexity

Process	Entities	This work	TMACS
Setup	DCA	$4t\mathcal{E}$	$t\mathcal{E}$
	AA	$(4 + 2N_\Sigma)\mathcal{E}$	$\mathcal{E}$
Decryption Key	AA	$(2 + 2N_u)\mathcal{M}$	$(2 + 2N_u)\mathcal{M}$
Generation	DU	$(2t + tN_u)\mathcal{M}$	$(2t + tN_u)\mathcal{M}$
Encryption	DO	$\mathcal{E} + (2l + 1)\mathcal{M}$	$\mathcal{E} + (2l + 1)\mathcal{M}$
Decryption	DU	$\mathcal{M}$	$(1 + 2l)\mathcal{E}$
	CSP	$(1 + 2l)\mathcal{E} + (\pi - \pi_c)\mathcal{M}$	-
Revocation	CSP	$(t + 2N_{\Sigma,R})\mathcal{M}$	N/A
	AA	$3\mathcal{M}N$	N/A
	DU	$(2t + tN_u)\mathcal{M}$	N/A

The comparison shows that our construction does not include any computation overhead compared to TMACS for performing data encryption and decryption key generation processes. Thanks to the outsourcing pre-decryption, our construction drastically reduces the amount of computations required to be performed by DU for decrypting a data item. However, it requires linearly in the number of attributes more group exponentiations than TMACS to perform the setup process. Again, we stress that this latter computation overhead can be tolerated as it occurs only once during the setup phase.

8   Conclusion

In this work, we propose the first CP-ABE fine-grained access control construction for outsourced data that enables the following features simultaneously. First, it ensures robustness for both decryption key issuing and access revocation while achieving forward secrecy. Second, it enables outsourced decryption to reduce the decryption overhead for data users that have limited computational resources. Third, it achieves adaptive security in standard models.

References

1. Ahmed, A.S., Aura, T.: Turning trust around: smart contract-assisted public key infrastructure. In: 2018 17th IEEE International Conference on Trust, Security and Privacy in Computing and Communications/12th IEEE International Conference on Big Data Science and Engineering (TrustCom/BigDataSE), pp. 104–111. IEEE (2018)
2. Al-Dahhan, R.R., Shi, Q., Lee, G.M., Kifayat, K.: Survey on revocation in ciphertext-policy attribute-based encryption. Sensors **19**(7), 1695 (2019)
3. Bethencourt, J., Sahai, A., Waters, B.: Ciphertext-policy attribute-based encryption. In: 2007 IEEE Symposium on Security and Privacy (SP 2007), pp. 321–334. IEEE (2007)
4. Bkakria, A.: Robust, revocable and adaptively secure attribute-based encryption with outsourced decryption. Cryptology ePrint Archive, Report 2022/456 (2022), https://ia.cr/2022/456
5. Boyen, X.: The uber-assumption family. In: Galbraith, S.D., Paterson, K.G. (eds.) Pairing 2008. LNCS, vol. 5209, pp. 39–56. Springer, Heidelberg (2008). https://doi.org/10.1007/978-3-540-85538-5_3
6. Cui, H., Deng, R.H., Li, Y., Qin, B.: Server-aided revocable attribute-based encryption. In: Askoxylakis, I., Ioannidis, S., Katsikas, S., Meadows, C. (eds.) ESORICS 2016. LNCS, vol. 9879, pp. 570–587. Springer, Cham (2016). https://doi.org/10.1007/978-3-319-45741-3_29
7. Han, J., Susilo, W., Mu, Y., Zhou, J., Au, M.H.: PPDCP-ABE: privacy-preserving decentralized ciphertext-policy attribute-based encryption. In: Kutyłowski, M., Vaidya, J. (eds.) ESORICS 2014. LNCS, vol. 8713, pp. 73–90. Springer, Cham (2014). https://doi.org/10.1007/978-3-319-11212-1_5
8. Hur, J., Noh, D.K.: Attribute-based access control with efficient revocation in data outsourcing systems. IEEE Trans. Parallel Distrib. Syst. **22**(7), 1214–1221 (2011)
9. Karchmer, M., Wigderson, A.: On span programs. In: [1993] Proceedings of the Eigth Annual Structure in Complexity Theory Conference, pp. 102–111. IEEE (1993)
10. Lewko, A., Sahai, A., Waters, B.: Revocation systems with very small private keys. In: 2010 IEEE Symposium on Security and Privacy, pp. 273–285. IEEE (2010)
11. Lewko, A., Waters, B.: Decentralizing attribute-based encryption. In: Paterson, K.G. (ed.) EUROCRYPT 2011. LNCS, vol. 6632, pp. 568–588. Springer, Heidelberg (2011). https://doi.org/10.1007/978-3-642-20465-4_31
12. Li, J., Yao, W., Han, J., Zhang, Y., Shen, J.: User collusion avoidance CP-ABE with efficient attribute revocation for cloud storage. IEEE Syst. J. **12**(2), 1767–1777 (2017)
13. Li, Q., Ma, J., Li, R., Liu, X., Xiong, J., Chen, D.: Secure, efficient and revocable multi-authority access control system in cloud storage. Comput. Secur. **59**, 45–59 (2016)
14. Li, W., Xue, K., Xue, Y., Hong, J.: TMACS: a robust and verifiable threshold multi-authority access control system in public cloud storage. IEEE Trans. Parallel Distrib. Syst. **27**(5), 1484–1496 (2015)
15. Liang, X., Cao, Z., Lin, H., Shao, J.: Attribute based proxy re-encryption with delegating capabilities. In: Proceedings of the 4th International Symposium on Information, Computer, and Communications Security, pp. 276–286 (2009)
16. Liang, X., Cao, Z., Lin, H., Xing, D.: Provably secure and efficient bounded ciphertext policy attribute based encryption. In: Proceedings of the 4th International Symposium on Information, Computer, and Communications Security, pp. 343–352 (2009)

17. Liu, Z., Cao, Z.: On efficiently transferring the linear secret-sharing scheme matrix in ciphertext-policy attribute-based encryption. IACR Cryptol. ePrint Arch. **2010**, 374 (2010)
18. Liu, Z., Wong, D.S.: Practical attribute-based encryption: traitor tracing, revocation and large universe. Comput. J. **59**(7), 983–1004 (2016)
19. Luo, S., Hu, J., Chen, Z.: Ciphertext policy attribute-based proxy re-encryption. In: Soriano, M., Qing, S., López, J. (eds.) ICICS 2010. LNCS, vol. 6476, pp. 401–415. Springer, Heidelberg (2010). https://doi.org/10.1007/978-3-642-17650-0_28
20. Nishide, T., Yoneyama, K., Ohta, K.: Attribute-based encryption with partially hidden Encryptor-specified access structures. In: Bellovin, S.M., Gennaro, R., Keromytis, A., Yung, M. (eds.) ACNS 2008. LNCS, vol. 5037, pp. 111–129. Springer, Heidelberg (2008). https://doi.org/10.1007/978-3-540-68914-0_7
21. Ostrovsky, R., Sahai, A., Waters, B.: Attribute-based encryption with non-monotonic access structures. In: Proceedings of the 14th ACM Conference on Computer and Communications Security, pp. 195–203 (2007)
22. Qin, B., Zhao, Q., Zheng, D., Cui, H.: (dual) server-aided revocable attribute-based encryption with decryption key exposure resistance. Inf. Sci. **490**, 74–92 (2019)
23. Sahai, A., Waters, B.: Fuzzy identity-based encryption. In: Cramer, R. (ed.) EUROCRYPT 2005. LNCS, vol. 3494, pp. 457–473. Springer, Heidelberg (2005). https://doi.org/10.1007/11426639_27
24. Tomida, J., Kawahara, Y., Nishimaki, R.: Fast, compact, and expressive attribute-based encryption. Des. Codes Cryptogr. **89**(11), 2577–2626 (2021). https://doi.org/10.1007/s10623-021-00939-8
25. Waters, B.: Ciphertext-policy attribute-based encryption: an expressive, efficient, and provably secure realization. In: Catalano, D., Fazio, N., Gennaro, R., Nicolosi, A. (eds.) PKC 2011. LNCS, vol. 6571, pp. 53–70. Springer, Heidelberg (2011). https://doi.org/10.1007/978-3-642-19379-8_4
26. White, D.: Top 5 cloud computing predictions for 2020 (2020). https://www.techfunnel.com/information-technology/top-5-cloud-computing-predictions-for-2020/.Accessed 11 Apr 2022
27. Xiong, H., Huang, X., Yang, M., Wang, L., Yu, S.: Unbounded and efficient revocable attribute-based encryption with adaptive security for cloud-assisted internet of things. IEEE Internet Things J. **9** (2021)
28. Yang, K., Jia, X., Ren, K.: Attribute-based fine-grained access control with efficient revocation in cloud storage systems. In: Proceedings of the 8th ACM SIGSAC Symposium on Information, Computer and Communications Security, pp. 523–528 (2013)
29. Yang, K., Jia, X., Ren, K., Zhang, B., Xie, R.: DAC-MACS: effective data access control for multiauthority cloud storage systems. IEEE Trans. Inf. Foren. Secur. **8**(11), 1790–1801 (2013)
30. Yeh, L.Y., Chiang, P.Y., Tsai, Y.L., Huang, J.L.: Cloud-based fine-grained health information access control framework for LightweightIoT devices with dynamic auditing andattribute revocation. IEEE Trans. Cloud Comput. **6**(2), 532–544 (2018). https://doi.org/10.1109/TCC.2015.2485199
31. Yu, S., Wang, C., Ren, K., Lou, W.: Attribute based data sharing with attribute revocation. In: Proceedings of the 5th ACM Symposium on Information, Computer and Communications Security, pp. 261–270 (2010)
32. Zhang, Y., Deng, R.H., Xu, S., Sun, J., Li, Q., Zheng, D.: Attribute-based encryption for cloud computing access control: a survey. ACM Comput. Surv. **53**(4), 1–41 (2020)

Libertas: Backward Private Dynamic Searchable Symmetric Encryption Supporting Wildcards

Jeroen Weener[1], Florian Hahn[1] , and Andreas Peter[1,2(✉)]

[1] Services and Cybersecurity, University of Twente, Enschede, The Netherlands
`{f.w.hahn,a.peter}@utwente.nl`
[2] Safety-Security-Interaction, University of Oldenburg, Oldenburg, Germany

Abstract. When outsourcing data, *Searchable Symmetric Encryption (SSE)* allows clients to query the server for their encrypted files without compromising data confidentiality. Several attacks against searchable encryption schemes have been proposed that leverage information leakage the schemes emit when operating. Schemes should achieve *Forward and Backward Privacy* to mitigate these types of attacks. Despite the variance of query types across SSE schemes, most forward and backward private schemes only support exact keyword search. In this research, we extend backward privacy notions and their underlying leakage functions to the *Wildcard Search* domain. Additionally, we present Libertas; a construction that provides backward privacy to any wildcard supporting SSE scheme. If the scheme is forward private, this property is inherited. We prove security in the established $\mathcal{L}$-adaptive security model with respect to a leakage function $\mathcal{L}$. We show that the performance overhead scales linearly with the number of deletions.

Keywords: Searchable Encryption · Backward Privacy · Wildcard Search

1 Introduction

Motivation and Related Work. The demand for Cloud Service Providers (CSPs) has increased in recent years. They offer convenient, scalable and on-demand data storage and processing. Sharing data with a CSP can be inappropriate, however, as the provider is not fully trusted. Encryption prevents them from accessing the data but in doing so, obstructs their ability to process it. Searchable Symmetric Encryption (SSE) allows clients to first encrypt and later search their data once placed at the CSP, allowing for selective data retrieval. SSE was first explored by Song et al. [16]. The server hosts data of the client in encrypted form. Later, the client can search the data for keywords and retrieve relevant data from the server without revealing the searched keywords or the content of the data. Goh [11] introduced the concept of an *index* to speed up searches. An index is a data structure where keyword identifiers are stored

© IFIP International Federation for Information Processing 2022
Published by Springer Nature Switzerland AG 2022
S. Sural and H. Lu (Eds.): DBSec 2022, LNCS 13383, pp. 215–235, 2022.
https://doi.org/10.1007/978-3-031-10684-2_13

per document identifier. Searches use the index to find the matching document identifiers instead of using the documents themselves. Most SSE schemes offer a trade-off between efficiency, e.g. achieving search times sublinear in the number of indexed keywords, and security, e.g. leaking the result set of an encrypted search query in form of the access pattern. Curtmola et al. [9] gave a security notion formalizing this trade-off for static datasets. Later, Kamara et al. [14] extended this notion for *Dynamic SSE* (DSSE) schemes that allow documents to be added and removed.

To allow for more query flexibility, several extensions to the basic single keyword search have been proposed. *Boolean queries* enable different kinds of boolean operators such as conjunctions, disjunctions and negations. Cash et al. [7] describe a scheme featuring boolean queries. *Substring queries* match keywords that contain the query as a substring. Prefix and suffix queries match keywords that either start or end with the query. Chase and Shen [8] describe a substring supporting scheme. *Wildcard queries* allow the client to insert different kinds of wildcard characters in the search query. For example, a wildcard character can replace exactly one character or multiple characters. The search query 'com*' matches keywords 'computer' and 'company', while the search query 'c_t' matches 'cat' and 'cut'. Several schemes using several constructions have been proposed that allow for wildcard queries. One such construction is by storing keywords in Bloom filters. Suga et al. [18] consider Bloom filters allowing for substring, fuzzy and wildcard queries. Hu et al. [12] introduce a scheme that is more efficient compared to Suga et al. and allows clients to update the database. The scheme by Bösch et al. [3] operates in the dynamic environment and implement wildcard support by generating and inserting all wildcard variants of a keyword upon database insertion. This transforms the problem of wildcard search into exact keyword search, but heavily burdens server storage depending on the type and number of allowed wildcards in queries. Zhao and Nishide [20] describe a wildcard supporting scheme capable of supporting two types of wildcards by cleverly storing keyword characteristics in Bloom filters. Faber et al. [10] propose a matching algorithm based on the conjunctive search scheme by Cash et al. [7]. Among other query types, Faber et al.'s scheme supports single keyword search, substring and wildcard queries, and supports any combination of these query types using boolean operators.

Unfortunately, search queries and updates potentially leak information such as the matching documents or the affected keywords. As shown by previous lines of research, despite a scheme conforming to the aforementioned security definitions by Curtmola et al. [9] and by Kamara et al. [14], this information leakage can allow for powerful *Leakage Abuse Attacks (LAAs)*. Islam et al. [13] describe the first so-called query recovery attack exploiting full background knowledge about indexed data to retrieve the keyword hidden in search queries. Cash et al. [6] extended this work by describing several LAAs, both passive and active. They improve the attack of Islam et al. and introduce plaintext recovery attacks; attacks that aim to recover the content of the stored documents. Zhang et al. [19] describe efficient file-injection attacks aiming to recover keywords from search queries, assuming little knowledge of stored content.

To defend against query recovery attacks, the security notion *forward privacy* was informally defined by Stefanov et al. [17] and later formalized by Bost [4]. Forward private schemes do not leak which keywords are considered during updates, making it impossible to link newly added data to earlier search queries. Later, Bost et al. [5] introduced *Backward Privacy (BP)* as another security notion for DSSE schemes. In backward private schemes, search queries cannot be executed over deleted entries, limiting the potential of (future) attacks. They introduce three levels of BP of decreasing strength: 1. BP with insertion pattern leakage, 2. BP with update pattern leakage, and 3. weak BP. However, despite all the advancements in flexible search queries as mentioned above, most forward and backward private schemes only consider the exact keyword search setting.

Our Contribution. This paper introduces Libertas; a construction for providing BP with update pattern leakage to any wildcard supporting DSSE scheme. It is proven secure against adaptive adversaries. We implement Libertas with the wildcard supporting DSSE scheme by Zhao and Nishide (Z&N) [20] and evaluate its performance. The source code of our implementation is publicly available on GitHub.[1] Our results show that Libertas' search performance overhead is hardly affected by increases in index size, result set size or the number of wildcards in a query. Libertas does experience noticeable overhead during searches when the index contains entries of removed document-keyword pairs. This overhead scales linearly with the number of deletions.

Organization of the Paper. In Sect. 2 we introduce searchable symmetric encryption and recall its security definitions - including forward and backward privacy. We then discuss the extension of the search functionality from exact-keyword towards wildcards in Sect. 3. Afterwards, in Sect. 4 we give our construction Libertas that provides backward privacy for any dynamic wildcard supporting SSE scheme and present a practical evaluation for a concrete instantiation in Sect. 5. In Sect. 6 we discuss real-world applications and possible further improvements before we conclude our research in Sect. 7.

2 Preliminaries

2.1 Searchable Symmetric Encryption (SSE)

Searchable symmetric encryption schemes allow clients to store documents at a third party in encrypted form and later search for them using queries. Search functionality is typically achieved by the use of an *index*. The exact implementation of the index differs per scheme, but it is typically a look-up table that links keyword identifiers to the identifiers of matching documents. The client can search these keyword identifiers to find the document identifiers of matching documents. These document identifiers can then be used to send the matching documents to the client. SSE schemes can be static or dynamic. Dynamic

---

[1] https://github.com/LibertasConstruction/Libertas.

SSE (DSSE) schemes differ from static schemes as they additionally allow for updates to the index after the initial setup phase. In this work, we only consider dynamic SSE schemes. Encryption (decryption) and uploading (downloading) of documents is often not relevant for the security analysis and thus treated as an independent step in the process. Typically, documents are encrypted using AES in CBC mode and stored on the server. SSE schemes consist of eight algorithms.

$K \leftarrow \mathsf{Setup}(\lambda)$ is run one time by the client, at the start of the scheme. It takes as input the security parameter λ and outputs the scheme's key K.

$\gamma \leftarrow \mathsf{BuildIndex}(\lambda)$ is run one time by the server, at the start of the scheme. It takes as input the security parameter λ and outputs an (at that point empty) index γ.

$\tau^{\mathsf{srch}} \leftarrow \mathsf{SrchToken}(K, w)$ is run by the client during search operations. It takes as input the scheme's key K and a keyword w that is to be searched for. The output is a search token τ^{srch}.

$\tau^{\mathsf{add}} \leftarrow \mathsf{AddToken}(K, \mathsf{ind}, w)$ is run by the client during add operations. It takes as input the scheme's key K and a document-keyword pair, consisting of a document identifier ind and a keyword w. The output is an add token τ^{add}.

$\tau^{\mathsf{del}} \leftarrow \mathsf{DelToken}(K, \mathsf{ind}, w)$ is run by the client during delete operations. It takes as input the scheme's key K and a document-keyword pair, consisting of a document identifier ind and a keyword w. The output is a delete token τ^{del}.

$R \leftarrow \mathsf{Search}(\gamma, \tau^{\mathsf{srch}})$ is run by the server after receiving the search token τ^{srch} from the client. Together with the index γ, this results in a result set R, which is a list of document identifiers: $R : (\mathsf{ind}_1, \ldots, \mathsf{ind}_n)$. Usually, the server sends back the encrypted documents corresponding to these document identifiers.

$\gamma' \leftarrow \mathsf{Add}(\gamma, \tau^{\mathsf{add}})$ is run by the server after receiving the add token τ^{add} from the client. This token is used to update index γ to a new index γ'.

$\gamma' \leftarrow \mathsf{Del}(\gamma, \tau^{\mathsf{del}})$ is run by the server after receiving the delete token τ^{del} from the client. This token is used to update index γ to a new index γ'.

SrchToken and Search together form the **Search** protocol of the SSE scheme. In the same way, AddToken and Add, and DelToken and Delete form the **Add** and **Delete** protocol of the SSE scheme, respectively.

Result-Hiding SSE Schemes. Result-hiding SSE schemes hide the document identifiers, normally uncovered during the Search algorithm, from the server. An example of such a scheme is the Masked Index Scheme by Bösch et al. [3]. Results are hidden by altering the **Search** protocol, adding new algorithms DecSearch and FetchDocuments in a second round. In these schemes, Search outputs encrypted document identifiers at the server that have to be sent to the client for decryption. The client, therefore, has control over what happens with the document identifiers and does not necessarily have to reveal them to the server. The server can, however, identify when the same document identifier is sent multiple times, as its encryption in the index does not change if no additional measures are taken. The modified algorithm Search (now having two rounds), and the new algorithms DecSearch and FetchDocuments are formally defined as

$R^* \leftarrow \mathsf{Search}(\gamma, \tau^{\mathsf{srch}})$ is run by the server, taking as input the index γ and a search token τ^{srch}, resulting in an encrypted result set R^*.

$R \leftarrow \mathsf{DecSearch}(K, w, R^*)$ is run by the client, taking as input the scheme's key K, the keyword that is searched for w and the encrypted result set R^*. The output of the algorithm is the list of identifiers of matching documents $R : (\mathsf{ind}_1, \dots, \mathsf{ind}_n)$.

$D \leftarrow \mathsf{FetchDocuments}(R)$ is run by the server, taking as input the document identifiers revealed by $\mathsf{DecSearch}$. The server outputs documents D corresponding to the document identifiers in R.

Note that, in this extended 2-round **Search** protocol, document identifiers are first revealed to the client rather than the server.

2.2   Leakage Functions

A *leakage function* $\mathcal{L}$ describes what information is leaked by an SSE scheme. Leakage can be abused to mount an attack. Schemes should therefore aim to leak as little as possible. Typically, there exists a trade-off between the security and the efficiency of the scheme. By allowing some leakage, the scheme can achieve greater efficiency, and to achieve higher security, one should restrict the leakage, which incurs a penalty for efficiency. The total leakage of a dynamic SSE scheme consists of $\mathcal{L}^{\mathsf{Srch}}$, $\mathcal{L}^{\mathsf{Add}}$ and $\mathcal{L}^{\mathsf{Del}}$, which are the leakage functions corresponding to the Search protocol, Add protocol and Delete protocol, respectively. Leakage functions keep an internal state Q. The Search protocol inserts (u, w) tuples in Q, where u is the timestamp of the operation and w is the searched keyword. Update operations append $(u, \mathsf{op}, (\mathsf{ind}, w))$ tuples to Q, where op is an indicator of the nature of the operation (add or delete) and (ind, w) is the document-keyword pair to either add or delete. The security of SSE schemes is typically measured by the amount of information they leak during operations. To describe this leakage, multiple leakage functions are often considered in the literature. The most common functions are the *search pattern* and *access pattern*, which both relate to search operations.

$$\mathsf{sp}(w) = \{u \mid (u, w) \in Q\},$$
$$\mathsf{ap}(w) = \{\mathsf{ind} \mid (u, \mathsf{add}, (\mathsf{ind}, w)) \in Q \wedge \ \nexists\, u' > u, \text{ s.t. } (u', \mathsf{del}, (\mathsf{ind}, w)) \in Q\}.$$

The search pattern $\mathsf{sp}(w)$ leaks the timestamps u at which the keyword w has been searched for. If a scheme leaks the search pattern, one is able to infer which search queries pertain to the same keyword. The access pattern $\mathsf{ap}(w)$ leaks the document identifiers ind of documents that contain keyword w at the time of the search.

2.3   Security Model

The security model for SSE schemes often considered in the literature is called $\mathcal{L}$-*adaptive security* [9]. An $\mathcal{L}$-adaptively-secure SSE scheme Σ leaks only explicitly defined leakage $\mathcal{L}$. In this model, an adversary $\mathcal{A}$ can adaptively trigger the different algorithms that make up the scheme with inputs of choice and observe their outputs. We define a real world game $\text{SSEReal}_{\mathcal{A}}^{\Sigma}(\lambda, n)$ and an ideal world game $\text{SSEIdeal}_{\mathcal{A},\mathcal{S},\mathcal{L}}(\lambda, n)$, where λ is the security parameter and n is the number of queries that are executed. In $\text{SSEReal}_{\mathcal{A}}^{\Sigma}(\lambda, n)$, Σ is executed honestly, while in $\text{SSEIdeal}_{\mathcal{A},\mathcal{S},\mathcal{L}}(\lambda, n)$, a simulator $\mathcal{S}$ simulates Σ using $\mathcal{L}$ as input. The task of the adversary is to output a bit b, distinguishing between a real transcript and a simulated one. Σ is $\mathcal{L}$-adaptively secure if the transcripts are indistinguishable. Algorithm 1 describes the security games $\text{SSEReal}_{\mathcal{A}}^{\Sigma}(\lambda, n)$ and $\text{SSEIdeal}_{\mathcal{A},\mathcal{S},\mathcal{L}}(\lambda, n)$, adapted for result-hiding SSE schemes. We use these games in the security proof of Libertas, which is a result-hiding scheme, in Sect. 4.3.

Definition 1 ($\mathcal{L}$-Adaptive Security). *An SSE scheme Σ is $\mathcal{L}$-adaptively-secure with respect to a leakage function $\mathcal{L}$, if for any polynomial-time adversary $\mathcal{A}$ issuing a polynomial number of queries $n(\lambda)$, there exists a probabilistic polynomial time simulator $\mathcal{S}$ such that:*

$$\left| \mathbb{P}[\text{SSEReal}_{\mathcal{A}}^{\Sigma}(\lambda, n) = 1] - \mathbb{P}[\text{SSEIdeal}_{\mathcal{A},\mathcal{S},\mathcal{L}}(\lambda, n) = 1] \right| \leq negl(\lambda).$$

$\text{SSEReal}_{\mathcal{A}}^{\Sigma}(\lambda,n)$

1: $K \leftarrow \text{Setup}(\lambda)$
2: $\gamma \leftarrow \text{BuildIndex}(\lambda)$
3: **for** $i = 1$ to n **do**
4:     $(\text{type}_i, \text{params}_i, \text{st}_{\mathcal{A}}) \leftarrow \mathcal{A}_i(\text{st}_{\mathcal{A}}, \gamma, \tau, \mathbf{R}^*, \mathbf{R})$, where τ, $\mathbf{R}^*$ and $\mathbf{R}$ consist of all tokens, encrypted result sets and result sets, respectively, generated in previous iterations.
5:     **if** $\text{type}_i = \text{Search}$ **then**
6:         $w_i \leftarrow \text{params}_i$
7:         $\tau_i^{\text{srch}} \leftarrow \text{SrchToken}(K, w_i)$
8:         $R_i^* \leftarrow \text{Search}(\gamma, \tau_i^{\text{srch}})$
9:         $R_i \leftarrow \text{DecSearch}(K, w_i, R_i^*)$
10:     **else if** $\text{type}_i = \text{Add}$ **then**
11:         $(\text{ind}_i, w_i) \leftarrow \text{params}_i$
12:         $\tau_i^{\text{add}} \leftarrow \text{AddToken}(K, \text{ind}_i, w_i)$
13:         $\gamma \leftarrow \text{Add}(\gamma, \tau_i^{\text{add}})$
14:     **else**
15:         $(\text{ind}_i, w_i) \leftarrow \text{params}_i$
16:         $\tau_i^{\text{del}} \leftarrow \text{DelToken}(K, \text{ind}_i, w_i)$
17:         $\gamma \leftarrow \text{Del}(\gamma, \tau_i^{\text{del}})$
18:     **end if**
19: **end for**
20: $b \leftarrow \mathcal{A}_{n+1}(\text{st}_{\mathcal{A}}, \gamma, \boldsymbol{\tau}, \boldsymbol{R}^*, \boldsymbol{R})$
21: **Return** b

$\text{SSEIdeal}_{\mathcal{A},\mathcal{S},\mathcal{L}}(\lambda,n)$

1: $(\widetilde{\gamma}, \text{st}_{\mathcal{S}}) \leftarrow \mathcal{S}_0(\lambda)$
2: **for** $i = 1$ to n **do**
3:     $(\text{type}_i, \text{params}_i, \text{st}_{\mathcal{A}}) \leftarrow \mathcal{A}_i(\text{st}_{\mathcal{A}}, \widetilde{\gamma}, \widetilde{\tau}, \widetilde{\boldsymbol{R}}^*, \widetilde{\boldsymbol{R}})$
4:     **if** $\text{type}_i = \text{Search}$ **then**
5:         $w_i \leftarrow \text{params}_i$
6:         $(\widetilde{\tau}_i^{\text{srch}}, \widetilde{R}_i^*, \widetilde{R}_i, \text{st}_{\mathcal{S}}) \leftarrow \mathcal{S}_i(\text{st}_{\mathcal{S}}, \mathcal{L}^{\text{Srch}}(w_i))$
7:     **else if** $\text{type}_i = \text{Add}$ **then**
8:         $(\text{ind}_i, w_i) \leftarrow \text{params}_i$
9:         $(\widetilde{\tau}_i^{\text{add}}, \widetilde{\gamma}, \text{st}_{\mathcal{S}}) \leftarrow \mathcal{S}_i(\text{st}_{\mathcal{S}}, \mathcal{L}^{\text{Add}}(\text{ind}_i, w_i))$
10:     **else**
11:         $(\text{ind}_i, w_i) \leftarrow \text{params}_i$
12:         $(\widetilde{\tau}_i^{\text{del}}, \widetilde{\gamma}, \text{st}_{\mathcal{S}}) \leftarrow \mathcal{S}_i(\text{st}_{\mathcal{S}}, \mathcal{L}^{\text{Del}}(\text{ind}_i, w_i))$
13:     **end if**
14: **end for**
15: $b \leftarrow \mathcal{A}_{n+1}(\text{st}_{\mathcal{A}}, \widetilde{\gamma}, \widetilde{\tau}, \widetilde{\boldsymbol{R}}^*, \widetilde{\boldsymbol{R}})$
16: **Return** b

Fig. 1. Adaptive Semantic Security Games for Result-Hiding DSSE Schemes

2.4   Forward Privacy

Forward privacy has been introduced by Stefanov et al. [17] and is further explored by Bost et al. [4]. Informally, a forward private scheme's update algorithm does not leak whether a newly inserted element matches previous search queries. Formally, forward privacy is defined as follows.

Definition 2 (Forward Privacy). *An $\mathcal{L}$-adaptively-secure SSE scheme is **forward-private** iff the add leakage function $\mathcal{L}^{\mathsf{Add}}$ and delete leakage function $\mathcal{L}^{\mathsf{Del}}$ can be written with stateless functions $\mathcal{L}'$, $\mathcal{L}''$ as:*

$$\mathcal{L}^{\mathsf{Add}}(\mathsf{ind}, w) = \mathcal{L}'(\mathsf{ind}) \qquad and \qquad \mathcal{L}^{\mathsf{Del}}(\mathsf{ind}, w) = \mathcal{L}''(\mathsf{ind}),$$

where ind *is the document identifier,* w *is the updated keyword.*

2.5   Backward Privacy (BP)

In addition to forward privacy, Bost et al. specify backward privacy (BP) [5]. BP limits what one can learn regarding updates on keyword w from a search query on that keyword. Informally, search queries in backward private schemes only reveal document-keyword pairs that have been added, but not subsequently deleted. Limiting the leakage on search queries alone is not sufficient, however, as observing the document-keyword pairs during update queries would trivially grant the server the information on whether a document has been deleted. Therefore, backward private schemes limit the leakage of both search and update queries. Obtaining a full backward private scheme requires hiding the update pattern (see Updates(w) hereafter), resulting in expensive SSE schemes. Bost et al. have defined three notions of BP with decreasing strength, depending on the amount of information that is leaked [5]. We consider the two strongest notions.

Backward privacy with insertion pattern leakage: Upon a search query for keyword w, leaks the document identifiers currently matching w, the timestamps at which they were inserted and the total number of updates on w.

Backward privacy with update pattern leakage: Upon a search query for keyword w, leaks the document identifiers currently matching w, the timestamps at which they were inserted and the timestamps of all the updates on w (but not their content).

The differences between these notions become clear when considering an example with the following updates: (add, ind_1, w_1), (add, ind_1, w_2), (add, ind_2, w_1), (del, ind_1, w_1). Upon a search query for keyword w_1, the first notion reveals ind_2, that it was inserted at time slot 3 and that there were three updates to w_1. The second notion additionally reveals that updates regarding w_1 occurred at time slot 1, 3 and 4. To formally define these notions, Bost et al. define the leakage functions UpHist(w), TimeDB(w) and Updates(w). UpHist(w) contains the timestamp, operation and document identifier of every update. TimeDB(w) outputs all documents currently matching w and the timestamp of insertion. Updates(w) results in a list of timestamps of updates on keyword w.

$$\mathsf{UpHist}(w) = \{(u, \mathsf{op}, \mathsf{ind}) \mid (u, \mathsf{op}, (\mathsf{ind}, w)) \in Q\},$$
$$\mathsf{TimeDB}(w) = \{(u, \mathsf{ind}) \mid (u, \mathsf{add}, (\mathsf{ind}, w)) \in Q \land$$
$$\nexists\, u' > u \text{ s.t. } (u', \mathsf{del}, (\mathsf{ind}, w)) \in Q\},$$
$$\mathsf{Updates}(w) = \{u \mid (u, \mathsf{op}, (\mathsf{ind}, w)) \in Q\}.$$

Note how the access pattern ap(w) can be constructed from TimeDB(w) and how TimeDB(w) and Updates(w) can be derived from UpHist(w). This means that UpHist(w) leaks strictly more than those leakage functions and that TimeDB(w) leaks strictly more than ap(w). A scheme leaking UpHist(w) therefore inherently also leaks TimeDB(w), ap(w) and Updates(w).

$$\mathsf{ap}(w) = \{\mathsf{ind} \mid (u, \mathsf{ind}) \in \mathsf{TimeDB}(w)\},$$
$$\mathsf{TimeDB}(w) = \{(u, \mathsf{ind}) \mid (u, \mathsf{add}, \mathsf{ind}) \in \mathsf{UpHist}(w) \land$$
$$\nexists\, u' > u \text{ s.t. } (u', \mathsf{del}, \mathsf{ind}) \in \mathsf{UpHist}(w)\},$$
$$\mathsf{Updates}(w) = \{u \mid (u, \mathsf{op}, \mathsf{ind}) \in \mathsf{UpHist}(w)\}.$$

The different notions of BP can be formally described using these leakage functions.

Definition 3 (Backward Privacy). *An $\mathcal{L}$-adaptively-secure SSE scheme is* **insertion pattern revealing backward-private** *iff the search, add and delete leakage functions $\mathcal{L}^{\mathsf{Srch}}$, $\mathcal{L}^{\mathsf{Add}}$ and $\mathcal{L}^{\mathsf{Del}}$ can be written as:*

$$\mathcal{L}^{\mathsf{Srch}}(w) = \mathcal{L}'(\mathsf{TimeDB}(w), a_w) \quad and \quad \mathcal{L}^{\mathsf{Add}}(\mathsf{ind}, w) = \perp \quad and \quad \mathcal{L}^{\mathsf{Del}}(\mathsf{ind}, w) = \perp,$$

where a_w denotes the number of updates on w and $\mathcal{L}'$ is stateless.

An $\mathcal{L}$-adaptively-secure SSE scheme is **update pattern revealing backward-private** *iff the search and update leakage functions $\mathcal{L}^{\mathsf{Srch}}$, $\mathcal{L}^{\mathsf{Add}}$ and $\mathcal{L}^{\mathsf{Del}}$ can be written with three stateless functions $\mathcal{L}'$, $\mathcal{L}''$ and $\mathcal{L}'''$ as:*

$$\mathcal{L}^{\mathsf{Srch}}(w) = \mathcal{L}'(\mathsf{TimeDB}(w), \mathsf{Updates}(w)),$$
$$\mathcal{L}^{\mathsf{Add}}(\mathsf{ind}, w) = \mathcal{L}''(w),$$
$$\mathcal{L}^{\mathsf{Del}}(\mathsf{ind}, w) = \mathcal{L}'''(w).$$

3   Wildcards

Different SSE schemes support different kinds of search queries. The simplest search query consists of one keyword. This is called *exact keyword search*: clients can search for one keyword and receive all documents containing this keyword. In our research, we consider DSSE schemes supporting *single keyword wildcard search*. This setting extends exact keyword search by additionally allowing that the searched keyword can contain wildcards. We consider two types of wildcards:

' _ ' and '*'. The first wildcard type, ' _ ', is used to indicate the presence of a single character. The second wildcard type, '*', is used to indicate the presence of zero or more characters. Suppose we upload $(\mathsf{ind}_1, \text{'cat'})$ and $(\mathsf{ind}_2, \text{'cut'})$. The query $q = \text{'c\_t'}$ would match both ind_1 and ind_2. Consider additionally uploading another document-keyword pair $(\mathsf{ind}_3, \text{'catering'})$. The query $q_2 = \text{'cat*'}$ matches with ind_1 and ind_3.

3.1 Wildcard Security

As searches of wildcard supporting SSE schemes operate on queries q rather than keywords w, we first describe a natural extension of the aforementioned leakage functions to the wildcard setting. We introduce the following notation: let w be a keyword and q be a query that can contain wildcards. If keyword w is contained in query q we denote this as $w \mathrel{\dot\subseteq} q$. 'cat' $\mathrel{\dot\subseteq}$ 'c_t'. We change the definition of the internal state Q of leakage functions to the following: the list Q stores every search query as a (u, q) pair, where u is the timestamp and q is the search string (a keyword, possibly containing wildcard characters). Update queries remain the same: a $(u, \mathsf{op}, (\mathsf{ind}, w))$ tuple, where op is the operation (add or del) and (ind, w) is the document-keyword pair. We define $\mathsf{sp}(q)$, $\mathsf{ap}(q)$, $\mathsf{UpHist}(q)$, $\mathsf{TimeDB}(q)$ and $\mathsf{Updates}(q)$ as wildcard adaptations of $\mathsf{sp}(w)$, $\mathsf{ap}(w)$, $\mathsf{UpHist}(w)$, $\mathsf{TimeDB}(w)$ and $\mathsf{Updates}(w)$, respectively.

$$\mathsf{sp}(q) = \{u \mid (u, q) \in Q\},$$
$$\mathsf{ap}(q) = \{\mathsf{ind} \mid (u, \mathsf{add}, (\mathsf{ind}, w)) \in Q \wedge$$
$$\nexists\, u' > u \text{ s.t. } (u', \mathsf{del}, (\mathsf{ind}, w)) \in Q \wedge w \mathrel{\dot\subseteq} q\},$$
$$\mathsf{UpHist}(q) = \{(u, \mathsf{op}, \mathsf{ind}) \mid (u, \mathsf{op}, (\mathsf{ind}, w)) \in Q \wedge w \mathrel{\dot\subseteq} q\},$$
$$\mathsf{TimeDB}(q) = \{(u, \mathsf{ind}) \mid (u, \mathsf{add}, (\mathsf{ind}, w)) \in Q \wedge$$
$$\nexists\, u' > u \text{ s.t. } (u', \mathsf{del}, (\mathsf{ind}, w)) \in Q \wedge w \mathrel{\dot\subseteq} q\},$$
$$\mathsf{Updates}(q) = \{u \mid (u, \mathsf{op}, (\mathsf{ind}, w)) \in Q \wedge w \mathrel{\dot\subseteq} q\}.$$

Similarly to their non-wildcard counterparts, $\mathsf{ap}(q)$, $\mathsf{TimeDB}(q)$ and $\mathsf{Updates}(q)$ can be constructed from $\mathsf{UpHist}(q)$. We can extend the notions of BP introduced earlier to the wildcard setting by using the leakage functions we defined.

Definition 4. *A wildcard supporting, $\mathcal{L}$-adaptively-secure SSE scheme is **insertion pattern revealing backward-private** iff the search, add and delete leakage functions $\mathcal{L}^{\mathsf{Srch}}$, $\mathcal{L}^{\mathsf{Add}}$ and $\mathcal{L}^{\mathsf{Del}}$ can be written as:*

$$\mathcal{L}^{\mathsf{Srch}}(q) = \mathcal{L}'(\mathsf{TimeDB}(q), a_q),$$
$$\mathcal{L}^{\mathsf{Add}}(\mathsf{ind}, w) = \bot,$$
$$\mathcal{L}^{\mathsf{Del}}(\mathsf{ind}, w) = \bot,$$

where a_q denotes the number of updates on q and $\mathcal{L}'$, $\mathcal{L}''$ and $\mathcal{L}'''$ are stateless.

Definition 5. *A wildcard supporting, $\mathcal{L}$-adaptively-secure SSE scheme is* **update pattern revealing backward-private** *iff the leakage functions $\mathcal{L}^{\mathsf{Srch}}$, $\mathcal{L}^{\mathsf{Add}}$ and $\mathcal{L}^{\mathsf{Del}}$ can be written with stateless functions $\mathcal{L}'$, $\mathcal{L}''$ and $\mathcal{L}'''$ as:*

$$\mathcal{L}^{\mathsf{Srch}}(q) = \mathcal{L}'(\mathsf{TimeDB}(q), \mathsf{Updates}(q)),$$
$$\mathcal{L}^{\mathsf{Add}}(\mathsf{ind}, w) = \mathcal{L}''(w),$$
$$\mathcal{L}^{\mathsf{Del}}(\mathsf{ind}, w) = \mathcal{L}'''(w).$$

4 Libertas: Constructing Wildcard Supporting Update Pattern Revealing Backward Private Schemes

Libertas is a construction for creating the first backward private, wildcard supporting DSSE schemes. Its idea is similar to that of the scheme $B(\Sigma)$ proposed by [5]. Rather than being an SSE scheme on its own, Libertas encapsulates an existing SSE scheme Σ that supports wildcards and document-keyword additions, to provide BP. The idea is as follows: rather than storing document identifiers, store encryptions of document-update pairs, regardless of whether the update was an insertion or a deletion. During searches, send all encrypted document-update pairs to the client for decryption. The client can select relevant document identifiers (those that are added, but not subsequently deleted) and send them to the server to retrieve the documents. This approach makes Libertas result-hiding.

4.1 Construction

Libertas is built from an encryption scheme E and an SSE scheme Σ. E is *which-key concealing* (sometimes referred to as *key-private encryption*), meaning that two encryptions do not leak whether they are encrypted using the same key [1]. Σ supports add operations and wildcard queries, and is $\mathcal{L}_\Sigma$-adaptively secure, where $\mathcal{L}_\Sigma = (\mathcal{L}_\Sigma^{\mathsf{Srch}}, \mathcal{L}_\Sigma^{\mathsf{Add}})$ is defined with stateless functions $\mathcal{L}'$ and $\mathcal{L}''$ as

$$\mathcal{L}_\Sigma^{\mathsf{Srch}}(q) = \mathcal{L}'(\mathsf{sp}_\Sigma(q), \mathsf{UpHist}_\Sigma(q)),$$
$$\mathcal{L}_\Sigma^{\mathsf{Add}}(\mathsf{ind}, w) = \mathcal{L}''(\mathsf{ind}, w).$$

Libertas is described in Algorithm 1. Here, $E_{K_{\mathsf{Lib}}}$ denotes an encryption using E under key K_{Lib}. Returned values are sent over the network.

4.2 Analysis

We analyze the theoretical cost of running Libertas in terms of storage, operations and communication. We compare these components with Σ, as most costs are identical to, or dependent on, Σ.

Storage. The client stores one extra key K_{Lib} and the counter c. The server stores an encryption in its index for every update (including deletions), rather than a document identifier for document-keyword pairs currently in the database.

Algorithm 1. Libertas

Setup(λ)

  1: $K_\Sigma \leftarrow \Sigma.\text{Setup}(\lambda)$

  2: $K_{\text{Lib}} \xleftarrow{\$} \{0,1\}^\lambda$

  3: $K = (K_\Sigma, K_{\text{Lib}})$

  4: $c \leftarrow 0$

BuildIndex(λ)

  1: $\gamma \leftarrow \Sigma.\text{BuildIndex}(\lambda)$

SrchToken(K, q)

  1: $\tau^{\text{srch}} \leftarrow \Sigma.\text{SrchToken}(K_\Sigma, q)$

  2: Return τ^{srch}

AddToken(K, ind, w)

  1: $\tau^{\text{add}} \leftarrow \Sigma.\text{AddToken}(K_\Sigma, E_{K_{\text{Lib}}}(c, \text{add}, \text{ind}, w), w)$

  2: $c \leftarrow c + 1$

  3: Return τ^{add}

DelToken(K, ind, w)

  1: $\tau^{\text{del}} \leftarrow \Sigma.\text{AddToken}(K_\Sigma, E_{K_{\text{Lib}}}(c, \text{del}, \text{ind}, w), w)$

  2: $c \leftarrow c + 1$

  3: Return τ^{del}

Search($\gamma, \tau^{\text{srch}}$)

  1: $R^* \leftarrow \Sigma.\text{Search}(\gamma, \tau^{\text{srch}})$

  2: Return R^*

DecSearch(K, R^*)

  1: Decrypt R^* using K_{Lib} and sort the entries in ascending order based on the value of c, resulting in $((c_1, \text{op}_1, \text{ind}_1, w_1), \ldots, (c_n, \text{op}_n, \text{ind}_n, w_n))$.

  2: Let W be the set of distinct keywords in R^*.

  3: For all $w \in W$, let $R_w = \{\text{ind} \mid \exists\, i \text{ s.t. } (\text{op}_i, \text{ind}_i, w_i) = (\text{add}, \text{ind}, w) \wedge \nexists\, j > i,\ (\text{op}_j, \text{ind}_j, w_j) = (\text{del}, \text{ind}, w)\}$.

  4: $R = \bigcup_{w \in W} R_w$

  5: Return R

FetchDocuments(R)

  1: Return all documents corresponding to the document identifiers in R.

Add($\gamma, \tau^{\text{add}}$)

  1: $\gamma \leftarrow \Sigma.\text{Add}(\gamma, \tau^{\text{add}})$

Delete($\gamma, \tau^{\text{del}}$)

  1: $\gamma \leftarrow \Sigma.\text{Add}(\gamma, \tau^{\text{del}})$

Operations. During the setup phase, the client generates an extra key K_{Lib}. For add and delete operations, the client performs an extra encryption and addition. For searches, rather than receiving the documents from the server, the client gets the encryptions of all relevant updates. The client decrypts the fetched updates and selects relevant document identifiers by going over the updates linearly.

Communication. In Σ, searches result in communication between client and server regarding the search token and the resulting documents. During searches in Libertas, between sending the search token and receiving the matching documents, client and server exchange additional information. The server sends all updates regarding keywords matching the searched query and the document identifiers of the matching documents. The client, in turn, sends the identifiers of matching documents to the server. This requires an extra round of communications. This can be a problem in specific settings where communication is slow, unstable, expensive, subject to time constraints or otherwise limited. In some cases, round trips can be combined. Suppose that Σ itself is result-hiding and its DecSearch algorithm only requires the client to decrypt an AES encryption for every result. This process can be done in the DecSearch algorithm of Libertas, therefore combining the second rounds of Σ and Libertas, requiring a total of two round trips rather than three.

4.3 Security

Theorem 1. *Let E_{K_Σ} be an IND-CPA secure, which-key concealing encryption scheme and Σ be a wildcard supporting, $\mathcal{L}_\Sigma$-adaptively secure scheme that supports add operations, with $\mathcal{L}_\Sigma = (\mathcal{L}_\Sigma^{Srch}, \mathcal{L}_\Sigma^{Add})$ defined as*

$$\mathcal{L}_\Sigma^{Srch}(q) = \mathcal{L}'(sp_\Sigma(q), UpHist_\Sigma(q)),$$
$$\mathcal{L}_\Sigma^{Add}(ind, w) = \mathcal{L}''(ind, w),$$

where $\mathcal{L}'$ and $\mathcal{L}''$ are stateless. Then, Libertas is $\mathcal{L}_{Lib}$-adaptively secure, with $\mathcal{L}_{Lib} = (\mathcal{L}_{Lib}^{Srch}, \mathcal{L}_{Lib}^{Add}, \mathcal{L}_{Lib}^{Del})$ defined as

$$\mathcal{L}_{Lib}^{Srch}(q) = (sp_{Lib}(q), TimeDB_{Lib}(q), Updates_{Lib}(q)),$$
$$\mathcal{L}_{Lib}^{Add}(ind, w) = w,$$
$$\mathcal{L}_{Lib}^{Del}(ind, w) = w.$$

Libertas *is therefore update pattern revealing backward-private.*

If Σ is additionally forward private, meaning it is $\mathcal{L}_{\Sigma_{fp}}$-adaptively secure, where $\mathcal{L}_{\Sigma_{fp}} = (\mathcal{L}_\Sigma^{Srch}, \mathcal{L}_{\Sigma_{fp}}^{Add})$, with $\mathcal{L}_{\Sigma_{fp}}^{Add}$ defined with stateless function $\mathcal{L}'''$ as

$$\mathcal{L}_{\Sigma_{fp}}^{Add}(ind, w) = \mathcal{L}'''(ind),$$

and where Libertas *is $\mathcal{L}_{Lib_{fp}}$-adaptively secure, where $\mathcal{L}_{Lib_{fp}} = (\mathcal{L}_{Lib}^{Srch}, \mathcal{L}_{Lib_{fp}}^{Add}, \mathcal{L}_{Lib_{fp}}^{Del})$, with $\mathcal{L}_{Lib_{fp}}^{Add}$ and $\mathcal{L}_{Lib_{fp}}^{Del}$ defined as*

$$\mathcal{L}_{Lib_{fp}}^{Add}(ind, w) = \bot, \qquad and \qquad \mathcal{L}_{Lib_{fp}}^{Del}(ind, w) = \bot,$$

meaning Libertas *is forward private as well.*

Proof. We describe a polynomial-time simulator $\mathcal{S}_{Lib}$ such that for all probabilistic polynomial-time adversaries $\mathcal{A}$, the output of $SSEReal_{\mathcal{A}}^{Lib}(\lambda, n)$ and the output of SSEIdeal$_{\mathcal{A},\mathcal{S}_{\mathsf{Lib}},\mathcal{L}_{\mathsf{Lib}}}(\lambda, n)$ are equal. Since Σ is $\mathcal{L}_{\Sigma}$-adaptively secure, there exists a polynomial-time simulator $\mathcal{S}_{\Sigma}$ that can simulate operations in Σ using $\mathcal{L}_{\Sigma}$. Consider the simulator $\mathcal{S}_{\mathsf{Lib}}$ that adaptively simulates a sequence of n simulated tokens $(\widetilde{\tau}_1, \ldots, \widetilde{\tau}_n)$, a sequence of m simulated encrypted result sets $(\widetilde{R}_1^*, \ldots, \widetilde{R}_m^*)$ and a sequence of m simulated decrypted result sets $(\widetilde{R}_1, \ldots, \widetilde{R}_m)$, where $m \leq n$, as follows:

- (Setup) the simulator generates a random key $K_{\mathcal{S}_{\mathsf{Lib}}}$.
- (Simulating τ^{srch}) given $\mathcal{L}_{\mathsf{Lib}}^{\mathsf{Srch}}(q) = (\mathsf{sp}_{\mathsf{Lib}}(q), \mathsf{TimeDB}_{\mathsf{Lib}}(q), \mathsf{Updates}_{\mathsf{Lib}}(q))$, construct $\widetilde{\mathcal{L}}_{\Sigma}^{\mathsf{Srch}}(q) = \mathcal{L}(\widetilde{\mathsf{sp}}_{\Sigma}(q), \widetilde{\mathsf{UpHist}}_{\Sigma}(q))$ with $\widetilde{\mathsf{sp}}_{\Sigma}(q) = \mathsf{sp}_{\mathsf{Lib}}(q)$ and $\widetilde{\mathsf{UpHist}}_{\Sigma}(q) = \{(u, \mathsf{add}, E_{K_{\mathcal{S}_{\mathsf{Lib}}}}(\bot_c, \bot_{\mathsf{op}}, \bot_{\mathsf{ind}}, \bot_w)) \,|\, u \in \mathsf{Updates}_{\mathsf{Lib}}(q)\}$.
  Then, rather than running $\Sigma.\mathsf{SrchToken}(K_{\Sigma}, q)$, run $\mathcal{S}_{\Sigma}(\mathsf{st}_{\mathcal{S}_{\Sigma}}, \widetilde{\mathcal{L}}_{\Sigma}^{\mathsf{Srch}}(q))$. Since every search for query q in Libertas results in a search for query q in Σ, the search patterns for Libertas and Σ are identical. $\mathsf{UpHist}_{\Sigma}(q)$ can be generated as the timestamps are identical to those of $\mathsf{Updates}_{\mathsf{Lib}}(q)$, the operation is always add and the encryption of meaningless data is indistinguishable from that of meaningful data, since E is IND-CPA secure. $(\bot_c, \bot_{\mathsf{op}}, \bot_{\mathsf{ind}}, \bot_w)$ are generated based on u, maintaining consistency between simulated search tokens of identical queries. By taking constructed leakage $\widetilde{\mathcal{L}}_{\Sigma}^{\mathsf{Srch}}$ as input, $\mathcal{S}_{\Sigma}$, and in turn $\mathcal{S}_{\mathsf{Lib}}$, can simulate search tokens $\widetilde{\tau}^{\mathsf{srch}}$ that are indistinguishable from real tokens τ^{srch}.
- (Simulating τ^{add}) given $\mathcal{L}_{\mathsf{Lib}}^{\mathsf{Add}}(\mathsf{ind}, w) = w$, construct $\widetilde{\mathcal{L}}_{\Sigma}^{\mathsf{Add}}(\mathsf{ind}, w) = \mathcal{L}(\widetilde{\mathsf{ind}}, \widetilde{w})$ with $\widetilde{\mathsf{ind}} = E_{K_{\mathcal{S}_{\mathsf{Lib}}}}(\bot_c, \bot_{\mathsf{op}}, \bot_{\mathsf{ind}}, \bot_w)$, and $\widetilde{w} = w$.
  Then, instead of running algorithm $\Sigma.\mathsf{AddToken}(K_{\Sigma}, E_{K_{\mathsf{Lib}}}(c, \mathsf{add}, \mathsf{ind}, w))$, run $\mathcal{S}_{\Sigma}(\mathsf{st}_{\mathcal{S}_{\Sigma}}, \widetilde{\mathcal{L}}_{\Sigma}^{\mathsf{Add}}(\mathsf{ind}, w))$. To clarify, ind is viewed as a document identifier from Σ's perspective, but as an encrypted tuple from Libertas's perspective. Since $E_{K_{\mathcal{S}_{\mathsf{Lib}}}}$ is CPA-secure, $\bot_c, \bot_{\mathsf{op}}, \bot_{\mathsf{ind}}$ and $\bot_w$ can be anything, as the resulting encryption will be indistinguishable from an encryption where an actual timestamp, update operation, document identifier and keyword are considered. Therefore, $\mathcal{S}_{\Sigma}$, and in turn Libertas, will be able to create add tokens $\widetilde{\tau}^{\mathsf{add}}$ that are indistinguishable from real tokens τ^{add}. We do not maintain consistency for add tokens as we did for search tokens, as add tokens are distinct by nature.
  In case Σ is forward private, we are given $\mathcal{L}_{\mathsf{Lib}_{fp}}^{\mathsf{Add}}(\mathsf{ind}, w) = \bot$ and we construct $\widetilde{\mathcal{L}}_{\Sigma_{fp}}^{\mathsf{Add}}(\mathsf{ind}, w) = \mathcal{L}(\widetilde{\mathsf{ind}})$ with $\widetilde{\mathsf{ind}} = E_{K_{\mathcal{S}_{\mathsf{Lib}}}}(\bot_c, \bot_{\mathsf{op}}, \bot_{\mathsf{ind}}, \bot_w)$.
- (Simulating τ^{del}) $\mathcal{S}_{\mathsf{Lib}}$ can construct a delete token $\widetilde{\tau}^{\mathsf{del}}$ that is indistinguishable from τ^{del} in the same way as it constructs add tokens.
- (Simulating R^*) given $\mathcal{L}_{\mathsf{Lib}}^{\mathsf{Srch}}(q) = (\mathsf{sp}_{\mathsf{Lib}}(q), \mathsf{TimeDB}_{\mathsf{Lib}}(q), \mathsf{Updates}_{\mathsf{Lib}}(q))$, construct $\widetilde{R}^* = \{E_{K_{\mathcal{S}_{\mathsf{Lib}}}}(\bot_c, \bot_{\mathsf{op}}, \bot_{\mathsf{ind}}, \bot_w) \,|\, u \in \mathsf{Updates}_{\mathsf{Lib}}(q)\}$, where $\bot_c$ is a fake timestamp, $\bot_{\mathsf{op}}$ is a fake update operation, $\bot_{\mathsf{ind}}$ is a fake document identifier and $\bot_w$ is a fake keyword. Since $E_{K_{\mathcal{S}_{\mathsf{Lib}}}}$ is IND-CPA secure, items in R^* and $\widetilde{R}^*$ are indistinguishable. As both result sets have the same length as well, R^* and $\widetilde{R}^*$ are indistinguishable. To maintain consistency of simulated

sets between identical search queries, we generate values $(\perp_c, \perp_{op}, \perp_{ind}, \perp_w)$ based on u, akin to what we did for simulating search tokens.

- (Simulating R) given $\mathcal{L}_{Lib}^{Srch}(q) = (sp_{Lib}(q), \text{TimeDB}_{Lib}(q), \text{Updates}_{Lib}(q))$, construct $\widetilde{R} = \{ind \mid (u, ind) \in \text{TimeDB}_{Lib}(q)\}$.

5   Evaluation

In order to empirically evaluate the cost of BP in Libertas, we implemented it with the wildcard supporting scheme by Zhao and Nishide (Z&N) [20] that stores one Bloom filter [2] for each document-keyword pair in the index. An overview of the scheme's algorithms, including the generation of the Bloom filters, can be found in Appendix A. Z&N is forward private and allows for updates on a document-keyword pair level rather than considering complete documents, making integration with Libertas easy. Also, it supports two wildcard types, allowing for greater query flexibility.

5.1   Setup

Implementation. A single-core implementation is written and tested in Python 3.8 with code available at https://github.com/LibertasConstruction/Libertas.

Hardware. The experiments were carried out on a laptop computer running Windows 10 with 8 GB of RAM and 4 Intel i7-4700MQ cores, operating at 2.4 GHz each. The implementation only used a single CPU core, however. Both the scheme's client and server ran in the same process, communicating directly via the Python script.

Parameters. We set the false positive rate of the Bloom filters to 0.01 and used keywords of length 5. The length of the keyword determines the size of the keyword characteristic set and thus the number of elements in the Bloom filter. With these settings, Bloom filters consist of 240 bits and use 7 hash functions. We used 2048 bit keys for all Z&N instances and 256 bit keys for AES encryptions in Libertas.

Dataset. For the experiments, we generated document-keyword pairs of the form $[(0, `00000'), (1, `00001'), \ldots, (99999, `99999')]$.

5.2   Experiments

We devised four experiments that measure the effect of changes to the index size, the wildcard query, the result set and the number of deletions, respectively. We measured the execution time of the search protocol of both schemes, averaged over 10 queries and 10 instances of the schemes. We considered the Search operation for Z&N and both the Search and DecSearch operations for Libertas$_{Z\&N}$. We disregarded the SrchToken operation as it is identical for both schemes.

Table 1. Avg. search times in *seconds* for (a) exact keyword search, (b) wildcard search with index size 10^4, and (c) varying result set size with index size 10^4.

Scheme	(a) Index size				(b) # of wildcards					(c) Result set size				
	10^2	10^3	10^4	10^5	0	1	2	3	4	10^0	10^1	10^2	10^3	10^4
Z&N	0.02	0.11	0.67	2.90	0.67	0.69	0.76	1.02	2.39	0.63	0.63	0.74	1.91	14.34
Libertas$_{Z\&N}$	0.02	0.11	0.67	2.91	0.66	0.69	0.76	1.05	2.78	0.63	0.63	0.74	1.93	15.34

Table 2. Avg. search times in *seconds* per number of deletions (index size 10^4).

Scheme	Number of deletions										
	0	1000	2000	3000	4000	5000	6000	7000	8000	9000	10000
Z&N	0.65	0.57	0.51	0.44	0.38	0.32	0.25	0.19	0.12	0.06	0.00
Libertas$_{Z\&N}$	0.63	0.70	0.76	0.81	0.88	0.95	1.01	1.07	1.12	1.20	1.24

Basic Search. To measure the basic search time, we inserted the first n_i pairs of the generated data set for different index sizes n_i. We measured the search time of a random keyword present in the index.

Wildcard Query Search. To measure the effect of wildcards, we considered a fixed index size of 10,000 but increasingly replaced more query characters with '_' wildcards, to increase the number of matching keywords. We chose not to include '*' wildcards, as the construction of Z&N uses the same concept for both wildcard types. While there is a measurable performance difference depending on the wildcard type, this effect will be identical for Z&N and Libertas$_{Z\&N}$. We are only interested in the number of matching keywords as this influences the performance of the DecSearch operation in Libertas.

Varying Result Set Size. We investigated the effect of matching multiple documents. The generated data set is modified slightly for this experiment. The last n_r pairs that are inserted consider the same keyword. This is the keyword we query for. We measured the search time for increasing n_r, with a fixed index size of 10,000.

Varying Number of Deletions. To evaluate the effect of deletions growing the index of Libertas, we measured search times for an increasing number of deletions. For this experiment, both schemes started out with their index containing the first 10,000 pairs of the generated data set. Then, we deleted pairs from the index using the delete protocol of the scheme.

5.3 Results

Tables 1 and 2 summarize our experimental results.

Basic Search. For exact keyword searches, Table 1(a) shows that Libertas$_{Z\&N}$ experiences no overhead compared to Z&N, regardless of the index size.

Wildcard Query Search. Table 1(b) shows that the overhead of Libertas$_{Z\&N}$ barely increases when considering queries containing wildcards such that they match multiple keywords. Note that, for the given dataset, every additional wildcard increases the number of matching keywords ten-fold.

Varying Result Set Size. Table 1(c) indicates that Libertas$_{Z\&N}$ and Z&N have a comparable performance regardless of the result set size.

Varying Number of Deletions. Table 2 shows the downside of an index that grows with deletions. Typically, search times decrease as items are deleted, as can be seen for Z&N. Due to Libertas' nature, however, its index increases, slowing down searches linearly with the number of deletions.

6   Discussion

Query Similarity. The wildcard leakage functions we introduced in Sect. 3.1 allow for query similarity leakage. We consider Definition 4. Here, information on query similarity is leaked in the following way. We consider queries q_1 and q_2. If $q_2 \dot\subseteq q_1$, then $\mathsf{TimeDB}(q_2) \subseteq \mathsf{TimeDB}(q_1)$. Note that the relation is not reversible; if an observer sees that $\mathsf{TimeDB}(q_2) \subseteq \mathsf{TimeDB}(q_1)$, it does not necessarily mean that $q_2 \dot\subseteq q_1$. An adversary can try to link result sets that are subsets of each other and assume that the corresponding queries are related; the query corresponding to the larger result set is likely a more general form of the query of the smaller set. This query similarity leakage might be abusable and compromise wildcard security. We leave it for future work to determine if this leakage undermines wildcard security and if so, to develop an LAA.

Real-World Application. Libertas$_{Z\&N}$ is ready for deployment in systems that require a backward private, wildcard supporting DSSE scheme today. The implementation provided with this paper uses a single CPU core. The implementation can easily be parallelized, however. During the Search algorithm, the server goes through all updates in the index (see line 2–3 in Search in Algorithm 2). This search can be split up between cores. If we assume a computer with 8 CPU cores, we can effectively cut search times by a factor of 8. Searches will take less than a second even with a large index or many deletions. Only when considering very large databases or environments where two round trips are undesirable would Libertas not provide a proper solution.

Clean-Up Procedure. The major drawback of Libertas is that its index grows with every update, as deletions in Libertas translate to insertions in Σ. This increases search times for both the Search algorithm run at the server and the DecSearch algorithm run at the client. We propose a clean-up procedure similar to that of Bost et al. [5] to combat this problem. During Search, the server removes all results from the index. Then, when running the FetchDocuments algorithm, the client additionally runs the AddToken algorithm for every relevant document-keyword pair. That is, every pair that was added, but not subsequently deleted. The server runs the Add algorithm to re-add the relevant document-keyword pairs to the index. This procedure cleanses the index during searches, removing updates that cancel each other out. If Libertas is constructed from a forward private scheme, we believe this procedure incurs no additional leakage, as additions do not leak information. This clean-up procedure restricts the choice of Σ, as the scheme should be able to remove individual entries from the index. A common example of a valid index structure is a list containing entries for every document-keyword pair, such as in Z&N. An example of a DSSE scheme with an unsuitable index structure is the scheme by Kamara et al. [14].

Insertion Pattern Revealing Backward Privacy. Libertas can achieve *insertion pattern revealing backward privacy* if Σ is forward private and does not leak $\mathsf{UpHist}_\Sigma(q)$ during search operations, but only $\mathsf{ap}_\Sigma(q)$. In our scenario, the difference between leakage functions $\mathsf{UpHist}_\Sigma(q)$ and $\mathsf{ap}_\Sigma(q)$ consists of only the timestamps of all updates, as update operations are always additions. If Σ does not leak these timestamps, then Libertas does neither. In the proof, rather than using $\mathsf{Updates}_{\mathsf{Lib}}(q)$ to construct $\mathsf{UpHist}_\Sigma(q)$, we can use $a_{q_{\mathsf{Lib}}}$ to construct $\mathsf{ap}_\Sigma(q)$ by generating $a_{q_{\mathsf{Lib}}}$ encryptions of $(\perp_c, \perp_{\mathsf{op}}, \perp_{\mathsf{ind}}, \perp_w)$ tuples. Hiding $\mathsf{UpHist}(q)$ in SSE schemes remains a challenge, however. Current solutions use ORAM but are not efficient [15].

7   Conclusion

In this research, we extended commonly used leakage functions and, in turn, backward privacy definitions, to consider wildcard queries as opposed to just exact keyword queries. We presented Libertas; a construction providing *update pattern revealing backward privacy* to any wildcard supporting scheme Σ. We proved the security of Libertas in the $\mathcal{L}$-*adaptive security model* and evaluated its performance compared to its underlying scheme Σ. We found that Libertas experiences an overhead that is linear in the number of deletions. The resulting scheme requires an additional round of communication during searches and its index grows with every update. Nonetheless, searches are fast, making Libertas suitable for real-world applications.

A   Z&N: Construction

We provide the construction of Z&N: a DSSE scheme supporting wildcard search. It is proposed by Zhao and Nishide in [20] and uses Bloom filters [2] and a regular index. The algorithms are described in Algorithm 2. An implementation of Z&N can be found at https://github.com/LibertasConstruction/Libertas. The scheme uses a hash function g. $\bar{g}$ denotes the first bit of a hash using g. The scheme uses g with r different keys to effectively create r different hash functions to use for Bloom filters. $\mathsf{BF}[p]$ denotes the bit in a Bloom filter at position p. ind $\|$ w indicates a concatenation of ind and w. The scheme uses keyword characteristic and token (query) characteristic sets, $S_K(w)$ and $S_T(q)$, to capture the structure of keywords and queries to support both '*' and '_' wildcard symbols. Every keyword characteristic set is stored in a Bloom filter.

A.1   Keyword Characteristic Set

$S_K(w)$ is made up of the two sets $S_K^{(o)}(w)$ and $S_K^{(p)}(w)$. The set $S_K^{(o)}(w)$ contains characters of a keyword w together with their position. For example, $S_K^{(o)}(\text{'diana'}) = \{\text{'1:d'}, \text{'2:i'}, \text{'3:a'}, \text{'4:n'}, \text{'5:a'}, \text{'6:\textbackslash0'}\}$. Note the terminator symbol indicating the end of the keyword. The set $S_K^{(p)}(w)$ consists of the sets $S_K^{(p1)}(w)$ and $S_K^{(p2)}(w)$. These sets consider pairs of characters. Let us take a look at these sets when using the keyword 'diana'.

$$S_K^{(p1)}(\text{'diana'}) = \{\text{'1:1:d,i'}, \text{'2:1:d,a'}, \text{'3:1:d,n'}, \text{'4:1:d,a'}, \text{'5:1:d,\textbackslash0'},$$
$$\text{'1:1:i,a'}, \text{'2:1:i,n'}, \text{'3:1:i,a'}, \text{'4:1:i,\textbackslash0'},$$
$$\text{'1:1:a,n'}, \text{'2:1:a,a'}, \text{'3:1:a,\textbackslash0'},$$
$$\text{'1:1:n,a'}, \text{'2:1:n,\textbackslash0'},$$
$$\text{'1:1:a,\textbackslash0'}\}$$

Here, the element '3:1:d,n' comes from the character pair 'di̱a̱na', where 3 is the distance between the characters and 1 indicates that it is the first occurrence of the pair with the given distance in this set.

$$S_K^{(p2)}(\text{'diana'}) = \{\text{'-:1:d,i'}, \text{'-:1:d,a'}, \text{'-:1:d,n'}, \text{'-:2:d,a'}, \text{'-:1:d,\textbackslash0'},$$
$$\text{'-:1:i,a'}, \text{'-:1:i,n'}, \text{'-:2:i,a'}, \text{'-:1:i,\textbackslash0'},$$
$$\text{'-:1:a,n'}, \text{'-:1:a,a'}, \text{'-:1:a,\textbackslash0'},$$
$$\text{'-:1:n,a'}, \text{'-:1:n,\textbackslash0'},$$
$$\text{'-:2:a,\textbackslash0'}\}$$

Here, the element '-:2:i,a' comes from the character pair 'di̱ana̱'. Distances are not considered in this set. The 2 indicates that this is the second occurrence of the pair in the set.

A.2   Token Characteristic Set

Next, we will show how to construct the token characteristic set $S_T(q)$ of a search query q. As this scheme does not support conjunctive keyword queries, q can be thought of as a keyword containing wildcards. Similar to $S_K(w)$, $S_T(q)$ is made up of the sets $S_T^{(o)}(q)$, $S_T^{(p1)}(q)$ and $S_T^{(p2)}(q)$. The construction of the sets is illustrated by an example with the query 'di*a_a*\0'.

The set $S_T^{(o)}(q)$ is constructed by extracting characters from q with a specified appearance order. $S_T^{(o)}(\text{'di*a\_a*\textbackslash0'}) = \{\text{'1:d'}, \text{'2:i'}\}$.

We define a *character group* as a group of subsequent characters that do not contain wildcards. 'di*a_a*\0' consists of the character groups 'di', 'a', 'a' and '\0'. For $S_T^{(p1)}(q)$, we consider the character group to the left and to the right of '_' wildcards. We generate all possible character pairs with their corresponding distance. Then, we do mostly the same for '*' wildcards: we consider

Algorithm 2. Z&N

$\text{Setup}(\lambda)$

1: $k_t \overset{\$}{\leftarrow} \{0,1\}^{\lambda}$, for $t \in [1, r]$
2: $K_H = \{k_t\}_{t \in [1, r]}$
3: $K_G \overset{\$}{\leftarrow} \{0,1\}^{\lambda}$
4: $K = (K_H, K_G)$

$\text{BuildIndex}(\lambda)$

1: $\gamma \leftarrow$ empty list

$\text{SrchToken}(K, q)$

1: $S_{T_q} \leftarrow S_T(q)$
2: For each element e_j of S_{T_q}:
3:     $p_t \leftarrow g(k_t, e_j)$, for $t \in [1, r]$
4:     $\tau^{\text{srch}}_{e_j,1} = (p_1, p_2, \dots, p_r)$
5:     $\tau^{\text{srch}}_{e_j,2} = (g(K_G, p_1), g(K_G, p_2), \dots, g(K_G, p_r))$
6:     $\tau^{\text{srch}}_{e_j} = (\tau^{\text{srch}}_{e_j,1}, \tau^{\text{srch}}_{e_j,2})$
7: $\tau^{\text{srch}} = (\tau^{\text{srch}}_{e_1}, \tau^{\text{srch}}_{e_2}, \dots, \tau^{\text{srch}}_{e_\ell})$
8: Return τ^{srch}

$\text{AddToken}(K, \text{ind}, w)$

1: $b_{\text{id}} \leftarrow g(K_G, \text{ind} \| w)$
2: $S_{K_w} \leftarrow S_K(w)$
3: For each element e_j of $S_K(w)$:
4:     $p_t \leftarrow g(k_t, e_j)$, for $t \in [1, r]$
5:     Initialize a Bloom filter BF of length b and set the bits at positions p_t to 1
6: For $p \in [1, b]$:
7:     $\text{mb}[p] \leftarrow \overline{g}(b_{\text{id}}, g(K_G, p))$
8:     $\text{BF}[p] \leftarrow \text{BF}[p] \oplus \text{mb}[p]$
9: $\tau^{\text{add}} = (\text{ind}, \text{BF}, b_{\text{id}})$
10: Return τ^{add}

$\text{DelToken}(K, \text{ind}, w)$

1: $b_{\text{id}} \leftarrow g(K_G, \text{ind} \| w)$
2: $\tau^{\text{del}} = b_{\text{id}}$
3: Return τ^{del}

$\text{Search}(\gamma, \tau^{\text{srch}})$

1: τ^{srch} consists of Bloom filter positions and hashes of these positions. We arrange these as $((p_1, g(K_G, p_1)), \dots, (p_i, g(K_G, p_i)))$
2: For all $(\text{ind}, \text{BF}, b_{\text{id}})$ in γ:
3:     Add ind to R if $\text{BF}[p_t] \oplus \overline{g}(b_{\text{id}}, g(K_G, p_t)) = 1$ for all $(p_t, g(K_G, p_t))$, where $t \in [1, i]$.
4: Return R

$\text{Add}(\gamma, \tau^{\text{add}})$

1: Add τ^{add} to γ

$\text{Delete}(\gamma, \tau^{\text{del}})$

1: $\tau^{\text{del}} = b_{\text{id}}$
2: Remove from γ the entry with Bloom filter identifier b_{id}

the character group left and right of the '*' wildcard. This time, however, we *concatenate* the character groups before generating the character pairs, thereby ignoring the wildcard itself in the distance computation. The resulting pairs are added to $S_T^{(p1)}$. The following example illustrates what this means exactly. Consider $S_T^{(p1)}$ ('di*a_a*\0'). The '_' wildcard is surrounded by 'a' and 'a'. $S_T^{(p1)}$ therefore contains '2:1:a,a'. The first '*' wildcard is surrounded by character group 'di' and character 'a', adding '1:1:d,i', '2:1:d,a' and '1:1:i,a' to the set. In the same fashion, '1:1:a,\0' is added.

To construct the set $S_T^{(p2)}(q)$, consider the search string without wildcard symbols. Then, follow the same procedure as with the construction of $S_K^{(p2)}(w)$.

References

1. Abadi, M., Rogaway, P.: Reconciling two views of cryptography. In: van Leeuwen, J., Watanabe, O., Hagiya, M., Mosses, P.D., Ito, T. (eds.) TCS 2000. LNCS, vol. 1872, pp. 3–22. Springer, Heidelberg (2000). https://doi.org/10.1007/3-540-44929-9_1

2. Bloom, B.H.: Space/time trade-offs in hash coding with allowable errors. Communications of the ACM **13**, 422–426 (1970)

3. Bösch, C., Brinkman, R., Hartel, P., Jonker, W.: Conjunctive wildcard search over encrypted data. In: Jonker, W., Petković, M. (eds.) SDM 2011. LNCS, vol. 6933, pp. 114–127. Springer, Heidelberg (2011). https://doi.org/10.1007/978-3-642-23556-6_8

4. Bost, R.: Σοφος: forward secure searchable encryption. In: Proceedings of the ACM SIGSAC Conference on Computer and Communications Security (2016)

5. Bost, R., Minaud, B., Ohrimenko, O.: Forward and backward private searchable encryption from constrained cryptographic primitives. In: Proceedings of the ACM SIGSAC Conference on Computer and Communications Security (2017)

6. Cash, D., Grubbs, P., Perry, J., Ristenpart, T.: Leakage-abuse attacks against searchable encryption. In: Proceedings of the ACM SIGSAC Conference On Computer and Communications Security (2015)

7. Cash, D., Jarecki, S., Jutla, C., Krawczyk, H., Roşu, M.-C., Steiner, M.: Highly-scalable searchable symmetric encryption with support for Boolean queries. In: Canetti, R., Garay, J.A. (eds.) CRYPTO 2013. LNCS, vol. 8042, pp. 353–373. Springer, Heidelberg (2013). https://doi.org/10.1007/978-3-642-40041-4_20

8. Chase, M., Shen, E.: Substring-searchable symmetric encryption. In: Proceedings on Privacy Enhancing Technologies (2015)

9. Curtmola, R., Garay, J., Kamara, S., Ostrovsky, R.: Searchable symmetric encryption: improved definitions and efficient constructions. In: Proceedings of the ACM SIGSAC Conference on Computer and Communications Security (2006)

10. Faber, S., Jarecki, S., Krawczyk, H., Nguyen, Q., Rosu, M., Steiner, M.: Rich queries on encrypted data: beyond exact matches. In: Pernul, G., Ryan, P.Y.A., Weippl, E. (eds.) ESORICS 2015. LNCS, vol. 9327, pp. 123–145. Springer, Cham (2015). https://doi.org/10.1007/978-3-319-24177-7_7

11. Goh, E.J.: Secure indexes. IACR Cryptol. ePrint Arch. (2003). https://ia.cr/2003/216

12. Hu, C., Han, L.: Efficient wildcard search over encrypted data. Int. J. Inf. Secur. **15**(5), 539–547 (2015). https://doi.org/10.1007/s10207-015-0302-0

13. Islam, M.S., Kuzu, M., Kantarcioglu, M.: Access pattern disclosure on searchable encryption: ramification, attack and mitigation. In: NDSS (2012)
14. Kamara, S., Papamanthou, C., Roeder, T.: Dynamic searchable symmetric encryption. In: Proceedings of the ACM SIGSAC Conference on Computer and Communications Security (2012)
15. Naveed, M.: The fallacy of composition of oblivious RAM and searchable encryption. IACR Cryptol. ePrint Arch (2015). https://ia.cr/2015/668
16. Song, D.X., Wagner, D., Perrig, A.: Practical techniques for searches on encrypted data. In: Proceedings of the IEEE Symposium on Security & Privacy. IEEE (2000)
17. Stefanov, E., Papamanthou, C., Shi, E.: Practical dynamic searchable encryption with small leakage. In: Proceedings of the Network and Distributed System Security Symposium (2014)
18. Suga, T., Nishide, T., Sakurai, K.: Secure keyword search using bloom filter with specified character positions. In: Takagi, T., Wang, G., Qin, Z., Jiang, S., Yu, Y. (eds.) ProvSec 2012. LNCS, vol. 7496, pp. 235–252. Springer, Heidelberg (2012). https://doi.org/10.1007/978-3-642-33272-2_15
19. Zhang, Y., Katz, J., Papamanthou, C.: All your queries are belong to us: the power of file-injection attacks on searchable encryption. In: Proceedings of the USENIX Security Symposium (2016)
20. Zhao, F., Nishide, T.: Searchable symmetric encryption supporting queries with multiple-character wildcards. In: Chen, J., Piuri, V., Su, C., Yung, M. (eds.) NSS 2016. LNCS, vol. 9955, pp. 266–282. Springer, Cham (2016). https://doi.org/10.1007/978-3-319-46298-1_18

End-to-End Protection of IoT Communications Through Cryptographic Enforcement of Access Control Policies

Stefano Berlato[1,3]($\boxtimes$) (ID), Umberto Morelli[3] (ID), Roberto Carbone[3] (ID), and Silvio Ranise[2,3] (ID)

[1] Department of Informatics, Bioengineering, Robotics and Systems Engineering, University of Genoa, Genoa, Italy
[2] Department of Mathematics, University of Trento, Trento, Italy
[3] Security and Trust Research Unit, Fondazione Bruno Kessler, Trento, Italy
{sberlato,umorelli,carbone,ranise}@fbk.eu

Abstract. It is crucial to ensure the security and privacy of communications in Internet of Things (IoT) scenarios that process an increasingly large amount of sensitive data. In this context, we propose a cryptographic enforcement mechanism of access control policies to guarantee the confidentiality and integrity of messages exchanged with the MQTT protocol in presence of external attackers, malicious insiders and "honest-but-curious" service providers. A preliminary performance evaluation with a prototype implementation in an open-source tool shows the overhead is acceptable in relevant use case scenarios and provides a higher level of security with respect to other approaches.

Keywords: Cryptographic Access Control · Internet of Things · End-to-end Protection · MQTT

1 Introduction

The capillary diffusion of Internet of Things (IoT) devices holds the potential to improve the well-being of society in several scenarios, like eHealth and smart cities. The undeniable benefits offered by IoT-based scenarios should be coupled with their security, though. Indeed, the environments in which these scenarios are deployed are traditionally assumed to be hostile due to the presence of external attackers. Moreover, being often unattended and equipped with limited computational resources, IoT devices are intrinsically vulnerable and exposed to high levels of risk. Hence, suitable security mechanisms should be adopted to ensure the protection of sensitive data (e.g., personal or confidential information) throughout their life cycle, i.e., when in-transit, in-use and at-rest. In particular, we note that IoT-based scenarios are especially focused on the transmission of data, which is one of the fundamental layers of their architecture [20]. In this context, communication security and data encryption are the two top

© IFIP International Federation for Information Processing 2022
Published by Springer Nature Switzerland AG 2022
S. Sural and H. Lu (Eds.): DBSec 2022, LNCS 13383, pp. 236–255, 2022.
https://doi.org/10.1007/978-3-031-10684-2_14

concerns for IoT scenarios, as clearly shown by the 2021 Eclipse IoT survey.[1] However, since the traditional client-server network paradigm does not properly fit the needs and peculiarities of IoT (e.g., limited computational and communication capabilities, unreliable channels, latency requirements), these scenarios usually employ more lightweight and efficient *publish-subscribe* protocols such as Message Queue Telemetry Transport (MQTT) [18].

Furthermore, we note that the complexity and dynamicity of IoT-based scenarios (considering also the latest trends in security such as Zero Trust) make it almost impossible to assume full trust on any agent involved. Instead, the agents operating in these scenarios are usually assumed to be untrusted or partially-trusted, where "partially-trusted" (or "honest-but-curious") denotes an agent which faithfully performs the assigned tasks but, at the same time, tries to access sensitive data, usually for profit [7,12]. In other words, besides being threatened by a plethora of external attackers, sensitive data in IoT-based scenarios must be secured from malicious insiders (e.g., disgruntled employees, harmful tenants) and honest-but-curious service providers as well (e.g., Cloud, Edge).

When no fully-trusted central entity is present, a decentralized approach has to be adopted to protect sensitive data. In this regard, the use of cryptography is fundamental to mitigate and prevent possible attacks on the confidentiality and integrity of data. Indeed, these two security properties are of the utmost importance, especially in scenarios involving personal information (e.g., users' health data) or providing vital services in which integrity is crucial (e.g., smoke sensors). A popular cryptographic-based solution to protect communications by guaranteeing confidentiality and integrity is Transport Layer Security (TLS). However, the adoption of TLS may be difficult in presence of constrained IoT devices that cannot support cumbersome handshakes and computationally expensive key derivation algorithms [13,18]. Moreover, TLS offers hop-to-hop protection (i.e., information is only encrypted when travelling through the network), thus it cannot protect sensitive data against partially-trusted agents.

In this paper, we address these issues by proposing a solution for the end-to-end protection of IoT communications through the cryptographic enforcement of Access Control (AC) policies. In detail, our contributions are as follows:

- we design a Cryptographic Access Control (CAC) scheme enforcing AC policies in IoT scenarios to prevent external attackers, malicious insiders and partially-trusted agents from breaching the confidentiality and the integrity of sensitive data;
- we implement the proposed CAC scheme in a modular and portable tool, which we make open-source and freely available;[2]
- we conduct a preliminary experimental evaluation to analyze the performance of our tool and investigate the (possible) overhead with respect to both the approach proposed in [9] and a traditional TLS-based solution.

As a final remark, we acknowledge that the use of cryptography alone to enforce AC policies makes the evaluation of permissions depending on dynamic

---

[1] https://outreach.eclipse.foundation/iot-edge-developer-2021.
[2] https://github.com/stfbk/CryptoAC.

and contextual (e.g., time-based) conditions difficult, if possible at all. The limited expressiveness of CAC can however be mitigated through the combination with more traditional (e.g., centralized) AC enforcement mechanisms, at the cost of addressing possible collusions between users and the (agents managing the) enforcement mechanisms. In other words, rather than supplanting existing approaches to AC like [9], CAC can complement and synergize with them to provide an even more complete and thorough protection of sensitive data.

The paper is structured as follows. In Sect. 2 we compare our approach with related work, while in Sect. 3 we introduce the background. In Sect. 4 we give an overview of our approach, while providing a more detailed description in Sect. 5. We briefly describe the implementation of our CAC scheme and present the performance evaluation in Sect. 6.[3] We conclude the paper with final remarks and future work in Sect. 7.

2   Related Work

During the analysis of the large number of papers devoted to secure data in IoT, we have collected the key properties discussed and present them in Table 1. For lack of space, we only provide a discussion of the most closely related works.

In [9], the authors propose to plug in into MQTT-based IoT scenarios a logically centralized entity for enforcing Attribute-Based Access Control (ABAC) policies. While a traditional AC mechanism allows for context awareness and (horizontal) scalability, the proposal requires full trust on the central agent and does not employ cryptography to guarantee integrity and confidentiality.

As constrained IoT devices can hardly support TLS, in [18] the authors propose an alternative security mechanism: each MQTT client is equipped with a smart card containing the public key of the broker which is used to agree upon a session key (unique for each client). The smart card relieves resource consumption, while symmetric cryptography ensures confidentiality (but not end-to-end

Table 1. Comparison with Related Work

	[9]	[18]	[8]	[19]	[15]	[11]	Our work
Channel encryption	✗	✓	✓	✓	✓	✓	✓
End-to-end encryption	✗	✗	✗	✓	✗	✓	✓
Integrity guarantee	✗	✓	✗	✓	✓	✓	✓
AC policy enforcement	✓	✗	✗	✗	✗	✗	✓
Scalable w.r.t. #subscribers	✓	✗	✗	✗	✓	✗	✓
Context Awareness	✓	✗	✗	✗	✗	✗	✓*
Suit constrained IoT devices	✓	✓	✓	✗	✓	✓	✓

*as mentioned in Sect. 1 and discussed at the end of Sect. 5.2, we can easily complement our CAC scheme with traditional AC enforcement mechanisms for context awareness

---

[3] An extended version of this work with more details on the CAC scheme is at https:// st.fbk.eu/complementary/assets/DBSEC2022/DBSEC2022_Extended.pdf.

encryption). However, the broker has to encrypt messages for each client separately, yielding a non-negligible overhead, and AC policies are not discussed.

In [8], the authors design a secure communication scheme for MQTT based on the Augmented Password-Only Authentication and Key Exchange (AugPAKE) protocol.[4] Each client establishes a symmetric key with the broker, while topics are associated with authorization tokens. As in [18], the per-client re-encryption makes the solution hardly scalable, and the broker can read MQTT messages. Finally, the authors do not discuss mechanisms to provide data integrity.

Even when the client-broker link is encrypted (e.g., via TLS), processing data in clear at the broker constitutes a privacy and security risk. As such, in [19] the authors propose the use of Trusted Execution Environments (TEEs) at the broker: whenever a client publishes a message to a topic, the message is encrypted with a symmetric key previously shared with the TEE and then sent to the broker over TLS. While achieving end-to-end encryption and integrity, this approach suffers from an overhead that can be up to $8\times$ in some scenarios.

In [15], the authors propose a framework for protecting MQTT-based IoT scenarios with 3 increasing security levels: the first provides data integrity, authenticity and accountability, the second adds confidentiality while the third offers long-term security. While having different security levels allows adapting the solution to the requirements of different IoT scenarios (e.g., latency, scalability), the proposed solution neither preserves the confidentiality of data from the MQTT broker nor considers the enforcement of AC policies.

In [11], the authors discuss the protection of data in an eHealth scenario where several wearable devices (e.g., smartwatches, pacemakers) communicate with a single predetermined entity (i.e. the doctor assigned to the patient) through symmetric cryptography. Similarly to our approach, this solution provides end-to-end encryption and integrity, and it is suitable for constrained IoT devices. However, it supports many-to-1 communication scenarios only.

In conclusion, the main difference between the work presented in this paper and the above works is that the latter do not provide end-to-end encryption while enforcing AC policies and supporting many-to-many communications. This is a novel contribution of our approach as shown in Table 1.

3   Background

We describe some concepts of AC and Role-Based Access Control (RBAC). We also overview the MQTT protocol and the Mosquitto MQTT broker.

3.1   Access Control

Samarati and De Capitani di Vimercati [17] defined AC as "the process of mediating every request to resources maintained by a system and determining whether the request should be granted or denied". A resource usually consists of data such

---

[4] https://datatracker.ietf.org/doc/draft-irtf-cfrg-augpake/.

as messages or files. In the following, we assume an AC policy $\mathbf{P}$ to be compiled into a RBAC model rather than an a ABAC model (as in [9]), since support for the enforcement of RBAC policies is readily available in several MQTT broker implementations, thus simplifying the experimental validation of our approach. In this work, the state of $\mathbf{P}$ can be described as a tuple $(\mathbf{U}, \mathbf{R}, \mathbf{F}, \mathbf{UR}, \mathbf{PA})$, where $\mathbf{U}$ is the set of users, $\mathbf{R}$ is the set of roles, $\mathbf{F}$ is the set of resources, $\mathbf{UR} \subseteq \mathbf{U} \times \mathbf{R}$ is the set of user-role assignments and $\mathbf{PA} \subseteq \mathbf{R} \times \mathbf{PR}$ is the set of role-permission assignments, being $\mathbf{PR} \subseteq \mathbf{F} \times \mathbf{OP}$ a derivative set of $\mathbf{F}$ combined with a fixed set of operations $\mathbf{OP}$ (both $\mathbf{PR}$ and $\mathbf{OP}$ are not included in the state of the AC policy as they remain constant over time). A user u can use a permission $\langle f, op \rangle$ if $\exists r \in \mathbf{R} : (u, r) \in \mathbf{UR} \wedge (r, \langle f, op \rangle) \in \mathbf{PA}$. Role hierarchies can always be compiled away by adding suitable pairs to $\mathbf{UR}$.

3.2 MQTT

MQTT is a lightweight *publish-subscribe* messaging protocol,[5] widely employed in scenarios involving (computationally constrained) IoT devices. MQTT expects a message to be published to a *topic*, which can be seen as a temporary communication channel, grouping messages logically related to each other (e.g., concerning a specific location, event or action). An IoT device (in this context called "MQTT client") can subscribe to a topic, thus expressing the will to receive messages published to that topic. Whenever a client wants to publish a message to a topic, it sends the message (and the name of the topic) to a server called "MQTT broker", which can be seen as the central node of a star network topology. When the broker receives the message and the name of the topic, it broadcasts the message to all MQTT clients that previously subscribed to that topic. Each topic can have one "retained" message, i.e., a message stored by the broker and sent to each client that subscribes to the topic.

Among MQTT broker implementations, it is common to find extensions supporting security mechanisms such as TLS and centralized enforcement of AC policies based on, e.g., roles and access control lists. For instance, Mosquitto[6] is an open-source (EPL/EDL licensed) message broker maintained by Eclipse that implements the MQTT protocol (versions 5.0, 3.1.1 and 3.1). Mosquitto provides a variety of functionalities including the DYNamic SECurity (DYNSEC) plugin, which enforces dynamic RBAC policies via a centralized enforcement point.

4 Overview

First, we discuss a smart building scenario (as in [9]) focusing on an IoT service commonly considered in the literature, i.e., Smart Lock (Sect. 4.1). Then, we give an overview of our CAC-based approach for the end-to-end protection of sensitive data exchanged by IoT devices through the MQTT protocol (Sect. 4.2)

---

[5] https://www.iso.org/standard/69466.html.
[6] https://mosquitto.org/.

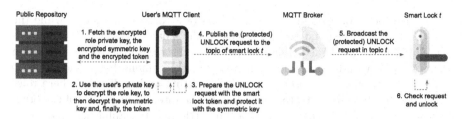

Fig. 1. Instance of an UNLOCK Request to a Smart Lock

in the context of the Smart Lock service previously described. Below, we keep the discussion at a high level to allow the reader to get a general understanding of the approach before delving into (complex) details in Sect. 5.

4.1 Smart Lock Service

Organizations operating in large buildings (e.g., government structures, hospitals, research centres) have to manage access to several locals, some of which might contain confidential documents, delicate equipment or health hazards. In this context, smart locks may be used to regulate and restrict access to rooms, laboratories and closets more efficiently than traditional locks [1–3] by enforcing RBAC policies that are administered mandatorily (this means that delegations are not relevant in this scenario). A smart lock can be seen as a cyber-physical device made of a smart cylinder and a microcontroller with limited computational, storage and communication capabilities.

A smart lock usually requires the use of a token to be unlocked, which is distributed to (authorized) users according to their qualifications. Generalizing, we can say that users are assigned to one or more roles by the system administrator, where the roles reflect the internal hierarchy of an organization (e.g., employee, canteen staff, human resources). For instance, in a research centre, the AC policy may assign to members of the cleaning service the permission to access all rooms in a building except for laboratories, while members of a research unit may have the permission to access their laboratory only. After having chosen a role to assume, a user can interact with the smart lock through a dedicated MQTT topic. For instance, a smart lock "LOCK_ID" located on the first floor of a building may be subscribed to the topic "building/firstfloor/$LOCK_ID". In this way, a user (who belongs to an authorized role) can publish to that topic UNLOCK and LOCK requests by presenting the related token.

4.2 Securing the Smart Lock Service

CAC involves the use of cryptography to enforce AC policies while guaranteeing the confidentiality and the integrity of sensitive data. In the Smart Lock service described in Sect. 4.1, the AC policy corresponds to the assignments between users and roles (e.g., cleaning service, research unit) and roles to permissions (e.g., which locals of a building the members of a role can un/lock), while the data to protect correspond to the tokens of the smart locks. Cryptography is then employed to implement role memberships, distribute the tokens according to the AC policy and secure them when transmitted among IoT devices.

More specifically, each user (i.e., MQTT client) and each role, where roles are defined by the administrator according to the internal hierarchy of the organization, is provided with a pair of asymmetric cryptographic keys. Instead, each smart lock is provided with a dedicated symmetric key and assigned to an MQTT topic (i.e., one key and topic for smart lock). The token of each smart lock is encrypted with the related symmetric key, which is in turn (separately) encrypted with the public keys of all roles that are authorized to interact with that smart lock. Similarly, the private keys of all roles to which a user belongs are (separately) encrypted with the user's public key. All encrypted information (i.e., tokens, symmetric keys and roles' private keys) are made available through a public repository. In addition, this information is digitally signed by the administrator of the policy to guarantee its integrity, and the digital signatures are stored together with the information.

Whenever a user wants to send an UNLOCK request to a smart lock, she first chooses one role which is authorized to open the lock. As shown in Fig. 1, she uses her private key to decrypt the private key of the role, which is in turn used to decrypt the symmetric key. Then, the user can decrypt the token of the smart lock with the symmetric key. Finally, the user exploits the knowledge of the token to interact with the smart lock (e.g., by engaging in a challenge-response protocol), using the same symmetric key to secure MQTT messages published to the topic of the smart lock. Neither the (partially trusted service provider hosting the) MQTT broker (e.g., the Cloud or Edge) nor possible Man-in-the-Middle (MitM) attackers nor malicious insiders can access the (encrypted) token, while digital signatures make tampering attempts obvious.

Unfortunately, the symmetric keys cannot be hard-coded into the smart locks or the users' MQTT clients, and must instead be dynamically distributed. Intuitively, a new key has to be created whenever a new smart lock is added to the building. Besides, whenever a permission is revoked, the involved symmetric key (as well as the token) must be renewed. Otherwise, revoked users could use cached keys to still be able to decrypt MQTT messages or collude with the service provider hosting the MQTT broker. The use of TEEs can potentially relieve this issue (e.g., see the Cloud-based CAC schemes proposed in [14] and [10]). However, constrained IoT devices are not likely to be equipped with a TEE. To renew a symmetric key, the administrator has to distribute new public or private information (e.g., the new symmetric key) to all users, along with version numbers to differentiate between old and new information. The new information and the version numbers are stored in the public repository as well. Asymmetric cryptography such as Identity-Based Encryption (IBE), Public Key Infrastructure (PKI)-based and Attribute-Based Encryption (ABE) is usually employed to regulate access to the new information (i.e., ensure only authorized users can decrypt the new symmetric key) and provide accountability (i.e., ensure that the new symmetric key was indeed created by the administrator).

5 Cryptographic Access Control for MQTT

We present the design of a role-based CAC scheme for the end-to-end encryption of sensitive data exchanged through MQTT in IoT-based scenarios. We choose MQTT since it is one of the most employed publish-subscribe protocols in IoT [16]. However, our scheme can adapt to other publish-subscribe protocols as well (e.g., AMQP[7]). The design of our CAC scheme is inspired to the work in [12] with several technical variations and two notable differences, namely the context of use (i.e., Cloud in [12] vs. IoT in this work) and the protection of data (i.e., at-rest in [12] vs. in-transit in this work). Below, we first discuss how to map RBAC elements to MQTT concepts (Sect. 5.1). Then, we present our CAC scheme (Sect. 5.2). Finally, we provide some considerations on the security of the scheme (Sect. 5.3). The symbols used in this Section are in Table 2.

5.1 Role-Based Access Control to MQTT

We map MQTT clients and MQTT topics to the set of users $\mathbf{U}$ and resources $\mathbf{F}$ of the RBAC policy, respectively. The set of roles $\mathbf{R}$ is instead defined by the administrator, as described in Sect. 4.1, thus roles are not mapped to any MQTT concept. The set of operations $\mathbf{OP}$ is composed by publish (Pub) and subscribe (Sub). Each user u and role r is provided with a pair of asymmetric keys $(\mathbf{k^{enc}}, \mathbf{k^{dec}})$ for en/decryption. Besides this key pair, the administrator A is provided with an additional pair of asymmetric keys $(\mathbf{k}_A^{ver}, \mathbf{k}_A^{sig})$ for verification/creation of digital signatures. Each topic f is assigned to a symmetric key $\mathbf{k}_f^{sym}$, used to encrypt each message m in f, resulting in $\mathbf{Enc}_{\mathbf{k}_f^{sym}}^S(m)$.

To assign a user u to a role r, r's decryption key $\mathbf{k}_r^{dec}$ is encrypted with u's encryption public key $\mathbf{k}_u^{enc}$, resulting in $\mathbf{Enc}_{\mathbf{k}_u^{enc}}^P(\mathbf{k}_r^{dec})$. To give permission to a role r over a topic f (e.g., to allow the users assigned to the role r to lock and unlock the smart lock corresponding to the topic f), f's symmetric key $\mathbf{k}_f^{sym}$ is encrypted with r's encryption public key $\mathbf{k}_r^{enc}$, resulting in $\mathbf{Enc}_{\mathbf{k}_r^{enc}}^P\left(\mathbf{k}_f^{sym}\right)$.

To handle revocations, we associate version numbers to (the keys of) roles and topics. The administrator only can create a new topic f by generating a new symmetric key $\mathbf{k}_{(f,v_f)}^{sym}$ and publishing a retained message to f containing the version number v_f, which is initially equal to 1. Whenever the key $\mathbf{k}_{(f,v_f)}^{sym}$ needs to be updated (due to, e.g., user's revocation), the administrator generates a new symmetric key $\mathbf{k}_{(f,v_f+1)}^{sym}$ and replaces the retained message with a new one, containing the (updated) version number v_f+1, i.e., the old version number plus 1. In this way, users are notified of the key renewal and can update their key accordingly. To delete a topic, the administrator removes the retained message, notifying all users to unsubscribe from the topic.

---

[7] https://www.amqp.org/.

5.2 Full Construction

As illustrated in Sect. 3.2, the Mosquitto MQTT broker can enforce dynamic RBAC policies through the DYNSEC plugin as a centralized entity. Therefore, to provide an additional security layer besides cryptography, we synchronize

Table 2. Symbols

Symbol	Description
e	A generic entity (either a user, a role or a topic)
u	A generic user
A	The administrator user
r	A generic role
f	A generic topic
v_e	A generic version number for the entity e
op	Either {Sub}, {Pub} or {Sub, Pub}
N	Null (i.e., empty) value
m	A generic plaintext
c	A generic ciphertext
$-$	Wildcard
$\mathbf{Gen^{Pub}}$	Generation of key pair for en/decryption
$\mathbf{Gen^{Sig}}$	Generation of key pair for signatures
$\mathbf{Gen^{Sym}}$	Generation of symmetric key
$k^{enc}_{(e,v_e)}$	Public encryption key of (e, v_e)
$k^{dec}_{(e,v_e)}$	Private decryption key of (e, v_e)
$k^{ver}_{(e,v_e)}$	Public verification key of (e, v_e)
$k^{sig}_{(e,v_e)}$	Private signing key of (e, v_e)
$k^{sym}_{(f,v_f)}$	Symmetric key of topic (f, v_f)
$\mathbf{Enc}^{P}_{k^{enc}_{(e,v_e)}}(-)$	Encryption with public key $k^{enc}_{(e,v_e)}$ of $-$
$\mathbf{Dec}^{P}_{k^{dec}(e,v_e)}(-)$	Decryption with private key $k^{dec}(e, v_e)$ of $-$
$\mathbf{Enc}^{S}_{k^{sym}_{(f,v_f)}}(m)$	Symmetric encryption with key $k^{sym}_{(f,v_f)}$ of m
$\mathbf{Dec}^{S}_{k^{sym}_{(f,v_f)}}(c)$	Symmetric decryption with key $k^{sym}_{(f,v_f)}$ of c
$\langle \mathbf{U_t, R_t, F_t, UR_t, PA_t} \rangle$	The state of the traditional AC policy
$\mathbf{U_t}$	Set of users; a member is a single value u
$\mathbf{R_t}$	Set of roles; a member is a single value r
$\mathbf{F_t}$	Set of topics; a member is a single value f
$\mathbf{UR_t}$	Set of user-role pairs; a member is a tuple (u, r)
$\mathbf{PA_t}$	Set of role-permissions; a member is a tuple $(r, \langle f, op \rangle)$
$\langle \mathbf{U_c, R_c, F_c, UR_c, PA_c} \rangle$	The state of the CAC policy
$\mathbf{U_c}$	Set of users; a member is a tuple $(u, k^{enc}_u, k^{ver}_u)$
$\mathbf{R_c}$	Set of roles; a member is a tuple $(r, k^{enc}_{(r,v_r)}, v_r)$
$\mathbf{F_c}$	Set of topics; a member is a tuple (f, v_f)
$\mathbf{UR_c}$	Set of user-role pairs; a member is a tuple $(u, r, \mathbf{Enc}^{P}_{k^{enc}_u}\left(k^{dec}_{(r,v_r)}\right), v_r)$
$\mathbf{PA_c}$	Set of role-permission pairs; a member is a tuple $(r, f, \mathbf{Enc}^{P}_{k^{enc}_{(r,v_r)}}\left(k^{sym}_{(f,v_f)}\right), v_r, v_A, op)$

the DYNSEC AC policy with the CAC policy. In this way, every modification performed in one policy is mirrored in the other. For instance, adding a user in the CAC policy implies adding a user in the DYNSEC policy as well, although the two actions are implemented differently. We highlight that the same kind of synchronization can also be implemented with other traditional AC enforcement mechanisms to enable the evaluation of permissions depending on contextual (e.g., time-based) conditions (e.g., such as the approach presented in [9]).

The state of the traditional AC policy enforced through the DYNSEC plugin can be described as a tuple $\langle \mathbf{U_t}, \mathbf{R_t}, \mathbf{F_t}, \mathbf{UR_t}, \mathbf{PA_t} \rangle$ (where the subscript $\mathbf{t}$ stands for "traditional"), while the state of the CAC policy can be described as a tuple $\langle \mathbf{U_c}, \mathbf{R_c}, \mathbf{F_c}, \mathbf{UR_c}, \mathbf{PA_c} \rangle$ (where the subscript $\mathbf{c}$ stands for "cryptographic"). Essentially, the CAC policy extends the traditional AC policy with additional metadata (e.g., digital signatures, public keys, version numbers). We report in Fig. 2 (Appendix A) the pseudocode of each action available in the CAC scheme which acts on both the state of the traditional AC policy and that of the cryptographic AC policy by updating the components of the tuples. An action α in Fig. 2 belongs to one of two categories:

- *administrative* - includes all actions performed by the administrator for the management of the AC and the CAC policies. First, the administrator initializes the system ($initA()$). Then, she can add and delete users ($addU(u)$, $delU(u)$), roles ($addR(r)$, $delR(r)$) and topics ($addP(f)$, $delP(f)$). Finally, she can assign and revoke users from roles ($assignU(u,r)$, $revokeU(u,r)$) as well as assign and revoke permissions from roles ($assignP(r, \langle f, op \rangle)$, $revokeP(r, \langle f, op \rangle)$));
- *operative* - includes all actions performed by the MQTT clients. After the administrator created the corresponding user in the AC policy, an MQTT client can generate her asymmetric keys ($init_u()$). Afterwards, she can subscribe to a topic f ($sub_u(f,c)$) and also publish messages ($pub_u(f,m)$), according to the policy defined by the administrator. Messages received from a topic are en/decrypted as described in Sect. 5.1.

All metadata are digitally signed by the administrator with her signature creation key $\mathbf{k}_A^{\mathbf{sig}}$ and verified with her verification key $\mathbf{k}_A^{\mathbf{ver}}$. The integrity of MQTT messages is protected by using (symmetric) authenticated encryption, which is (usually) implemented through Message Authentication Codes (MACs) [6]; for the sake of simplicity, in Fig. 2 we omit these details and also other trivial checks like the uniqueness of identifiers.

5.3   Security Considerations

Our CAC scheme allows administrators to enforce RBAC policies both traditionally and cryptographically. This capability restricts access to MQTT topics to authorized users only. Besides, it provides end-to-end protection for guaranteeing confidentiality and integrity of MQTT messages from both external attackers and the (partially-trusted agent managing the) MQTT broker. We assume that cryptographic primitives are perfect, i.e., the confidentiality and integrity of encrypted MQTT messages cannot be violated except by (computationally infeasible) brute force attacks. Then, the traditional AC policy enforced by DYNSEC allows only authorized users to publish and subscribe to topics. We note that, without the corresponding symmetric key, an unauthorized user could not produce a valid MQTT message anyway.

In our CAC scheme, accountability—the ability to map MQTT messages to the corresponding publishers—is currently not ensured cryptographically, since messages are (hashed and) signed with symmetric keys known by all authorized users, as presented in Sect. 5.2. However, since users have to authenticate toward the MQTT broker, the broker itself can provide accountability by mapping each MQTT message to the MQTT client (thus, the user) that published it. Nonetheless, a scenario based on a Zero Trust model may call for a stronger guarantee of accountability. In this case, users can easily be provided with an additional pair of asymmetric keys and required to sign MQTT messages to guarantee accountability through cryptography, at the cost of incurring additional overhead. The modification to the CAC scheme for implementing this requirement would be straightforward and can be seen as an instance of the AC model introduced in [4,5] that considers the features of the client used by a subject to access a certain resource. Despite a subject (e.g., a general practitioner) can be entitled to read a sensitive resource (e.g., the healthcare information of a patient), it can be denied such a right because of the low level of protection offered by the client (e.g., personal smartphone) or it can be granted when an adequate client is used (e.g., desktop operated by the hospital). Finally, we note that protection against replay attacks has to be provided by smart-lock supported mechanisms (e.g., timestamps, challenge-response protocol) and it is out of the scope of this paper.

As illustrated in Table 2, the CAC policy contains public (e.g., public keys) or encrypted (e.g., encrypted private keys) information only. Indeed, as shown in Sect. 5.2, the symmetric keys of topics are encrypted with the public keys of authorized roles, while the private keys of roles are encrypted with the authorized users' public keys. Therefore, by construction, only authorized users can decrypt roles' private keys and, consequently, access symmetric keys to en/decrypt MQTT messages. In other words, even though the CAC policy is public, only authorized users can obtain secret keys (i.e., the roles' private keys and the topics' symmetric keys). Adding permissions to the CAC policy is a straightforward operation, as it consists in encrypting private information (i.e., secret keys) with the public key of the newly authorized users (or roles). On the other hand, the revocation of permissions requires careful management of cryptographic material. We consider the worst-case scenario in which a user u previously cached all secret keys she could access, both of roles and topics. Hence, when revoking permissions from u (or from one of the roles that u is assigned to), we need to renew the affected secret keys. In detail, when revoking a permission $\langle f, op \rangle$ from a role r (i.e., when invoking the function $revokeP(r, \langle f, op \rangle)$) in our CAC scheme, we distinguish two cases:

- if r already had permission op' so that $op' \subseteq op$, we generate a new key $\mathbf{k}^{\mathbf{sym}}_{(f,v_f+1)} \leftarrow \mathbf{Gen}^{\mathbf{Sym}}$ for f, which we distribute to all *other* authorized roles. In this way, users belonging to r do not have access to the new key;
- if r already had permission op' so that $op' \cap op \neq \emptyset$, we simply update $\mathbf{PA_t}$ and $\mathbf{PA_c}$ by removing the permissions in op from op'.

Similarly, when revoking a user u from a role r (i.e., when invoking the function $revokeU(u, r)$), we generate new keys $(\mathbf{k}^{\mathbf{enc}}_{(r,v_r+1)}, \mathbf{k}^{\mathbf{dec}}_{(r,v_r+1)}) \leftarrow \mathbf{Gen}^{\mathbf{Pub}}$ for r and distribute them to all *other* authorized users. In this way, u does not have access to r's new private key. Finally, we renew the symmetric keys of all topics that r had permission over with a procedure similar to the *revokeP* function.

6   Implementation and Experimental Evaluation

The pseudocode presented in Appendix A has been paired with an MQTT client and deployed as standalone, open-source software named *"CryptoAC"*.[8] Altogether, the CAC scheme involves three entities: *CryptoAC*/MQTT client, the MQTT broker and the public repository. Below, we provide details on the implementation (or configuration) of each of these entities and their interactions (Sects. 6.1, 6.2, 6.3). Finally, we present our preliminary performance evaluation of *CryptoAC* (Sect. 6.4).

6.1   CryptoAC

CryptoAC has been developed in Kotlin multiplatform[9] due to the intrinsic portability and the possibility of a native deployment avoiding the computational overhead of a Java Virtual Machine (JVM). This is especially true since Kotlin mainly targets Linux environments,[10] which are the most deployed in IoT.[11]

As the cryptographic provider, we choose Sodium,[12] a modern cryptographic library whose security has been thoroughly audited.[13] To invoke Sodium's APIs easily, we use an open-source Kotlin multiplatform wrapper.[14] Sodium uses the Elliptic Curves Diffie-Hellman (ECDH) algorithm (X25519) to generate public-private keys and the Edwards-curve Digital Signature Algorithm (EdDSA) for digital signatures (Ed25519). Like many cyphers in TLS 1.3, Sodium supports (AEAD), which is a more robust and secure variant of authenticated encryption (recall the discussion in Sect. 5.2) allowing to bind the ciphertext to the context where it is supposed to be used (to, e.g., avoid replay attacks). We observe

---

[8] The code is freely available at https://github.com/stfbk/CryptoAC.
[9] https://kotlinlang.org/docs/multiplatform.html.
[10] https://www.jetbrains.com/lp/devecosystem-2019/.
[11] https://outreach.eclipse.foundation/iot-edge-developer-2021.
[12] https://libsodium.gitbook.io/doc/.
[13] https://www.privateinternetaccess.com/blog/libsodium-audit-results/.
[14] https://github.com/ionspin/kotlin-multiplatform-libsodium.

that the usage of AEAD is in line with the requirements contained in the call for Lightweight Cryptography to protect small electronics (thus including IoT devices) issued by NIST.[15]

In this regard, Sodium proposes the use of the XSalsa20 symmetric stream cypher (i.e., Salsa20 with 192-bit nonce extension) together with the Poly1305 universal hash function as the best option, instead of using 256-bit AES in Galois/Counter Mode (GCM) with, e.g., the SHA-384 hash function. The latter is typically used in TLS 1.3 deployments labelled as TLS_AES_256_GCM_SHA384, and it will be used in our experiments as discussed at the end of Sect. 6.4 below. One of the reasons for this choice is that, although hardware acceleration for AES is often available in modern processors, its performance on platforms that lack such hardware is considerably lower. Another issue is that many software-only AES implementations are vulnerable to cache-collision timing attacks. Instead, XSalsa20 is faster than (non-accelerated) AES and it achieves homogeneous performance independently of the underlying hardware, enhancing portability.

Finally, we use Eclipse Paho[16] as MQTT client. It is worth noting that *CryptoAC* caches symmetric keys of topics at the client-side to avoid having to obtain them (as described in Sect. 5.1) every time a message is received or needs to be published. In this way, we increase the efficiency of the implementation by eliminating superfluous cryptographic computations. When symmetric keys are renewed (e.g., after a revocation), the cache is invalidated. All secret keys are securely stored in a Java Keystore.

CryptoAC can also run as an administrative tool by acting as a web server allowing the administrator to manage the (traditional and cryptographic) AC policy. All the inputs to the interface are validated with OWASP-approved regular expressions[17] to avoid web-based attacks (e.g., injection, Cross-Site Scripting).

6.2   MQTT Broker

We choose Mosquitto[18] as MQTT broker. As introduced in Sect. 5.2, we enable the DYNSEC plugin for traditional AC enforcement on top of CAC. This additional security layer guarantees redundancy and allows restricting the permissions of the users (i.e., to specify whether a user can subscribe, publish or perform both actions on a topic). Of course, a user could potentially collude with the (service provider hosting the) MQTT broker to bypass the DYNSEC AC policy enforcement and gain publish and/or subscribe privileges. However, we highlight that this kind of collusions may happen regardless of whether the DYNSEC plugin is enabled, and that the colluding user should have the symmetric key of

---

[15] https://www.nist.gov/news-events/news/2018/04/nist-issues-first-call-lightweight-cryptography-protect-small-electronics.

[16] https://www.eclipse.org/paho/.

[17] https://owasp.org/www-community/OWASP_Validation_Regex_Repository.

[18] https://mosquitto.org/.

the topic anyway to en/decrypt messages on that topic (i.e., the CAC policy should already give publish or subscribe permissions to the colluding user on that topic). Intuitively, the same may happen if secret or symmetric keys are stolen or leaked from an IoT device. However, the physical and cyber security of IoT devices themselves (e.g., concerning physical attackers or firmware vulnerabilities) is out of the scope of this paper. Finally, access to the MQTT broker is protected by individual passwords.

6.3   Public Repository

We use Redis[19] to store metadata related to the CAC scheme. Redis is primarily an in-memory storage, a characteristic that allows for low response time to queries. The metadata of each user (i.e., the public keys) are stored under a unique Redis key, while a list collects all users' Redis keys. We follow the same approach for the metadata of roles, topics, user-role assignments and role-topic permissions. Finally, access to the Redis datastore is protected by individual passwords.

6.4   Performance Evaluation

The authors in [9] deploy a reference monitor as a proxy between the MQTT clients and the MQTT broker. For this reason, they evaluate the scalability when varying the number of publishers and subscribers, i.e., when increasing the computational load on the reference monitor. Differently, *CryptoAC* is deployed as (part of) an MQTT client; therefore, we distribute the computation at the edge nodes and achieve scalability by design.[20] Consequently, our preliminary evaluation aims at assessing the computational overhead on a single IoT device, where the cryptographic operations of CAC could strongly affect performance. In detail, we consider the following experimental configurations:

- *C1*: in this configuration, our baseline, the communication channel between the MQTT client and the MQTT broker is protected by neither TLS nor CAC, and the broker enforces AC policies through the DYNSEC plugin;
- *C2*: in this configuration, the communication channel between the MQTT client and the MQTT broker is protected with unilateral TLS 1.3 (i.e., MQTT clients verifies the broker's certificate but they are not required to provide a certificate in turn) and the MQTT broker enforces AC policies through the DYNSEC plugin. This configuration corresponds to the traditional solution for the protection of data in-transit, even though the confidentiality of data is not preserved from the partially-trusted service provider hosting the broker. For fairness, we remark that in this configuration we do not measure the overhead due to the TLS handshake and session key derivation algorithms

---

[19] https://redis.io/.

[20] Increasing the number of clients would only assess the scalability of the MQTT broker since the encryption/decryption are performed client-side.

between MQTT clients and the MQTT broker, as it has already been found by other works that TLS as a whole is hardly usable by constrained IoT devices [13,18]. Therefore, we just measure the transmission time *after* having fully established a TLS session;
- *C3*: in this configuration, we use the CAC scheme presented in Sect. 5 to provide end-to-end encryption while the MQTT broker enforces AC policies through the DYNSEC plugin.

Experimental Settings. We are interested in measuring the overhead of cryptographic techniques for data protection (i.e., TLS in *C2* and CAC in *C3*) with respect to the baseline *C1*. Therefore, we reuse the same infrastructure and experimental settings across the three configurations to avoid possible measurement discrepancies. For instance, using another MQTT client (e.g., Mosquitto_sub[21] and Mosquitto_pub[22]) instead of Eclipse Paho could create biases in the measurements, as its implementation may be more (or less) performant than Paho. For this reason, we employ *CryptoAC* to implement all three configurations. In detail (and only during the performance evaluation), we remove all cryptographic computations from *CryptoAC* to implement *C1*. Similarly, we disable the CAC scheme but enable TLS in *CryptoAC* to implement *C2*. Finally, we use the original implementation of *CryptoAC* to implement *C3*. By doing so, we ensure that the underlying infrastructure remains the same across the different configurations and we are guaranteed to precisely measure the overhead of TLS (*C2*) and our CAC scheme (*C3*) with respect to the baseline (*C1*). Finally, we highlight that we compile *CryptoAC* to Java bytecode for ease of use, and leave the native deployment (which may be more suitable for IoT devices) for future work, as it is mainly an implementation effort.

We use Mosquitto 2.0.11 as the MQTT broker, running on an endpoint with Intel Xeon E3-1240 V2 (4 cores with Hyper-Threading @ 3.40 GHz) as CPU and 16 GB of RAM. A Raspberry Pi 3 Model B+ (Cortex-A53 ARMv8 64-bit SoC @ 1.4 GHz with 1 GB of RAM) hosts two instances of *CryptoAC* (i.e., two MQTT clients): one that publishes to a topic a message with, as payload, a timestamp *T1* acquired just before (possibly encrypting and) publishing the message, and a second one that subscribes to that topic and acquires another timestamp *T2* after receiving and (possibly decrypting) the message from the broker. The network connections between the MQTT clients and the MQTT broker are configured as described in the Smart Lock service in Fig. 1.

Results and Discussion. As in [9], we measure the transmission time as the difference between *T2* and *T1*, with the two MQTT clients (a publisher and a subscriber) sharing the same host, avoiding therefore a possible time drift (i.e., avoiding the use of two hosts that lose clock synchronization over time). We repeat the measurements for *C1*, *C2* and *C3* with 1,000 individual MQTT messages: the average of *C1* is 11.1 ms, *C2* is 11.8 ms and *C3* is 13.5 ms;[23]

---

[21] https://mosquitto.org/man/mosquitto_sub-1.html.
[22] https://mosquitto.org/man/mosquitto_pub-1.html.
[23] https://st.fbk.eu/complementary/assets/DBSEC2022/experimental_results.xlsx.

As expected, the baseline *C1* has the lowest average transmission time due to avoiding cryptographic operations. Once removed the burden of the TLS handshake and key derivation procedure, *C2* incurs negligible overhead. We believe that this is mainly due to the performance of the host running Mosquitto, and the fact that the TLS session was using the TLS_AES_256_GCM_SHA384 cypher, for which the processor of the host supports hardware acceleration.[24] The use of CAC in *C3* yields an average overhead with respect to *C1* and *C2* of 2.4 ms and 1.7 ms, respectively. We believe that this is an acceptable overhead in a Smart Lock service, especially when considering the greater security guarantees offered by CAC. We also believe we can reduce this overhead by optimizing the code of *CryptoAC* and fine-tuning the parameters of the cryptographic algorithms employed. We leave the validation of these ideas as future work.

Finally, we investigate two variants of *C3*, i.e., one which disables DYNSEC to measure its overhead on the broker (configuration *C3B*) and one that removes the caching mechanism for symmetric keys to consider the worst-case scenario in which *CryptoAC* obtains a symmetric key for a topic for the first time, as described in Sect. 5.1 (configuration *C3C*). The results show that in *C3B* there is a negligible improvement of 0.1 ms on average, an indicator that DYNSEC does not have a significant impact on the performance of Mosquitto. The average transmission time on *C3C* is 20.9 ms on average, 7.4 ms more than *C3*, which denotes that a worst-case scenario is still acceptable for the Smart Lock service.

7   Conclusion and Future Directions

In this paper, we proposed a CAC scheme for IoT scenarios based on MQTT to secure sensitive data against external attackers, malicious insiders and partially trusted agents while providing end-to-end encryption and enforcing role-based AC policies. We implemented the scheme in an open-source tool and conducted a preliminary performance evaluation. In our experiments, the use of CAC introduces an overhead of 1.7 ms with respect to a scenario employing TLS (but without considering the handshake and key derivation algorithms), and 2.4 ms when the channel is not secured. These results are in line with the requirements of the smart lock use case and the additional security guarantees offered by CAC.

We plan to extend our work in several directions including the use of ABE to allow more expressive and fine-grained ABAC policies and of TEEs to guarantee confidentiality and integrity in IoT scenarios, as in [19], and provide different levels of security, as in [15]. We also intend to adapt the technique for optimizing deployments of cryptographic enforcement mechanisms in the cloud of [7] to IoT scenarios.

Acknowledgements. This work has been partially supported by "Futuro & Conoscenza Srl", jointly created by the FBK and the Italian National Mint and Printing House (IPZS), Italy.

---

[24] https://ark.intel.com/content/www/us/en/ark/products/65730/intel-xeon-processor-e31240-v2-8m-cache-3-40-ghz.html.

A   Pseudocode of the Cryptographic Access Control Scheme

---

initA()
- Generate encryption key pair $(\mathbf{k}_A^{\mathbf{enc}}, \mathbf{k}_A^{\mathbf{dec}}) \leftarrow \mathbf{Gen}^{\mathbf{Pub}}$, signature key pair $(\mathbf{k}_A^{\mathbf{ver}}, \mathbf{k}_A^{\mathbf{sig}}) \leftarrow \mathbf{Gen}^{\mathbf{Sig}}$
- Add $(A, \mathbf{k}_A^{\mathbf{enc}}, \mathbf{k}_A^{\mathbf{ver}})$ to $\mathbf{U_c}$, $(A, \mathbf{k}_A^{\mathbf{enc}}, 1)$ to $\mathbf{R_c}$ and $(A, A, \mathbf{Enc}_{\mathbf{k}_A^{\mathbf{enc}}}^{\mathbf{P}}(\mathbf{k}_A^{\mathbf{dec}}), 1)$ to $\mathbf{UR_c}$
- Add A to $\mathbf{U_t}$ and (A, A) to $\mathbf{UR_t}$

init$_u$()
- Generate encryption key pair $(\mathbf{k}_u^{\mathbf{enc}}, \mathbf{k}_u^{\mathbf{dec}}) \leftarrow \mathbf{Gen}^{\mathbf{Pub}}$
- Replace $(u, \mathbf{N}, \mathbf{N})$ with $(u, \mathbf{k}_u^{\mathbf{enc}}, \mathbf{N})$ in $\mathbf{U_c}$

addU(u)
- Add $(u, \mathbf{N}, \mathbf{N})$ to $\mathbf{U_c}$
- Add u to $\mathbf{U_t}$

delU(u)
- Delete $(u, -, -)$ from $\mathbf{U_c}$
- For every role r that u is a member of:
  * *revokeU(u, r)*
- Delete u from $\mathbf{U_t}$ and $(u, -)$ from $\mathbf{UR_t}$

addR(r)
- Generate encryption key pair $(\mathbf{k}_{(r,1)}^{\mathbf{enc}}, \mathbf{k}_{(r,1)}^{\mathbf{dec}}) \leftarrow \mathbf{Gen}^{\mathbf{Pub}}$
- Add $(r, \mathbf{k}_{(r,1)}^{\mathbf{enc}}, 1)$ to $\mathbf{R_c}$ and $(A, r, \mathbf{Enc}_{\mathbf{k}_A^{\mathbf{enc}}}^{\mathbf{P}}(\mathbf{k}_{(r,1)}^{\mathbf{dec}}), 1)$ to $\mathbf{UR_c}$
- Add r to $\mathbf{R_t}$ and (A, r) to $\mathbf{UR_t}$

delR(r)
- Delete $(r, -, -)$ from $\mathbf{R_c}$
- Delete all $(-, r, -, -)$ from $\mathbf{UR_c}$
- For every file f that r has access to:
  * *revokeP(r, ⟨f, {Sub, Pub}⟩)*
- Delete r from $\mathbf{R_t}$ and $(-, r)$ from $\mathbf{UR_t}$

revokeU(u, r)
- Generate new role keys $(\mathbf{k}_{(r,v_r+1)}^{\mathbf{enc}}, \mathbf{k}_{(r,v_r+1)}^{\mathbf{dec}}) \leftarrow \mathbf{Gen}^{\mathbf{Pub}}$
- For all $(u', r, -, -) \in \mathbf{UR_c} : u' \neq u$:
  * Add $(u', r, \mathbf{Enc}_{\mathbf{k}_{u'}^{\mathbf{enc}}}^{\mathbf{P}}(\mathbf{k}_{(r,v_r+1)}^{\mathbf{dec}}), v_r + 1)$ to $\mathbf{UR_c}$
- For all $f \in \mathbf{F} : (r, f, -, -, -, op) \in \mathbf{PA_c}$
  * Generate new symmetric key $\mathbf{k}_{(f,v_f+1)}^{\mathbf{sym}} \leftarrow \mathbf{Gen}^{\mathbf{Sym}}$ for f
  * Replace (f, v_f) with $(f, v_f + 1)$ in $\mathbf{F_c}$
  * Add $(r, f, \mathbf{Enc}_{\mathbf{k}_{(r,v_r+1)}^{\mathbf{enc}}}^{\mathbf{P}}(\mathbf{k}_{(f,v_f+1)}^{\mathbf{sym}}), v_f + 1, v_r + 1, op)$ to $\mathbf{PA_c}$
  * For all $(r', f, -, -, v_r', op') \in \mathbf{PA_c} : r' \neq r$:
    · Add $(r', f, \mathbf{Enc}_{\mathbf{k}_{(r',v_r')}^{\mathbf{enc}}}^{\mathbf{P}}(\mathbf{k}_{(f,v_f+1)}^{\mathbf{sym}}), v_f + 1, v_r', op')$ to $\mathbf{PA_c}$
- Replace $(r, -, -)$ with $(r, \mathbf{k}_{(r,v_r+1)}^{\mathbf{enc}}, v_r + 1)$ in $\mathbf{R_c}$
- Delete all $(-, r, -, v_r)$ from $\mathbf{UR_c}$
- Delete all $(r, -, -, -, v_r, -)$ from $\mathbf{PA_c}$
- Delete (u, r) from $\mathbf{UR_t}$

assignP(r, ⟨f, op⟩)
- If r already has $⟨f, op'⟩$ permission, i.e., there exists $(r, f, c, v_f, v_r, op') \in \mathbf{PA_c}$ and $(r, ⟨f, op'⟩) \in \mathbf{PA_t}$:
  * Replace (r, f, c, v_f, v_r, op') with $(r, f, c, v_f, v_r, op \cup op')$ in $\mathbf{PA_c}$ and $(r, ⟨f, op'⟩)$ with $(r, ⟨f, op \cup op'⟩)$ in $\mathbf{PA_t}$
- Else:
  * Add $(r, f, \mathbf{Enc}_{\mathbf{k}_{(r,v_r)}^{\mathbf{enc}}}^{\mathbf{P}}(\mathbf{k}_{(f,v_f)}^{\mathbf{sym}}), v_f, v_r, op)$ to $\mathbf{PA_c}$ and $(r, ⟨f, op⟩)$ to $\mathbf{PA_t}$

Fig. 2. Role-based Cryptographic Access Control for IoT Using MQTT

addP(f)
- Generate symmetric key $k^{sym}_{(f,1)} \leftarrow Gen^{Sym}$
- Add $(f,1)$ to F_c, $(A, f, Enc^P_{k^{enc}_A}\left(k^{sym}_{(f,1)}\right), 1, v_A, \{Sub, Pub\})$ to PA_c
- The broker publishes retained message $(f,1)$ to topic f
- Add $(A, \langle f, \{Sub, Pub\}\rangle)$ to PA_t

delP(f)
- Delete $(f,-,-)$ from F_c and $(-,f,-,-,-,-)$ from PA_c
- Delete $(-,\langle f,-\rangle)$ from PA_t
- The broker deletes retained message $(f,-,-)$ from the topic f

assignU(u,r)
- Find (A, r, c, v_r) in UR_c
- Decrypt $m = Dec^P_{k^{dec}_A}(c)$
- Add $(u, r, Enc^P_{k^{enc}_u}(m), v_r)$ to UR_c
- Add (u,r) to UR_t

sub$_u$(f,c)
- When receiving c on f from the broker, find a role r such that the following hold:
  * u is in role r, i.e., there exists $(u, r, Enc^P_{k^{enc}_u}\left(k^{dec}_{(r,v_r)}\right), v_r)$ in UR_c
  * r has read access to the topic f, i.e., there exists $(r, f, Enc^P_{k^{enc}_{(r,v_r)}}\left(k^{sym}_{(f,v_f)}\right), v_f, v_r, op)$ where $op \cap \{Sub\} \neq \emptyset$
- Decrypt role key $k^{dec}_{(r,v_r)} =$ $Dec^P_{k^{dec}_u}\left(Enc^P_{k^{enc}_u}(k^{dec}_{(r,v_r)})\right)$
- Decrypt file key $k^{sym}_{(f,v_f)} =$ $Dec^P_{k^{dec}_{(r,v_r)}}\left((Enc^P_{k^{enc}_{(r,v_r)}}\left(k^{sym}_{(f,v_f)}\right))\right)$
- Decrypt message $m = Dec^S_{k^{sym}_{(f,v_f)}}(c)$

revokeP(r, ⟨f, op⟩)
- Given $(r, f, c, v_f, v_r, op') \in PA_c$ and $(r, \langle f, op'\rangle) \in PA_t$, if $op' \subseteq op$:
  * Delete $(r, \langle f, op'\rangle)$ from PA_t and (r, f, c, v_f, v_r, op') from PA_c
  * Generate new symmetric key $k^{sym}_{(f,v_f+1)} \leftarrow Gen^{Sym}$
  * Replace all $(r', f, -, -, v_{r'}, op'')$ with $(r', f, Enc^P_{k^{enc}_{(r',v_{r'})}}\left(k^{sym}_{(f,v_f+1)}\right), v_f+1, v_{r'}, op'')$ in PA_c
  * Replace $(f,-)$ with $(f, v_f + 1)$ in F_c
- Else if $op \cap op' \neq \emptyset$:
  * Replace $(r, \langle f, op'\rangle)$ with $(r, \langle f, op' \setminus op\rangle)$ in PA_t and (r, f, c, v_f, v_r, op') with $(r, f, c, v_f, v_r, op' \setminus op)$ in PA_c

pub$_u$(f,m)
- Find a role r such that the following hold:
  * u is in role r, i.e., there exists $(u, r, Enc^P_{k^{enc}_u}\left(k^{dec}_{(r,v_r)}\right), v_r)$ in UR_c
  * r has write access to topic f, i.e., there exists $(r, f, Enc^P_{k^{enc}_{(r,v_r)}}\left(k^{sym}_{(f,v_f)}\right), v_f, v_r, op)$ where $op \cap \{Pub\} \neq \emptyset$
- Decrypt role key $k^{dec}_{(r,v_r)} =$ $Dec^P_{k^{dec}_u}\left(Enc^P_{k^{enc}_u}(k^{dec}_{(r,v_r)})\right)$
- Decrypt file key $k^{sym}_{(f,v_f)} =$ $Dec^P_{k^{dec}_{(r,v_r)}}\left((Enc^P_{k^{enc}_{(r,v_r)}}\left(k^{sym}_{(f,v_f)}\right))\right)$
- Encrypt message $c = Enc^S_{k^{sym}_{(f,v_f)}}(m)$
- Send c to the broker
- The broker receives c and verifies the following:
  * u is assigned to r, i.e., there exists (u,r) in UR_t
  * r has write access to topic f, i.e., there exists $(r, \langle f, op\rangle)$ in PA_t so that $op \cap \{Pub\} \neq \emptyset$
- If verification is successful, the broker sends c to all clients subscribed to topic f

Fig. 2. (_continued_)

References

1. Ahmad, T., Morelli, U., Ranise, S.: Deploying access control enforcement for IoT in the cloud-edge continuum with the help of the CAP theorem. In: Proceedings of the 25th ACM Symposium on Access Control Models and Technologies, pp. 213–220. ACM (2020)
2. Ahmad, T., Morelli, U., Ranise, S., Zannone, N.: A lazy approach to access control as a service (ACaaS) for IoT: an AWS case study. In: Proceedings of the 23nd ACM on Symposium on Access Control Models and Technologies, SACMAT 2018, pp. 235–246. Association for Computing Machinery, New York (2018)
3. Ahmad, T., Morelli, U., Ranise, S., Zannone, N.: Extending access control in AWS IoT through event-driven functions: an experimental evaluation using a smart lock system. Int. J. Inf. Secur. **21**(2), 379–408 (2021)
4. Armando, A., Grasso, M., Oudkerk, S., Ranise, S., Wrona, K.: Content-based information protection and release in NATO operations. In: Proceedings of the 18th ACM Symposium on Access Control Models and Technologies - SACMAT 2013, p. 261. ACM Press (2013)
5. Armando, A., Oudkerk, S., Ranise, S., Wrona, K.: Formal modelling of content-based protection and release for access control in NATO operations. In: Danger, J.-L., Debbabi, M., Marion, J.-Y., Garcia-Alfaro, J., Zincir Heywood, N. (eds.) FPS-2013. LNCS, vol. 8352, pp. 227–244. Springer, Cham (2014). https://doi.org/10.1007/978-3-319-05302-8_14
6. Bellare, M., Namprempre, C.: Authenticated encryption: relations among notions and analysis of the generic composition paradigm. J. Cryptol. **21**(4), 469–491 (2008)
7. Berlato, S., Carbone, R., Lee, A.J., Ranise, S.: Formal modelling and automated trade-off analysis of enforcement architectures for cryptographic access control in the cloud. ACM Trans. Priv. Secur. **25**(1), 1–37 (2021)
8. Calabretta, M., Pecori, R., Veltri, L.: A token-based protocol for securing MQTT communications. In: 2018 26th International Conference on Software, Telecommunications and Computer Networks (SoftCOM), pp. 1–6. IEEE (2018)
9. Colombo, P., Ferrari, E.: Access control enforcement within MQTT-based internet of things ecosystems. In: Proceedings of the 23nd ACM on Symposium on Access Control Models and Technologies, pp. 223–234. ACM (2018)
10. Djoko, J.B., Lange, J., Lee, A.J.: NeXUS: practical and secure access control on untrusted storage platforms using client-side SGX. In: 2019 49th Annual IEEE/IFIP International Conference on Dependable Systems and Networks (DSN), pp. 401–413. IEEE (2019)
11. Elemam, E., Bahaa-Eldin, A.M., Shaker, N.H., Sobh, M.A.: A secure MQTT protocol, telemedicine IoT case study. In: 2019 14th International Conference on Computer Engineering and Systems (ICCES), pp. 99–105. IEEE (2019)
12. Garrison, W.C., Shull, A., Myers, S., Lee, A.J.: On the practicality of cryptographically enforcing dynamic access control policies in the cloud. In: 2016 IEEE Symposium on Security and Privacy (SP), pp. 819–838 (2016)
13. Heer, T., Garcia-Morchon, O., Hummen, R., Keoh, S.L., Kumar, S.S., Wehrle, K.: Security challenges in the IP-based internet of things. Wirel. Pers. Commun. **61**(3), 527–542 (2011)
14. Kurnikov, A., Paverd, A., Mannan, M., Asokan, N.: Keys in the clouds: auditable multi-device access to cryptographic credentials. In: Proceedings of the 13th International Conference on Availability, Reliability and Security, pp. 1–10. ACM (2018)

15. Malina, L., Srivastava, G., Dzurenda, P., Hajny, J., Fujdiak, R.: A secure publish/-subscribe protocol for internet of things. In: Proceedings of the 14th International Conference on Availability, Reliability and Security, pp. 1–10. ACM (2019)
16. Palmieri, A., Prem, P., Ranise, S., Morelli, U., Ahmad, T.: MQTTSA: a tool for automatically assisting the secure deployments of MQTT brokers. In: 2019 IEEE World Congress on Services (SERVICES), vol. 2642–939X, pp. 47–53 (2019)
17. Samarati, P., de Vimercati, S.C.: Access control: policies, models, and mechanisms. In: Focardi, R., Gorrieri, R. (eds.) FOSAD 2000. LNCS, vol. 2171, pp. 137–196. Springer, Heidelberg (2001). https://doi.org/10.1007/3-540-45608-2_3
18. Sanjuan, E.B., Cardiel, I.A., Cerrada, J.A., Cerrada, C.: Message queuing telemetry transport (MQTT) security: a cryptographic smart card approach. IEEE Access 8, 115051–115062 (2020)
19. Segarra, C., Delgado-Gonzalo, R., Schiavoni, V.: MQT-TZ: hardening IoT brokers using ARM TrustZone: (practical experience report). In: 2020 International Symposium on Reliable Distributed Systems (SRDS), pp. 256–265. IEEE (2020)
20. Zeadally, S., Das, A.K., Sklavos, N.: Cryptographic technologies and protocol standards for internet of things. Internet Things 14, 100075 (2019)

Quantum Security

Integrating and Evaluating Quantum-safe TLS in Database Applications

Anselme Tueno[1]([✉]), David Boehm[1], and Shin Ho Choe[2]

[1] SAP Security Research, SAP SE, Karlsruhe, Germany
{`anselme.tueno,david.boehm`}`@sap.com`
[2] Department of Mathematics, Technical University of Munich, Munich, Germany
`shinho.choe@tum.de`

Abstract. Quantum computing promises to build computers capable of solving complex problems much faster than today's computers. This will benefit to many real-world applications such AI, machine learning, optimization problems, complex financial modelling, etc. Quantum computing will also have an impact on cryptology by allowing to break many public-key encryptions in use today. As a response to this threat the cryptography community is investigating Post-Quantum Cryptography (PQC). PQC provides encryption schemes that run on conventional computers and are believed to be secure against attacks from both classical and quantum computers. Such schemes are therefore called quantum-safe or quantum-resistant. In this work, we experiment with quantum-safe TLS to secure the communication for PostgreSQL which is an open source client-server database management system. In a client-server database, the database resides on a server, and client applications can access the database by sending requests to the server. These requests usually include requesting or modifying data. To establish a quantum-safe client-server communication, we first integrate quantum-safe TLS in PostgreSQL source code and evaluate connections between client and server. Our evaluation goal consists of measuring the overhead of TLS connections, especially when using quantum-safe algorithms. We experiment with different certificate chain lengths (from 0 to 4). Since NIST recommends applying hybrid schemes (combining both quantum-weak, i.e., current public-key crypto, and quantum-safe schemes) during the transition to quantum-safe algorithms, we also evaluate hybrid algorithms but first focus on lattice-based schemes (KYBER for key exchange and DILITHIUM for authentication) as they are believed to be the only TLS-ready alternative. Finally, we consider three security levels (128, 192, and 256), and evaluate both the running time and the bandwidth. Our results confirm that lattice-based schemes are promising, but come with significantly higher communication overhead.

Keywords: Post-quantum Crypto · Database · PostgreSQL · Public-key Encryption · Digital Signature · Key Exchange · Key Encapsulation Mechanism · TLS

© IFIP International Federation for Information Processing 2022
Published by Springer Nature Switzerland AG 2022
S. Sural and H. Lu (Eds.): DBSec 2022, LNCS 13383, pp. 259–278, 2022.
https://doi.org/10.1007/978-3-031-10684-2_15

1   Introduction

To protect our sensitive data on computer systems and the Internet, cryptography provides encryption and signature schemes. Cryptography is the last line of defense against data breaches. When all other security measures have failed, encryption provides the last barrier that protects company secrets against unauthorized access. An encryption scheme consists of algorithms for key generation, encryption and decryption [4,11]. There are symmetric (also known as shared key schemes) and asymmetric aka public key schemes. Both have advantages and disadvantages such that in a real world setting they are used in a hybrid way. Public key schemes base their security on mathematical problems that are difficult to solve on a computer. Since its invention, public key cryptography has been relying on two problems, namely prime factorization [29] and discrete logarithm [8,10,13,14].

In 1994, American mathematician Peter Shor published efficient quantum algorithms that allow to find the prime factorization or the discrete logarithm of any integer [31,32]. When quantum computers become powerful enough to run Shor's algorithm for commonly used key lengths, cryptographic schemes that rely on the difficulty of prime factorization or discrete logarithm will be broken. Public-key cryptography, however, is present in a multitude of application fields. It has impact on the Internet, e-mail, key management, secure shell, virtual private networks, distributed ledgers, code signing, and basically any scenario that requires secure communication. That is, a powerful quantum computer represents an apocalyptic cybersecurity threat to our IT infrastructure [22].

As a response to the quantum threat on cryptography, NIST has initiated a process to solicit, evaluate, and standardize one or more quantum-resistant public-key cryptographic algorithms [18]. In its call for proposal, NIST requested schemes that implement one or more of the following functionalities: public-key encryption, key encapsulation mechanism (KEM), and digital signature. The cryptography community is now investigating what is called Post-Quantum Cryptography (PQC). PQC provides encryption schemes that run on conventional computers and are believed to be secure against attacks from both classical and quantum computers. Such schemes are therefore called quantum-safe, quantum-resistant or post-quantum. While Shor's algorithm theoretically breaks current cryptography, it requires a powerful quantum computer, that is still difficult to build. PQC is all about preparing for the time when quantum computers are powerful enough to be useful for cryptographic attacks.

While NIST's standardization effort is aimed at designing new cryptographic algorithms that are secure against quantum attacks, there is another major challenge to consider, namely the migration of existing infrastructures to the new algorithms [22]. Replacing broken cryptography and integrating new one is not only a difficult but also a time-consuming task, especially since PQC schemes come with different requirements and security assumptions than existing ones. The lack of crypto-agility in cryptographic APIs, makes transition to new schemes a challenge. Therefore, NIST and many experts recommend to start preparing now [22,24].

In this work, we experiment with quantum-safe TLS to secure the communication for PostgreSQL which is an open source client-server database management system. In a client-server database, the database resides on a server, and client applications can access the database by sending requests to the server. These requests usually include selecting, inserting, updating, and deleting data. To establish a quantum-safe communication between client and server, we first integrate quantum-safe TLS in PostgreSQL source code and evaluate database connections and queries. Our evaluation goal consists of measuring the overhead of TLS connections, especially when using quantum-safe algorithms. We experiment with different certificate chain lengths (from 0 to 4). Since NIST recommends applying hybrid schemes (combining both quantum-weak, i.e., current public-key crypto, and quantum-safe schemes) during the transition to quantum-safe algorithms, we also evaluate hybrid algorithms but first focused on lattice-based schemes (KYBER for key exchange and DILITHIUM for authentication) as they are believed to be the only TLS-ready alternative. Finally, we considered three security levels (128, 192, and 256), and evaluated both the running time and the bandwidth.

Our contributions are as follows. We investigate post-quantum cryptography for database applications. We focus our investigation on PostgreSQL which is an open source and popular client-server database. As other client-server databases, PostgreSQL relies on the OpenSSL library such that our work is relevant for those databases as well. Using the liboqs crypto library [33], we integrate post-quantum TLS to secure the communication between a client and the database server. We ensure the integration to be crypto-agile such that one can choose which algorithms to use without recompiling the code. We evaluate quantum-safe client connections to the server and data query under realistic conditions.

The remainder of the paper is structured as follows. We review preliminaries in Sect. 2 before presenting PostgreSQL in Sect. 3. We describe our integration in Sect. 4 and present our evaluation results in Sect. 5. In Sect. 6, we present related work before concluding our work in Sect. 7.

2   Preliminary

In this section, we discuss some preliminaries including PQC, the state of NIST standardization, the Open Quantum Safe project and the TLS protocol.

2.1   Post-quantum Cryptography

Current standard quantum-weak public-key cryptography includes RSA DH, ElGamal and related encryption systems. All these systems rely either on the integer factorization or the discrete logarithm problems. PQC relies on different computational problems that are believed to be hard to break even for a quantum computer.

Famillies of PQC schemes. There exist five families of PQC schemes: lattice-based, code-based, hash-based, multivariate, and isogeny-based schemes. Lattice-based schemes [6,15,26,30] are based on computational problems related to mathematical objects called lattices. In mathematics, a lattice is a set of points in an n-dimensional space with a periodic structure. Graphically, a lattice can be described as the set of intersection points of an infinite, regular (but not necessarily orthogonal) n-dimensional grid. Code-based schemes [17] are based on error-correcting codes which are quite well understood as the foundation of coding theory. Error-correcting codes are used to ensure reliable transmission of information across noisy channels. Hash-based schemes [12] rely on the security of cryptographic hash functions. Multivariate schemes [9] are based on the difficulty of solving a system of multivariate polynomial equations over a finite field. Isogeny-based schemes [7] are based on the hardness of computing isogenies between a pair of isogenous elliptic curves. An isogeny is a map that transforms a curve into another one while preserving their mathematical structure.

PQC schemes differ not only on different mathematical problems, but also in their resource's requirements (e.g., size of keys, ciphertext and signature and computational cost), their maturity and the confidence in their security strength. The resource requirements are important as they influence the integration into existing infrastructures. In general, PQC schemes require more resources compared to existing public key schemes. Therefore, quantum-safe security comes with additional performance overhead. Hash-based and code-based schemes are very mature as they have been developed and investigated for many years. Moreover, hash-based schemes require minimal assumptions. Multivariate schemes have also been introduced many years ago and their underlying math problem is well understood. However, their mathematical structure has been used to break many schemes in the past. Lattice-based schemes are younger than multivariate schemes. But there exist proofs of their security strength resulting in a growing confidence. Moreover, the lattice family allows the design of more advanced cryptographic tools like fully homomorphic encryption. While the hash-based family can only be used for digital signatures, with the remaining families one can theoretically implement both signature and encryption. However, in the current state of development, only the lattice family offers schemes for signature and encryption, that are still secure. Code-based and isogeny-based families provide only encryption, while the multivariate-based family provides only signature.

PQC Standardization. Inspired by two earlier standardization processes for AES and SHA3, NIST announced the PQC project on February 2016 with the goal to standardize post-quantum algorithms for public-key encryption and digital signatures [18]. In [19], NIST specifies five security levels. Level one, three and five correspond to the security of AES128, AES192 and AES256, respectively. Levels two and four correspond to the security of SHA256/SHA3-256 and SHA384/SHA3-384, respectively. Out of the 82 initial submissions, only 15 schemes are still under consideration for standardization. Initially, 23 algorithms for signature and 59 for encryption were submitted by the submission deadline in December 2017 of which 69 in total were accepted for the first round. On

January 2019, the number of algorithms was reduced to 26 (17 encryption and 9 signature algorithms) for the second round. On July 22, 2020, NIST moved the PQC standardization process to the third round by announcing a list of 7 finalists and 8 alternates [20]. The finalists consist of four schemes for public-key encryption (Classic McEliece [17], CRYSTALS-KYBER [30], NTRU [5], SABER [6]) and three schemes for digital signature (CRYSTALS-DILITHIUM [15], Falcon [26], Rainbow [9]). The 8 alternate candidates are not in the finalists' list but might still be considered for standardization in a fourth round.

2.2   Open Quantum Safe

While NIST's effort aims at designing new cryptographic schemes, there exist community projects with the goal of assessing and evaluating those schemes in a real world setting. The Open Quantum Safe Project (OQS) [33] is such an open-source software project for prototyping quantum-resistant cryptography, which includes liboqs, a C library of quantum-resistant algorithms. Liboqs is an open source C library that provides a common interface for key encapsulation mechanism and digital signature schemes. It also contains open source implementations of a variety of post-quantum schemes that are part of the NIST standardization. The liboqs library has been used to integrate PQC into several open-source applications and protocols, including the OpenSSL, BoringSSL, and OpenSSH libraries. Moreover, OQS provides language wrappers for liboqs that cover several programming languages such as Python, C#, C++, Go and Java.

2.3   Transport Layer Security

The first integration of OQS occurred into OpenSSL which is an open source crypto library. It consists of libcrypto for cryptographic algorithms and libssl for SSL/TLS implementation. TLS [28] is the current standard protocol for establishing secure communication on the Internet. The current version is TLS 1.3, which this paper focuses on. TLS consists of three basic steps: connection establishment, TLS handshake and the encryption of application data using symmetric cryptography. While the first and last steps are not threatened by quantum computers, as long as the symmetric encryption keys used in the last step are long enough, the second step consists of authentication and key exchange that both rely on public-key cryptography.

The three main steps of TLS are illustrated in Fig. 1. In the first step, the client contacts the server with the Client_Hello message consisting of specific parameter including the protocol version, a random nonce, a session ID, and a list of cipher suites and compression methods. To reduce network traffic, the client also sends its key material (Client_Key_Share) for the key establishment in the assumption that the corresponding algorithm is supported by the server. In the second step, the server replies with the Server_Hello that is similar to the Client_Hello and chooses the best possible protocol version. Additionally, the server sends its key material for key establishment (Server_Key_Share), the server certificate chain (Server_certificate) for authentication, a confirmation message for the encryption of subsequent messages (Change_Cipher_Spec), and the indication of its readiness for secure communication (Finished). The server reply is signed by its private key. In the last step, the client also transmits a confirmation for encryption of subsequent messages (Change_Cipher_Spec) and its readiness to communicate securely (Finished).

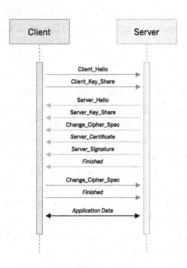

Fig. 1. A simplified illustration of TLS 1.3

3   PostgreSQL

A database stores data that can later be queried or modified. In this section, we briefly present the PostgreSQL DBMS and refer to [35] for further details.

3.1   Overview

PostgreSQL [35] is an object-relational database management. It is an open source database that supports a large part of the SQL standard and offer many modern features including complex queries, foreign keys, triggers etc. PostgreSQL is extendable in many ways by adding new programming constructs including data types, functions, operators. The architecture is the client-server model (Fig. 2). The server manages database files, accepts connections client applications and performs database actions on behalf of the client. The client can access the database, select, update, delete data. Client applications are diverse in nature, from command-line tools to web servers accessing the database to display web pages. Some client applications are included in the PostgreSQL distribution. As is it the case for client-server applications, the client and the server can be hosted by different machine on the network. They, therefore communicate over a TCP/IP network connection.

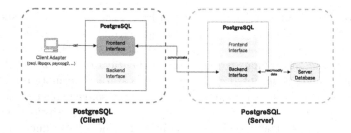

Fig. 2. Client-Server Architecture of PostgreSQL

3.2 Database Server

The database server program is called postgres. The server can handle multiple concurrent connections from clients. To achieve this, the server starts a new process for each connection. From this point on, the client and the new server process communicate without intervention by the original postgres process. Thus, the supervisor server process is always running, waiting for new client connections, whereas client and associated server processes come and go. Apparently, all of this is transparent to the user. The server must be installed and configured to work properly. The installation can be done using binary packages or the source code. At code level, the server can be accessed using a backend interface. Similarly, there is a frontend interface for client programs.

3.3 Client Interface

PostgreSQL provides a programming interface for clients to establish a connection with the server. This interface is called libpq. It is a C application programmer's interface which offers a set of library functions. These functions can be used by client programs to connect to the server and query the database. Libpq is also the interface to many other client applications written in different programming languages including C++, Perl and Python. Client programs must include the header file libpq−fe.h and must link with the libpq library. The client communicates with the server by sending messages back and forth between the frontend and the backend interface. This communication is defined by the PostgreSQL frontend-backend protocol that is described in the subsequent section.

3.4 Frontend-Backend Protocol

PostgreSQL clients communicate with the server through a message-based protocol which is supported over TCP/IP as well as Unix-domain sockets. The default TCP port number is 5432, but any non-privileged port is allowed. The current version of the protocol is 3.0, but a single server can support different versions. The parties therefore agree on the version to use during the first protocol interaction. If the client requests a version not supported by the server, the connection is rejected or the server may ask the client to choose another version among a list of supported versions. As illustrated in Fig. 3, the protocol consists of these two main phases: connection (startup) and query (normal operation). The client connects with a startup packet which allows to negotiate the protocol version. In addition, the server may require user authentication to the database. If a connection request is accepted, the server sends status information and notifies its readiness for accepting queries. In the query phase, the client sends a query which the server processes before replying with a row description followed by the requested data. The server then notifies the end of the query phase and its readiness for further queries. The client may want the communication to be encrypted. In this case, it initiates the connection phase with an SSL Negotiation Packet. If the server is configured to support TLS, they perform a TLS handshake so that the subsequent communication, including the connection and query phases described above, is fully encrypted.

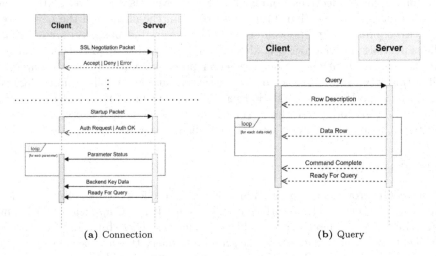

(a) Connection   (b) Query

Fig. 3. Illustration of the Frontend-backend Protocol

4 Integration

In this section, we describe our integration of quantum-safe TLS into PostgreSQL, to secure the communication between client and server.

4.1 Architecture

We start our integration by presenting and describing the architecture in Fig. 4. As mentioned before, PostgreSQL has a backend and frontend interface for managing server and client respectively. Both interfaces rely on the OpenSSL library for cryptographic services including TLS. Open Quantum Safe offers a version of

OpenSSL where the liboqs library has been integrated and therefore allows utilizing quantum-safe schemes. To integrate TLS into the frontend-backend protocol, PostgreSQL uses its internal interface libpq which also provides an interface for other security APIs. Our integration therefore takes place in the libpq interface. Before the server can work with TLS, it must be configured properly, which is described in more detail in the following section.

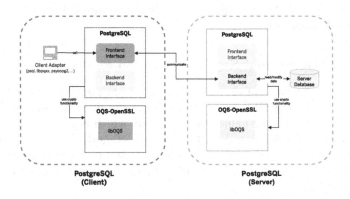

Fig. 4. Architecture of the Integration

4.2 Configuration

PostgreSQL allows secure communication between the client and the server using TLS. This requires installing OpenSSL on both systems and enabling TLS when building PostgreSQL. The server must then be configured using the configuration file postgresql.conf which on UNIX systems is located in /usr/local/pgsql/data/. The configuration file consists of several parameters among which the most relevant for our integration are: enabling TLS, specifying the location of the server's public-key certificate and the corresponding private-key file, and setting the name of the key exchange algorithm. Besides, there are further parameters such as TLS min/max version, passphrase, etc. When TLS is enabled, the server listens for TLS and non-TLS connection requests on the same TCP port and negotiates with the client on whether to encrypt the communication [35].

4.3 Digital Signature

To integrate quantum-safe authentication, we need to create post-quantum certificates. Recall that Open Quantum Safe offers a version of OpenSSL that integrates quantum-safe schemes. We can therefore create quantum-safe signatures using usual OpenSSL commands. An example for creating a DILITHIUM certificate and private-key file looks as follows:

```
openssl req −x509 −new −newkey dilithium2
−keyout server.key −out server.crt
−nodes −subj "/CN=test" −days 365
```

server.key and server.crt are the default file names for the server private-key file and the corresponding public-key certificate. The generated certificate and private-key file must then be copied to the /usr/local/pgsql/data/ directory. No modifications to the PostgreSQL source code are required. This is, however, not the case for key exchange.

4.4 Key Exchange and Key Encapsulation Mechanisms

The server gets the name of the algorithm for key exchange (KEX) or key encapsulation mechanism (KEM) from the configuration file postgresql.conf. This is defined using a parameter named ssl_ecdh_curve which points out that only the Elliptic-Curve Diffie-Hellman (ECDH) scheme is supported as key exchange algorithm. Moreover, ECDH is hard-coded into the source code of PostgreSQL, which concerns both the frontend and the backend part. Besides, there is no client-side configuration file.

As mentioned before, PostgreSQL provides the libpq interface to allow using crypto APIs such as OpenSSL. Concerning the backend, the functionality for OpenSSL support is implemented in the file be−secure−openssl.c. There is a function named initialize_ecdh() that uses the ssl_ecdh_curve config parameter to set the DH parameters by providing the curve name to OpenSSL. This is done using the OpenSSL function SSL_CTX_set_tmp_ecdh. OpenSSL offers the generic function SSL_CTX_set1_groups to set KEX using its algorithm ID. It requires a list of algorithms as input parameter for specifying the set of supported key exchange algorithms. Therefore, we replace the ECDH-specific function by the generic one and set the required list of algorithms correctly.

For the frontend, the functionality for supporting OpenSSL is implemented in the file fe−secure−openssl.c. Usually, clients and servers that communicate via TLS respectively hold a list of supported schemes for key exchange. In the context of ECC, these schemes are also referred to as curves or groups. Both sides have to support PQC schemes for quantum-safe communication. Therefore, the configuration of the supported KEX/KEM algorithms has been inserted after the configuration of the client-side SSL context, which holds various configuration and data relevant to TLS session establishment. In order to enable changing the KEX/KEM algorithm at runtime, the program will read a config file on the client side, containing the group, curve or KEM algorithm name. The remaining part for the client-side integration of PQC is equivalent to the server-side modifications described above, namely converting the algorithm name to its ID, adding the ID to a list, and passing it to OpenSSL using the function SSL_CTX_set1_groups.

In summary, we integrated PQC by identifying the entry points for TLS. Then we modified the frontend and backend parts by removing hard-coded specifications of ECDH, adding generic support for key exchange algorithms, and adding a configuration file on the client side.

5 Evaluation

In this section, we first present the evaluation methodology and our test program. Then we discuss the results of our extensive evaluation in a real-word setting.

5.1 Test Methodology

Our evaluation methodology consists of measuring the overhead of TLS connections, comparing the overhead of classical, i.e. quantum-weak algorithms to the overhead of quantum-safe algorithms. When using TLS, we experimented with different certificate chain lengths (from zero to four), where the length of zero indicates that TLS is not used at all, a length of one means the server certificate is a self-signed root certificate, and length $n > 1$ means there are $n - 2$ intermediate certificates between the root and server certificates (Fig. 5). Recall that a certificate chain is a list of certificates used to authenticate an entity. The chain begins with the certificate of that entity, and each certificate in the chain is signed by the entity identified by the next certificate in the chain. The last certificate in the chain is called root and is usually self-signed. Figure 5 shows the structure of certificate chains for a given chain length. As recommended by NIST, transition to quantum-safe security should be done using hybrids that combine both quantum-weak (i.e., current public-key crypto) and quantum-safe algorithms. In the pre-quantum era, quantum-weak algorithms are still secure and compliant with existing standardizations, while quantum-safe algorithms protect against the sudden maturity of quantum computers. Therefore, we also evaluate hybrids but focused on lattice-based schemes (KYBER for key exchange and DILITHIUM for authentication) as they are believed to be the only TLS-ready alternative. Finally, we considered three different security levels (i.e., AES128, AES192, and AES256), and evaluated both the running time and the bandwidth (i.e., communication size or the number of bits sent during a TLS connection).

Chain Length	Certificate Entities
0	No TLS
1	Self-signed Root
2	Self-signed Root $\xrightarrow{certify}$ Server/Client
3	Self-signed Root $\xrightarrow{certify}$ Intermediate CA $\xrightarrow{certify}$ Server/Client
4	Self-signed Root $\xrightarrow{certify}$ Intermediate CA (1) $\xrightarrow{certify}$ Intermediate CA (2) $\xrightarrow{certify}$ Server/Client

Fig. 5. Common Types of Certificate Chains

5.2   Setup

The evaluation was conducted in two experiments using two separate machines, a client and a server machine that perform a TLS handshake with each other. The experiments cover two different cases of network connections: a local area network (LAN) connection where both machines are located in Frankfurt (Germany), and a wide area network (WAN) connection where the server is located in Frankfurt and the client connects to the server from Oregon (USA). In the LAN, we must record a latency of 0.9 to 1.0 ms, while the WAN adds a latency of 140 to 150 ms for message exchange between two peers. Each machine was chosen to be an AWS EC2 cloud instance, running on the Ubuntu 18.04 OS, having two CPU cores, 8 GB of RAM, and a scalable Intel XEON processor @ 3.0 GHz. All the measurements were performed with a real time clock in order to examine the impact on real conditions of a network communication.

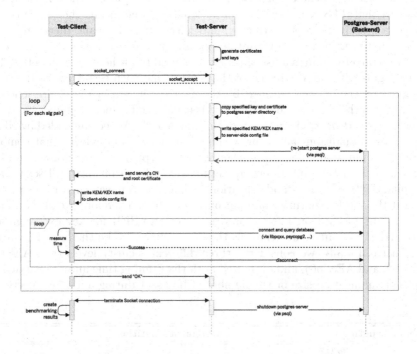

Fig. 6. Sequence Diagram of the Client-Server Test Program

5.3   Test Program

To evaluate the integration, we implemented a client-server test program. It consists of a Test-Client and a Test-Server which are both implemented in C++ and Python using PostgreSQL client APIs libpqxx [1] and psycopg2 [34]. As illustrated in Fig. 6, the Test-Server first generates certificates and keys for all algorithm pairs to be evaluated, and accepts a connection request from the Test-Client. An algorithm pair consists of a signature and a KEX/KEM, e.g., DILITHIUM and KYBER. For each algorithm pair, the Test-Server configures the PostgreSQL server, by making the certificates and keys available, and specifying the KEX/KEM algorithm in the server-side configuration file. Then the Test-Server starts the PostgreSQL server and transmits the server's certificate to the Test-Client. The Test-Client specifies the KEX/KEM in its client-side configuration file for PostgreSQL clients. Now, the Test-Client is able to directly connect to the PostgreSQL database server and send SQL queries. We then run several connections and queries, and measure the performance. Finally, the Test-Client sends a completion message which causes the database server to shut down, the connection between Test-Client and Test-Server to terminate, and the Test-Client to create benchmarking results.

5.4 Results

Figures 7, 8 and 9 show the elapsed time for a TLS Handshake in a LAN with 0.98 ms network latency. We performed similar experiments in a WAN setting with 140 ms network latency and present the result in Appendix A. Figure 7 illustrates the case when the signature is RSA vs. DILITHIUM and the KEX/KEM is ECDH vs. KYBER. For security level 1, Handshake with RSA/ECDH is almost 2 times slower than using PQC. For security level 3 and 5, the situation is even worse with a factor of at least 12 (level 3) and 61 (level 5). Figure 8 illustrates the case when the signature is ECDSA vs. DILITHIUM and the KEX/KEM is ECDH vs. KYBER. Using security level 1, the handshake performance with ECDSA/ECDH is comparable with post-quantum crypto. However, with security level 3 and 5, the handshake with ECDSA/ECDH is about two times and three times slower, respectively. Figure 9 illustrates the case when the signature is RSA/ECDSA vs. Hybrids and the KEX/KEM is ECDH vs. Hybrids. We consider hybrids with combined algorithms at the same security level (e.g.: ECDSA-DILITHIUM, RSA-DILITHIUM, ECDH-KYBER). Since in hybrid mode, both algorithms are executed in parallel, the runtime is comparable to that of the slowest algorithm. Therefore, the result for hybrids is comparable to the results in Figs. 7 and 8.

We started the evaluation by measuring the insecure connection (i.e., no TLS) between the client and the server which takes on average around 244 ms in WAN and 113 ms in LAN. Adding TLS increases this by at least a factor of six. At security level 128, the running time of the quantum-safe TLS connection is comparable to quantum-weak. At higher security levels (192, 256), quantum-safe TLS is faster (at least three times, five times respectively). The running time for hybrids (i.e., a combination of both quantum-safe and quantum-weak as above) is comparable to quantum-weak only.

In Fig. 10, we compare the communication size during the handshake. As expected already, the bandwidth of quantum-safe schemes is higher than that of quantum-weak ones. In our experiment, quantum-safe TLS has 6, 8, 9 times higher bandwidth for security levels 128, 192, 256, respectively. This is because

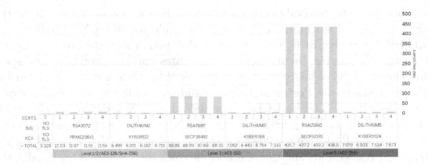

Fig. 7. Elapsed time in milliseconds for a TLS handshake on LAN, comparing RSA/ECDH and DILITHIUM/KYBER with different certificate chain lengths and different security levels. PRIME256V1, SECP384R1, SECP521R1 are curves for ECDH.

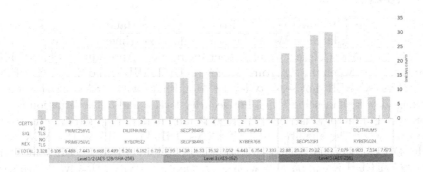

Fig. 8. Elapsed time in milliseconds for a TLS handshake on LAN, comparing ECD-SA/ECDH and DILITHIUM/KYBER with different certificate chain lengths and different security levels. PRIME256V1, SECP384R1, SECP521R1 are curves for ECDH.

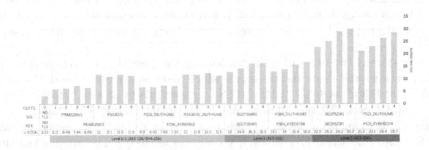

Fig. 9. Elapsed time in milliseconds for a TLS handshake on LAN, comparing ECD-SA/ECDH and DILITHIUM/KYBER in hybrid mode, with different certificate chain lengths and different NIST security levels. Each hybrid combines a classic and a quantum-safe algorithm. P256_DILITHIUM2 (resp. P256_KYBER512) stands for 256-bit ECDSA (resp. ECDH) together with DILITHIUM2 (resp. KYBER512).

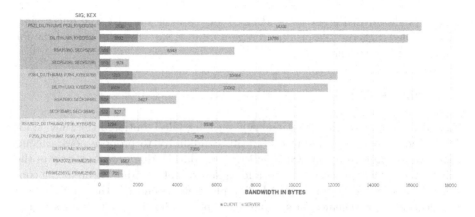

Fig. 10. Bandwidth of the TLS handshake, i.e., the amount of bytes that is exchanged during the handshake by the client (in blue) and the server (in yellow). Algorithms are grouped by NIST security levels, from low level (light gray) to high level (dark gray). (Color figure online)

quantum-safe schemes have much larger sizes for keys, ciphertexts and signature texts. This result confirms that lattice-based crypto is a promising option for TLS as they offer an acceptable trade-off between running time and bandwidth. However, quantum-safe algorithms are still being analyzed by the cryptographic community for their security. One aspect that is not clear yet is their resistance to side-channel attacks. Moreover, the standardization process is still ongoing.

We also evaluated database query after quantum-safe TLS Handshake. Using network traffic analyzers, we first checked the traffic for being indeed encrypted as expected. That is, the analyzers display the traffic as plaintext when TLS is not used, but show only TLS metadata when the traffic is encrypted with TLS. For the actual data in the database, we have the choice between applying pgbench or using test data. pgbench is a PostgreSQL built-in tool, that allows to run benchmark tests. It can be used to generate a database with four tables,

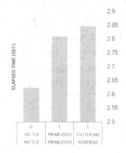

Fig. 11. Elapsed time in seconds for querying the database and receiving a result of size 100 MB, with activated and deactivated TLS.

insert random data and send queries to the database. Since the query phase happens after the TLS handshake, the query communication is encrypted symmetrically using AES. Therefore, the only difference between quantum-weak and quantum-safe for this phase is the length of the encryption key. However, we were still interested in measuring the overhead of quantum-safe TLS versus non-TLS (i.e., insecure communication). Our experiments showed that this overhead is small. As shown in Fig. 11 for a SELECT query with 100 MB, the query time with enabled TLS on LAN is on average around 2.8 s, while the query time for disabled TLS is around 2.6 s.

6   Related Work

To address the quantum threat on cryptography, NIST initiated the PQC standardization process by calling the crypto community to propose new schemes that are quantum-resistant [18]. The PQC standardization process is now in the third round, in which seven finalists and eight alternate candidates are being considered for standardization [20]. NIST is planning to end the third round soon by selecting a few schemes for standardization and allowing a few other schemes to move to a fourth round. Since current quantum-safe signature schemes have either large keys or larger signature text, they do not fit for every application. After the third round, NIST will therefore call for general-purpose signature schemes that are not based on structured lattices. In PQC, there are basically two main lines of work, namely designing schemes [6,7,9,12,15,17,26,30] or crypto-analyzing them [2,3,16,27], and experimenting with those schemes by integrating them into applications, or rather migrating applications to quantum-safe schemes. NIST will also provide guidance for transition. The NCCoE is a part of NIST, which is a collaborative hub for industry, government and academia to work together on the most pressing cybersecurity issues. The NCCoE has initiated the development of practices to ease migration from quantum-weak to quantum-safe schemes [21]. In [33], Stebila and Mosca proposed a library for PQC and its integration into standard libraries such as OpenSSL and OpenSSH. Paul et al. integrated PQC into WolfSSL and investigated a migration strategy that consists of using mixed certificate chains [23]. Other works have targeted specific use cases by including PQC in cyber-physical systems [25]. Our work is also experimental and targets another application, namely databases. We rely on [33] to integrate PQC in the secure communication of PostgreSQL.

7   Conclusion

In this work, we integrated PQC algorithms into PostgreSQL and experimentally assessed the performance of quantum-safe TLS handshake and query. In our evaluation, we focused on lattice-based schemes and considered different security levels as well as various certificate chain lengths. Moreover, we conducted our experiments under realistic conditions, i.e., LAN and WAN. Our results confirm that lattice-based schemes are promising, but come with significantly higher communication overhead. In future work, we will consider other quantum-safe algorithms, but also other test cases, such as stress tests, side-channel analysis, mutual authentication, and mixed certificate chains. Moreover, we will also consider integrating PQC into other crypto functionalities of PostgreSQL, including PGP, or even other types of applications that rely on cryptography.

A   Results for the WAN Setting

Figures 12, 13 and 14 show the elapsed time for a TLS Handshake in a WAN with 140 ms network latency. Figure 12 illustrates the case when the signature is RSA vs. DILITHIUM and the KEX/KEM is ECDH vs. KYBER. For security level 1, the handshake with RSA/ECDH is comparable to PQC, except for certificate chains with a length of 4, where PQC is a little slower. For security level 3, the handshake with RSA/ECDH is faster for certificate chain lengths of 1 and 2, and slower for lengths 3 and 4. At level 5, Handshake with RSA/ECDH is slower than PQC. Figure 13 illustrates the case when the signature is ECDSA vs. DILITHIUM and the KEX/KEM is ECDH vs. KYBER. With security level 1, the handshake with ECDSA/ECDH is comparable to RSA/ECDH, i.e., also comparable to PQC except for certificate chains with a length of 4, where PQC is a little slower. At security level 3, we observe comparable performance for certificate chain lengths 1 and 2, and a faster ECDSA/ECDH handshake for certificate chain lengths 3 and 5. Concerning level 5, Handshake with ECDSA/ECDH is a little faster than PQC. Figure 14 illustrates the case when the signature is RSA/ECDSA vs. Hybrids and the KEX/KEM is ECDH vs. Hybrids. As for the LAN case, we consider hybrids with combined algorithms at the same security level (e.g.: ECDSA-DILITHIUM, RSA-DILITHIUM, ECDH-KYBER) and the result is comparable to the results in Figs. 12 and 13.

We remark that, in the WAN setting, the handshake with PQC is a little slower than using classic algorithms. This is different in the LAN setting. We attribute this difference to the larger communication size that needs to be sent over a long distance. That is, the communication overhead of the handshake with PQC is noticeable in the WAN but not in the LAN setting.

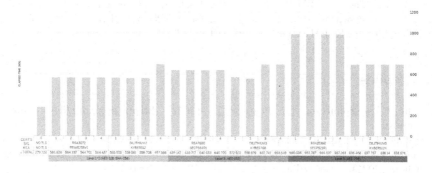

Fig. 12. Elapsed time in milliseconds for a TLS handshake on WAN, comparing RSA/ECDH and DILITHIUM/KYBER with different certificate chain lengths and different security levels. PRIME256V1, SECP384R1, SECP521R1 are curves for ECDH.

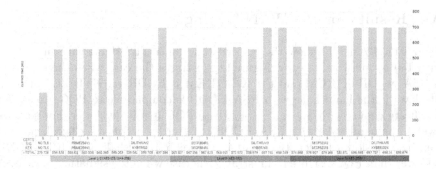

Fig. 13. Elapsed time in milliseconds for a TLS handshake on WAN, comparing ECD-SA/ECDH and DILITHIUM/KYBER with different certificate chain lengths and different security levels. PRIME256V1, SECP384R1, SECP521R1 are curves for ECDH.

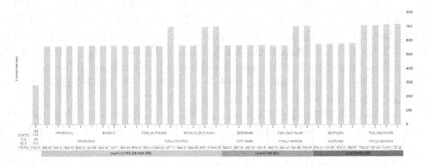

Fig. 14. Elapsed time in milliseconds for a TLS handshake on WAN, comparing ECD-SA/ECDH and DILITHIUM/KYBER in hybrid mode, with different certificate chain lengths and different NIST security levels. Each hybrid combines a classic and a quantum-safe algorithm. P256_DILITHIUM2 (resp. P256_KYBER512) stands for 256-bit ECDSA (resp. ECDH) together with DILITHIUM2 (resp. KYBER512).

References

1. The C++ connector for PostgreSQL (2022). http://pqxx.org/development/libpqxx/
2. Beullens, W.: Improved cryptanalysis of UOV and rainbow. In: Canteaut, A., Standaert, F.-X. (eds.) EUROCRYPT 2021. LNCS, vol. 12696, pp. 348–373. Springer, Cham (2021). https://doi.org/10.1007/978-3-030-77870-5_13
3. Beullens, W.: Breaking rainbow takes a weekend on a laptop. Cryptology ePrint Archive, Report 2022/214 (2022). https://ia.cr/2022/214
4. Boneh, D., Shoup, V.: A graduate course in applied cryptography (2017). https://crypto.stanford.edu/~dabo/cryptobook/
5. Chen, C., Danba, O., Hoffstein, J., et al.: NTRU algorithm specifications and supporting documentation (2019). https://pq-crystals.org/kyber/data/kyber-specification-round3-20210804.pdf

6. D'Anvers, J., Karmakar, A., Roy, S.S., Vercauteren, F.: Saber: module-LWR based key exchange, CPA-secure encryption and CCA-secure KEM. In: Proceedings of Progress in Cryptology - AFRICACRYPT 2018–10th International Conference on Cryptology in Africa, Marrakesh, Morocco, 7–9 May 2018, pp. 282–305 (2018). https://doi.org/10.1007/978-3-319-89339-6_16
7. Jao, D., Azarderakhsh, R., et al.: Supersingular isogeny key encapsulation (2020). https://sike.org/files/SIDH-spec.pdf
8. Diffie, W., Hellman, M.E.: New directions in cryptography. IEEE Trans. Inform. Theory **22**(6), 644–654 (1976)
9. Ding, J., Schmidt, D.: Rainbow, a new multivariable polynomial signature scheme. In: Proceedings of Applied Cryptography and Network Security, Third International Conference, ACNS 2005, New York, NY, USA, 7–10 June 2005, pp. 164–175 (2005). https://doi.org/10.1007/11496137_12
10. ElGamal, T.: A public key cryptosystem and a signature scheme based on discrete logarithms. In: Blakley, G.R., Chaum, D. (eds.) CRYPTO 1984. LNCS, vol. 196, pp. 10–18. Springer, Heidelberg (1985). https://doi.org/10.1007/3-540-39568-7_2
11. Goldreich, O.: Foundations of Cryptography: Volume 2, Basic Applications. Cambridge University Press, New York (2004)
12. Aumasson, J.-P., Bernstein, D.J., et al.: SPHINCS+- submission to the 3rd round of the NIST post-quantum project (2020). https://sphincs.org/data/sphincs+-round3-specification.pdf
13. Koblitz, N.: Elliptic curve cryptosystems. Math. Comput. **48**(177), 203–209 (1987)
14. Koblitz, N., Menezes, A., Vanstone, S.A.: The state of elliptic curve cryptography. Des. Codes Cryptogr. **19**(2/3), 173–193 (2000)
15. Ducas, L., Kiltz, E., Lepoint, T., et al.: Crystals-dilithium - algorithm specifications and supporting documentation (version 3.1) (2021). https://pq-crystals.org/dilithium/data/dilithium-specification-round3-20210208.pdf
16. Marzougui, S., Ulitzsch, V., Tibouchi, M., et al.: Profiling side-channel attacks on dilithium: A small bit-fiddling leak breaks it all. Cryptology ePrint Archive, Report 2022/106 (2022). https://ia.cr/2022/106
17. McEliece, R.J.: A public-key cryptosystem based on algebraic coding theory. The Deep Space Network Progress Report DSN PR 42-44. NASA (1978). https://tmo.jpl.nasa.gov/progress_report2/42-44/44N.PDF
18. NIST: Post-quantum cryptography (2016). https://csrc.nist.gov/projects/post-quantum-cryptography
19. NIST: Submission requirements and evaluation criteria for the post-quantum cryptography standardization process (2016). https://csrc.nist.gov/CSRC/media/Projects/Post-Quantum-Cryptography/documents/call-for-proposals-final-dec-2016.pdf
20. NIST: Status report on the second round of the NIST post-quantum cryptography standardization process (2020). https://nvlpubs.nist.gov/nistpubs/ir/2020/NIST.IR.8309.pdf
21. NIST NCCoE: Migration to post-quantum cryptography project description draft (2021). https://www.nccoe.nist.gov/publications/project-description/migration-post-quantum-cryptography-project-description-draft
22. Ott, D., Peikert, C., et al.: Identifying research challenges in post quantum cryptography migration and cryptographic agility. CoRR abs/1909.07353 (2019). http://arxiv.org/abs/1909.07353
23. Paul, S., Kuzovkova, Y., Lahr, N., et al.: Mixed certificate chains for the transition to post-quantum authentication in TLS 1.3. Cryptology ePrint Archive, Report 2021/1447 (2021). https://ia.cr/2021/1447

24. Paul, S., Niethammer, M.: On the importance of cryptographic agility for industrial automation. at - Automatisierungstechnik **67**(5), 402–416 (2019). https://doi.org/10.1515/auto-2019-0019. https://www.degruyter.com/document/doi/10.1515/auto-2019-0019/html

25. Paul, S., Scheible, P.: Towards post-quantum security for cyber-physical systems: integrating PQC into industrial M2M communication. In: Chen, L., Li, N., Liang, K., Schneider, S. (eds.) ESORICS 2020. LNCS, vol. 12309, pp. 295–316. Springer, Cham (2020). https://doi.org/10.1007/978-3-030-59013-0_15

26. Fouque, P.-A., Hoffstein, J., Kirchner, P., et al.: Falcon: fast-fourier lattice-based compact signatures over NTRU (2020). https://falcon-sign.info/falcon.pdf

27. Ravi, P., Jhanwar, M.P., Howe, J., et al.: Side-channel assisted existential forgery attack on Dilithium - a NIST PQC candidate. Cryptology ePrint Archive, Report 2018/821 (2018). https://ia.cr/2018/821

28. Rescorla, E.: The Transport Layer Security (TLS) Protocol Version 1.3. RFC 8446, August 2018. 10.17487/RFC8446. https://www.rfc-editor.org/info/rfc8446

29. Rivest, R.L., Shamir, A., Adleman, L.: A method for obtaining digital signatures and public-key cryptosystems. Commun. ACM **21**(2), 120–126 (1978)

30. Avanzi, R., Bos, J., Ducas, L., et al.: Crystals-kyber (version 3.02) - submission to round 3 of the NIST post-quantum project (2021). https://pq-crystals.org/kyber/data/kyber-specification-round3-20210804.pdf

31. Shor, P.W.: Algorithms for quantum computation: Discrete logarithms and factoring. In: 35th Annual Symposium on Foundations of Computer Science, Santa Fe, New Mexico, USA, 20–22 November 1994, pp. 124–134 (1994). https://doi.org/10.1109/SFCS.1994.365700

32. Shor, P.W.: Polynominal time algorithms for discrete logarithms and factoring on a quantum computer. In: Proceedings of Algorithmic Number Theory, First International Symposium, ANTS-I, Ithaca, NY, USA, 6–9 May 1994, p. 289 (1994). https://doi.org/10.1007/3-540-58691-1_68

33. Stebila, D., Mosca, M.: Post-quantum key exchange for the internet and the open quantum safe project. In: Selected Areas in Cryptography - SAC 2016–23rd International Conference, St. John's, NL, Canada, 10–12 August 2016, Revised Selected Papers, pp. 14–37 (2016). https://doi.org/10.1007/978-3-319-69453-5_2

34. psycopg2 - python-postgresql database adapter (2021). https://pypi.org/project/psycopg2/

35. The PostgreSQL Global Development Group: Postgresql 14.2 documentation (2022). https://www.postgresql.org/files/documentation/pdf/14/postgresql-14-A4.pdf

Feel the Quantum Functioning: Instantiating Generic Multi-Input Functional Encryption from Learning with Errors

Alexandros Bakas$^{(\boxtimes)}$, Antonis Michalas, Eugene Frimpong, and Reyhaneh Rabaninejad

Tampere University of Technology, Tampere, Finland
{alexandros.bakas,antonios.michalas,eugene.frimpong,
reyhaneh.rabbaninejad}@tuni.fi

Abstract. Functional Encryption (FE) allows users who hold a specific decryption key, to learn a specific function of encrypted data while the actual plaintexts remain private. While FE is still in its infancy, it is our strong belief that in the years to come, this remarkable cryptograhic primitive will have matured to a degree that will make it an integral part of access-control systems, especially cloud-based ones. To this end, we believe it is of great importance to not only provide theoretical and generic constructions but also concrete instantiations of FE schemes from well-studied cryptographic assumptions. Therefore, in this paper, we undertake the task of presenting two instantiations of the generic work presented in [5] from the Decisional Diffie-Hellman (DDH) problem that also satisfy the property of verifiable decryption. Moreover, we present a novel multi-input FE (MIFE) scheme, that can be instantiated from Regev's cryptosystem, and thus remains secure even against quantum adversaries. Finally, we provide a multi-party computation (MPC) protocol that allows our MIFE construction to be deployed in the multi-client model.

Keywords: Functional Encryption · Learning With Errors · Multi-Party Computation · Verifiable Decryption

1 Introduction

In contrast to traditional cryptographic techniques, Functional Encryption (FE) is an emerging cryptographic primitive enabling selective computations over

This work was partially funded from the Technology Innovation Institute (TII), Abu Dhabi, United Arab Emirates, for the project ARROWSMITH: Living (Securely) on the edge.
This work was partially funded by the Harpocrates project, Horizon Europe.

© IFIP International Federation for Information Processing 2022
Published by Springer Nature Switzerland AG 2022
S. Sural and H. Lu (Eds.): DBSec 2022, LNCS 13383, pp. 279–299, 2022.
https://doi.org/10.1007/978-3-031-10684-2_16

encrypted data. FE has been described [8] as generalized public-key cryptography that offers modern encryption capabilities such as cryptographic access control through Attribute-Based Encryption (ABE) [18] where the decryption algorithm results vary according to the decryption key used each time. Each decryption key sk_f is connected to a function f. Unlike traditional public-key cryptography, the use of sk_f on a ciphertext $\mathsf{Enc}(x)$ does *not* recover x but a function $f(x)$. In this way, the actual value x remains private. A more recent work [14] has introduced the general and promising notion of multi-input FE (MIFE). Here, when ciphertexts $\mathsf{Enc}(x_1), \ldots, \mathsf{Enc}(x_n)$ are provided, sk_f can be used to recover $f(x_1, \ldots, x_n)$. MIFE appears to be a perfect match for real-life applications, particularly cloud-based, as multiple users store large volumes of data in remote and possibly corrupted entities. However, the majority of research in the topic revolves around building *generic* schemes that do not support specific functions except for sums [5], inner-products [1–3] and quadratic polynomials [19]. Though practically FE could lead to innovative, hands-on and creative applications, it still fails to meet those goals. We are persuaded that FE is of great importance and that only a group of modern encryption schemes can lead us into an uncharted technological terrain. We hence attempted to narrow inconsistencies between theory and practice.

Quantum-Secure Constructions: Along with the numerous advantages that technological evolution has to offer, it is no secret that we are slowly moving towards quantum age, where quantum computers will eventually replace today's digital machines. Quantum computers should not be seen simply as *more powerful supercomputers* since they represent a whole new paradigm in computing. In particular, quantum computers are, at least in theory, capable of performing computations not attainable by traditional computer, no matter their processing power. To this end, it is important to start replacing quantum-vulnerable mathematical problems, used in traditional public-key encryption, with mathematical problems that are believed to be intractable from both classical and quantum machines. As a result, over the past years, researchers have begun showing great interest in designing encryption schemes based on such problems. This is particularly evident in the case of Homomorphic Encryption [13], where state-of-the-art constructions rely on the hardness assumption of the *"Learning with Errors"* (LWE) problem and its variation over rings of polynomials in finite fields (RLWE) [9,11]. With this in mind, in this paper we present a detailed construction of a MIFE scheme that can be instantiated from a public-key encryption scheme that remains secure under the LWE hardness assumption.

Contributions Our contribution can be summarized as follows:

C1: The first contribution of this paper is an instantiation of the MIFE scheme presented in [5] from the Decisional Diffie-Hellman Problem (DDH). Our instantiation is based on a variation of the ElGamal cryptosystem [12], called additively homomorphic ElGamal, whose IND-CPA security is proven under the hardness assumption of DDH.

C2: We prove that our instantiation from DDH satisfies the property of verifiable decryption in a zero-knowledge fashion. In particular, using our DDH instantiation, a user can verify that the functional decryption was honestly computed without having access to the decryption key. This is extremely important in cases where the decryptor is an untrusted third party such as a Cloud Service Provider (CSP). Satisfying the property of verifiable decryption in FE, is an important step towards assuming stronger threat models, by removing trust from, traditionally, fully trusted entities.

C3: The main contribution of our work is a modified version of the generic scheme from [5] that can be instantiated from LWE. More precisely, similarly to [5], the main building block of our modified scheme is an IND-CPA secure public-key encryption scheme PKE. However, our work shows that Regev's cryptosystem can be used as the PKE. While this modification may seem like a trivial extension, it needs to be treated carefully, because, in contrast to [5], where the multiplication of the public keys (and the ciphertexts) is feasible, in Regev's cryptosystem the public keys are non-squared matrices of equal dimensions, therefore multiplication is not possible. To overcome this challenge, we provide novel definitions and properties in the place of *Linear Key Homomorphism* (LKH) and *Linear Ciphertext Homomorphism* (LCH) used in [5]. Finally, we present a formal security proof for our novel construction.

C4: We also present a secure Multi-Party Computation (MPC) that can be used as a generic compiler that turns a single-client MIFE, whose functional decryption key is formed as a linear combination of n different secret keys, to a multi-client one. The idea is that instead of having one user generating n public/private key pairs (pk_i, sk_i), to distribute the process to n different users where each user generates a unique (pk_i, sk_i). Then, using our MPC construction, users cooperate with each other and send a masked version of the functional decryption key to an untrusted third party, responsible for executing functional decryption. Upon reception the untrusted party can recover the functional decryption key without learning anything about each individual sk_i, assuming that at least two users are honest.

2 Related Work

The most direct ancestor of FE is undoubtedly ABE. In [18], Sahai and Waters presented a ground-breaking idea according to which the data owner could express how they wish to share data directly in the encryption algorithm. In particular, the data owner would provide a predicate f[1] describing how the data will be shared. Moreover, each user would receive a list of credentials L. Then, decryption of a ciphertext encrypted with predicate f is possible if and only if $f(L) = 1$. Functional encryption was then formalized as a generalization of public-key encryption in [18] and [8]. Since then, numerous studies with general definitions and generic constructions of FE have been proposed [14,15,17,20].

---

[1] In mathematical logic, a predicate is a function that tests for some condition involving its arguments and returns 1 si the condition is true and 0 otherwise.

Despite the promising works published, there is a clear lack of research proposing FE schemes to support specific functions. This step would be necessary to allow FE to transcend its limitations and provide the foundations to reach its full potential. To the best of our knowledge, currently the number of supported functionalities is limited to sums [4–6], inner products [1–3] and quadratic polynomials [19]. In this work, we fist present an instantiation from DDH for the generic scheme presented in [5] and then we propose a MIFE scheme for the sum of a vector's components that can be instantiated from LWE.

3 Preliminaries

Notation. If $\mathcal{Y}$ is a set, we use $y \xleftarrow{\$} \mathcal{Y}$ if y is chosen uniformly at random from $\mathcal{Y}$. The cardinality of a set $\mathcal{Y}$ is denoted by $|\mathcal{Y}|$. For a positive integer m, $[m]$ denotes the set $\{1, \ldots, m\}$. Vectors are denoted in bold as $\mathbf{x} = [x_1, \ldots, x_n]$. A PPT adversary $\mathcal{ADV}$ is a randomized algorithm for which there exists a polynomial $p(z)$ such that for all input z, the running time of $\mathcal{ADV}(z)$ is bounded by $p(|z|)$. A function $negl(\cdot)$ is called negligible if $\forall c \in \mathbb{N}, \exists \epsilon_0 \in \mathbb{N}$ such that $\forall \epsilon \geq \epsilon_0 : negl(\epsilon) < \epsilon^{-c}$.

3.1 Public-Key Encryption

Definition 1 (Public-Key Encryption Scheme). *A public-key encryption scheme* PKE *for a message space* $\mathcal{M}$, *consists of three algorithms* PKE = (Gen, Enc, Dec). *A* PKE *scheme is said to be correct if:*

$$Pr[\mathsf{Dec}(\mathsf{sk}, c) \neq m \mid [(\mathsf{pk}, \mathsf{sk}) \leftarrow \mathsf{Setup}(1^\lambda)] \wedge [m \in \mathcal{M}] \wedge [c \leftarrow \mathsf{Enc}(\mathsf{pk}, m)]] = negl(\lambda)$$

Definition 2 (selective-Indistinguishability-Based Security). *Let* PKE *be a public-key encryption scheme. We define the following experiments:*

$Exp^{s-IND-CPA-\beta}(\mathcal{ADV})$

Initialize(λ, x_0, x_1)
$(\mathsf{pk}, \mathsf{sk}) \xleftarrow{\$} \mathsf{Gen}(1^\lambda)$
Return pk
Challenge()
$c_\beta \xleftarrow{\$} \mathsf{Enc}(\mathsf{pk}, m_\beta)$

Finalize(β')
$\beta' = \beta$

The advantage ϵ of $\mathcal{ADV}$ is defined as:

$$\epsilon = \left| Pr[Exp^{s-ind-CPA-0}(\mathcal{ADV}) = 1 - Pr[Exp^{s-ind-CPA-1}(\mathcal{ADV}) = 1] \right|$$

We say that PKE *is s-IND-CPA-β secure if*

$$\epsilon = negl(\lambda)$$

Definition 3 (Linear Ciphertext Homomorphism (LCH)). *We say that a* PKE *scheme has linear ciphertext homomorphism if:*

$$\prod_{i=1}^{n} \mathsf{Enc}(\mathsf{pk}_i, x_i)$$

$$= \mathsf{Enc}\left(\prod_{i=1}^{n} \mathsf{pk}_i, \sum_{i=1}^{n} x_i\right)$$

Definition 4 (Linear Key Homomorphism (LKH)). *Let* $(\mathsf{pk}_1, \mathsf{sk}_1)$ *and* $(\mathsf{pk}_2, \mathsf{sk}_2)$ *be two public/private key pairs that have been generated using* PKE.Gen. *We say that* PKE *has linear key homomorphism if* $\mathsf{sk}_1 + \mathsf{sk}_2$ *is a private key to a public key computed as* $\mathsf{pk}_1 \cdot \mathsf{pk}_2$.

A direct result of Definitions 3 and 4 is that if a PKE scheme is linear ciphertext and key homomorphic, then the public keys of PKE live in multiplicative group $\mathbb{G}_{pub} = (\mathbb{G}, \cdot, 1_{\mathbb{G}_{pub}})$ and the private keys in an additive group $\mathbb{H}_{priv} = (\mathbb{H}, +, 0_{\mathbb{H}_{priv}})$.

3.2   Multi-Input Functional Encryption

Definition 5 (Multi-Input Functional Encryption). *A Multi-Input Functional Encryption scheme MIFE for a message space* $\mathcal{M}$ *is a tuple MIFE = (*Setup, Enc, KeyGen, Dec*) such that:*

- Setup(1^λ): *The* Setup *algorithm is a probabilistic algorithm that on input the security parameter* λ, *outputs a master public/private key pair* (mpk, msk).
- Enc(mpk, x): *The encryption algorithm* Enc *is a probabilistic algorithm that on input the master public key* mpk *and a message* $\mathbf{x} = \{x_1, \ldots, x_n\} \in \mathcal{M}$, *outputs a ciphertext* $\mathbf{c} = \{c_1, \ldots, c_n\}$.
- KeyGen(msk, f): *The key generation algorithm* KeyGen *is a deterministic algorithm that on input the master secret key* msk *and a function* f, *outputs a functional key* sk_f.
- Dec(sk_f, c): *The decryption algorithm* Dec *is a deterministic algorithm that on input a functional key* sk_f *and a ciphertext* $\mathbf{c}$, *outputs* $f(x_1, \ldots, x_n)$.

A MIFE scheme is said to be correct if:

$$Pr[\mathsf{Dec}(\mathsf{sk}_f, \mathbf{c}) \neq f(\mathbf{x}) \mid [(\mathsf{mpk}, \mathsf{msk}) \leftarrow \mathsf{Setup}(1^\lambda)]$$
$$\wedge [\mathbf{c} \leftarrow \mathsf{Enc}(\mathsf{mpk}, \mathbf{x})] \wedge [\mathsf{sk}_f \leftarrow \mathsf{KeyGen}(\mathsf{msk}, f)]] = negl(\lambda)$$

Just like in the case of PKE we base our security definition on the selective-IND-CPA formalization:

Definition 6 (MIFE Indistinguishanility-Based Security). *For a MIFE scheme MIFE = (Setup, Enc, KeyGen, Dec) we define the following experiments:*

$Exp^{s-IND-FE-CPA-\beta}(\mathcal{ADV})$

Initialize(λ, x_0, x_1)

mpk, msk $\xleftarrow{\$}$ Setup(1^λ)

$L \leftarrow \emptyset$

Output mpk

Key Generation(f)

$\overline{L \leftarrow L \cup \{f\}}$

sk$_f \xleftarrow{\$}$ KeyGen(msk, f)

Output sk$_f$

Challenge()

$c_\beta \xleftarrow{\$}$ Enc(mpk, x_β)

Finalize(β')

If $\exists f \in L$:

$f(x_0) \neq f(x_1)$

Output $\perp$

Else

$\beta' = \beta$

The advantage ϵ of $\mathcal{ADV}$ is defined as:

$$\epsilon = \left| Pr[Exp^{s-ind-FE-CPA-0}(\mathcal{ADV}) = 1 - Pr[Exp^{s-ind-FE-CPA-1}(\mathcal{ADV}) = 1] \right|$$

We say that MIFE is s-IND-FE-CPA-β secure iff $\epsilon = negl(\lambda)$

3.3 Background on LWE

For a real number $x \in \mathbb{R}$, we denote by $\lfloor x \rfloor$ the largest integer not greater than x and by $\lfloor x \rceil = \lfloor x + 1/2 \rfloor$ the integer closest to x with ties broken upward.

Definition 7 (Hermite Normal Form (HNF)). *Let $A \in \mathbb{Z}_q^{n \times m}$. Assume that the leftmost n columns $A_1 \in \mathbb{Z}_q^{n \times n}$ of $A = [A_1 | A_2] \in \mathbb{Z}_q^{n \times m}$ form an invertible matrix over $\mathbb{Z}_q$. We can then replace A with its HNF as:*

$$A_1^{-1} \cdot A = [I_n | \overline{A} = A_1^{-1} \cdot A_2] \tag{1}$$

Definition 8 (LWE Distribution). *Let $\mathcal{G}$ be a discrete Gaussian of width $\kappa \cdot q$ for some $\kappa < 1$ (error rate). For a vector $s \in \mathbb{Z}_q^n$ called the secret, the LWE distribution $\mathcal{D}$ over $\mathbb{Z}_q^n \times \mathbb{Z}_q$ is sampled by choosing $a \in \mathbb{Z}_q^n$ uniformly at random, choosing $e \leftarrow \mathcal{G}$ and outputting $(a, b = \langle s, a \rangle + e \mod q)$.*

Definition 9 (Decision-LWE). *Given m independent samples $(a_i, b_i) \in \mathbb{Z}_q^n \times \mathbb{Z}_q$, where every sample is sampled either from $\mathcal{D}$ or from the uniform distribution, distinguish which is the case with non-negligible advantage.*

Regev's Cryptosystem. Regev's cryptosytem is parametrized by an LWE dimension n, a modulus q and an error distribution $\mathcal{G}$ over $\mathbb{Z}$. Note that public-keys are $\widetilde{O}(n^2)$ bits and ciphertexts $\widetilde{O}(n)$ bits where the $\widetilde{O}$ notation ignores logarithmic factors.

- The private key is a uniformly random LWE secret $s \in \mathbb{Z}^n$, and the public key is m samples $(\overline{\mathbf{a_i}}, b_i = \langle \mathbf{s}, \overline{\mathbf{a_i}} \rangle + e_i) \in \mathbb{Z}_q^{n+1}$ drawn from $\mathcal{D}$ and collected as the columns of a matrix

$$A = \begin{bmatrix} \overline{A} \\ b^T \end{bmatrix} \in \mathbb{Z}_q^{(n+1) \times m} \tag{2}$$

By definition, the private and the public keys satisfy the relation:

$$(-\mathbf{s}, 1)^T \cdot A = \mathbf{e}^T \approx 0 (\mod q) \tag{3}$$

- To encrypt a bit $m \in \mathbb{Z}_2$ using the public key A, a user first chooses a uniformly random $\mathbf{r} \in \{0, 1\}^m$ and outputs:

$$\mathbf{c} = A \cdot \mathbf{r} + \left(0, m \cdot \left\lfloor \frac{q}{2} \right\rfloor\right) \in \mathbb{Z}_q^{n+1} \tag{4}$$

- To decrypt a ciphertext using a secret key $\mathbf{s}$ the user computes:

$$
\begin{aligned}
(-\mathbf{s}, 1)^T \cdot \mathbf{c} \\
&= (-\mathbf{s}, 1)^T \cdot A \cdot r + m \cdot \left\lfloor \frac{q}{2} \right\rfloor \\
&= \mathbf{e}^T \cdot r + m \cdot \left\lfloor \frac{q}{2} \right\rfloor \\
&\approx m \cdot \left\lfloor \frac{q}{2} \right\rfloor (\mod q)
\end{aligned}
\tag{5}
$$

where the relations holds because $\mathbf{s}, \mathbf{e}^T$ and $\mathbf{r}$ are small. Upon calculating $m \cdot \left\lfloor \frac{q}{2} \right\rfloor$ the user simply checks whether the result is close to 0 or 1.

In [16] Regev proved that his cryptosystem is semantically secure, assuming that the decision LWE is hard. More specifically, Regev proved that the hardness of decision LWE is implied by the worst-case quantum hardness of lattice problems.

4   Base Construction

In this Section, we briefly recall the generic construction from [5].

Construction. Let PKE = (Gen, Enc, Dec) be an IND-CPA secure cryptosystem, that also fulfils the LCH and LKE properties. Then define MIFE as MIFE = (Setup, Enc, KeyGen, Dec) where:

1. Setup($1^\lambda, n$): The setup algorithm invokes the PKE's key generation algorithm Gen and generates n public/private key pairs as $(pk_1, sk_1), (pk_2, sk_2) \ldots$, (pk_n, sk_n). The public keys are then used to create and output a master public/private key pair (mpk, msk), where mpk = (params, $pk_1, \ldots, pk_n$) and msk = $(sk_1, \ldots, sk_n)^2$.

---

[2] The public parameters params depend on the choice of the PKE scheme.

2. $\mathsf{Enc}(\mathsf{mpk}, \mathbf{x})$: The encryption algorithm Enc, takes as input the master public key mpk and a vector $\mathbf{x}$ and outputs $\mathbf{c} = \{c_1, \ldots, c_n\}$, where $c_i = \mathsf{Enc}(\mathsf{pk}_i, x_i)$.
3. $\mathsf{KeyGen}(\mathsf{msk})$: The key generation algorithm, takes as input the master secret key msk and outputs a functional key sk as $\mathsf{sk} = \sum_1^n \mathsf{sk}_i{}^3$.
4. $\mathsf{Dec}(\mathsf{sk}, \mathbf{c})$: The decryption algorithm takes as input the functional key sk and an encrypted vector $\mathbf{c}$ and outputs $\mathsf{PKE.Dec}(\mathsf{sk}, \prod_{i=1}^n \mathbf{c})$.

Correctness. Correctness follows directly since:

$$\mathsf{MIFE.Dec}(\mathsf{sk}, \mathbf{c}) = \mathsf{PKE.Dec}\left(\mathsf{sk}, \prod_{i=1}^n \mathsf{PKE.Enc}(\mathsf{pk}_i, x_i)\right)$$

$$= \mathsf{PKE.Dec}\left(\mathsf{sk}, \mathsf{PKE.Enc}(\prod_{i=1}^n \mathsf{pk}_i, \sum_{i=1}^n x_i)\right) = \sum_{i=1}^n x_i$$

where we used the LCH property. Since the LKE property holds, we know that sk is a valid secret key that decrypts $\prod_{i=1}^n \mathbf{c}$.

Theorem 1. *Let* PKE *be an IND-CPA secure public key cryptosystem that is additive key and additive ciphertext homomorphic. Moreover, let* MIFE *be the base Multi-Input Functional Encryption construction from [5] which is obtained though* PKE. *Then* MIFE *is s-IND-FE-CPA secure.*

A detailed proof can be found in [5].

5   Instantiation from DDH

We are now ready to present an instantiation of the generic construction from [5] from DDH. In particular, we will present an instantiation using the Additively Homomorphic El Gamal cryptosystem as the public-key encryption scheme PKE. For the needs of our proof, we rely on the fact that El Gamal remains secure under randomness reuse, as proven in [7].

Theorem 2. *Let* MIFE *be the generic construction from Sect. 4. Then* MIFE *can be instantiated from El Gamal's cryptosystem.*

Proof. It suffices to prove that El Gamal satisfies the LCH and LKH properties defined in Definitions 3 and 4 respectively.

Let q be a prime and $\mathbb{G}$ a group of order q where the DHH assumption is hard. Moreover, let g be a generator of $\mathbb{G}$. Then we have that the private key space is the group $(\mathbb{Z}_q, +, 0_{\mathbb{Z}})$ while the public key space is the group $(\mathbb{G}, \times, 1_{\mathbb{G}})$. Then, an El Gamal ciphertext for a message x is:

$$c = (g^r, \mathsf{pk}^r \cdot g^x)$$

---

[3] We omit the description of the function since in this case we are only focusing on the sum.

where r is a random value used to ensure that the encryption algorithm is probabilistic.

- **LCH:** If Enc is the Encryption algorithm of El Gamal, then we have:

$$\mathsf{Enc}(\mathsf{pk}_1, x_1) \cdot \mathsf{Enc}(\mathsf{pk}_2, x_2) = g^{r\mathsf{sk}_1} g^{x_1} \cdot g^{r\mathsf{sk}_2} g^{x_2} = g^{r(\mathsf{sk}_1 + \mathsf{sk}_2)} \cdot g^{x_1 + x_2}$$
$$= \mathsf{Enc}(\mathsf{pk}_1 \mathsf{pk}_2, x_1 + x_2).$$

- **LKH** In the El Gamal cryptosystem we have that for a public/private key pair $(\mathsf{pk}, \mathsf{sk})$ the following condition holds:

$$\mathsf{pk} = g^{\mathsf{sk}}$$

Let $(\mathsf{pk}_1, \mathsf{sk}_1), (\mathsf{pk}_2, \mathsf{sk}_2)$ be two public/private key pairs for an El Gamal instantiation such that $\mathsf{pk}_1, \mathsf{pk}_2 \in (\mathbb{G}, \cdot, 0_\mathbb{G})$ and $\mathsf{sk}_1, \mathsf{sk}_2 \in (\mathbb{Z}, +, 0_\mathbb{Z})$. Then we have:

$$\mathsf{pk}_1 \cdot \mathsf{pk}_2 = g^{\mathsf{sk}_1} \cdot g^{\mathsf{sk}_2} g^{(\mathsf{sk}_1 + \mathsf{sk}_2)}$$

Moreover, since the groups $(G, \cdot, 0_G)$ and $(Z, +, 0_Z)$ are closed with respect to multiplication and addition operations respectively, we conclude that $(\mathsf{pk}_1 \mathsf{pk}_2, \mathsf{sk}_1 + \mathsf{sk}_2)$ is a valid public/private key pair.

5.1   Verifiable Decryption

As already mentioned, instantiating the generic MIFE construction from Sect. 4 using DDH, allows users to verify the decryption result in an zero-knowledge manner. This is extremely important as it allows us to considers a stronger threat models. In particular, assuming a malicious curator of a cloud database colludes with the CSP, could result to publishing modified statistics in an attempt to mislead data analysts. Hence, we show that an analyst that only possess a function $f(\mathbf{x})$ along with the public parameters of the encryption scheme, can verify that $f(\mathbf{x})$ is indeed the decryption of $\mathsf{Enc}(\mathsf{mpk}, (\mathbf{x} = x_1, \ldots, x_n))$ under the function f, without having access neither to the master secret key, nor the functional decryption key for the underlying function. This is done by simply calculating and verifying the equality of two discrete logarithms. More precisely, and given that the final ElGamal ciphertext is given by:

$$(u, v) = (g^r, \mathsf{pk}^r \cdot g^{f(x)}), \tag{6}$$

the analyst needs to verify that:

$$\log_{\mathsf{pk}} \left[\left(g^{f(x)} \right)^{-1} \cdot \mathsf{pk}^r \cdot g^{f(x)} \right] = \log_g(g^r) \tag{7}$$

as follows:

$$\log_{\mathsf{pk}} \left[\left(g^{f(x)} \right)^{-1} \cdot \mathsf{pk}^r \cdot g^{f(x)} \right] = \log_g(g^r) \Rightarrow \log_{\mathsf{pk}} \left[\frac{1}{g^{f(x)}} g^{f(x)} \cdot \mathsf{pk}^r \right] = \log_g(g^r) \Rightarrow$$
$$\log_{\mathsf{pk}}(\mathsf{pk}^r) = \log_g(g^r) \Rightarrow r = r$$

$$\tag{8}$$

Indeed, it can be seen that if a malicious party tampers with the result $f(x)$ and replaces it with $f(x)'$, then the term $\left(g^{f(x)'}\right)^{-1}$ will not cancel out along with $g^{f(x)}$ and hence, the equality will not hold.

5.2 Instantiation from CL Framework

In the previous section, we presented an additively homomorphic instantiation which was obtained by encoding the message in the exponent of an ElGamal encryption $(g^r, \mathsf{pk}^r \cdot g^{f(x)})$ where g is a generator of a cyclic group $\mathbb{G}$. However, this instantiation only supports a limited (*logarithmic*) number of additions. The reason is that one has to recover $f(x)$ from $g^{f(x)}$ and since Discrete Logarithm (DL) problem must be intractable in $\mathbb{G}$, it is essential to limit the size of message in the exponent to ensure an efficient decryption.

To enable an *unbounded* number of additions modulo prime q from the ciphertexts, Castagnos and Laguillaumie proposed the CL framework [10]. They assume a group $\mathbb{G}$ where the Decisional Diffie-Hellman (DDH) assumption holds and there exists a subgroup $\mathbb{H}$ of $\mathbb{G}$ in which the DL problem is easy. In the introduced cryptosystem, the message space is $\mathbb{Z}_q$, where the prime q can be *scaled* to meet the application needs, as its size is independent of the security parameter.

5.2.1 Background on CL Framework

CL framework is based on a DDH group with an easy DL subgroup which is defined as a pair of algorithms (Gen, Solve) described as:

- CL.Gen($1^\lambda, q$): this algorithm inputs security parameter λ and q as a μ-bit prime for $\lambda \leq \mu$, and outputs public parameters as $\mathsf{pp} = (q, \widehat{\mathbb{G}}, \mathbb{G}, \mathbb{G}^q, \mathbb{H}, \widetilde{s}, g, h, g_q)$, where
  - $\widehat{\mathbb{G}}$ is a finite group of order $\widehat{n} = q \cdot \widehat{s}$, such that $gcd(q, \widehat{s}) = 1$. Besides, $\widetilde{s}$ is defined to be an upper bound for $\widehat{s}$ with the condition that the distribution of $\{g^r, r \xleftarrow{\$} \{0, \ldots \widetilde{s} \cdot q\}\}$ is computationally indistinguishable from uniform distribution on $\widehat{\mathbb{G}}$.
  - $\mathbb{G}$ is a cyclic group of order $n = q \cdot s$ with generator g, such that s divides $\widehat{s}$.
  - $\mathbb{G}^q := \{x^q | x \in \mathbb{G}\}$ is a cyclic group of order s with generator g_q.
  - $\mathbb{H}$ is a unique cyclic group of order q with generator h, where $g = g_q \cdot h$.
- CL.Solve(q, pp, X): this is a deterministic polynomial time algorithm that solves the DL problem in subgroup $\mathbb{H}$:

$$\Pr\left[x = x' \ \middle| \ \mathsf{pp} \xleftarrow{\$} \mathsf{Gen}(1^\lambda, q), x \xleftarrow{\$} \mathbb{Z}_q, X \leftarrow h^x, x' \leftarrow \mathsf{Solve}(q, \mathsf{pp}, X)\right] = 1,$$

Definition 10 (Hard Subgroup Membership Problem (HSM)). *Let λ be a positive integer and q be a μ-bit prime for $\lambda \leq \mu$. Also* (Gen, Solve) *generates* a DDH group with an easy DL subgroup. The advantage of a PPT adversary $\mathcal{A}$ is defined as:

$$\epsilon = |\text{Pr}\left[b = b' \middle| \begin{array}{l} \text{pp} \xleftarrow{\$} \text{Gen}(1^\lambda, q), x \xleftarrow{\$} \mathcal{D}, x' \xleftarrow{\$} \mathcal{D}_q \\ b \xleftarrow{\$} \{0,1\}, X_0 \leftarrow g^x, X_1 \leftarrow g_q^{x'} \\ b' \leftarrow \mathcal{A}(q, \text{pp}, X_b, \text{Solve}(.)) \end{array}\right] - 1/2|,$$

where distribution $\mathcal{D}$ is such that the distribution of $\{g^x, x \xleftarrow{\$} \mathcal{D}\}$ is computationally indistinguishable from uniform distribution on $\mathbb{G}$ (same for $\mathcal{D}_q, \{g_q^x, x \xleftarrow{\$} \mathcal{D}_q\}$, and $\mathbb{G}^q$). $HSM - CL$ assumption holds for (Gen, Solve), if for all PPT adversay $\mathcal{A}$, $Adv_{\mathcal{A}}^{\text{HSM}-\text{CL}} \leq negl(\lambda)$, where $negl(\lambda)$ is a negligible function.

- CL.KeyGen(pp) this algorithm samples $\alpha \xleftarrow{\$} \mathcal{D}_q$ and computes g_q^α. It then returns the key pair (sk, pk), where sk $:= \alpha$ and pk $:= g_q^\alpha$.
- CL.Enc(pk, m) on input m from the message space $\mathbb{Z}_q$ and the public key, this algorithm samples randomness $r \xleftarrow{\$} \mathcal{D}_q$ and returns $(c_1, c_2) = (g_q^r, h^m \cdot \text{pk}^r)$.
- CL.Dec(sk, (c_1, c_2)) this algorithm computes $M \leftarrow c_2/c_1^{\text{sk}}$. It then runs $m \leftarrow$ Solve(q, pp, M), and returns m.

The CL PKE scheme described above is proven to be semantically secure under chosen plaintext attacks (IND-CPA) under the $HSM - CL$ assumption [10].

Theorem 3. Let MIFE be the generic construction from Sect. 4. Then MIFE can be instantiated from CL.PKE scheme.

Proof is omitted as it is very similar to that of Theorem 2.

6   MIFE for Sums

We will now present a modified version of the base construction from Sect. 4 that can be instantiated from LWE. In particular, our construction will use Regev's cryptosystem as the public-key encryption scheme PKE. For the purposes of our version we first need to define new properties in the place of Definitions 3 and 4. The reason for this is that in Regev's cryptosystem, the public keys (and the ciphertexts) are non-squared matrices of equal dimensions and hence, we cannot define multiplication between two public keys or ciphertexts respectively.

Definition 11 (Additive ciphertext homomorphism (ACH)). *We say that a PKE scheme has additive ciphertext homomorphism if:*

$$\sum_{i=1}^n \text{Enc}(\text{pk}_i, x_i)$$

$$= \text{Enc}\left(\sum_{i=1}^n \text{pk}_i, \sum_{i=1}^n x_i\right)$$

Definition 12 (Additive Key Homomorphism (AKH)). *Let* $(\mathsf{pk}_1, \mathsf{sk}_1)$ *and* $(\mathsf{pk}_2, \mathsf{sk}_2)$ *be two public/private key pairs that have been generated during* PKE.Gen. *We say that* PKE *has additive key homomorphism if* $\mathsf{sk}_1 + \mathsf{sk}_2$ *is a private key to a public key computed as* $\mathsf{pk}_1 + \mathsf{pk}_2$.

Definition 13 (Modified MIFE for the summation of a vector's components (mMIFE)). *Let* PKE $=$ (Gen, Enc, Dec) *be an IND-CPA secure cryptosystem, that also fulfils the ACH and AKE properties. Then we define our* mMIFE *as* mMIFE $=$ (Setup, Enc, KeyGen, Dec) *where:*

1. Setup($1^\lambda, n$): *The* Setup *algorithm invokes the* PKE*'s* Gen *algorithm and generates n public/private key pairs as* $(\mathsf{pk}_1, \mathsf{sk}_1), \ldots, (\mathsf{pk}_n, \mathsf{sk}_n)$. *It outputs a master public/private key pair as* mpk, msk, *where* mpk $=$ (params, $\mathsf{pk}_1, \ldots, \mathsf{pk}_n$) *and* msk $=$ $(\mathsf{sk}_1, \ldots, \mathsf{sk}_n)$.
2. Enc(mpk, $\mathbf{x}$): *The Encryption algorithm* Enc, *takes as input the master public key* mpk *and a vector* $\mathbf{x}$ *and outputs* $\mathbf{c} = \{c_1, \ldots, c_n\}$, *where* $c_i = $ Enc(pk_i, x_i).
3. KeyGen(msk): *The Key Generation algorithm, takes as input the master secret key* msk *and outputs a functional key* sk *as* sk $= \sum_1^n \mathsf{sk}_i$.
4. Dec(sk, $\mathbf{c}$): *The Decryption Algorithm takes as input the functional key* sk *and an encrypted vector* $\mathbf{c}$ *and outputs* PKE.Dec(sk, $\sum_{i=1}^{n} \mathbf{c}$)

Correctness. The correctness of our construction follows directly since:

$$\mathsf{Dec}\,(\mathsf{sk}, \mathbf{c}) = \mathsf{PKE.Dec}\left(\mathsf{sk}, \sum_{i=1}^{n} \mathbf{c}\right) = \mathsf{PKE.Dec}\left(\mathsf{sk}, \sum_{i=1}^{n} \mathsf{PKE.Enc}(\mathsf{pk}_i, x_i)\right)$$

$$= \mathsf{PKE.Dec}\left(\mathsf{sksk}, \mathsf{PKE.Enc}\left(\sum_{i=1}^{n} \mathsf{pk}_i, \sum_{1}^{n} x_i\right)\right) = \sum_{1}^{n} x_i$$

Where we used the ACH property of PKE. Moreover, since the AKH property holds, we know that $\mathsf{sk}_{\|\cdot\|}$ is a valid secret key that decrypts $\sum_{i=1}^{n} \mathbf{c}$.

Theorem 4. *Let* PKE *be an IND-CPA secure public key cryptosystem that is additive key and additive ciphertext homomorphic. Moreover, let* mMIFE_{ℓ_1} *be our modified Multi-Input Functional Encryption scheme for the ℓ_1 norm of a vector space which is obtained though* PKE. *Then* mMIFE_{ℓ_1} *is s-IND-FE-CPA secure.*

Proof Sketch: To prove Theorem 4 we will rely on a combination of the games presented in Definitions 2 and 6. In particular, we assume two algorithms $\mathcal{A}$ and $\mathcal{B}$ are executed simultaneously but independently in which $\mathcal{B}$ is the adversary in game 2 and $\mathcal{A}$ is the both the adversary in game 6 and the challenger in game 6. Hence, $\mathcal{A}$ needs to simulate a perfect view of game 6. We prove that the advantage of $\mathcal{B}$ is bounded by the advantage of $\mathcal{A}$ and hence, if $\mathcal{B}$ wins then $\mathcal{A}$ also wins. However, this contradicts with the assumption that PKE is IND-CPA.

Due to space constrains, the full proof can be found in Appendix A.

6.1   Instantiation from LWE

What remains to be done to show that our novel construction can be instantiated from LWE is prove the following theorem:

Theorem 5. *Let* mMIFE *be our modified construction for the summation of a vector's components. Then our construction can be instantiated using Regev's cryptosystem.*

Proof. To prove our theorem, it suffices to show that Regev's cryptosystem is both additive-ciphertext and key homomorphic. Just like in the case of the DDH instantiation, we rely on the fact that the randomness is shared between users, and hence, two users can use the same randomness to produce their ciphertexts.

ACH. A ciphertext from Regev's cryptosystem is of the form $c = Ar + (0, x \cdot \lfloor \frac{q}{2} \rceil)$. For visual clarification, we can write the above relation as $c = Ar + g(x)$, where $g(x) = x \cdot \left(\lfloor \frac{q}{2} \rceil \right)$. Hence, for two ciphertexts $\mathbf{c_1}, \mathbf{c_2}$ we get:

$$\mathbf{c_1} + \mathbf{c_2} = A_1 r + g(x_1) + A_2 r + g(x_2) = (A_1 + A_2)r + g(x_1 + x_2) \qquad (9)$$

And thus, Regev's cryptosystem is additive ciphertext homomorphic.

AKH. The secret keys on Regev's cryptosystem are samples uniformly from $\mathbb{Z}_q^n$. Since $\mathbb{Z}_q^n$ is closed under addition, we know that $\sum_1^n \mathsf{sk}_i = \sum_1^n \mathbf{s}_i \in \mathbb{Z}_q^n$. What remains to be done, is to show that $\sum_1^n \mathsf{sk}_i$ is a valid private key for a public key of the form $\sum_1^n (A\mathsf{sk}_i + \mathbf{e}_i)$, which is true as long as $\sum_1^n \mathbf{e}_i$ remains small. This can be seen from the fact that a private/public key pair needs to satisfy the following:

$$\left(-\sum_1^n \mathsf{sk}_i, 1 \right)^T \cdot A = \sum_1^n \mathbf{e}^T \approx 0 (\mod q) \qquad (10)$$

Hence, we see that Regev's cryptosystem satisfies both the ACH and AKH properties and as a result, it can be used to instantiate our modified construction mMIFE.

Security of the Instantiation. A direct result of Theorems 4 and 5 is that by instantiating our construction using Regev's cryptosystem, then our scheme is quantum-secure.

7   From Single-Client to Multi-client MIFE

In this section, we present a generic tranformation that tranforms our construction from being solely multi-input to also being multi-client. The main challenge in this setting is the generation of the functional decryption key. Our solution relies on an MPC in which all users input a masked version of their secret key sk_i. Then, they send the masked keys to a central authority, that outputs the functional decryption key as the sum of all sk_i's without learning anything about each individual sk_i. More precisely, the problem we are trying to solve is formally described below:

Probelm Statement 1 (**MIFE$_{\ell_1}$ with Multi-Client Support**). *Let $\mathcal{U} = \{u_1, \ldots, u_n\}$ be a set of users. Each user $u_j \in \mathcal{U}$ generates a public/private key pair $(\mathsf{pk}_j, \mathsf{sk}_j)$ for a public-key encryption scheme satisfying the properties defined in Definitions 3 and 4, and uses pk_j to encrypt a message x_j. Additionally, assume that all generated ciphertexts are outsourced and stored in a remote location operated by an untrusted (i.e. possible malicious) CSP. Furthermore, we assume that an analyst* **A** *(e.g. a user from $\mathcal{U}$) wishes to perform statistics on the data stored on the CSP. Our multi-client construction shows how a legitimate analyst can do this without learning any valuable information about the individual values x_j.*

MPC. Upon request of **A**, each user $u_i \in \mathcal{U}$ generates a random number r_i and breaks it into n shares as $r_i = r_{i,1} + \cdots + r_{i,n}$. Each share will be sent to a different user from the set $\mathcal{U} = \{u_1, \ldots, u_n\}$. Upon receiving $n-1$ different shares, each user u_i mask her private key sk_i as $b_i = \mathsf{sk}_i + r_i - \sum_{j=1}^{n} r_{j,i}$, and sends the masked key to **A**. When **A** has gathered all the masked keys, she computes the functional decryption key sk as $\mathsf{sk} = \sum_1^n \mathsf{b_i}$. The MPC is illustrated in Fig. 1.

MPC

A generates $r_A \xrightarrow{\$} \mathbb{Z}$
A writes r_A as $r_A = r_{i,1} + \cdots + r_{i,n}$
for $j \in [1, n-1]$ **do:**
  Send $r_{i,j}$ to u_j
for $u_j \in \mathcal{U}/\{\mathbf{A}\}$ **do:**
  u_j generates $r_j \xrightarrow{\$} \mathbb{Z}$
  Express r_j as $r_j = r_{j,1} + \cdots + r_{j,n}$
  Send r_{j_i} to $u_i, \forall u_i \in \mathcal{U}/\{\mathbf{A}\}$
  Compute masked version of the key as $b_j = \mathsf{sk}_j + r_j - \sum_{\ell=1}^{n} r_{k_i}$ after having received every share from the rest of the users
  Send b_j to **A**
A computes the functional decryption key as $\sum_1^n b_j = \sum_1^n \mathsf{sk}_j = \mathsf{sk}$

Fig. 1. Functional Decryption Key Generation in the Multi-Client Setting

It is important to highlight that splitting and distributing the random numbers to the different users, allows the users to work in parallel for the MPC and hence, we overcome the limitations that would emerge by using a ring topology.

Theorem 6. *Let $\mathcal{ADV}$ be an adversary that corrupts at most $n-2$ users out of those in $\mathcal{U}$. Then, $\mathcal{ADV}$ cannot infer any information about the secret keys of the legitimate users.*

Due to space constrains, a detailed proof can be found in Appendix B.

8 Experimental Results

In this section, we present a brief evaluation of an implementation of the instance of the generic construction described in Sect. 5. To this end, we implement the core functions of the construction on a standalone Linux machine, and measure the performance when applied to a real dataset. Our evaluations focused on the Setup, Encryption, and KeyGen functions. The experiments described in this section were conducted on an Intel Core i5-8279U CPU @ 2.40 GHz x2 Ubuntu 20.04 Desktop with 2 GB RAM. Additionally, we utilized an Additive EC-Elgamal C library[4] to implement the basic cryptographic operations needed to implement the proposed construction. To closely mimic the multi-party nature of our construction, we perform our experiments on a real-world dataset obtained from the European Centre for Disease Prevention and Control[5], and conduct each experiment 50 times to find an average.

Setup Phase: Experiments in this phase focused on analyzing the processing time for generating a unique pair of keys for each row, and encrypting a specific chosen value on that row. In this instance, we chose the number of *deaths* as our value of interest. In total, the selected dataset has 61901 rows, however to provide a comprehensive evaluation of the setup process, we performed our experiments on a varying number of rows from 10000 to the maximum number of rows. The number of rows directly corresponds to the number of unique key pair and ciphertexts being computed. The processing time for generating 10,000 unique keypairs and computing 10,000 ciphertexts was 2.353 s while the processing time was 12.791 s for 60,000 ciphertexts (Fig. 2).

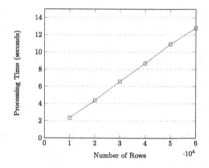

Fig. 2. Setup Phase

Functional Key Generation: In this phase, we measured the execution time for computing the Functional Decryption key in the KeyGen function and time taken to compute the final ciphertext in the Encryption algorithm. As with the Setup function, we evaluated both functions for a varying number of keys and ciphertexts from 10,000 to 60,000 based on the unique keys and ciphertexts generated. For 10,000 keys, it took 0.226 s to compute the function decryption key (Fig. 3a) and 0.415 s to generate the final ciphertext (Fig. 3b). While for

---

[4] https://github.com/lubux/ecelgamal.
[5] https://www.ecdc.europa.eu/en/publications-data/download-todays-data-geographic-distribution-covid-19-cases-worldwide.

60,000 keys and ciphertexts, it took 1.316 s and 2.379 s respectively (Fig. 3a and Fig. 3b).

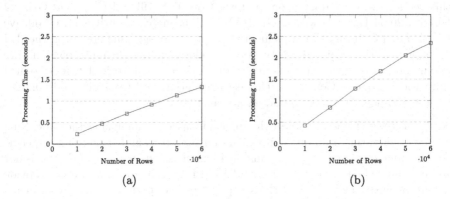

(a)   (b)

Fig. 3. (a) KeyGen Function (b) Encryption Function

Science and Reproducible Research: To support open science and reproducible research, and provide other researchers with the opportunity to use, test, and hopefully extend our scheme, our source code is publicly available online[6].

9   Conclusion

The future will inevitably bring to the fore the need to exploit the power and functionality of a modern cryptographic technique such as FE. It is our firm belief that future access-control systems, especially cloud-based ones will rely less on traditional encryption and more on computations over encrypted data. To this end, it is of great significance, to start designing schemes that remain secure even against quantum attackers, an imminent threat closer than ever before.

A   Proof of Theorem 4

Proof. The proof begins with $\mathcal{B}$ sending $(0, z)$ to the challenger $\mathcal{C}$, where z is an element sampled at random from the message space of PKE. Upon receiving $(0, \mu)$, $\mathcal{C}$ generates a public/private key pair $(\mathsf{pk}_\mathcal{C}, \mathsf{sk}_\mathcal{C})$, flips a truly random coin b and encrypts either 0 or μ under $\mathsf{pk}_\mathcal{C}$ according to the result of the random coin to produce c_b. Finally, $\mathcal{C}$ forwards the pair $(\mathsf{pk}_\mathcal{C}, c_b)$ back to $\mathcal{B}$. Upon reception, $\mathcal{B}$ invokes $\mathcal{A}$ and as a result, receives two messages $\mathbf{x_0}$ and $\mathbf{x_1}$ such that $\|x_0\|_1 = \|x_1\|_1$[7]. To make sure that $\mathcal{B}$ only issues functional decryption keys queries for

---

[6] https://github.com/iammrgenie/FeelQuantum.

[7] Note here that we abuse the notation of the ℓ_1 norm to denote the sum $\sum_1^n x_i$ where $\mathbf{x} = (x_1, \ldots, x_n)$.

vectors such that $\|\mathbf{x_0}\|_1 = \|\mathbf{x_1}\|_1$, we impose the restriction that $\mathcal{B}$ only issues queries to a vector space $\mathcal{V} \subset \mathcal{M}$ of dimension n such that $\forall \mathbf{x} \in \mathcal{V}, \|\mathbf{x}\|_1 = 0$ and is not able to decrypt in other vector spaces. As a next step, $\mathcal{B}$ produces a basis of $\mathcal{V}$ as $(\mathbf{x_1} - \mathbf{x_0}, r_1, \ldots, r_{n-1})$.

Key Generation. The first thing $\mathcal{B}$ needs to do, is to generate the master public key mpk. To do so, $\mathcal{B}$ samples $n-1$ linearly independent vectors $\mathbf{r_1}, \ldots, \mathbf{r_{n-1}}$ such that $\forall i \in [1, n-1] : r_i \in \mathcal{V}$ and each $\mathbf{r_i}$ is also linearly independent to $\mathbf{x_1} - \mathbf{x_0}$. The canonical vectors of the basis are then $\mathbf{e} = \left[\boldsymbol{\alpha} \cdot (\mathbf{x_1} - \mathbf{x_0}) + \sum_1^{n-1} z_j \right]$, where $\boldsymbol{\alpha} = (\alpha_1, \ldots, \alpha_n)$ and $\alpha_i = \frac{x_{1,i} - x_{0,i}}{\|x_{1,i} - x_{0,i}\|_2^2}$. Subsequently, $\mathcal{B}$ executes $(\mathsf{pk}_{z_j}, \mathsf{sk}_{s_j}) \leftarrow$ PKE.Gen, $\forall j \in [1, n-1]$ and sets:

$$\mathsf{pk}_i = \alpha_i \cdot \mathsf{pk}_\mathcal{C} + \sum_j^{n-1} \mathsf{pk}_{z_j} \quad \text{and} \quad \mathsf{mpk} = (\mathsf{pk}_1, \ldots, \mathsf{pk}_n). \tag{11}$$

Note that while $\mathsf{sk}_\mathcal{C}$ is not known to $\mathcal{B}$, due to the AKH property of PKE $\mathcal{B}$ is unknowingly setting $\mathsf{sk}_i = \alpha_i \cdot \mathsf{sk}_\mathcal{C} + \sum_1^{n-1} \mathsf{sk}_{z_j}$

Functional Decryption Keys. $\mathcal{B}$ receives queries for functional decryption keys from $\mathcal{A}$. To reply to such a query, all $\mathcal{B}$ has to do, is set $\mathsf{sk} = \sum_1^{n-1} \mathsf{sk}_{z_j}$.

Challenge Ciphertexts. At some point $\mathcal{A}$ outputs two messages $\mathbf{x_0}$ and $\mathbf{x_1}$ such that $\|\mathbf{x_0}\|$ to $\mathcal{B}$. According to the game in the Definition 6, $\mathcal{B}$ is supposed to flip a random coin $\beta \in \{0, 1\}$, and reply to $\mathcal{A}$ with c_β. However, recall that $\mathcal{B}$ not only needs to simulate a perfect view for $\mathcal{A}$, but also extract as much information as possible in order to win its own indistinguishability game of the public-key encryption scheme PKE. To do so, $\mathcal{B}$ flips the truly random coin β but instead of replying with c_β, sets the challenge ciphertext to be:

$$c = \alpha \cdot c_b + \mathsf{PKE.Enc}\left(\sum_{i=1}^{n-1} \mathsf{pk}_{z_j}, 0 \right) + \mathsf{PKE.Enc}(0_{el}, \mathbf{x_\beta}) \tag{12}$$

where 0_{el} in Eq. 12 denotes the zero element of the space in which the public keys live.

Finally, $\mathcal{A}$ outputs a guess for β. If $\mathcal{A}$ correctly guess $\odot$, then $\mathcal{B}$ guesses that $\mathcal{C}$ encrypted 0. Otherwise, if $\mathcal{A}$ fails to guess β, then $\mathcal{B}$ guesses that $\mathcal{C}$ encrypted μ. For a clearer presentation, we distinguish between two cases based on $\mathcal{C}$'s choice.

C1: $\mathcal{C}$ encrypted 0: Assuming that $\mathcal{C}$ encrypted 0, then Eq. 12 becomes:

$$c = \mathsf{PKE.Enc}(\alpha \cdot \mathsf{pk}_\mathcal{C}, 0) + \mathsf{PKE.Enc}\left(\sum_{i=1}^{n-1} \mathsf{pk}_{z_j}, 0 \right) + \mathsf{PKE.Enc}(0_{el}, \mathbf{x_\beta})$$

$$= \mathsf{PKE.Enc}(\alpha \cdot \mathsf{pk}_\mathcal{C} + \sum_{i=1}^{n-1} \mathsf{pk}_{z_j} + 0_{el}, 0 + 0 + \mathbf{x_\beta}) = \mathsf{PKE.Enc}(\mathsf{pk}_i, \mathbf{x_\beta})$$

It is evident, that in this case, $\mathcal{B}$ simulates a perfect view of the environment for $\mathcal{A}$, and hence, if $\mathcal{A}$ can guess β with advantage $\epsilon_{\mathcal{A}}$, then the advantage of $\mathcal{B}$, $\epsilon_{\mathcal{B}}$ in guessing that $\mathcal{C}$ will be exaclty the same. Thus:

$$\epsilon_{\mathcal{A}} = \epsilon_{\mathcal{B}} \tag{13}$$

C2: $\mathcal{C}$ encrypted μ: Following the same procedure as in the previous case, if $\mathcal{C}$ encrypted μ instead of 0, then the challenge ciphertext from Eq. 12 becomes:

$$c = \mathsf{PKE.Enc}(\alpha \cdot \mathsf{pk}_{\mathcal{C}}, \alpha \cdot \mu) + \mathsf{PKE.Enc}\left(\sum_{i=1}^{n-1}\mathsf{pk}_{z_j}, 0\right) + \mathsf{PKE.Enc}(0_{el}, \mathbf{x}_{\beta})$$

$$= \mathsf{PKE.Enc}(\alpha \cdot \mathsf{pk}_{\mathcal{C}} + \sum_{i=1}^{n-1}\mathsf{pk}_{z_j} + 0_{el}, \alpha \cdot \mu + 0 + \mathbf{x}_{\beta})$$

$$= \mathsf{PKE.Enc}(\mathsf{pk}_i, \alpha \cdot \mu + \mathbf{x}_{\beta}) = \mathsf{PKE.Enc}(\mathsf{pk}_i, \mathbf{x}')$$

However, recall that α is defined as: $\alpha = \frac{\mathbf{x}_1 - \mathbf{x}_0}{\|\mathbf{x}_1 - \mathbf{x}_0\|_2^2}$
Hence, $\mathbf{x}'$ is:

$$\mathbf{x}' = \mathbf{x}_{\beta} + \alpha \cdot \mu = \frac{\mu}{\|\mathbf{x}_1 - \mathbf{x}_0\|_2^2}(\mathbf{x}_1 - \mathbf{x}_0) + \mathbf{x}_{\beta}$$

$$= \frac{\mu}{\|\mathbf{x}_1 - \mathbf{x}_0\|_2^2}(\mathbf{x}_1 - \mathbf{x}_0) + \mathbf{x}_0 + \beta(\mathbf{x}_1 - \mathbf{x}_0)$$

If we now set $v = \frac{\mu}{\|\mathbf{x}_1 - \mathbf{x}_0\|_2^2} + \beta$, we see that the challenge message $\mathbf{x}'$ becomes:

$$\mathbf{x}' = v \cdot \mathbf{x}_1 + (1 - v)\mathbf{x}_0 \tag{14}$$

which is exactly the message that corresponds the the challenge ciphertext. Note that $\mathbf{x}' \in V$ since it is a linear combination of elements that live in V and whose coefficients sum up to one. Hence, $\mathbf{x}'$ is well defined. Finally, β is information theoretically hidden as the distributions of u is independent of β. Hence, in this case we have that:

$$\epsilon_{\mathcal{B}} = 0 \tag{15}$$

Combining Eqs. 13 and 15 we end up with $\epsilon_{\mathcal{B}} = \epsilon_{\mathcal{A}}$. Hence, the best advantage one can get against the CPA security of our construction presented in Definition 13, is bounded by the best advantage one can get against the IND-CPA security of the public key encryption scheme PKE. In other words, we proved that if $\mathcal{A}$ breaks our MIFE construction, then there exists a PPT algorithm $\mathcal{B}$ that that wins the IND-CPA game of PKE and hence, PKE cannot be IND-CPA secure, which contradicts with our initial assumption that PKE is IND-CPA secure. □

Functional Keys for Vectors in Different Vector Spaces: As mentioned, $\mathcal{A}$ is only allowed to request functional keys for vectors living in a vector space $V \subset M$, where $\forall \mathbf{x} \in V : \|\mathbf{x}\|_1 = 0$. Notice that by allowing $\mathcal{A}$ to obtain functional decryption keys for vectors $x \notin V$, our scheme can be trivially broken. However, this would imply that $\mathcal{B}$ can generate such functional decryption keys, which is *impossible* since $\mathcal{B}$ does not know sk_C. Hence, the generated functional keys can only decrypt ciphertexts whose plaintexts are elements of V. This is a valid assumption since otherwise, we would demand security in a scenario where the master secret key is known to the adversary.

B   Proof of Theorem 6

Proof. Recall that each user receives $n - 1$ shares from the remaining users. Assuming that $\mathcal{ADV}$ has colluded with $n - 2$ users, we conclude that $\mathcal{ADV}$ will know the $n \cdot (n - 2)$ shares of the compromised users. Moreover, $\mathcal{ADV}$ will also know the $n - 4$ shares sent from the legitimate users u_l and u_ℓ to the compromised ones. In other words, $\mathcal{ADV}$ knows all the exchanged shares except from the ones that u_l and u_ℓ keep for themselves as well as the ones exchanged between u_l and u_ℓ. More specifically, the shares $r_{l,l}$ and $r_{\ell,\ell}$ are kept with u_l and u_ℓ respectively, while the shares $r_{\ell,l}$ and $r_{l,\ell}$ are exchanged between u_l and u_ℓ. We notice that:

$$s_l = \underline{\mathsf{sk}_l} + \underline{r_l} - (r_{1,l} + \cdots + \underline{r_{l,l}} + \cdots + \underline{r_{\ell,l}} + \cdots + r_{n,l}) \tag{16}$$

and

$$s_\ell = \underline{\mathsf{sk}_\ell} + \underline{r_\ell} - (r_{1,\ell} + \cdots + \underline{r_{l,\ell}} + \cdots + \underline{r_{\ell,\ell}} + \cdots + r_{n,\ell}) \tag{17}$$

Where the underlined terms are the ones that $\mathcal{ADV}$ does not know. Equations 16 and 17 can also be written as:

$$s_l = \underline{\mathsf{sk}_l} + \sum_{j \neq l, \ell}^{n} (r_{l,j} - r_{j,l}) + \underline{r_{l,\ell} - r_{l,\ell}} \quad \text{and} \quad s_\ell = \underline{\mathsf{sk}_\ell} + \sum_{j \neq \ell, l}^{n} (r_{\ell,j} - r_{j,\ell}) + \underline{r_{\ell,l} - r_{\ell,l}}$$

We see that for $\mathcal{ADV}$ to find the the secret keys sk_l and sk_ℓ, she needs to solve a system of two equations with four unknown terms. Hence, we conclude that even in the extreme scenario where $n - 2$ users are corrupted, $\mathcal{ADV}$ cannot infer any information about the keys of the legitimate users. $\square$

References

1. Abdalla, M.D., Fiore, D., Gay, R., Ursu, B.: Multi-input functional encryption for inner products: function-hiding realizations and constructions without pairings. In: Advances in Cryptology – CRYPTO 2018 (2018)
2. Abdalla, M., Bourse, F., De Caro, A., Pointcheval, D.: Simple functional encryption schemes for inner products. In: Katz, J. (ed.) PKC 2015. LNCS, vol. 9020, pp. 733–751. Springer, Heidelberg (2015). https://doi.org/10.1007/978-3-662-46447-2_33

3. Abdalla, M., Gay, R., Raykova, M., Wee, H.: Multi-input inner-product functional encryption from pairings. In: Coron, J.-S., Nielsen, J.B. (eds.) EUROCRYPT 2017. LNCS, vol. 10210, pp. 601–626. Springer, Cham (2017). https://doi.org/10.1007/978-3-319-56620-7_21

4. Bakas, A., Michalas, A.: Multi-input functional encryption: efficient applications from symmetric primitives. In: 2020 IEEE 19th International Conference on Trust, Security and Privacy in Computing and Communications (TrustCom), pp. 1105–1112 (2020). https://doi.org/10.1109/TrustCom50675.2020.00146

5. Bakas, A., Michalas, A., Dimitriou, T.: Private lives matter: a differential private functional encryption scheme. In: Proceedings of the Twelfth ACM Conference on Data and Application Security and Privacy. p. 300–311. CODASPY 2022, Association for Computing Machinery, New York, NY, USA (2022). https://doi.org/10.1145/3508398.3511514, https://doi.org/10.1145/3508398.3511514

6. Bakas, A., Michalas, A., Ullah, A.: (F)unctional sifting: a privacy-preserving reputation system through multi-input functional encryption. In: Asplund, M., Nadjm-Tehrani, S. (eds.) NordSec 2020. LNCS, vol. 12556, pp. 111–126. Springer, Cham (2021). https://doi.org/10.1007/978-3-030-70852-8_7

7. Bellare, M., Boldyreva, A., Staddon, J.: Randomness re-use in multi-recipient encryption Schemeas. In: Desmedt, Y.G. (ed.) PKC 2003. LNCS, vol. 2567, pp. 85–99. Springer, Heidelberg (2003). https://doi.org/10.1007/3-540-36288-6_7

8. Boneh, D., Sahai, A., Waters, B.: Functional encryption: definitions and challenges. In: Ishai, Y. (ed.) TCC 2011. LNCS, vol. 6597, pp. 253–273. Springer, Heidelberg (2011). https://doi.org/10.1007/978-3-642-19571-6_16

9. Brakerski, Z., Gentry, C., Vaikuntanathan, V.: (leveled) fully homomorphic encryption without bootstrapping. In: ITCS 2012 (2012)

10. Castagnos, G., Laguillaumie, F.: Linearly homomorphic encryption from DDH. In: Nyberg, K. (ed.) CT-RSA 2015. LNCS, vol. 9048, pp. 487–505. Springer, Cham (2015). https://doi.org/10.1007/978-3-319-16715-2_26

11. Cheon, J.H., Kim, A., Kim, M., Song, Y.: Homomorphic encryption for arithmetic of approximate numbers. In: Takagi, T., Peyrin, T. (eds.) ASIACRYPT 2017. LNCS, vol. 10624, pp. 409–437. Springer, Cham (2017). https://doi.org/10.1007/978-3-319-70694-8_15

12. Elgamal, T.: A public key cryptosystem and a signature scheme based on discrete logarithms. IEEE Trans. Inf. Theory **31**(4), 469–472 (1985)

13. Gentry, C.: Fully homomorphic encryption using ideal lattices. In: Proceedings of the Forty-First Annual ACM Symposium on Theory of Computing. STOC 2009, pp. 169–178. Association for Computing Machinery, New York, NY, USA (2009)

14. Goldwasser, S., et al.: Multi-input functional encryption. In: Nguyen, P.Q., Oswald, E. (eds.) EUROCRYPT 2014. LNCS, vol. 8441, pp. 578–602. Springer, Heidelberg (2014). https://doi.org/10.1007/978-3-642-55220-5_32

15. Goldwasser, S., Kalai, Y.T., Popa, R.A., Vaikuntanathan, V., Zeldovich, N.: How to run turing machines on encrypted data. In: Canetti, R., Garay, J.A. (eds.) CRYPTO 2013. LNCS, vol. 8043, pp. 536–553. Springer, Heidelberg (2013). https://doi.org/10.1007/978-3-642-40084-1_30

16. Regev, O.: On lattices, learning with errors, random linear codes, and cryptography. J. ACM **56**(6) (2009). https://doi.org/10.1145/1568318.1568324

17. Sahai, A., Seyalioglu, H.: Worry-free encryption: functional encryption with public keys. In: Proceedings of the 17th ACM Conference on Computer and Communications Security, pp. 463–472 (2010)

18. Sahai, A., Waters, B.: Fuzzy identity-based encryption. In: Cramer, R. (ed.) EURO-CRYPT 2005. LNCS, vol. 3494, pp. 457–473. Springer, Heidelberg (2005). https://doi.org/10.1007/11426639_27

19. Sans, E.D., Gay, R., Pointcheval, D.: Reading in the dark: classifying encrypted digits with functional encryption. IACR Cryptol. ePrint Arch. **2018**, 206 (2018)

20. Waters, B.: A punctured programming approach to adaptively secure functional encryption. In: Gennaro, R., Robshaw, M. (eds.) CRYPTO 2015. LNCS, vol. 9216, pp. 678–697. Springer, Heidelberg (2015). https://doi.org/10.1007/978-3-662-48000-7_33

Security Operations and Policies

ReLOG: A Unified Framework for Relationship-Based Access Control over Graph Databases

Stanley Clark, Nikolay Yakovets, George Fletcher, and Nicola Zannone[✉]

Eindhoven University of Technology, 5600 MB Eindhoven, The Netherlands
{s.clark,hush,g.h.l.fletcher,n.zannone}@tue.nl

Abstract. Relationship-Based Access Control (ReBAC) is a paradigm to specify access constraints in terms of interpersonal relationships. To express these graph-like constraints, a variety of ReBAC models with varying features and ad-hoc implementations have been proposed. In this work, we investigate the theoretical feasibility of realising ReBAC systems using off-the-shelf graph database technology and propose a unified framework through which we characterise and compare existing ReBAC models. To this end, we formalise a ReBAC specific query language, ReLOG, an extension to regular graph queries over property graphs. We show that existing ReBAC models are instantiations of queries over property graphs, laying a foundation for the design of ReBAC mechanisms based on graph database technology.

1 Introduction

Relationship-Based Access Control (ReBAC) [14] has been proposed to support the specification of policies that naturally express relationships between a requester and a resource. For example, in a healthcare scenario, a typical notion used to specify policies is 'treating physician', where a doctor (the requester) wanting access to a patient's file (the resource) must either be the family doctor or a referred specialist of the patient. This constraint can be more naturally expressed by encoding the relationships between the resource and requester rather than through ad-hoc attributes as typically done in Attribute-Based Access Control (ABAC).

In general, ReBAC policies encode graph-like access conditions and are evaluated by determining whether the specified conditions occur in the graph encoding the current state of the system [15]. Therefore, ReBAC policies can naturally be viewed as graph queries over graph databases (DBs), an increasingly popular technology leveraging known complexity results, optimisation techniques and understandable performance for the efficient and scalable querying and analysis of graph data [4]. Graph databases thus have the potential to serve as a foundation for the design general-purpose ReBAC mechanisms.

However, to date it still remains unclear to what extent graph DB technology can be applied to evaluate ReBAC policies. A lack of consensus on the precise

S. Sural and H. Lu (Eds.): DBSec 2022, LNCS 13383, pp. 303–315, 2022.
https://doi.org/10.1007/978-3-031-10684-2_17

definition of ReBAC [14] has led to the proposal of a variety of domain-specific, rather than general-purpose, ReBAC models and underlying ad-hoc implementations. These models range from specifying simple conjunctions of relationships over social networks [2,8] to variants of first-order logic [3,16] operating over graphs specified in contexts such as medical records [12]. This diversity of models and policy languages has led to significant difficulties in comparing the expressiveness of ReBAC proposals and assessing their relation to graph query languages, with subtle but important differences easily overlooked.

To address these concerns, this work presents a *unified framework* for understanding and comparing existing proposals for ReBAC in the context of graph databases. We first develop an understanding of which types of ReBAC policies should be supported. Given a classification of such policy types, we then study how existing ReBAC models fit into this space. Our unified framework provides the essential ReBAC characteristics which we use as a basis for the definition and formalisation of an abstract query language suitable for modelling and theoretically reasoning about ReBAC policies. In particular, we show how to encode the different policy types in an abstract Datalog-style property-graph query language (with some proposed extensions) to help compare their expressiveness. This language offers formal well-defined semantics and complexity results over the property-graph model (PGM) [4], a leading industry standard for modelling graph data collections. This abstract query language poses a baseline for future implementations of ReBAC using widely-used concrete query languages such as Cypher and SPARQL.

2   Background

As the baseline for our framework, we employ the property-graph model and regular property-graph queries, the de facto graph data model and abstract query language. Hereafter, we provide an overview and refer to [4] for their formal definitions.

Property-Graph Model. Let $\mathcal{O}$ be a set of objects, $\mathcal{L}$ be a finite set of labels, $\mathcal{K}$ be a set of property keys, and $\mathcal{N}$ be a set of values; all pairwise disjoint. A property graph comprises a set of vertexes ($\mathcal{V} \subseteq \mathcal{O}$) and a set of edges ($\mathcal{E} \subseteq \mathcal{O}$) encoding relationships ($\eta : \mathcal{E} \to \mathcal{V} \times \mathcal{V}$) between them. Each vertex and edge can have multiple labels ($\lambda : \mathcal{V} \cup \mathcal{E} \to \mathcal{P}(\mathcal{L})$), also called *types*, and properties ($\nu : (\mathcal{V} \cup \mathcal{E}) \times \mathcal{K} \to \mathcal{N}$). The restriction of the types of nodes and the types of edges between them forms the *graph schema*.

As an example, consider the graph in Fig. 1 showing a social network modelling users posting on forums. The graph can be defined in terms of vertexes $(1, \ldots, 7)$, each with the label person (e.g., Anna) or forum (e.g., Forum 1). person vertexes have *name* and optionally *date of birth* properties, while forum vertexes have a *name* property. The graph also encodes labelled edges between vertexes: knows represents bi-directional relationships between users, likes shows which user likes a forum, hasMember represents the members of a forum, and hasModerator shows which user is the moderator of a forum.

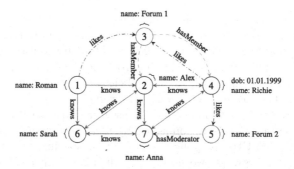

Fig. 1. Social network with nodes of type `person` (in black) and of type `forum` (in red) (Color figure online)

Regular Property-Graph Logic. Queries over the PGM are commonly specified using *Regular Property-Graph Logic* (RPGLog), a variant of non-recursive Datalog extended with transitive closure (through Kleene star operator, p^*) specialised to query graph properties [4]. An RPGLog query, or *program*, is a set of *rules* written over the graph schema, where each rule has a *head*, at least one *body* predicate and any number of *constraint* predicates. Each body predicate specifies the topology of vertexes and edges over which constraint predicates place restrictions based on property values or vertex equality. Queries over the topology are known as *basic graph patterns* (BGPs).

As an example consider the query to check the existence of a path between two people who (indirectly) know each other, with one of those people liking a forum. An RPGLog program for this query consists of a single rule, namely:

$$\texttt{result}() \leftarrow \texttt{knows}^*(x, y), \texttt{person}(x), \texttt{person}(y), \texttt{likes}(x, z), \texttt{Forum}(z)$$

3   Relationship-Based Access Control

A ReBAC model consists of three core elements [14]: *(i)* the set of information that specifies the access rights for each subject with respect to an object, or the *protection state* [12]; *(ii)* the entities involved in the authorisation decision; and *(iii)* a way to specify policies. Authorisation decisions are made by matching policies against the protection state in the context of an *access request* consisting of a requester and a resource.

ReBAC models typically propose a *policy language* over the protection state. Policies are written over the *schema* of the protection state. Based on the policy language, we can classify ReBAC models into three main classes: *simple user-oriented models*, *arbitrary graph query models* and *provenance-based models*. We study one representative model from each of the presented ReBAC model classes to derive a representative view of the entire spectrum of proposed ReBAC models.

Simple User-Oriented Models. Models in this class operate over graphs with a limited form of path conditions, have a strict syntax and often enforce requirements such as maximum path length [2,7,9]. They are well suited to regulate permissions in social networks where the protection state is a social graph representing user-to-user relationships and policies are specified in terms of simple relationships such as *friend* and *friend-of-a-friend.*

A representative ReBAC model in this class is user-to-user ReBAC (UURAC) [9], which defines a set of users connected by *multiple types* of *directed user-to-user* relationships. A UURAC policy, or graph rule, specifies the dis/conjunction of a series of paths between two users. We call this notion *node identity* where the policy is evaluated with respect to both the social graph and a function which provides the value of certain nodes, e.g. the requester or resource owner. Each path is a regular expression allowing quantification over single relationship types and associated with a mandatory maximum path length, together called a path specification. Each path specification can be negated such that the specified path should not exist within the maximum path length.

Example 1. Consider a policy allowing access to a forum with a moderator if the requester *(i)* is not (indirectly) known by the moderator in 2 hops, but *(ii)* is connected to the moderator. In UURAC, this policy can be expressed as follows:

$$(req, (\neg(\mathfrak{knows}^{-1}+, 2) \wedge (\mathfrak{T}, 1))$$

The start node *req* defines that the path is evaluated between the requester and the resource owner *owner* (the forum moderator). In terms of the graph in Fig. 1, access is granted when $req =$ Roman, $owner =$ Anna and denied otherwise.

This policy is a typical example of a user-defined social network policy regulating access to content. It is *non-monotonic* [12], where adding relationships to the graph might cause policy evaluation to switch from permit to deny. In this case, if the requester would become connected to the forum moderator then their access would be revoked. The policy is *relational* [12], evaluating paths between the requester and resource owner, greatly reducing the search space and thereby guaranteeing tractability. The policy also shows that, using UURAC, it is only possible to specify paths which have a *restricted depth* due to the mandatory maximum path length. Moreover, due to the use of the so-called *no-repeated-node* semantics where a node cannot be visited twice, only paths which do not contain cycles can be found (this limitation is further discussed in Sect. 5). Importantly, the policy also specifies a path matching *any relationship*. Thus, UURAC policies can ask for arbitrary connections regardless of the current protection state which allows the specification of policies requiring that some indirect connection exists between users.

Arbitrary Graph Query Models. Models in this class support, to a large extent, arbitrary first-order logic over arbitrary labelled (property) graphs [5,11,12,16, 17]. This allows the specification of policies encoding, e.g., *common friends.*

A representative model in this class is Extended Hybrid Logic (EHL) [16], which is composed of Hybrid Logic (HL) [5] extended with path conditions [11].

The hybrid logic model defining the protection state can be seen as a graph in which every node is assigned to a unique identifier. Accordingly, it is trivial to observe that the graph in Fig. 1 can be encoded as an EHL model where the nominals are the identifiers assigned to each node (i.e., 1, ..., 7) such that we can refer to the node with the name Roman by the nominal 1. By adding non-user entities to the model, EHL allows specifying conditions between the requester and the resource itself instead of the resource owner as in UURAC.

Example 2. Consider a policy expressing that access to a forum is granted if the requester *(i)* knows the forum moderator not named Bob and *(ii)* knows two users also known by the forum moderator. This policy can be expressed in EHL as follows:

$$@_{req}\langle knows\rangle \downarrow v_1(\langle hasModerator\rangle^{-1}res \wedge \neg Bob \wedge$$

$$@_{req}\langle knows\rangle \downarrow v_2(\langle knows\rangle^{-1}v_1 \wedge @_{req}\langle knows\rangle(\langle knows\rangle^{-1}v_1 \wedge \neg v_2)))$$

which defines a regular expressions over the set of relationship labels. The $\downarrow v$ symbol 'stores' the current node for later reference with $@_v$ which 'jumps' to the node represented by the variable v, similar to $@_n$, which jumps to the nominal n. Note that path conjunction is only required to support transitive closure over arbitrary paths. Additionally, only inverse relationship labels are considered since every inverse path can be transformed into a path consisting of only inverse relationship labels [11]. In the context of Fig. 1, this policy grants access when $req = $ Alex, $res = $ Forum 2 and denies access otherwise.

This example shows that EHL supports several characteristics which makes it naturally suited for expressing policies in a variety of complex scenarios. Indeed, EHL allows distinguishing intermediate nodes in the path, which we refer to as *node binding* capabilities, and is thus able to express desirable policy types such as *k-clique* and *k-common friends* [9]. The lack of a restriction on maximum relationship depth along with the inclusion of transitive closure means that EHL is also able to express *non-finitary* policies [12] such as 'allow access if the requester and owner of the resource know each other'. EHL is also able to express a variety of *owner-checkable* policies [12].

Provenance-Based Models. Models in this class specify access control policies on a provenance graph, which relates artefacts to depict their provenance through the system [3,6,8]. The paths encoding these policies can be seen as ReBAC policies as they define access requirements in terms of nodes and relationships to traverse in the protection state.

A representative model in this class is provenance-based access control (PBAC) [3], which provides an ABAC language encoding provenance-based access constraints as path conditions evaluated through user-defined functions [13]. Path conditions are built on the Open Provenance Model. The provenance graph can be seen as an acyclic edge-labelled property graph where role labels are edge properties and the three supported relationship types (i.e., *used*, *wasGeneratedBy*, and *wasControlledBy*) are the edge labels. PBAC allows to combine these relationships using Boolean connectors and existential and universal quantifiers. On evaluation, quantified variables are replaced with concrete node values.

Example 3. Consider the policy representing that only the owner of a resource can access it. Using PBAC, this policy can be specified as follows:

$$\exists p : wasGeneratedBy^\circ(res, p) \land wasControlledBy^{owner}(p, req)$$

where the domain of p is a set of process variables specified during policy evaluation.

An immediate observation is that the domain of quantified variables should be ascertained. Thus, each variable may have an *arbitrary variable domain*, with a mapping of variables to the values they can take, specified during policy evaluation. This characteristic allows expressing policies that, for instance, deny access to a particular concrete set of users. In addition, the inclusion of universal quantification, although not increasing the expressiveness of the language, allows specifying *all-of-type* policies with greater ease than in EHL. All-of-type policies are policies such as 'allow access if the user knows all members of a group', specifying a condition which should hold for every entity.

Discussion. Table 1 presents a classification of ReBAC models according to the types of expressible policies and the data that can be used in their evaluation. These characteristics, extracted from both the literature [1,2,9,12] and our study, represent the constraints that ReBAC models should be able to express. Notably, we identify three characteristics which are not explicitly defined in prior work: a desirable policy type *all-of-type*; a solidified notion of node identity, allowing to dynamically assign (sets of) node values at runtime; and the ability to encode the relationship depth for transitive closures of arbitrary relationships.

Figure 2 visualises four of the policy types that can be considered as policy templates [2] which can be extended with other features such as negation and more expressive paths. Policies encoding k-common connectors (Fig. 2a) specify that the requester and resource should have some number of common distinct connections. Those encoding k-cliques (Fig. 2b) specify that each node should be connected to every other node in the policy. Policies encoding *abstract path* (Fig. 2c) check if there is some remote pair of users n arbitrary hops away which satisfy relationship r_1 within a certain 'distance' from the user the policy is assigned to. Policies encoding *all-of-type* (Fig. 2d) specify universal quantification. We explicitly consider several characteristics pertaining to the model's data use to help exemplify that, while ReBAC policy languages make distinctions between these characteristics, graph query languages operating over the PGM make no such assumptions. A further important data characteristic is *any relationship* which ensures that in case new relationship types are added, policies will retain the same semantics compared to enumerating all relationship types in the current protection state.

Table 1. Supported ReBAC characteristics by ReBAC policy specification languages

Characteristic		UURAC	EHL	PBAC	RPGLog
Policy Types	Common connectors [9]	-	✓	-	✓
	Clique [9]	-	✓	-	✓
	Abstract path [2]	✓	-	-	-
	Non-finitary [12]	-	✓	✓	✓
	Non-monotonic [12]	✓	✓	✓	-
	Owner-checkable [12]	-	✓	✓	-
	Relational [12]	✓	✓	✓	-
	All-of-type	-	✓	✓	-
Data Use	Restricted relationship depth [9]	✓	✓	✓	✓
	Exact relationship depth	-	✓	✓	✓
	Any relationship	✓	-	-	-
	Arbitrary variable domain	-	-	✓	-
	Node identity	✓	✓	✓	-
	Node & relationship properties [1]	-	✓	-	✓
	Object-to-Object relationships [9]	-	✓	✓	✓
	Directed relationships [9]	✓	✓	✓	✓
	Multiple relationship types [9]	✓	✓	✓	✓

The middle three columns of Table 1 give an overview of these constraints. An immediate observation is that no one ReBAC model is strictly more expressive than another. UURAC is the only language able to express *any relationship* and in turn the *abstract path* policy type. Owner-checkable policies are not expressible since policies in this model are evaluated with respect to the requester and resource owner. On the other hand, EHL is the only language which can express policies requiring to distinguish nodes, i.e. common connectors and cliques, and fully supports arbitrary properties of nodes and relationships, with PBAC only supporting a limited set of properties. While both EHL and PBAC support universal quantifiers to specify both non-finitary and non-monotonic policies, PBAC is the only language that supports an at runtime defined domain for each variable.

RPGLog, despite being a general-purpose graph query language, cannot express all desired ReBAC characteristics as shown in the last column of Table 1. Therefore, in the next sections we introduce an abstract query language which extends RPGLog to encompass the desired features and formally classify ReBAC languages in terms of these features.

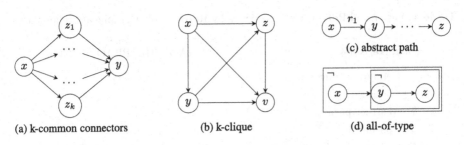

(a) k-common connectors   (b) k-clique   (d) all-of-type

Fig. 2. The main policy types supported by ReBAC

4   ReLOG: A Graph Query Language for ReBAC

In this section, we formalise ReBAC-Log (*ReLOG*), which extends RPGLog (cf. Section 2) to fully support all identified ReBAC features, thus providing a suitable language through which to compare ReBAC models (cf. Sect. 5). Supporting all identified ReBAC features in Table 1 requires the following general adjustments to RPGLog:

- any body or constraint predicate can be negated, supporting policies with *negation*;
- a query is evaluated in the context of both a graph and a mapping for a set of nodes from the graph to variables in the query, which are called *parameterised queries* and can therefore bind the requester and resource to specific nodes in the graph;
- addition of a dedicated label *any* to specify policies matching any label in the graph;
- rules used as transitive intensional (those that appear in rule's head) predicates (IDB) can only be built from other non-constraint positive body predicates such that rules using transitive closures represent *Regular Path Queries* (RPQs) matching paths conforming to a regular expression between nodes;
- non-transitive IDB predicates can be of arbitrary arity, such that variables can be compared across negated rules, so-called *cross-rule vertex references*; and
- a rule may be a constraint predicate on its own, allowing to specify *non-path* programs which test a node present as part of the parameters to a query in terms of its properties.

These extensions provide a language which finds a natural balance of expressiveness between the restrictive nature of RPGLog and the excess of pure Datalog. By remaining within the bounds of Datalog, we are able to theoretically reason about the expressiveness and known complexity results of (subsets of) Datalog which can then be directly applied to ReBAC policies [16]. The proposed extensions are supported through the formal ReLOG language syntax which is defined as follows:

Definition 1. A ReLOG rule has the form:

$$head \leftarrow body_1, \ldots, body_n, constraint_1, \ldots constraint_m$$

for some $n \geq 0$, $m \geq 0$ and $n + m > 0$. The *head* of a rule is of the form:

$$\texttt{head} ::= p(x_1, \ldots, x_m) \mid result()$$

where $p \in \mathcal{L}$ is a label, $x_1, \ldots, x_m \in V$ are vertex variables for $m \geq 0$ appearing in a constraint or body predicate and *result* is a reserved label not in $\mathcal{L}$. By supporting heads of arbitrary arity, variables in negated predicates can be referenced in outer scopes. Each body predicate $body_i$ for $1 \leq i \leq n$ is of the form:

$$
\begin{aligned}
\texttt{rpq} \quad &::= l(x, y) \texttt{ [AS } e \texttt{] } \mid l^*(x, y) \\
\texttt{path} \quad &::= p(z_1, \ldots, z_j) \mid l(x) \\
\texttt{body} \quad &::= \texttt{rpq} \mid \texttt{path} \mid \neg\texttt{rpq} \mid \neg\texttt{path}
\end{aligned}
$$

where $x, y, z_1, \ldots, z_j \in V$ are vertex variables for some $j \geq 0$, $e \in E$ is an edge variable, and $p \in \mathcal{L}$ and $l \in \mathcal{L} \cup \{\texttt{any}\}$ are labels. Compared to RPGLog, body predicates can be negated, non-transitive predicates can have arbitrary arity, and a new reserved label $\texttt{any} \notin \mathcal{L}$ matches arbitrary edges in the graph. Each predicate $constraint_i$ for $1 \leq i \leq m$ is of the form:

$$\texttt{constraint} ::= x.k \; \theta \; val \mid y_1 = y_2 \mid y_1 \neq y_2$$

where $x \in V \cup E$ are vertex or edge variables, $k \in \mathcal{K}$, $val \in \mathcal{N}$, $\theta \in \{=, \neq, <, >, \leq, \geq\}$ and $y_1, y_2 \in V$ are vertex variables. Vertex inequality is added, and variables used in a constraint predicate do not necessarily have to appear in the head of the rule, provided a runtime mapping for those variables is specified. A ReLOG query is a finite non-empty non-recursive set of rules such that at least one rule has head $result()$.

To give an intuition about the semantics of a ReLOG query and the relevance of the proposed extensions, we present some example policies utilising the additional features of ReLOG compared to RPGLog (for the full formal semantics see [10]).

For instance, consider a ReBAC policy granting access to a resource if the requester is over twenty years old and is somehow connected to a user who knows at most one other user. This can be encoded in ReLOG as a non-monotonic owner-checkable policy:

$$
\begin{aligned}
&\texttt{result}() \leftarrow \texttt{any}(req, z), \neg\texttt{knowsTwoUsers}(z), \texttt{old}() \\
&\texttt{knowsTwoUsers}(z) \leftarrow \texttt{knows}(x, z), \texttt{knows}^*(z, y) \\
&\texttt{old}() \leftarrow req.\texttt{age} \geq 20
\end{aligned}
$$

This ReLOG query uses a number of features not supported by RPGLog. The **any** predicate shows that the requester is *somehow* connected to a user. Negation is used to exclude those connections who know more than one user using a cross-rule vertex reference for the non-binary predicate knowsTwoUsers to bind the middle vertex z rather than x and y. Additionally, the last rule demonstrates

Table 2. RPGLog/ReLOG features required to support ReBAC policy languages

Feature		UURAC	EHL	PBAC
RPGLog	BGP semantics - homomorphic	✓	✓	✓
	Mutual exclusion constraints		✓	
	Path semantics - arbitrary	✓	✓	✓
	Path features - $\{\epsilon, s, \overline{s}, \pi; \pi, \pi | \pi\}$	✓	✓	✓
	Path features - RPQ		✓	✓
ReLOG	Path negation - simple	✓	✓	✓
	Path negation - nested		✓	✓
	Parameterised queries - node	✓	✓	✓
	Parameterised queries - sets			✓
	Cross-rule node reference		✓	✓
	Any predicate	✓		
	Non-path program		✓	✓

the ability of ReLOG to encode non-path constraints, and by extension policies, only relying on the properties of nodes. To correctly encode the meaning of this policy, the ReLOG query should be evaluated in the context of a mapping where parameter *req* is mapped to the requester.

As another example, consider a scenario where multiple users collaborate in moderating forums. We can define a policy granting access to a forum if the requester is a forum moderator and knows all moderators who (indirectly) collaborate with the moderator of the requested forum via some other forums. This policy can be encoded in ReLOG as:

$$\texttt{result}() \leftarrow \texttt{person}(req), \texttt{hasModerator}(x, req), \neg\texttt{notKnown}()$$

$$\texttt{notKnown}() \leftarrow \texttt{connectedMods}^*(x, y), \texttt{hasModerator}(res, y), \neg\texttt{knows}(req, x)$$

$$\texttt{connectedMods}(x, y) \leftarrow \texttt{hasModerator}(z, x), \texttt{hasModerator}(z, y), x \neq y$$

with a mapping from the requester and resource specified in the access request to the *req* and *res* vertexes respectively. To compute **result**(), nested negation is used to encode universal quantification over *all* moderators. The unary predicate **person**(*req*) refers to the type of vertex as opposed to an IDB predicate, e.g. knowsTwoUsers(*z*) in the previous example. To compute notKnown(), we take the transitive closure of connectedMods(*x*, *y*) which encodes an RPQ hasModerator^{-1}/hasModerator. The transitive closure of predicates representing such RPQs in ReLOG follows *arbitrary path semantics*, meaning that there are no restrictions on repetition of nodes or edges in the matched path. Node inequality $x \neq y$ is used to impose that the rule only returns distinct moderators. This condition is necessary since ReLOG relies on *homomorphic* semantics, where two variables can be instantiated to refer to the same node. To encode that moderators are connected *via some other forums*, in the last rule z is mapped to a set of forums determined at runtime.

5   Application of the ReLOG Framework to ReBAC Models

We investigated how the three classes of ReBAC policy languages discussed in Sect. 3 along with the underlying data model can be mapped to ReLOG. This mapping allows us to establish the features of graph query languages needed to encode the characteristics of those languages. For the lack of space, we refer to [10] for the mapping and examples and only present the key findings of our analysis. Table 2 presents the smallest subset of graph query language features needed to support each studied ReBAC model along with which of RPGLog and ReLOG supports it. This table naturally captures the essence of mapping, showing that ReLOG can express all constraints expressible by UURAC, EHL and PBAC.

ReLOG demonstrates the generality of graph query languages in encoding the characteristics of ReBAC (cf. Table 1) into distinguishing features. For instance, ReLOG uses *homomorphic* query evaluation semantics consistent with most ReBAC models (models using no-repeated-node semantics primarily do so to ensure termination of their policy evaluation algorithms [9,11]). By being able to specify BGPs and (in)equalities between nodes (so-called *mutual exclusion constraints*) policies specifying common connectors and cliques can be encoded. By supporting RPQs, ReLOG can specify non-finitary policies through path transitive closure as well as paths with restricted and exact relationship depth. Using *(nested) path negation* one can encode both non-monotonic and all-of-type policies. ReLOG's support for *parameterised queries* allows to express owner-checkable and relational policies by being able to bind variables to (sets of) values (similar to parameterised policies [2]). The inclusion of an 'any' predicate label allows to specify UURAC policies and rules can consist solely of constraint predicates which allows to write EHL policies specifying constraints based on the properties of a single vertex only.

Table 2 shows that no one policy language is contained in the other. Some example policies from non-overlapping fragments of the policy languages are:

- $PBAC\backslash EHL \cup UURAC$: Two users know a user in a runtime assigned set of users;
- $EHL\backslash PBAC \cup UURAC$: Two users have two different friends in common;
- $UURAC\backslash PBAC \cup EHL$: Two users are connected by any relationship within 2 hops;
- $EHL \cap PBAC\backslash UURAC$: The user knows all users belonging to a particular group

where $UURAC$, EHL and $PBAC$ denote the set of queries expressible in UURAC, EHL and PBAC respectively.

6 Conclusion

In this work, we studied the feasibility of modelling ReBAC in an abstract graph query language suitable for use in off-the-shelf graph databases. To this end, we devised a unified framework for comparing ReBAC models and graph query languages. We showed how ReBAC concepts map to more general graph concepts, thereby directing a shift in research to focus on ReBAC using graph DB engines. In the future, we plan to use our framework as a tool to assess the suitability of several concrete graph query languages for evaluating ReBAC policies, e.g. Cypher and SPARQL. We also plan to study how we can apply ReBAC to support fine-grained access control in graph databases.

References

1. Ahmed, T., Sandhu, R.S., Park, J.: Classifying and comparing attribute-based and relationship-based access control. In: CODASPY, pp. 59–70. ACM (2017)
2. Aktoudianakis, E., Crampton, J., Schneider, S.A., Treharne, H., Waller, A.: Policy templates for relationship-based access control. In: PST, pp. 221–228. IEEE (2013)
3. Bertolissi, C., den Hartog, J., Zannone, N.: Using provenance for secure data fusion in cooperative systems. In: SACMAT, pp. 185–194. ACM (2019)
4. Bonifati, A., Fletcher, G.H.L., Voigt, H., Yakovets, N.: Querying Graphs. Synthesis Lectures on Data Management, Morgan & Claypool Publishers, San Rafael (2018)
5. Bruns, G., Fong, P., Siahaan, I., Huth, M.: Relationship-based access control: its expression and enforcement through hybrid logic. In: CODASPY, pp. 117–124. ACM (2012)
6. Cadenhead, T., Khadilkar, V., Kantarcioglu, M., Thuraisingham, B.: A language for provenance access control. In: CODASPY, pp. 133–144. ACM (2011)
7. Carminati, B., Ferrari, E., Perego, A.: Enforcing access control in Web-based social networks. ACM Trans. Inf. Syst. Secur. 13(1), 6:1–6:38 (2009)
8. Cheng, Y., Bijon, K., Sandhu, R.: Extended ReBAC administrative models with cascading revocation and provenance support. In: SACMAT, pp. 161–170. ACM (2016)
9. Cheng, Y., Park, J., Sandhu, R.S.: An access control model for online social networks using user-to-user relationships. IEEE Trans. Dependable Secur. Comput. 13(4), 424–436 (2016)
10. Clark, S., Yakovets, N., Fletcher, G., Zannone, N.: A Unified Framework for Relationship-Based Access Control over Graph Databases (2022). https://gitlab.tue.nl/stanrogo/relog-framework/-/blob/main/Unified_ReBAC_Framework_Full.pdf
11. Crampton, J., Sellwood, J.: Path conditions and principal matching: a new approach to access control. In: SACMAT, pp. 187–198. ACM (2014)
12. Fong, P.W.L., Siahaan, I.S.R.: Relationship-based access control policies and their policy languages. In: SACMAT, pp. 51–60. ACM (2011)
13. Kaluvuri, S.P., Egner, A.I., den Hartog, J., Zannone, N.: SAFAX - an extensible authorization service for cloud environments. Frontiers ICT 2, 9 (2015)
14. Lobo, J.: Relationship-based access control: more than a social network access control model. Wiley Interdiscip. Rev. Data Mining Knowl. Discov. 9(2), e1282 (2019)

15. Paci, F., Squicciarini, A.C., Zannone, N.: Survey on access control for community-centered collaborative systems. ACM Comput. Surv. **51**(1), 6:1–6:38 (2018)
16. Pasarella, E., Lobo, J.: A datalog framework for modeling relationship-based access control policies. In: SACMAT, pp. 91–102. ACM (2017)
17. Rizvi, S.Z.R., Fong, P.W.L.: Efficient authorization of graph-database queries in an attribute-supporting ReBAC model. ACM Trans. Priv. Secur. **23**(4), 18:1–18:33 (2020)

Security Operations Center Roles and Skills: A Comparison of Theory and Practice

Andreas Reisser[1,2](✉), Manfred Vielberth[1], Sofia Fohringer[2], and Günther Pernul[1]

[1] Lehrstuhl für Wirtschaftsinformatik I, Universität Regensburg,
Universitätsstr. 31, 93053 Regensburg, Germany
{manfred.vielberth,guenther.pernul}@ur.de
[2] Krones AG, Böhmerwaldstraße 5, 93073 Neutraubling, Germany
{andreas.reisser,sofia.fohringer}@krones.com
http://www.krones.com/

Abstract. The increasing number of interfaces between IT assets leads to a broader area prone to attacks. To address the raising security challenges, enterprises are building up Security Operations Centers (SOC) to detect and defend against cyber-attacks. In this paper, we present an empirical study based on expert interviews to investigate the differences between the roles and skills needed within a SOC in academic research and practice. Our results indicate that there is a consensus. The roles and necessary skills of the SOC analyst emerge from the investigation as a particularly critical success factor. In addition we were able to present and validate a minimum configuration for SOC roles. We also elaborate the importance of SOC interfaces into the organization to facilitate an efficient SOC operation.

Keywords: SOC · Security Operations Center · Roles · Skills · Expert interview

1 Introduction

Corporate cybersecurity is becoming increasingly complex and ever more critical. In addition to the technologies required to maintain an adequate level of security, the cybersecurity talent shortage will worsen [3,16]. This means that, besides the provision of sufficiently well-trained experts, it is crucial to organize personnel as well as possible. Security Operations Centers (SOCs) have emerged as a unit in which security experts are organized within a company to detect and prevent incidents. So far, however, it can be seen that the improvement of SOCs is mainly practice-driven and research in this area is primarily focused on improving individual technologies. In order to address this problem, it is necessary to establish a comparison between theory and practice. The focus lies on

Supported by the research project INSIST.

the roles that are present in a SOC. This enables a better understanding of the distribution of tasks within a SOC, and provides a basis for recording the various functions. However, to enable academic research to advance this area, a transfer of knowledge from practice to research and vice versa is necessary. In order to build this bridge, this paper, therefore, aims to analyze and align both the view from the literature and the view from practice.

The remainder of this paper is structured as follows. Section 2 provides an overview of related work. Section 3 presents the SOC roles that can be derived from the literature. Building on this, Sect. 4 describes the conducted expert interview. Finally, Sect. 5 presents the results, comparing theory and practice. Section 6 concludes the paper.

2   Related Work

Since the structured analysis of roles defined in literature is presented in detail in Sect. 3, only a superficial view of related work will be given here. The literature deals with roles in a SOC primarily in a marginal way. For example, most of the works [2,9,14] that deal with SOC roles present a framework for a SOC, each of which contains roles, whereby the definition is primarily based on the individual functional requirements. Furthermore, the literature deals with sub-areas of SOCs that are directly related to SOC roles [13]. For example, Ganesan et al. [6] proposes an optimization of Alert Data Management in a SOC, showing the interfaces to the respective SOC roles. There is also a stream of research that focuses on educational SOCs. For example, DeCusatis et al. [5] propose an educational SOC, defining the roles of each trainee. A similar direction is taken by Sundaramurthy et al. [19], who compare a real-world SOC with an educational SOC to examine the human factors in its daily operation. Hámornik and Krasznay [9] look at the roles of a SOC from a slightly different perspective by proposing a floor plan for SOCs, looking at the locational arrangement of a SOC's staff. Also, two literature reviews exist that provide a general overview of SOC while looking at the roles within a SOC as a subtopic. Shahjee and Ware [17] conduct these with the underlying idea of merging SOCs and Network Operations Centers to take advantage of synergies. Vielberth et al. [20] provide a general view on SOCs, considering roles within a SOC as part of the PPT (People, Processes, and Technologies) framework. Summing up, in the literature, the roles of a SOC are primarily addressed peripherally. To the best of our knowledge, there has not yet been a methodical review of roles in a SOC in literature as well as in practice, which we aim to address in this paper.

3   Roles in a SOC

The following role definitions are based on a structured literature review, the documentation of which we provide publicly[1]. While tools help SOCs to perform

---

[1] https://go.ur.de/socroles.

better, people are still an essential part. In the following the core roles of a SOC are analyzed. According to literature the number of people and roles in a SOC varies. However, the core team of most SOCs consists of a SOC manager, SOC analysts, and a SOC engineer along with a CISO [11,18,19] (cf. Fig. 1). The CISO is part of the management level and is usually not directly assigned to the SOC. He focuses on the full scope of corporate level cybersecurity, usually has control over what constitutes the SOC and interacts with the SOC's management [4]. The SOC manager is considered the head of the SOC and is responsible for the definition of roles, task, responsibilities, staffing and the reporting interface towards the upper management levels [4,18]. The actual SOC operation consists of analysts, who can be split into different escalation levels (Tier-1 to Tier-3) and a SOC engineer [10]. SOC analysts are responsible for identifying threats, analyzing security incidents and recommending actions [11,19]. A SOC engineer handles the testing and deployment of new technology platforms [11]. However, the separation is not always clear-cut and many of the tasks may overlap in smaller organizations [10].

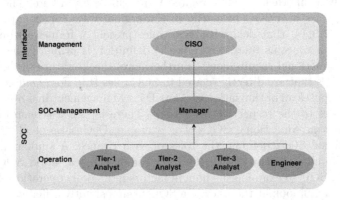

Fig. 1. SOC core roles (based on [21])

Depending on the maturity and the size of the SOC, this means more specific roles and locations [8]. Theses roles can be divided into technical (e.g. Digital Forensic Expert, Pen-Testers, etc.), advisory (e.g. Security Architects and Consultants), and supporting roles (e.g. project Managers, Audit Experts, etc.).

4   Approach Qualitative Research

First of all, a population has to be defined, which helps to select participants who are eligible for qualitative research. The prerequisite for this is a common characteristic or combination of characteristics [15]. In accordance with the focus of this work employees working in or with a SOC will be interviewed. By interviewing people from the same population it is ensured that the results are comparable [15]. In terms of data collection, a distinction can be made between visual and verbal methods [7]. In the present work data collection is planned with a verbal method, in the form of expert interviews[2] of experts from several big players in the industry (e.g. T-Systems GmbH, McKinsey & Company, Airbus SE, Datev GmbH, Rhode&Schwarz GmbH, Krones AG, etc.).

Interview Guideline: A guideline is used to structure the interviews and steer it in the right direction and make them comparable. The guide is divided into four sections: In the first section introduces the interview. Also, permission to record is requested. The main part of the interview is represented by questions about roles in a SOC in practice. Here the tasks and responsibilities of the roles are evaluated, but also new roles, which may not yet have emerged from theory, are identified. Furthermore, the collaboration and organization of the SOC team are examined in more detail. The literature review determined that the SOC analysts have a critical role in a SOC. Based on this, key qualifications and challenges of analysts in practice are analyzed.

Selection of the Experts: Eight experts were recruited for an interview all of which have been involved in the topic of SOC for at least two years. In addition, they can be identified as experts by their roles, which are shown in Table 1.

Table 1. Interviewed experts

Expert-ID	Company position	Industry
E1	Head of CERT/SOC	IT services for communes
E2.1	Information Security Analytics and Defense Manager	Electrical engineering
E2.2	Team lead Information Security Operations	Electrical engineering
E3	Head of Cybersecurity	Legal and tax consulting, auditing
E4	Competence lead Incident Response Team	SOC-service
E5	Consultant construction SOC CDC	IT-service
E6	Head of Cyber Defense Operations	Telecommunications
E7	Technical Lead SOC	IT-service
E8	Consultant Cyber Risk Practice	Management/consulting

5 Evaluation of the Qualitative Research

5.1 SOC Role Structure

The interviews have shown that it is not possible to derive a uniform SOC role structure as it depends mainly on the size of the SOC. Therefore, both a minimum and a maximum structure are derived.

---

[2] The transcripts of the interviews can be provided upon request for data protection reasons.

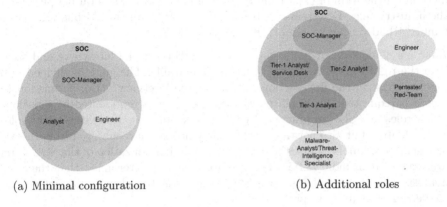

(a) Minimal configuration   (b) Additional roles

Fig. 2. SOC role structure

Each SOC where the interviewees are working includes analysts, engineers and a SOC leader. Thus, a minimal framework for a basic SOC structure can be deduced, illustrated in Fig. 2a. These roles typically deal with the main functions of a SOC (e.g. Monitoring & Detection, Analysis, and Response & Reporting). The analysts are not distinguished in multiple levels until a certain SOC size. Furthermore, the engineer's tasks in the early phase can be taken over by the analysts. Therefore the SOC engineer can be considered as an internal shared role in the minimal configuration in contrast to the external placement in a more advanced setup. In addition, there is a head of the SOC who is responsible for the overall management.

5.2   SOC Analysts

SOC analysts take a crucial role in a SOC as already evident from the literature review (see Sect. 3). Therefore, in the following, the key qualifications of analysts in practice are examined in more detail. The key skills are summarized with the frequency with which they were mentioned by the experts in Table 2. As the interviewees also note, the individual skills depend strongly on the developmental stage of the analyst.

Six experts agree that analysts must have a **broad picture of IT**:

- *"Analysts need to have a broad picture of IT, so you have to know how the networks work, but you also have to know roughly how an active directory works, how does routing work, what does a firewall do, so basically a very broad-based knowledge, some of which doesn't have to go into depth."*
- *"The technical know-how, of course. I can't expect him to know all systems, but I can expect him to have security know-how and especially network know-how."*
- *"He must have IT affinity and must understand operating systems and applications. He must be able to program scripting language."*

Table 2. Key qualifications of analysts

Key qualifications	Frequency of mention
Broad picture of IT	6
Ability to work in a team	5
Communication	5
Creativity/Innovation	5
Resilience/stress resistance	4
Passion for IT security	3
Time management	2
Self-employment	2
Conflict Management	2
Analytical mind	1
Reliability	1
Appraisal skills	1

Furthermore, **ability to work in a team** plays an important role for analysts. This is a soft skill, but is considered by many experts to be the most important.

- *"I would consider the ability to work in a team as the key qualification, because without this ability to work in a team in this close exchange, the whole thing doesn't work. Knowledge I can still train, but the team ability has to be set from the beginning."*
- *"The team ability, because of course it's also about sharing information or also working together with others."*

In addition, there is a high level of consensus regarding the key qualifications **creativity** and **innovation**.

- *"Curiosity, creativity, so being like a free-creating artist. Having new ideas, free thinking, because by always doing the same things, you don't achieve anything as an analyst"*
- *"40% of the work I like to call it is being open for gimmicks, to try things out yourself, to develop things further, to do a bit of research and development and to continue to educate yourself. You need this time because it's the only way to get creative. So creativity is also a key qualification that you should bring along."*
- *"The motivation to keep up to date, to think one step further in terms of know-how, not as deep as the analysts or the engineers on level 2 and 3, but I think here it helps of course to follow digital IT trends, to stay on top of things."*

Five experts also describe that the analyst must have a high level of communication skills. The ability to communicate goes hand in hand with the ability to deal with conflict. Analysts must also have a great passion for cybersecurity.

In addition, an analyst should work independently and reliably. Another expert explains that they must have a sharp analytical mind in order to be able to understand data and statistics and draw important conclusions. Furthermore, analysts should be able to handle stressful situations and be resilient.

5.3 Interfaces of a SOC in Practice

The interview results show that the interfaces can be divided into internal and external interfaces. The interfaces vary depending on the size of the organization.

Internal interfaces within the company:

- Management/CISO
- Departments/IT and IT Operations/NOC
- Security Researcher
- Service Desk
- Penetration-Testers
- Incident Management/Incident Response:
- Local Security Officers
- Human Resources Department

Interfaces/SOC exchange outside the company:

- Association (e.g. other SOCs, CERTs, etc.)
- Government Authorities/Federal office for information security (german: BSI)
- Forums
- Malware Information Sharing Platform (MISP)

5.4 Alignment of Theory and Practice of SOC Roles

There is a consensus among the experts that they agree with the alignment shown in Fig. 1 and their SOC. The experts see the core roles from theory as relevant and the mapped construct as working. The similarities and differences between roles in theory and practice are explained in more detail below.

- **Management level:** Zimmerman et al. [21] describe that the CISO decides on policies and procedures regarding a SOC and sets the SOC strategy. One expert explains that the CISO does not have any function operationally in a SOC. The implementation of the SOC strategy is carried out by operations. Practice and theory agree that the CISO mainly deals with strategic decisions and acts as an interface of a SOC. One expert explains that the CISO should have ultimate decision-making authority, which is often not the case in practice. Basically, there is a conflict of goals between IT operations and IT security. In order to override this, the CISO must be superior.
- **SOC management level:** The interviews show that in practice, the SOC manager role often merges with the CISO role in the early stages, which differs from theory. Three experts explain that a manager is only necessary

to lead the SOC staff once it exceeds a certain size. The experts believe that the SOC manager must have certain competencies such as interpersonal and communication skills and a understanding of IT and Cybersecurity. This is consistent with theory [12]. Muniz [11] describes that in larger SOCs, team and shift leaders often support the SOC manager. This is also evident from the interviews.

- **Operational level:**
  - **Analysts:** Four SOC experts organize analysts into tiers from Tier-1 to Tier-3, providing consensus with theory [10]. However, the experts emphasize that this emerges only with the size of the SOCs. Two experts outsource Tier-1 tasks to the service desk, as well as another expert plans to do so in the future. One expert explains that companies that out-source Tier-1 to an external company often have the problem that they do not understand the organization and thus cannot interpret the alerts correctly. In addition, two experts describe that the roles of Tier-2 and Tier-3 analysts often overlap. One SOC even combines the two tiers into one team so that each can implement all tasks. Tier-2 and Tier-3 must intervene as soon as a Tier-1 analyst escalates the analysis. They should also have specialized knowledge in various areas such as malware analysis. Practice has shown that in smaller organizations all analysts have access to all instruments, as the analysts often additionally manage IT operations. In larger organizations, analysts care less about connecting new systems and often cannot access certain servers due to admin rights. This is usually handled by SOC engineers or the outsourced engineering department. One expert explained that analysts do not make the decision to take action in case of a threat, but only provide decision options. Whether to shut down a critical system, for example, is decided by the organization's management. Another SOC drives in SOC operations organizationally a team structure, from Red, Blue and Black team. The expert sees a match between the roles of the Blue team and Tier 1 and Tier 2 analysts, the Red team with Tier 3 analysts, and the Black team with the SOC engineer. Red and Blue teams should usually work together, but in practice there is often a competitive situation between the two teams.
  - **Engineer:** The core technology of a SOCs is largely the SIEM system including rules. Experts agree that this requires roles that specifically take care of this system and have the expertise to generate the correlation rules and develop them further. Accordingly, it makes sense to hire a role that is dedicatedly responsible for this, otherwise it may happen that no further steps are taken after configuration and the SOC loses effectiveness. Hamornik et al. [9] describe that the main task of an SOC engineer is to define and refine correlation and detection rules, especially in the context of SIEM. Agyepong et al. [1] show in their framework that these tasks and log collection are not usually part of an analyst's job. All SOCs of experts have independent roles or departments that are responsible for these tasks. Muniz [11] et al. describes that there are also SOCs that do not perform the engineering activities within the SOC. In practice, this

is confirmed as two SOCs of the experts, both of which are larger SOCs, separate engineering from their SOC because the focus of the SOCs is heavily on monitoring and analysis. Accordingly, SOC engineers are often separated off, which deals with data acquisition and onboarding of new systems.

- **Other roles:** Agyepong et al. [1] explained that malware analysis is often performed outside the SOC. Through the interviews, on the other hand, it became apparent that specific technical roles, such as malware analyst, are taken on by someone who is one of the more experienced analysts. If malware analysis is not required, then this person usually works in Level-3. Another participant explained that roles that cannot perform their activities at all times cannot be SOC roles by definition, but rather are CERT roles. A SOC is Security Operations, which means that the SOC usually operates 24/7. An Incident Responder, does not deal with an incident continuously, but only over a period of time. Thus, roles such as incident responder or malware analyst would be typical CERT roles, as they do not operate 24/7.

- **New Roles:** A new role that emerged from the interviews is the Data Analyst, which analyses historical SOC data. The expert describes that this can be considered a Tier-2 1/2. Another expert describes that a point-of-contact role has been introduced in their SOC, which an analyst takes during an incident to inform the SOC manager of the current status. For SOCs that provide a service to external customers, additional roles are added that manage the customer relationship and are responsible for the individual customers such as the Service Delivery Manager role, which is often taken by the analysts.

In summary, there is a consensus between the core roles in theory and practice. Sundarmurthy et al. [18] and Muniz [11] describe that the number of employees in a SOC varies and there can be a variety of different roles in a SOC, depending on the size and organization. This can be confirmed in practice as the interviewees are of different SOC sizes and roles. However, in smaller SOCs, the roles are defined in a less fine-grained manner, allowing them to take on multiple tasks and responsibilities. Especially in the early stages, certain roles merge with each other, such as the SOC manager with the CISO. In addition, especially in the early stages, certain roles merge with each other, such as the SOC manager with the CISO. In addition, there are different structures in SOC operations, such as a team structure or a tiering from Tier-1 to Tier-3, where often Tier-1 analysts are outsourced to the service desk and Tier-2 and Tier-3 analysts form a team. Three experts describe that the division of analysts into different tier levels occurs only in larger SOCs. Here, the analyst role takes a very crucial role in a SOC. In larger SOCs, special roles are added that focus on additional functions in the SOC. In smaller SOCs, these often take the role only for a specific period of time and usually work as Tier-3 analysts. In larger SOCs, there are dedicated roles for this purpose. Furthermore, it was found that the interfaces and the interface roles to a SOC take a very crucial role to run an efficient SOC. One expert emphasized that numerous interfaces are necessary for a functional SOC operation.

5.5   Minimal Configuration SOC Roles

Basically, the minimum configuration of roles in an SOC refers to the skills of the analysts. If the analysts have very high expertise, including engineering, there is no need for a dedicated role for these tasks to begin with. Thus, the most important generic roles, as confirmed by three experts, are the analysts, as they are already dealing with the subject matter and can be pushed in the direction of additionally taking over the engineering and try to derive rules to detect anomalies more automatically and document them. Another expert, on the other hand, sees this the other way around and explains that if it is a matter of staffing only one person in the SOC in the initial phase, that the SOC engineer takes the most important role because, on the one hand, he manages the tools and use cases and, on the other hand, he can take over the analysis himself. In addition, one expert describes that both an analyst and a SOC engineer are necessary in the initial phase because the analyst is usually not necessarily the technical component for operations. Basically, the experts agree with Fig. 2a, which also represents a minimal role construct for building a SOC.

6   Conclusion and Future Research

Establishing a SOC is a challenging project in an organization. The building block of people is crucial here to run an efficient SOC. On the one hand, the SOC team must have a high level of expertise, but it must also be able to withstand the various challenges. These and other factors lead to high complexity when filling roles in a SOC. In addition, IT security is in a constant state of flux, which is why employees must undergo continuous training. In this work, roles in an SOC were studied in academic research and practice. Based on a systematic literature review, core roles and additional roles in a SOC were identified. Building upon these results, the identified roles were verified using an empirical expert interview. Thereby, it was deduced how SOCs are organized in practice and whether the core roles from the theory are reflected in practice.

Future fields of research can be a closer investigation of the role SOC-analyst as it has emerged as a crucial role of a SOC. Also studying the interaction between a SOC's role characteristics and SOC maturity models or examining a possible influence of Operation Technology orientated SOC (OT-SOC) on the existing role characteristics can be next steps and at the same time worthwhile research tasks.

Acknowledgement. This work is partly performed under the INSIST project, which is supported under contract by the Bavarian Ministry of Economic Affairs, Regional Development and Energy (DIK0338/01). In addition, we would like to thank Krones AG Department of Information Management, Krones India Pvt. Ltd. Global SOC and all the involved companies for their support.

326 A. Reisser et al.

References

1. Agyepong, E., Cherdantseva, Y., Burnap, P., Reinecke, P.: Towards a framework for measuring the performance of a security operations center analyst (2020)
2. AlSabbagh, B., Kowalski, S.: A framework and prototype for a socio-technical security information and event management system (ST-SIEM). In: 2016 European Intelligence and Security Informatics Conference (EISIC), pp. 192–195. IEEE (2016)
3. Caminiti, S.: CNBC technology executive council: Cyber threats, ongoing war for talent, biggest concerns for tech leaders (2021). https://www.cnbc.com/2021/03/25/cyber-threats-war-for-talent-are-biggest-concerns-for-tech-leaders-.html
4. Cassetto, O.: Security operations center roles and responsibilities (2019). https://www.exabeam.com/security-operations-center/security-operations-center-roles-and-responsibilities/. Accessed 16 Nov 2020
5. DeCusatis, C., Cannistra, R., Labouseur, A., Johnson, M.: Design and implementation of a research and education cybersecurity operations center. In: Hassanien, A.E., Elhoseny, M. (eds.) Cybersecurity and Secure Information Systems. ASTSA, pp. 287–310. Springer, Cham (2019). https://doi.org/10.1007/978-3-030-16837-7_13
6. Ganesan, R., Shah, A., Jajodia, S., Cam, H.: Optimizing alert data management processes at a cyber security operations center. In: Jajodia, S., Cybenko, G., Liu, P., Wang, C., Wellman, M. (eds.) Adversarial and Uncertain Reasoning for Adaptive Cyber Defense. LNCS, vol. 11830, pp. 206–231. Springer, Cham (2019). https://doi.org/10.1007/978-3-030-30719-6_9
7. Hussy, W., Schreier, M., Echterhoff, G.: Forschungsmethoden in Psychologie und Sozialwissenschaften für Bachelor. Springer, Heidelberg (2013). https://doi.org/10.1007/978-3-642-34362-9
8. Hámornik, B.P., Krasznay, C.: Prerequisites of virtual teamwork in security operations centers: knowledge, skills, abilities and other characteristics (2017)
9. Hámornik, B.P., Krasznay, C.: A team-level perspective of human factors in cyber security: security operations centers. In: Nicholson, D. (ed.) AHFE 2017. AISC, vol. 593, pp. 224–236. Springer, Cham (2018). https://doi.org/10.1007/978-3-319-60585-2_21
10. Kokulu, F.B., et al.: Matched and mismatched SOCs: a qualitative study on security operations center issues. In: Proceedings of the ACM Conference on Computer and Communications Security, pp. 1955–1970. Association for Computing Machinery (2019). https://doi.org/10.1145/3319535.3354239
11. Muniz, J., McIntyre, G., AlFardan, N.: Security Operations Center Building, Operating, and Maintaining your SOC, vol. 1. Cisco Press, Indianapolis (2015)
12. Mutemwa, M., Mtsweni, J., Zimba, L.: Integrating a security operations centre with an organization's existing procedures, policies and information technology systems. In: 2018 International Conference on Intelligent and Innovative Computing Applications, ICONIC 2018, pp. 1–6 (2019). https://doi.org/10.1109/ICONIC.2018.8601251
13. Nugraha, I.P.E.D.: A review on the role of modern SOC in cybersecurity operations. Int. J. Current Sci. Res. Rev. 4(5), 408–414 (2021)
14. Olt, C.: Establishing security operation centers for connected cars. ATZ Electron. Worldwide 14(5), 40–43 (2019)
15. Raithel, J.: Quantitative Forschung: Ein Praxiskurs (2008)

16. Sayegh, E.: Forbes magazine: predicting what 2022 holds for cybersecurity (2021). https://www.forbes.com/sites/emilsayegh/2022/01/06/predicting-what-2022-holds-for-cybersecurity/?sh=7f58a5972b72
17. Shahjee, D., Ware, N.: Integrated network and security operation center: a systematic analysis. IEEE Access **10**, 27881–27898 (2022)
18. Sundaramurthy, S.C.: An anthropological study of security operations centers to improve operational efficiency (2017). http://scholarcommons.usf.edu/etdscholarcommons.usf.edu/etd/6958
19. Sundaramurthy, S.C., Case, J., Truong, T., Zomlot, L., Hoffmann, M.: A tale of three security operation centers. In: Proceedings of the 2014 ACM Workshop on Security Information Workers, pp. 43–50 (2014)
20. Vielberth, M., Bohm, F., Fichtinger, I., Pernul, G.: Security operations center: a systematic study and open challenges. IEEE Access **8**, 227756–227779 (2020)
21. Zimmerman, C.: Ten Strategies of a World-Class Cybersecurity Operations Center (2014). https://www.mitre.org/sites/default/files/publications/pr-13-1028-mitre-10-strategies-cyber-ops-center.pdf

Author Index

Printed in the United States
by Baker & Taylor Publisher Services